For A)

Wit

from

Mike

CH00402466

SIX AUTHORS IN SEARCH OF JUSTICE

MICHAEL NEWMAN

Six Authors in Search of Justice

Engaging with Political Transitions

HURST & COMPANY, LONDON

First published in the United Kingdom in 2016 by
C. Hurst & Co. (Publishers) Ltd.,
41 Great Russell Street, London, WC1B 3PL
© Michael Newman, 2016
All rights reserved.
Printed in India

The right of Michael Newman to be identified as the author
of this publication is asserted by him in accordance with the
Copyright, Designs and Patents Act, 1988.

A Cataloguing-in-Publication data record for this book
is available from the British Library.

ISBN: 9781849046329 *hardback*

This book is printed using paper from registered sustainable
and managed sources.

www.hurstpublishers.com

CONTENTS

CONTENTS

ACKNOWLEDGEMENTS

Many people have helped me during the journey of this project from an initial vague idea into this book. My interest in the subject really began with a trip to South Africa in 2003. I went there with a strong, but ill-informed, belief that the Truth and Reconciliation Commission had been an extraordinary achievement in the transformation of the country after the end of apartheid. While there I learned that everything was far more complex than I had realised. One particularly powerful experience was a trip to Robben Island, where a former political prisoner, who was now a tourist guide, explained that he had been sentenced to a twenty-five year term at the age of eighteen. His description of the horrific conditions on the island was graphic and shocking, but it was one particular aspect of his account that really made me question my own assumptions. He explained that three police had not only beaten him up, but had subsequently inflicted such injuries on his father that he had been blinded and confined to a wheelchair for the rest of his life. Later they had 'confessed' to the Truth and Reconciliation Commission and were now running a lucrative private security firm. As he recounted this harrowing tale, it was obvious that there was an enormous gulf between the official message that he drew from the episode and his personal pain in recalling it. As an ANC member, he explained that this was a 'new South Africa' and that it was necessary to move on from the past; as an individual he clearly felt that it was totally unjust to offer freedom to these brutal agents of the former regime while the lives of so many remained blighted. Until this encounter, I had simply taken it for granted that the approach of the South African Truth and Reconciliation Commission, and

ACKNOWLEDGEMENTS

other similar initiatives elsewhere, was a wholly positive development—vastly preferable to revenge and retribution. I still believe this, but the former political prisoner made me realise that the whole question of justice in political transitions is far more complex than I had assumed. I am very grateful to him for setting me on the path that eventually led to this work.

This book, however, refused to remain within the confines of any single discipline or even any conventional field of study. It soon became evident that transitions from repressive states raised many questions about justice beyond a pre-occupation with the atrocities perpetrated by a previous regime. Clearly, many others have also been concerned that the focus is sometimes too narrow within conventional approaches to transitional justice and I am grateful to the organisers and participants of several conferences and discussions from which I derived a great deal in the early stages of the book: the 2nd Biennial War Crimes Conference, 'Justice? *Whose* Justice? Punishment, Mediation or Reconciliation' at the Institute of Advanced Legal Studies in London, 3–5 March 2011; the Transformative Justice Network of the Worldwide Universities Network, and particularly its two-day conference at Leeds University, 12–13 May 2011; and numerous events organised by the London Transitional Justice Network. I also want to thank Sylvia Servaes for some very helpful suggestions and also for alerting me to relevant material from the German organisation, FriEnt, the Working Group on Peace and Development. As usual, I have also learned an enormous amount through teaching and I am grateful to my students, both at London Metropolitan University and, more recently, at the London Center of New York University, for stimulating discussions on many relevant issues.

I have always believed that literature provides rich insights into social and political problems, but this is the first time that I have attempted to demonstrate this in my writing. My inclination to do so was reinforced by participation in a book group for the past five years with Marj Mayo, Elizabeth Wilson, Drew and Prue Stevenson and my wife, Ines Newman. Our interesting debates stimulated me to explore justice and transition through literature and I am very grateful to them all. At the same time, I was delighted that Rama Mani, Dan Smith and Randolph Kent—theorists and practitioners in the field of peacebuilding, development and

ACKNOWLEDGEMENTS

humanitarian issues—also believed that writers could illuminate the issues and I thank them for their encouragement.

I am, of course, also indebted to Luigi Pirandello, for the title of my book, which I took from his play, *Six Characters in Search of An Author: A Comedy in the Making*. I certainly do not share his political views, which also differ substantially from the ideas of most of the authors highlighted in this study, but Pirandello made many illuminating points about the complex relationships between truth and reality, which have some relevance to this work. The title is also appropriate as I wanted to focus on six authors in some depth, rather than spreading the net more widely. However, it was not easy to select just six and I would particularly like to thank David Edmonds, Howard Davies and Tony Murray for their suggestions, even if I did not eventually include them all. I am also grateful to Paul Ashton for alerting me to the importance of Ngũgĩ wa Thiong'o and to three people for the choice of Jorge Semprún: Monica Threlfall for originally recommending him, Csilla Kiss for urging me to continue when I was uncertain about his relevance, and Daniela Omlor for helping with a point of interpretation and lending me a copy of her book about his work. I would also like to thank Howard Davies and my daughter, Kate Newman, for help with some translations.

Once again I owe much to Michael Dwyer of Hurst Publishers, who was enthusiastic about the project before I had really defined it or decided which authors to include. I am also grateful to Alasdair Craig and Jon de Peyer of Hurst for their help in the editorial and production processes, and to the two referees for their supportive and constructive comments on an earlier draft, which led to some definite improvements in the final version. I would also like to thank my sister-in-law, Hannah Edmonds, for her invaluable assistance, once again, with the proof-reading.

Finally, my thanks go to my family—my brother, Jeff, my children and their partners for their support, and my grandchildren for being so delightful. Above all, as always, my greatest gratitude is to Ines, both for her belief in this project and her help—in so many ways—in turning it into a reality.

London, May 2016

ABBREVIATIONS

ANC	African National Congress
AP	Alianza Popular (People's Alliance)
CEDA	Confederación Española de Derechas Autónomas (Spanish Confederation of Autonomous Right-wing Groups)
Cheka	From Russian language initials for All-Russian Extraordinary Commission for Combating Counter-Revolution and Sabotage
CNI	Central Nacional de Informaciones (National Information Centre)
Comisión	Comisión Nacional de Verdad y Reconciliación (National Commission on Truth and Reconciliation [Chile])
Comintern	Communist International
CNR	Conseil National de la Résistance (National Council of the Resistance)
CNT	Confederación Nacional del Trabajo (National Confederation of Labour)
COSAW	Congress of South African Writers
DINA	Dirección de Inteligencia Nacional (National Intelligence Directorate)
ERC	Esquerra Republicana de Catalunya (Republican Left of Catalonia)
FPMR	Frente Patriótico Manuel Rodríguez (Manuel Rodríguez Patriotic Front)
ICC	International Criminal Court

ABBREVIATIONS

ICTJ	International Center for Transitional Justice
IU	Izquierda Unida (United Left)
KADU	Kenya African Democratic Union
KANU	Kenya African National Union
KCA	Kikuyu Central Association
KISA	Kikuyu Independent Schools Association
KKEA	Kikuyu Karing'a Education Association
MAPU	Movimiento de Acción Popular Unitaria (Popular Unitary Action Movement)
MAPU/OC	MAPU Obrero Campesino (MAPU Worker-Peasant)
MIR	Movimiento de Izquierda Revolucionaria (Revolutionary Left Movement)
MK	Umkhonto we Sizwe (Spear of the Nation)
NARC	National Rainbow Coalition (Kenya)
NEP	New Economic Policy
PCE	Partido Comunista Español (Spanish Communist Party)
PCF	Parti Communiste Français (French Communist Party)
PDC	Partido Demócrata Cristiano (Christian Democratic Party)
POUM	Partido Obrero de Unificación Marxista (Workers' Party of Marxist Unification)
PP	Partido Popular (People's Party)
PS	Partido Socialista de Chile (Socialist Party of Chile)
PSOE	Partido Socialista Obrero Español (Spanish Socialist Workers' Party)
SACP	South African Communist Party
TJRC	Truth, Justice and Reconciliation Commission (Kenya)
TRC	Truth and Reconciliation Commission (South Africa)
UCD	Unión de Centro Democrático (Union of the Democratic Centre)
UDF	United Democratic Front
UMOJA	United Movement for Democracy in Kenya
UP	Unidad Popular (People's Unity)

1

LITERATURE, JUSTICE AND TRANSITION

[T]he particularities of what oppression does to us, the consequences, the injustice we feel, the wounds we carry, the trauma we have ... can be very well dealt with in literature ... It doesn't show you the gruesome image without any meaning: it shows the meaning of this experience and I think that is what we need—we need to understand.

Choman Hardi[1]

Philosophy appears to concern itself only with the truth, but perhaps expresses only fantasies, while literature appears to concern itself only with fantasies, but perhaps it expresses the truth.

Antonio Tabucchi[2]

This book is primarily about problems of justice and injustice in relation to political transitions and transformations. In recent years considerable attention has been paid to these issues, particularly in relation to addressing past atrocities through such means as trials, truth and reconciliation commissions, amnesties, and memorials. While considering such means of dealing with the past, this work takes a broader approach to justice and injustice. It is also unusual because the issues are considered through a discussion of the lives and works of six writers. It is not a work of literary criticism or cultural studies because the writings are considered largely for the light that they throw on political and ethical issues, in the conviction that such a study complements more conven-

1

tional approaches to the problems. For each author lived under a repressive regime, was prepared to take substantial risks in order to contribute in some way to its overthrow, and survived a transition. They all thought deeply about the evolving situations in their countries, with viewpoints derived from a combination of lived experience and intellectual and artistic creation. Their writings thus provide a valuable addition to academic analyses and external policy advice that too often fail to take sufficient account of such reflective understanding and the specificity of each situation.

There is inevitably an arbitrary element in the choice of the authors and countries, and the book does not include some of the most historically significant transitions, such as the partition of India, the Chinese revolution, or the collapse of communism in Europe. The aim was to deal with a limited number of authors, who worked in more than one genre, publishing both fiction and non-fiction, in order to explore their thinking in some depth. However, only a limited amount of the work of each author is discussed and the approach varies both in respect of the length of the period covered and the types of writing that are discussed. The purpose is to highlight the authors' evolving conceptions of justice and injustice, which are both complementary and contrasting.

This chapter begins with brief introductions to the six authors and continues by considering some general questions about the relationship between literature and politics, explaining the position taken in this book in relation to some of the relevant controversies. It then turns to the concepts of injustice, justice and transitions, providing some definitions in order to facilitate discussion in the rest of the book.

The six authors[3]

The first author is Victor Serge (1890–1947). Born in Belgium of Russian heritage, he was an anarchist before World War I, but arrived in Russia in 1919 as an enthusiastic supporter of Bolshevism, and for several years he worked for the new state. However, his incipient doubts then developed into rebellion and, as a member of the Left Opposition faction, he was expelled from the Bolshevik Party in 1928, and was subsequently incarcerated in prison and later in a Siberian gulag before eventually being allowed to return to Western

Europe in 1936. By then he had written numerous works—historical essays, political commentaries and novels—which denounced the Stalinist dictatorship in the most forceful and compelling manner. Through a consideration of several of these works and his later celebrated autobiography, the chapter on Serge explores his political evolution over a comparatively long period. It seeks to explain the way in which the repression under Stalin both re-awakened some of his earlier ideas about the nature of justice and injustice and also forced him to think about questions that he had not really confronted in his initial zeal for Bolshevism.

While Serge has still not achieved the reputation that he deserves, the second author, Albert Camus (1913–60), is one of the most internationally influential writers of the twentieth century, with an oeuvre that includes novels, plays, philosophy and political essays. He also became a highly controversial figure politically, initially because of his growing anti-Communism and break with Jean-Paul Sartre (1905–80) at the beginning of the 1950s, but subsequently because of his opposition to Algerian independence. However, before any of this took place, Camus had achieved a reputation as an active opponent of the Vichy regime, particularly through his role in writing for, and subsequently editing, a Resistance newspaper. World War II and its immediate aftermath are the major focus of the chapter in this book because these were years in which Camus initially crystallised his views on justice and injustice. Having come to the decision that the Nazi occupation and Vichy regime constituted so clear a form of injustice that they must be opposed violently, he regarded the Resistance as the embodiment of justice. The stance that he took meant that he risked his life, and many of his associates were imprisoned or executed. However, after the Liberation, he quickly became alienated from the forces that he had supported, particularly because of his growing antipathy to the purges and trials in the early post-war period. These later reflections on the nature of justice and violence played a key role in his subsequent political evolution.

The Kenyan author and public intellectual, Ngũgĩ wa Thiong'o (1938–) (subsequently referred to as Ngũgĩ), has been a major figure in African and post-colonial literature; he has written novels, plays, political tracts, and also works of literary and cultural theory. The chap-

3

ter devoted to Ngũgĩ covers a long period because there have necessarily been important shifts in his interpretations and perceptions of injustice and justice over time. As a teenager he experienced the British oppression and atrocities in the Emergency period of the 1950s. In these years the main focus of 'injustice' seemed to be located in colonialism. Yet, while Ngũgĩ hoped that independence would open a new era, some of his early work already revealed his doubts, and both his experience of the Kenyatta regime and exposure to such influences as Frantz Fanon (1925–61) and Marxism, while studying and working abroad, meant that Ngũgĩ soon emerged as a leading critic of the new regime. This also meant that his interpretation of injustice became more complex as he explored the meaning and implications of 'neocolonialism'. In particular, he concentrated on the notion that the subjection of Africa was perpetrated through culture and language as well as economic and political exploitation. When he attempted to give practical expression to such ideas through community theatre in the Gĩkũyũ language, he was arrested and detained for almost a year. While imprisoned he decided that the way to challenge the subjugation was subsequently to write his novels in Gĩkũyũ, rather than English. Forced into exile in 1982, Ngũgĩ has continued to contest injustice in Kenya, but has not maintained adherence to a single framework, and there have also been some significant shifts in his thinking.

The fourth author is Jorge Semprún (1923–2011), who wrote novels, screenplays, autobiographical memoirs and historical and political essays. The son of José María de Semprún Gurrea, an official in the Spanish Republic, Semprún's whole family left the country in 1936 during the Civil War. Initially they went to the Netherlands, where Semprún Gurrea continued to represent the Republic, but when the Dutch government recognised Franco in 1939, they moved to France. There Semprún became bilingual and the majority of his work was written in French.

The main focus of the chapter is on his attitude towards the Franco regime and the transition to democracy, but Semprún's approach was circuitous and the product of an extraordinary life. He initially viewed events in Europe primarily through the prism of Spanish republicanism, but his intense opposition to Francoism soon broadened into antifascism in general and at the age of nineteen he joined the communist forces in the armed resistance in France. In 1943 he was captured, tortured and deported to Buchenwald concentration camp, where he was incarcerated for two years. The horror of this period remained with him for the rest of his life and he would subsequently view Francoism as part of a wider European form of evil and injustice. His political activity between 1953–62 was devoted to the clandestine organisation of the Communist Party in Spain, again involving major risks. Disagreements with the leadership then led to his expulsion from the party in 1965 and a subsequent evolution in his political views. He now became increasingly anti-communist, and believed that the post-Franco transition must be based on a broad coalition, initially led by the Centre-Right. He would serve as Minister of Culture in the socialist government from 1988–91. His stance was paradoxical, for the Spanish transition was made possible by politically inspired amnesties and amnesia about the past, while much of Semprún's writing and thinking stressed the crucial importance of collective memory as an ingredient of justice.

Ariel Dorfman (1942–) has worked across numerous genres, including poetry, literary and cultural criticism, novels, essays, plays, and films. The focus of this chapter is on his work in relation to Chile, but Dorfman has a complex identity. Having spent much of his childhood in the US, where he lives and works once more, he is bilingual and writes in English and Spanish. At the age of twenty-eight, Dorfman was an enthusiastic supporter of the left-wing government of Salvador Allende in Chile, eventually becoming the cultural and media adviser to Allende's Chief of Staff. However, the Pinochet coup in September 1973 threatened his life and forced him into exile. While abroad, he sought to maintain solidarity with democratic and left-wing forces in Chile, and also to keep alive the memory of the 'disappeared' and those killed by the dictatorship. However, there was also a significant evolution in his attitudes, for although he continued to believe that the Allende government stood for justice and that the subsequent dictatorship was its antithesis, he feared that Pinochet's support rested on profound forces both within Chilean society and in the international capitalist economy. Like Ngũgĩ, he attributed great importance to culture, particularly the way in which ideas were expressed politically and through popular media. By now he no longer regarded himself as a

Marxist revolutionary, having become a social-movement activist with a strong commitment to human rights as the means to bring about justice. The downfall of the dictatorship enabled him to return to Chile in the summer of 1990, but this exposed tensions between his position and the new consensus on the centre-left, for Dorfman could not accept the silence about the past. The negative reaction in Chile to his attempt to raise this question in his play, *Death and the Maiden*, played a key role in his decision to remain in the US after all.[4] It was only when the historical injustices were confronted more fully after 1998 that he began to feel more positive about the new regime in Chile.

The final author is the celebrated South African writer, Nadine Gordimer (1923–2014), who published numerous novels, short stories and essays. Her opposition to apartheid for its overt oppression, its economic and political discrimination, and its dehumanising impact upon the majority population, was central to her work from the 1950s until the first democratic elections in 1994, and she played an important role in communicating all this to an international audience. Although she was never arrested, her work was sometimes suppressed, and she took risks in shielding others from the security services and speaking out on behalf of victims of the regime. Her interpretation evolved over the period, becoming more imbued with socialist influences in the later years of apartheid, but she always believed that inequality on ethnic grounds was the most fundamental form of injustice. However, one of the key features of Gordimer's work was the exploration of wider society through a focus on the lives of, and interactions between, individuals. Because of her observation of the corrupting influence of an unjust social environment upon those who live in it, and perhaps also because of her understanding of the complexity of each individual, she never believed in the possibility of any form of utopia. She was inclined to give the benefit of the doubt to the post-apartheid regime and remained relatively silent about its own injustices for a long period after the political transition. The chapter will focus largely on the evolution of Gordimer's thought during the later years of apartheid and the transition.

The situations in which each of the above authors lived and wrote differed greatly and there were substantial differences in their outlooks and trajectories. Nor are the writers in this study 'representative' of their societies or even of particular classes and groups within them. In fact, they were atypical in many ways. All were broadly on the political left, all were secular in outlook, and all were highly courageous in confronting the dangers to which they were exposed by repressive regimes. All were, at least in part, also external to their societies. Serge's formative experiences were in Western Europe rather than Russia and much of his writing was in French; Camus came from Algeria rather than the mainland of France; Ngũgĩ has spent more of his life in Britain and the US than in Kenya; Semprún lived outside Spain more than in his native country and also wrote more in French than Spanish; Ariel Dorfman is Jewish, writes both in Spanish and English, and lives in the US rather than Chile; Gordimer, who was also Jewish, was a white South African in a majority black country. All were thus partially outsiders, but the book concentrates on their writing because they provide and communicate important insights into the issues, and those who are partially 'outside' and partially 'inside' may often be particularly discerning.

The authors share a further characteristic: they all lived through transitions. Having initially lived under a repressive regime in the hope or expectation that its removal would lead to justice, they were therefore subsequently able to reflect upon the new system. Of course, there were major differences, both in the transitions themselves and the way they were experienced and perceived by the authors. Serge arrived in Russia after the Bolshevik revolution had taken place. Having already participated in anarchist revolutionary uprisings in Western Europe, he hoped to play a role in a transition to socialism, but in fact witnessed the establishment of the brutally repressive Stalinist state. Camus identified the Resistance with justice and believed that the Liberation from Vichy and Nazi control would bring about a new era, but he was soon disillusioned with what he saw. For Ngũgĩ the situation was complex, for he came to regard the successor regime more as a continuation of the previous one than as the first step to genuine trans-formation. Gordimer, in contrast, viewed the new regime in 1994 as a decisive step forward, even though she grew disillusioned later. Semprún was well aware of the extent of continuity between the Francoist regime and its successor, but was nevertheless prepared to regard it as a genuine transition to democracy. Dorfman's position, however, was more equivocal because of his belief that Pinochet continued to dominate the new Chilean state even after 1990.

There were thus many types of transition, in the countries themselves and in the experiences and perspectives of the authors. As the book will show, there were both similarities and instructive differences in some of the conclusions that they reached.

Literature and the political sphere

The subject matter of this work spans several disciplines, but issues about injustice, justice and transition might normally be regarded as closer to the realms of politics (my own academic background) than to literature. Certainly, no attempt is made to evaluate the aesthetics of the contribution made by each author. Yet the fact that they were simultaneously accomplished writers and politically engaged is of great importance for this study and it is necessary to explain the position taken here in relation to various controversies about this combination.

It is notoriously difficult to identify the shared qualities of outstanding writers, but Nadine Gordimer is surely right to emphasise the importance of exceptionally acute skills of observation.[5] Because good writers observe people and society so well, they are also able to encapsulate the essence of character, relationships, issues, and problems and thus provide insights that may elude academics. As Chekhov put it: 'Specialists exist for special questions; it is their business to judge of the commune, the future of capitalism, the evil of drink, of boots, of the diseases of women ... An artist must judge only of what he understands.'[6] But, while such powers of observation and understanding are preconditions of successful writing, the ability to communicate thoughts, feelings, atmosphere, and ideas through the written word is obviously also crucial. Jean-Paul Sartre expressed this eloquently:

> One is not a writer for having chosen to say certain things, but for having chosen to say them in a certain way. And, to be sure, the style makes the value of the prose. But it should pass unnoticed. Since words are transparent since the gaze looks through them, it would be absurd to slip in among them some panes of rough glass. Beauty is in this case only a gentle and imperceptible force. In a painting it shines forth at the very first sight; in a book it hides itself; it acts by persuasion like the charm of a voice or a face.

It does not coerce; it inclines a person without his suspecting it, and he thinks that he is yielding to arguments when he is really being solicited by a charm that he does not see.[7]

He was referring primarily to fiction, but the importance of such qualities is also clear when a skilful author writes non-fiction. Thus in *Politics and the Novel*, after quoting a long, vivid passage from Trotsky's *History of the Russian Revolution*, Irving Howe comments that the work was 'history in the grand style and like all histories in the grand style, also a work of the literary imagination'. In comparison, he argues, the novels of André Malraux, Ignazio Silone and Arthur Koestler 'can be read as footnotes, half tragic half ironic, to Trotsky's paragraph'.[8] He did not state this in support of Trotsky's political stance, but in appreciation of his ability to evoke sympathetic attitudes to the revolution through his literary prowess. This ability is equally evident today as, for example, in the work of the novelist Ahdaf Soueif on the aborted revolution in Egypt.[9] In theory, this is an account of the 'Egyptian spring' in the form of a diary; in fact, because of Soueif's skill in combining personal reminiscences and stories with political and historical interpretations, and through her juxtaposition of past and present, the book provides the texture and atmosphere of the hopes and disappointments in a way that far surpasses conventional non-fictional reportage.

All six authors in this book possess the observational skills, perceptive understanding and stylistic qualities that are necessary for conveying such insight, although their writing is quite different. For Camus, for example, the importance of the ideas that he sought to convey was fundamental and they structured the text. Even if his novels are not always easy to interpret, it is evident that he is conveying his thinking through his terse prose. Jorge Semprún, in contrast, whether in his fiction or non-fiction, seeks to evoke attitudes through commentary and memories—often combining horrific events and everyday life. Yet in each of the six cases, both the content and quality of the writing conveys something beyond conventional academic insights into the problems.

Outstanding writing becomes more controversial when the political realm is tackled in works of fiction, and all six authors have conveyed their ideas about justice and injustice through works of fiction as well as in their essays and commentaries. This approach is anathema to a major school of thought that has insisted that the expression of political ideas effectively 'kills' a novel and that the two are incompatible. Many outstanding novelists have themselves propounded this viewpoint and, in *Novelists on the Novel*, Miriam Allot brings together quotations from Ivan Turgenev, Anton Chekhov, Ford Madox Ford, Thomas Hardy, André Gide and Aldous Huxley, revealing either complete opposition to the introduction of political ideas into novels or advocacy of extreme caution.[10] Nor is this view confined to the distant past, for it has recently been expressed in academic contributions to literary theory and by the 1990 Nobel Prize-winning author, Octavio Paz.[11] In Sartre's view, however, writers should be taking a politically-committed stance on issues of justice and injustice and using their literary skills to evoke appropriate attitudes: 'the writer can guide you and, if he describes a hovel, make it seem the symbol of social injustice and provoke your indignation.'[12] And, more generally, he argued that writers had a particular mission:

[I]f I am given this world with its injustices, it is not so that I might contemplate them coldly, but that I might animate them with my indignation, that I might disclose them and create them with their nature as injustices, that is, as abuses to be suppressed...

He continued:

It would be inconceivable that this unleashing of generosity provoked by the writer could be used to authorise an injustice, and that the reader could enjoy his freedom while reading a work which approves or accepts or simply abstains from condemning the subjection of man by man.[13]

Sartre himself was attacking the dominant French literary tradition as essentially 'bourgeois' and the authors in this book—particularly Victor Serge and Ngũgĩ—have been keen to break away from conventional middle-class ideas of the novel. Nor would any of them accept the suggestion that fiction and politics are two entirely distinct realms. The closest to doing this was Gordimer, who always insisted that she was not primarily a 'political' person and was led towards this sphere only through observing social and personal relationships and coming to understand the ways in which these were shaped by political power and structures. However, much turns here upon the definition of the 'political'. Certainly, her novels were regarded as highly political by the South African state, and much of her writing was motivated by her passionate sense of injustice against racial oppression and discrimination under apartheid. She felt uncomfortable about having to tailor her comments to fit any 'line' or to think about the political impact of her statements, and she sought full artistic freedom for her writing. But so did all the other authors in this book. Of course, the definition of politics is contested, from the feminist idea of 'the personal is political' at one end of the spectrum to narrowly institutional claims at the other. The position taken here is that questions of injustice, justice and transition concern politics and ethics and permeate the writing of all six authors.

In fact, however, all of them were aware that there are problems in combining political and literary themes in works of fiction, as Stendhal famously warned when he suggested that politics in a work of literature was 'like a pistol-shot in the middle of a concert, something loud and vulgar and yet a thing to which it is not possible to refuse one's attention.'[14] The point, as suggested by Maarten van Delden and Yvon Grenier, is that those with strong political viewpoints may tend to see the world in binary categories with a clear solution, while artistic perspectives tend to be 'more indefinite, hybrid, *human* pictures in which the reader is invited to question herself or himself and the world rather than being told what to think and to do'.[15] There is no single way of resolving this tension but there are various kinds of political literature that simultaneously contribute to art and provide a better understanding of politics.[16] The six authors have sought to achieve this in different ways, all of which are innovative. However, there is a crucial further point, which goes beyond merely accepting that the political and the literary can be successfully combined. For a passionate commitment surely often provides both the force behind the work and the insights that it provides.

George Orwell expressed this particularly clearly in his 1946 essay, 'Why I Write':

> What I have wanted to do throughout the past ten years is to make political writing into an art. My starting point is always a feeling of partisanship, a sense of injustice. When I sit down to write a book, I do not say to myself, 'I am going to produce a work of art'. I write it because there is some lie that I want to expose, some fact to which I want to draw attention and my initial concern is to get a hearing.

He concluded:

> [L]ooking back through my work, I see that it is invariably where I lacked a *political* purpose that I wrote lifeless books and was betrayed into purple passages, sentences without meaning, decorative adjectives and humbug generally.[17]

This is an unusually categorical statement, but many others have insisted that the attempt to come to terms with existential dilemmas, imbued with political and ethical dimensions, has fuelled their need to write. For example, in *Palestinian Walks*, a beautifully crafted and original exposition and denunciation of Israeli injustice through bureaucratic regulation, Raja Shehadeh explains how his outrage at the apparent failure of his work on human rights led him to turn to writing. In his case, this has been a means of constructively controlling and using anger about the deprivation of the land of the Palestinian people.[18] The original motivation for two of Aminatta Forna's major works was still more personal. As the daughter of the Sierra Leonean politician Mohamed Forna, who was framed and then executed by the dictator Siaka Stevens, she spent years trying to make sense of her traumatic early life. After sustained research to pinpoint exact responsibility for her father's death, she was eventually able to come to terms with the past and the present in two remarkable books—the non-fictional *The Devil Who Danced on the Water* and a novel, *The Memory of Love*.[19] Both volumes highlight issues about injustice, memory and reconciliation that resemble some of the themes of Dorfman and Semprún, who were themselves driven to write by memories of both personal and collective traumas. Finally, Christa Wolf, who was pilloried in the West, above all in the Federal Republic, for wanting to maintain a separate East German socialist state rather than embracing unification, was surely expressing a deep conviction about her writing when she told Jürgen Habermas in December 1991:

> I only gradually worked my way out of bias, dogmatic prejudice, credulity, inhibition—gradually and with great difficulty, pain, and existential conflicts. I can remember clearly each stage in this process, including the relapses, halfway measures, anxieties. Literature helped me. When you write, you can't lie, or you get blocked.[20]

A variety of intense emotions about political and ethical issues thus often provides the impetus to communicate a deeply-felt 'truth' about a situation through writing.

There is clearly a difference between historical truth and literary truth. In general, we make an assumption when reading a work of history that the author has made every effort to ensure that there is good evidence for the apparently factual statements that are made about the events that took place. When reading novels we do not make this assumption except when the author refers to public events or tells us that something really occurred. What, then, did Nadine Gordimer mean when she insisted that she felt that everything in her novels was 'true' in a way that was not the case in her non-fiction, where she felt constrained?[21] Her point surely was that in a novel she felt free to allow the situations and the characters to develop in ways shaped primarily by her imagination, but that they could direct us to an important 'truth' about the nature of the society and relationships depicted.[22] Yet this feeling has also been expressed by those who might be regarded as the most overtly 'political' of the six authors. Thus both Serge and Ngũgĩ, who had previously written mainly non-fiction, turned to novels because they found that they could convey 'reality' far more forcefully and vividly through fiction than in an analytical essay. Both attempted to express their 'truths' in novels, and the fictional writing of all six writers was inseparable from their political engagement around issues of justice and injustice.

Concepts of injustice, justice and transition

We all tend to use the language of justice to support our demands for political and social changes, but this does not, of course, mean that we are all using the same concept or theoretical framework. To take one obvious example: the proponents of neo-liberalism argue that justice will be maximised by limiting the role of the state in the economy, while most socialists hold that justice depends on enhancing socioeconomic equality and that this requires state intervention. Nor is this simply a difference between two conceptions of the means to attain justice, for it also involves distinct ideas about the constituent elements of justice itself. Furthermore, these two frameworks are primarily the product of Western intellectual development, and justice from a global historical perspective is a far wider field of study and contestation.

The six authors were not primarily theorists and did not attempt to underpin their arguments with the kind of precision and logic demanded by specialists. Nevertheless, they had passionate convictions about injustice and justice, frequently using such discourse in their writing. This section identifies some of the partially overlapping ideas that are the most relevant for this book. It begins with a brief consideration of injustice and then turns to six concepts of justice that were utilised by the authors, sometimes explicitly and sometimes implicitly. My selection and interpretation of these notions may sometimes be contentious, but the purpose of the classification is to provide a foundation for the discussion of the authors' ideas and also to establish some terminological definitions. The book will then consider the work of each writer in a separate chapter before returning to some of the general conceptual issues in the conclusion.

Injustice

It is widely assumed that it is necessary to have a clear notion of the nature of justice in order to contest injustice and that the two ideas are opposites. However, in different ways two recent theoretical works have challenged this assumption, and their central propositions have relevance for this study. In his important book, *The Idea of Justice* (2009), Amartya Sen argues that there is no need for a single defining notion of justice in order to strive against injustice.[23] His own claim, developed through detailed philosophical arguments, drawing on Western and non-Western traditions, is that, both within states and globally, there are obvious, flagrant and remediable injustices of hunger, poverty and inequality that require action, but that recognition of the injustices and appropriate action to address them requires no agreement on a single transcendent conception of justice. In *The Concept of Injustice* (2013), Eric Heinze goes further, arguing that much traditional political theory has been based on a misconception that has subordinated injustice to justice, assuming that injustice is simply the opposite of justice.[24] In his view, this idea is both mistaken and dangerous. The assumption that they are binary opposites has resulted in a failure to examine the idea of injustice in depth since the focus has been almost exclusively on justice. Justice has been defined either in terms of some overall ideal conception or 'unity' (as, for example, in Plato's *Republic*) or through some kind of measurement—for example, as the attainment of a particular income distribution. In either case, it is then assumed that injustice will be eradicated by the realisation of the conditions believed to constitute 'justice'. This, Heinze suggests, is dangerous because injustice will remain however justice is defined. The constant attempt to find new ways to measure or define justice will invariably lead to further injustice.

Heinze is certainly not arguing against the pursuit of justice or even the necessity of defining it in terms of unity or measurement. Rather he is suggesting that a necessary condition for understanding injustice is to abandon the ancient supposition that it has any straightforward relationship of mutual exclusion with a conceptually prior notion of justice. This is a contentious notion, which it is not necessary to pursue here, but the separation of the ideas of justice and injustice by both Sen and Heinze is particularly illuminating in relation to the writers discussed in this book, who were living under repressive dictatorships.

In general, resistance to oppression is based upon a conviction that the existing regime constitutes multiple forms of injustice. These may include social and economic forms, such as extreme poverty and inequality, but may also involve brutal penal systems, arbitrary legal processes, and the denial of any outlets for political opposition. Sometimes, of course, those who join or support movements to overthrow such regimes do so on the basis of a particular aspect of injustice. Thus Albert Camus's decision to join the Resistance was based, above all, on his growing belief that the Nazi occupation was unjust because of its brutality, while Nadine Gordimer's opposition to the South African regime was motivated primarily by her conviction that discrimination on the basis of ethnicity was completely intolerable. But they subsequently tended to broaden their opposition into wider demands than those that initially precipitated their involvement. Or, to take one other example, Ngũgĩ regarded the fundamental injustice of the situation in Kenya in the late 1950s as that of British colonialism and the lack of independence; subsequently he came to regard the phenomenon of neo-colonialism as incorporating other dimensions of injustice.

In such situations, then, injustice appears to be both concrete and multidimensional, while justice is, perhaps necessarily, viewed in less precise ways. Typically, if the regime itself is regarded as the key source of injustice, its overthrow will be seen as a necessary precondition for

15

the attainment of justice, but the constituent elements of this desirable goal may be left rather vague.

In the case of each author and each regime the trajectory was individual and complex. In 1919, for example, Victor Serge believed that the Bolshevik revolution would lead to the end of the injustices that he identified with Tsarist Russia and capitalism more generally: it was only later that he came to realise that Stalinism constituted a completely new system of horrific injustices. Most of the authors had major changes in belief over time, often as a result of their own experiences and of wider political developments. Thus, for example, while Jorge Semprún had been a communist when opposing Franco for over two decades, by the time the transition to democracy in Spain took place he had abandoned Marxism in favour of social democracy. Similarly, having originally opposed Pinochet from a Marxist standpoint, Ariel Dorfman eventually returned to Chile in 1990 as a human rights activist. Yet the initial motivation for these writers to take the risks that they did, was their passionate commitment to end injustice rather than because they had a clear conception of justice. Nevertheless, at various stages their positions oscillated around the ideas of justice outlined under the headings below.

Most of the authors had hybrid notions of justice, incorporating elements of more than one theoretical position. This was sometimes because they themselves combined differing conceptual frameworks, but also because there are overlaps between the frameworks themselves. The positions of most of the authors were also fluid, in some cases shifting considerably. Nor do all aspects of their conceptions of justice fit neatly into any of the conventional frameworks. For example, Camus's emphasis on the 'absurd', Ngũgĩ's inclusion of culture, language and history, and Semprún's incorporation of memory and truth transcend these categorisations of justice. Nevertheless, most of the authors oscillated between some of the positions summarised below.

Rights, liberties and constitutions: a liberal conception of justice

It is generally acknowledged that liberalism is not a single theory, but has developed over several centuries in different countries and has been shaped by their various cultural traditions and trajectories. Furthermore, it contains no agreed conception of justice. In fact, one theorist recently noted that, since the mid-nineteenth century, 'disagreement over what justice requires has divided liberals more than any other issue'.[25] Two of the most influential American political theorists of the second half of the twentieth century, John Rawls (1921–2002) and Robert Nozick (1938–2002), may thus both be described as liberals, but their worldviews and conceptions of justice were quite different. There have also been quite different starting points for the construction of liberal arguments for justice, perhaps most notably between the utilitarian tradition that has attempted to judge laws and policies by their consequences and the Kantian tradition that has sought to do so through moral reasoning. Yet even this difference is perhaps less fundamental than a further one: the question of whether the economic roots of liberalism have continuing primacy in its outlook or whether these may be superseded by political and social aspects.

From its origins liberalism has been closely associated with capitalism, but this economic system of private ownership and market relationships has also been associated with the development of political and social ideas about individual freedom and constitutional government. The question of which aspect in liberal theory is seen as the more fundamental may also affect the way in which it is described. Many proponents of liberalism tend to emphasise political and social aspects—government by consent, the separation of powers, toleration of diverse lifestyles—while many critics concentrate on the inequalities created and perpetuated by the economic system. In my own view, the tensions between these different components are an integral part of liberalism.

John Locke (1632–1704) established many of its key elements, if only in an embryonic and partial form, and his theory certainly contained both economic and political dimensions. His notion of 'natural rights' was conceived as a defence against the tyranny of absolute monarchy, but it rested on private property ownership as one of the inalienable individual rights that he sought to protect. Nevertheless, he also provided a foundation for government by consent, constitutionalism, a degree of toleration, and a system of law and punishment. All this rested on two fundamental assumptions. The first was a suspicion of power: rulers and ruling bodies needed to be controlled and power divided in order to protect people against the 'Leviathan' state. Secondly, individuals should be free to pursue their own self-interest so long as this did not deprive others of what they needed for life and liberty. These two assumptions also implied a third: that justice itself was viewed in a limited way, for it was defined primarily in negative terms as the need to erect barriers against tyranny or other agreed forms of injustice. This was a step towards a more general tendency within liberalism to emphasise formal, procedural ideas of justice over substantive ones about the nature of justice itself. Nevertheless, over time the definition of these forms of injustice evolved markedly. Increasing theoretical acceptance of the equality of rights for all individuals meant that liberal principles were invoked against slavery, restrictions on suffrage, the subjection of women, and racist discrimination. Following the principles in John Stuart Mill's classic text, *On Liberty* (1859), liberals also came to accept that infringements of personal freedom should be tolerated only when others are harmed by an individual's actions, and these principles facilitated the introduction of greater equality of treatment in relation to sexuality, and general lifestyle issues in many countries. The concept of rights has often been of crucial importance in establishing a normative reason for implementing of such changes. Yet this progression could not overcome the tensions at the heart of liberalism.

In political terms, the autonomy of individuals, and doctrines about rights, liberties and the constitutional division of power might be viewed as essential guarantees against injustice. But capitalism is based on unequal property ownership, producing and sustaining socioeconomic inequality, and this has long posed a key question for liberal ideas. Is a liberal conception of justice one that accepts the effects of the capitalist system on the grounds that any interference with its operation will contravene the rights of individuals? This is essentially the position of Nozick in his influential book, *Anarchy, State, and Utopia* (1974), which is really a text for libertarianism and the minimal state.[26] Or do liberal values about freedom and the equality of rights mean that justice must be attained through distributive procedures, thereby favouring the interests of the disadvantaged? This is essentially the position of John Rawls in *A Theory of Justice* (1971), which places liberalism within the general framework of social justice (see below).[27] For libertarian liberals, this concern for distributive justice leads to socialism, but other liberals argue that the egalitarian concern is the way to maintain a viable doctrine in the twenty-first century.[28] Put another way, it could be asked whether a liberal theory of rights is just about political and civil rights or whether it embraces wider social goals. More generally this also raises the question, passionately debated within the United Nations ever since the Universal Declaration of Human Rights in 1948, as to whether the concept of human rights has emancipated itself from its Western, male, individualist roots.[29] Such questions have relevance for the way in which a liberal approach to justice was regarded by the authors in this book.

None of them adopted liberalism wholeheartedly. Gordimer's approach to apartheid was originally rooted in liberal principles of non-discrimination and anti-racism, but from the mid-1960s until after the end of apartheid she vehemently condemned liberalism and liberals. This was based primarily on her antipathy to the political stance of liberals in South Africa, which she regarded as an ineffective and unprincipled attempt to compromise with a system of gross injustice. She sometimes expressed this in terms of a total rejection of liberalism *per se*, but many of her deepest convictions were rooted in liberal thought. The attitudes of the other authors were still more complex, particularly because they all adhered to a form of Marxism at some stage and, from this perspective, generally regarded liberalism as a doctrine of the capitalist status quo. Yet none of them consistently and wholly rejected it.

Camus, Semprún and Dorfman increasingly favoured liberal doctrine as their Marxism waned. At one point Camus viewed his position as the need to make a choice between 'justice' (which he identified with social and economic equality) and 'liberty'. After World War II he emphasised the latter, subsequently adhering to a general position that was broadly liberal in its attitudes towards the state, law and the individual, although he reached these conclusions through his own distinct form of ethical reasoning. Similarly, as Semprún turned against communism, he too tended to stress liberal conceptions, while also reaching this destination through a unique personal journey. Dorfman's journey was a little more complex, since his trajectory was from Marxism to human rights activism. This certainly meant that he adopted generally liberal principles with respect to the state and the individual, but he also reflected the general ambiguity of human rights in relation to the various political doctrines. His abandonment of Marxism did not therefore mean that the conception of justice to which he now adhered was wholly identifiable with liberalism, for his notion of human rights was broad and eclectic.

In both his anarchist and Bolshevik phases, Serge was totally opposed to liberalism and its conceptions of rights and justice. However, his initial anarchist beliefs were also imbued with a strong commitment to the individual and freedom, although these were later subordinated to his general support for the Bolshevik revolution and the principles it professed. Nevertheless, his subsequent opposition to Stalinism was increasingly expressed in ideas that partially incorporated liberal principles, even though he never regarded them in this way. This was the case when he called for forms of political pluralism, legal independence, an active civil society, and stressed the importance of individual freedom. No doubt some of these ideas were also rooted in his earlier anarchism, and he never utilised them to oppose Marxism. Nevertheless, there were elements of a liberal conception of justice and rights in these later ideas.

Ngũgĩ's trajectory was a little similar. When he rejected British colonialism, he condemned liberalism as an ideological mask for coercive and repressive power, and these denunciations intensified during the later 1960s and 1970s. At this stage he seemed to regard liberal doctrines as having little intrinsic value, viewing them primarily as a means to advance capitalism, imperialism and neo-colonialism, which also embodied notions of Western superiority. Yet, like Serge, his position shifted as the brutality of the regime in independent Kenya became increasingly apparent. He therefore advocated legal, political and civil rights, and divisions of power. This did not mean that he either regarded such ideas as inherently liberal or that he substituted them for other notions of justice. But he certainly adopted them as necessary for combating injustice and facilitating progress.

Social justice

While some have regarded 'social justice' as a continuation and development of the principle of 'distributive justice', originating with

Aristotle, there is also a strong case for arguing that it emanated from the industrial and French revolutions and has been embodied in a mixture of political traditions—republicanism, some versions of liberalism, and non-Marxist forms of socialism and social democracy.[30] Because its antecedents and contemporary exponents cover a range of positions, in my view it is more helpful to regard it as a general spectrum of positions than to attempt to define it as constituting a precise one. It is also true that some of the most influential recent theorists of justice, who have effectively put forward concepts that incorporate important contributions to 'social justice', including John Rawls, have not used this as their primary defining terminology.[31]

The concept of social justice has traditionally been associated with the claim that the current distribution of resources and opportunities within a given society is unfair and that political authorities have both a capacity and duty to redistribute them in such a way as to bring about greater equality and to alleviate poverty. While the origins of the concept were primarily European, it later acquired far wider application. For example, in 2006 the United Nations Department of Economic and Social Affairs published a report entitled *Social Justice in an Open World*, in which it argued that most proponents of social justice held the view

> that when people engage in economic activity for survival, personal and professional growth, and the collective welfare of society, inequality is inevitable but should remain within acceptable limits that may vary according to the particular circumstances. In the modern context, those concerned with social justice see the general increase in income inequality as unjust, deplorable and alarming. It is argued that poverty reduction and overall improvements in the standard of living are attainable goals that would bring the world closer to social justice. However, there is little indication of any real ongoing commitment to address existing inequalities. In today's world, the enormous gap in the distribution of wealth, income and public benefits is growing ever wider, reflecting a general trend that is morally unfair, politically unwise and economically unsound. Injustices at the international level have produced a parallel increase in inequality between affluent and poor countries.[32]

It also argued that 'all developments relating to justice occur in society, whether at the local, national, or global level', thus suggesting that the concept of social justice applies both within specific countries and between them.[33] More specifically, it argued that social justice was not

21

possible without strong and coherent redistributive policies conceived and implemented by public agencies; and a fair, efficient and progressive taxation system allowing a state to perform its duties through the provision of public services and by offering protection and support to those temporarily or permanently in need. This, it claimed, also involved international redistributive justice through development assistance.[34]

The concept of 'social justice' historically stressed distributional issues and the importance of such measures as social protection, higher wage levels and progressive taxation to alleviate the problems of poverty and inequality. But, like Marxism and other socialist traditions that focused on class as the primary social cleavage, from the 1970s onwards traditional notions of social justice provoked criticism from new social movements, which argued that the emphasis on socioeconomic inequalities ignored or under-played other vital questions about discrimination and disadvantage, such as those concerning gender, ethnicity and sexuality. However, legitimate justice claims by such groups could fail to address the distributional issues that not only produced inequality between social classes, but were also interrelated with the disadvantages experienced by and within the identity groups themselves. For example, while women typically tend to face discrimination in the labour market, the situation of working-class women is quite different from that of those from a privileged background with high educational qualifications. Justice claims that treat women as a homogenous category will therefore fail to address this kind of differential disadvantage, and this is equally true if other identity groups are viewed in this way. Recent notions of social justice have therefore often stressed the necessity to tackle inequalities of both class and identity by considering the interrelationships between the two. There has also been greater emphasis on those suffering from the various forms of disadvantage themselves participating in social movements to bring about change, thereby being empowered in the process. This has been theorised by Nancy Fraser, who has argued that 'recognition' can demonstrate the extent to which a society values different people, but that this needs to be understood in relation to economic class, rather than under the guise of identity politics.[35] This gives rise to an enlarged concept of social justice based on a form of recognition through fairness, which incorporates emancipation, social protection and controlled markets.[36] Similarly, environmental concerns have also meant that sustainability has entered into the definition, as recognised in *Social Justice in an Open World*.[37]

All the authors in this book were committed to greater social justice. Certainly, at times most of them expressed their position in terms of a Marxist concept of class, which differs from that of social justice, but only Serge maintained an adherence to Marxism for the majority of his writing career and, in my view, even he adopted a social justice perspective in his final years. As already noted, Gordimer never adhered to Marxism, but from the mid-1960s she emphasised the importance of social and economic equality. In the cases of Camus and Semprún, the values of freedom and truth ultimately tended to eclipse their commitment to social justice without, however, leading them to abandon it completely. Taken overall, therefore, the pursuit of social justice was of great importance to all of them and, particularly in the cases of Ngũgĩ and Dorfman, its international application in relation to North–South relations was also significant, with both also increasingly emphasising the gender, cultural and environmental dimensions that have been incorporated into more recent concepts of social justice.

A Marxist conception: class and justice

It is a little paradoxical to talk of a Marxist conception of justice since many Marxists have denied its existence.[38] Marx himself often condemned the idea, claiming that this, like the notion of a universal morality autonomous from class relations, was a bourgeois misconception. Within a capitalist society, he argued, the payment that the worker received for his or her labour power was 'just' because it was functional to the prevailing system of production. Furthermore, it was anti-revolutionary to criticise the system as a whole on the grounds of its 'injustice' or to call for a socialist alternative on the basis of 'justice': the Marxist claim was rather that the proletariat as the agency for historical transformation would bring about a new form of society in which the wage relationship would ultimately cease to exist and in which human beings would achieve freedom. Nor, according to some Marxist thinkers, is it reasonable even to argue that there was an implicit conception of justice in Marxist theory. For a critique of capitalism in terms of the principle of justice would, it has been argued, entail the denial of the central claim that class conflict was the agency for revolutionary change.[39]

There are some strong arguments on both sides of this debate but, for two reasons, this book assumes that there is a Marxist conception of justice. First, as Norman Geras has demonstrated, Marx's own statements were contradictory and there are convincing reasons for suggesting that he did, in fact, have such a theory.[40] Certainly, he denounced any suggestion that ethical ideas in themselves could bring about revolutionary change, and he sometimes indeed appeared to argue that justice simply needed to be viewed as part of the system of production that it served. However, Marx's own passionate condemnation, both of the capitalist system as a whole, and of the 'robbery' of the workers within it, surely stemmed from convictions about justice. As Geras also argues, Marx insisted that this needed to be understood through his materialist conception of history, but both the critique of capitalism and the ultimate goal of communism were underpinned by a distributive form of justice based on convictions about equality and need.[41] Secondly, the five authors in this book who believed themselves to be Marxist at some time were certainly driven to this conviction because they regarded it as the way of bringing about justice, viewing the notions of class, revolution and justice as inextricably linked. The extent to which they probed into its body of theory was variable, but when this book refers to the Marxist conception of justice in relation to any of them, this will suggest that the author in question was, at that time, committed to a form of revolutionary change to transform the class system of capitalism. In some cases, other aspects may also be discussed in this context: for example, the role of culture, ethnicity or colonial and neo-colonial relationships, as informed by a Marxist perspective.

Legal justice

The idea of justice is often identified with law and is sometimes even taken as indistinguishable from it. However, the US Supreme Court Judge, Oliver Wendell Holmes, drew a distinction between them, writing in a letter, 'I have said to my brethren ... that I hate justice, which means that I know that if a man begins to talk about that, for one reason or another he is shirking thinking in legal terms'.[42] Holmes wanted to concentrate on law, but Derrida, who also distinguished between the two concepts, was more concerned with justice:

> But justice is not the law. Justice is what gives us the impulse, the drive or the movement to improve the law, that is to deconstruct the law. Without a call for justice we would not have any interest in deconstructing the law ... Justice is not reducible to the law, to a given system of legal structure.[43]

Most people would accept that there is a relationship between law and justice even though it is extremely complex and elusive.[44]

The term 'legal justice' is not very widely used and, as Robin West has argued, it can be interpreted in a conservative way to block progressive reform.[45] This is equally true of the more common term, 'the rule of law', which tends to be interpreted more narrowly. The problem is that a legal system is embedded in the cultural, economic and political structures and practices of a society and is difficult to detach from them. Clearly it is possible to have a society in which there is a codified legal system with trained judges, lawyers and court processes, but where the laws themselves are fundamentally unjust. Even in societies that combine comparatively well-functioning legal systems with democratic political institutions and advanced welfare systems, the problem remains. Thus legal institutions generally take an established system of distribution as given and simply seek to apply the laws that govern it, so that there is an inherently conservative role in their function in relation to any society.

As David Luban demonstrates, there is therefore probably no satisfactory way of reconciling two fundamental tensions between the concept of legal justice and broader notions of justice. The first is between the rule of law, which subordinates particular cases to general rules, and the moral demand to treat particular cases according to their individual merits; and the second is between the values of consistency, predictability and stability of legal justice and the more ambitious, and sometimes utopian, values of justice itself.[46] However, such philosophical problems do not undermine the relevance of the concept of legal justice in this book. This is because the book's whole approach is based on the notion that justice has many dimensions rather than a single defining essence and, viewed in this way, legal justice makes an important contribution. For a society surely lacks overall justice in any meaningful sense when, for example, the legal processes are corrupt and controlled by political leaders for their own purposes, and punishment is brutal and arbitrary.

The notion of 'legal justice' as used here suggests that there are relationships between the state and the legal sphere, and procedures, rules and norms within it, that guarantee a degree of integrity to the sphere as a whole. In this respect, the eight procedural requirements proposed by Lon Fuller are helpful. These are that legal enactments must be general in scope; public; prospective rather than retrospective; clear; consistent; relatively constant; capable of being obeyed; and enforced as written. These conditions, he argues, enable law to serve as a baseline around which citizens may organise their activities.[47] While such conditions do not eliminate the tensions between legal justice and wider conceptions of justice, they provide some guidelines for evaluating legal systems and their contribution to justice more generally. Other considerations may include the question of whether, in any particular system, the aim is simply to provide order in society through law and its enforcement or whether it is designed to promote legally protected rights and to safeguard human dignity within the legal processes, including through systems of punishment; and also the extent to which people are themselves able to contribute to determining the content of laws. Asking such questions then helps to define some of the minimum necessary conditions for the attainment of legal justice. Of course, there remains the danger that such conditions might appear to bias the definition and practice towards particular systems. However, the refusal to comply with the necessary minimum conditions makes it unlikely that any form of legal justice will be secured, thereby also undermining the possibility of attaining wider forms of justice.

In most cases, the authors discussed in this book did not begin with any particular interest in this aspect of justice but, through a combination of their own experiences and the evolution of the states with which they were preoccupied, this soon changed. Serge had opposed prison before the Bolshevik revolution (having already experienced it for long periods himself), and the nature of the subsequent repression, particularly under Stalin, which he again experienced personally, led him to regard some form of legal justice as essential. In the case of

Camus, the question of punishment, initially by the Nazi Occupation forces and the Vichy regime, and then by the Liberation, would play a key role in the evolution of his thinking about justice itself and politics more generally. This was also true of Ngũgĩ who was incarcerated in appalling conditions in post-independence Kenya and who subsequently campaigned for the rights of prisoners and exiles and incorporated a concern for fair legal processes and punishments into his work. For Gordimer, the campaign against pass laws (designed to enforce segregation) and the political trials of the early 1960s played an important role in her political evolution, as did the trial of the lawyer Bram Fischer, which she incorporated into her novel *Burger's Daughter*.[48] Semprún said little specifically about legal justice, but his own detention in Buchenwald, as the antithesis of any such notion, was the defining experience of his life. Finally, for Dorfman the brutality of extra-legal killings, disappearances and torture would haunt him through his own enforced exile and shape his ideas about law and punishment following Chile's transition to democracy.

Historical justice

The very existence of the concept of 'historical justice' is contested, with sceptics often arguing that the idea of trans-generational responsibility for past injustices is flawed.[49] However, demands for recognition, reparations and apologies for wrongs of the past have been an increasing feature of contemporary life. Many of these have been within the framework of transitional justice (discussed in the next section), but the phenomenon has been more general: most notably in relation to slavery, colonialism and other past atrocities against whole peoples. Examples include demands for Turkey to recognise the Armenian massacres as genocide; for Australia and the US to acknowledge their decimations of indigenous populations; and for Israeli to recognise the Palestinian *Nakba*.[50] In contrast, the way in which Germany has acknowledged its guilt for the Holocaust is widely regarded as ground-breaking in terms of the birth of historical justice.

One of the major ambiguities in the concept is in relation to the victims of the original injustice. Claims have often been lodged by or on behalf of groups or whole peoples and their descendants. For example, African slaves transported to the Caribbean or North America were the original victims, but the recognition or recompense was to be granted to their descendants. However, many memorials and systems of reparations in post-dictatorship societies have been for victims of repression as individuals without any clear sense that they may have a collective identity. Perhaps it simply needs to be recognised that historical justice may operate in relation to individuals, groups and whole peoples.[51] However, important implications may follow from the extent to which a collective injustice is recognised and how that collective identity is seen to be constituted. If it is acknowledged that a whole people has experienced historical injustice, for example through slavery or colonialism, recognition of the continuing negative effects may be more likely. It is for this reason that governments do not normally want to acknowledge this kind of responsibility for a collective historical injustice. If, on the other hand, the damage is simply to individuals, any recompense will probably be short-term. The identification of a group—between the individual and a whole people—may also be significant, for this may carry a collective history that has nothing to do with ethnicity or nationality. For example, the Franco regime sought to suppress the whole history of Spanish republicanism, silencing the collective political memory and identity of republicans. The Historical Memory Law, which was finally introduced more than thirty years after Franco's death, was not therefore simply a recognition of historical injustice to individuals, but also to a large collective group defined primarily by political allegiance.

In different ways, a reclaiming of history was important to all the authors in this book. Thus much of Serge's writing, both his fiction and non-fiction, attempted to recreate the memory of suppressed political ideas and debates. Similarly, Camus initially believed it vital that the values and memories of the Resistance should be recognised and embodied in post-war France; subsequently he became disillusioned when, in his view, this was done in a distorted way. Gordimer was very conscious of the multiple historical injustices embedded within apartheid and of their legacy after its formal downfall. For the other three authors, a notion of historical justice has been more central. In Ngũgĩ's view, the colonial experience, with its multiple forms of injustice, perpetrated particularly through the transmission of its own version of history and culture, continued to poison the whole post-independence period. In a rather different way, Semprún also saw the recovery of the past, including the suppressed memory of the Second Spanish Republic, as a key part of his life and work. Finally, Dorfman believed that his 'promise to the dead'—those who had been killed and the 'disappeared'—provided a reason for staying alive to tell the story of what had happened.

Transitional justice

Since this book is concerned with justice and transitions, there might be an expectation that the notion of transitional justice would be the central framework for a discussion of the ideas of the authors. In fact, this is far more problematic than it might appear. The difficulty is that the concept has often been underpinned by a set of normative assumptions belonging to a particular era and ideology, which are unhelpful in respect of some of the authors and situations, although the general concerns identified by the field of transitional justice are certainly of relevance.

The International Center for Transitional Justice (ICTJ), one of the most influential non-governmental bodies that seeks to promote and advise on transitional justice, defines the term as follows:

> Transitional Justice refers to the set of judicial and non-judicial measures that have been implemented by different countries in order to redress the legacies of massive human rights abuses. These measures include criminal prosecutions, truth commissions, reparations programs, and various kinds of institutional reforms. Transitional justice is not a 'special' kind of justice, but an approach to achieving justice in times of transition from conflict and/or state repression. [52]

It elaborates on the basic approaches, which include: criminal prosecutions, particularly of perpetrators considered to be the most responsible; reparations, including material elements, such as cash payments or health services; symbolic events, such as public apologies or a day of remembrance; institutional reform of abusive state institutions, such as armed forces, police and courts; and truth commissions to investigate and report on systematic patterns of abuse, recommend changes and help understand the underlying causes of serious human rights violations.[53] Such matters are clearly important in relation to changes of regime, but transitional justice emerged at the end of the Cold War and was one element in a more fundamental set of assumptions about transition.[54]

This was a time when the dominant discourse suggested a trend towards only one kind of political regime throughout the world. The notion of 'transition' was thus taken as synonymous with that of 'transition to liberal-democracy' from an implicitly homogenous alternative of 'dictatorship'. Within this framework, human rights were defined above all in civil and political terms, as a mobilising call, and the tendency was to brush aside the differences between different types of non-liberal regime in a general affirmation that (liberal) democracy guaranteed those rights.

The birth of transitional justice sought to replace various other ways of understanding and shaping transitions, three of which are of particular relevance in this book.[55] One was the Marxist concept of revolutionary transformation from capitalism to socialism, which thus focused on a quite different type of transition. In the era of the collapse of communism and triumph of the West, those who played the key roles in devising the package of ideas that emerged as transitional justice simply ignored or buried the Marxist concept as irrelevant to the form of transition that was being considered and advocated. A second important model that was discarded was that of development through state-led investment and control in developing and post-colonial countries. This idea, which had been highly influential during the 1960s and 1970s, also included the notion of 'transition' from 'third world' status to higher levels of growth and development. However, in the era of neo-liberalism, which gathered increasing momentum from the late 1970s, this was replaced by the new emphasis on open markets, privatisation and the roll-back of the state. A third omission concerned the role of social movements and mass mobilisation in bringing about change. The emphasis was upon bargaining to create a new elite consensus based upon the recognition of individual rights and responsibilities. The general assumption was that the transition would be to a familiar form of institutional mechanisms rather than that it should involve a variety of social and political forces shaping new institutions and mechanisms. Transitional justice was therefore one part of an epochal shift in which a new orthodoxy centred on neo-liberal economies and liberal–democratic political systems. Furthermore, it has often appeared to remain wedded to the assumptions of that era, implicitly associating transitional justice with democratisation and liberalism.

The kinds of transition and justice considered by the authors who are discussed in this book do not necessarily fit into this model for, as already noted, Marxism, socialism and social justice were important themes in their outlooks. Similarly, the situations in Russia, Kenya, South Africa and Chile were deeply affected by issues of development in which there was a widespread conviction, generally shared by the authors, that the state needed to play a key role. Certainly, some of them—particularly Camus, Semprún and Dorfman—came to conclusions about how to deal with past atrocities that overlapped substantially with themes emphasised by the proponents of transitional justice. But in other cases, and particularly that of Ngũgĩ, the congruence was less marked, and his vehement opposition to colonialism and neo-colonialism continued to define his most fundamental attitudes to both justice and transition. Furthermore, the focus of this book is not simply upon the writers' notions of justice at the time of transition, but is also on their evolving conceptions of justice over much longer periods. Their ideas cannot therefore be squeezed into the straightjacket of transitional justice that emerged between the end of the Cold War and the turn of the twenty-first century. Nevertheless, there are two reasons for arguing that transitional justice is highly relevant for this book.

First, its focus upon dealing with past mass atrocities in relation to stabilisation, reconciliation, sustainable peace and law within a new regime were preoccupations for many of the authors. In some cases, this again long pre-dated the existence of the term and even the concept. Thus as Serge's opposition to Stalinism grew, he started questioning the early Bolshevik treatment of counter-revolutionaries and wondered whether a softer approach might have created a less brutal society. For Camus, as already noted, the whole question of the purges, trials and executions was of central importance in the evolution of his outlook, and he came to believe in reconciliation rather than retribution. And at the time of Kenyan independence, one of Ngũgĩ's immediate concerns was the way in which Kenyatta instituted official amnesia about the crimes of the British. Gordimer wholly endorsed the South African Truth and Reconciliation Commission as an essential aspect in transition, while Semprún accepted the necessity for the amnesty in Spain, but not the silence about the past. Finally, Dorfman's preoccupations in Chile in 1990 were exactly those at the heart of transitional justice: whether legal justice and truth were being subordinated to peace and stabilisation and how this might be avoided.

Secondly, in recent years there has been a considerable growth of critical views within the field of transitional justice. A seminal early work of this kind was *Beyond Retribution: Justice in the Shadow of War* (2002) by Rama Mani, which dealt with the particular weaknesses of transitional justice in relation to low income countries in the Global South. Subsequently, there have been numerous critiques of transitional justice, as conventionally defined, both in respect of approaches in particular countries and its application more generally.[56] Many have discussed the ways in which the treatment of past atrocities should be combined with tackling other fundamental problems, and it has even been suggested that the trend in academic research is now to include issues of social justice, development and economics in transitional justice.[57] All this suggests that there is considerable contestation within the field and that use of the terminology does not necessarily imply acceptance of the ideological assumptions that were certainly dominant in the origins of the field and are often still associated with it.[58]

In this book, I therefore take the term transitional justice to refer to a range of possible ways of dealing with past atrocities at the time of, or following, a change of regime. It also suggests an attempt to formulate appropriate policies in both legal and non-legal spheres rather than, for example, an approach based wholly on retribution or revenge. Defined in this way, it is certainly of relevance to the authors' work.

The authors discussed in this book were living and writing in political contexts that shaped their lives, but they were prepared to take risks for their beliefs in the hope that their writing would have some impact, however limited. Their commitment to combating injustice, and their views about the nature of justice and the ways of achieving it, were never therefore simply abstract or academic. Nor were they static, for they also constantly reflected on their own experiences and the wider context, reconsidering their own ideas in the light of developments. Of course, such reflections did not mean that they all reached similar conclusions:

the situations of their societies differed both before and after the transitions, as did their initial ideological outlooks and their ultimate thinking.
Yet, as will become evident, there were also many overlaps and related
themes, which will be considered in the conclusion. It is now time to
explore the thinking of each author in a separate chapter.

2

VICTOR SERGE, THE BOLSHEVIK REVOLUTION
AND STALINISM

Attitudes towards the Bolshevik revolution have been so influenced by
the subsequent history of the Soviet Union that it is now commonplace
to assume the inevitability of this course of events and to suggest that all
the ingredients of Stalinism existed in 1917. The prevalence of this notion
owes much to Cold War propaganda and writers have played a role in
reinforcing the Western anti-communist account. Classics such as Arthur
Koestler's *Darkness at Noon* and George Orwell's *Animal Farm* promoted
the message that the revolutionary ideal was doomed and the critical
works of Soviet authors, such as Boris Pasternak in *Dr Zhivago* and, above
all, Aleksandr Solzhenitsyn in his numerous books, have reinforced this
perspective.[1] Of course, this simple equation of Leninism with Stalinism
has never been uncontested. In particular, Trotskyist movements have
normally insisted that the degeneration only began with Stalin's ascendancy, thereby seeking to uphold the pristine purity of Bolshevism. In
contrast to such over-simplifications from both ends of the ideological
spectrum, the writings of Victor Serge do not fit into any pigeonhole,
either politically or in terms of genre.[2] For he was simultaneously a participant, witness, historian, journalist, political analyst and novelist. This
makes his work extraordinarily illuminating, and he posed some questions of great relevance for any discussion of justice in a revolutionary

transition. Through his writing it is possible to appreciate why a committed participant initially regarded the Bolshevik revolution as a triumph for justice and later came to view the outcome as the most extreme form of injustice.

Life, politics and literature

Political evolution

Victor Serge (originally Kibalchich) was born in 1890 in Belgium, the son of Russian parents.[3] His father was an anti-Tsarist exile and the revolutionary tradition was a profound part of his heritage. The family lived in extreme poverty, with Serge fending for himself from an early age. He was a voracious reader and at the age of fifteen was attracted to anarchism through a pamphlet by Kropotkin. But he was, he later recalled, already conscious of the existence of social conflict and the need for struggle.[4] This is a key factor in relation to his subsequent trajectory, for Serge's initial starting point was not to view the political realm as one of peaceful evolution or compromise, but to regard repression and violence as pervasive in capitalist society—whether in terms of the treatment of dissident opinion at home or in the phenomenon of imperialism abroad.

In 1909 he moved to Paris, where he taught French to Russians and translated Russian novels and poems. He quickly became prominent in anarchist circles, writing for and subsequently editing the *L'Anarchie* newspaper. His articles at this stage were not particularly consistent, but his most prominent theme was an absolute rejection of existing society. In December 1911 a group which included two of his childhood associates, Raymond Callemin and Octave Garnier, robbed and killed a young bank messenger; three days later the two men hid in the house that Serge shared with his partner, Rirette Maitrejean.[5] He defended their action in a strident article, denouncing those who invoked the law and sanctity of life as 'ignobly hypocritical, since they kill in its name by hunger, work, subjection, and prison', and he proclaimed that he was 'with the bandits'.[6] Subsequently, the police raided the offices of *L'Anarchie*, claimed to find two revolvers, and arrested Serge and Rirette, who were held in captivity until the trial in February

1913. Rirette was then released, but Serge was sentenced to a further four years' imprisonment.[7]

On his release in January 1917, he went to Barcelona where he was attracted by the anarcho-syndicalism of the Confederación Nacional del Trabajo (CNT), and he renounced the more individualist anarchism that he had advocated in Paris.[8] He admired local working-class militancy and supported Salvador Seguí, who led an attempted uprising in the city in which Serge was again arrested.[9] However, he came to believe that Seguí had no viable revolutionary strategy and, while still in Barcelona, heard the news of the first revolution in Russia and determined to get there himself. As a first step he returned to France, but in October 1917 he was re-arrested as a Bolshevik sympathiser and held in captivity for another fifteen months.[10] At this stage, he was attracted by the militant message of Bolshevism, but he knew little about it. Nevertheless, he initiated a Russian revolutionary group in the prison camp where he became involved in intense debates on the subject.

By now he was sufficiently prominent to be included in a prisoner exchange deal, arranged in October 1918, between the French authorities and the new Bolshevik regime. Amongst the group were a Jewish veteran of the 1905 Russian revolution, Alexander Russakov, and his daughter, Liuba, whom Serge would soon marry.[11] After the group arrived in Petrograd in January 1919, Serge's talents were immediately put to use by the Bolsheviks and over the next three years he worked for the party in the Commissariat of Foreign Affairs, in propaganda work, in the archives of the Tsarist secret police, and most notably on the Executive Committee of the Communist International (Comintern).[12] Although his first published writings from Russia were largely propagandist, he already indicated concerns about some aspects of policy, which were greatly reinforced in 1921, particularly by the aftermath of the rising in March, when the sailors of the Kronstadt base staged a rebellion against the regime (see below).

He spent much of the period from 1922 until the end of 1925 outside the Soviet Union, mainly in central Europe, where he continued to work for the Comintern. On his return, the Left Opposition immediately sought him out, but, when this was banned at the end of 1927, his position became extremely precarious.[13] The following year he was arrested, expelled from the Bolshevik Party, and imprisoned—the immediate cause being a series of articles he had written on China, implicitly attacking Stalin's catastrophic policy there.[14] Fortunately, by now his writings had already secured a readership in France and he was released from prison after only two months because of this external support, although he then almost died from an intestinal occlusion.[15] However, this spell in prison and his serious illness led him to make the important decision to concentrate on writing.

Until about 1932, though totally opposed to Stalin and the system that was being constructed through super-industrialisation and collectivisation, he still believed that there might be some possibility of regenerating the party. However, by February 1933, concerned that he would probably soon be arrested, he wrote a last testament for his friends in Paris, asking them to publish it if he disappeared. His accompanying letter reveals a new stage in his political thinking, for it constituted a definitive break with the party, which he no longer believed to have any future:

> I sympathise with all who go against the current, looking to preserve the ideas, principles, and the spirit of the October Revolution. I think that ... it is a must to review everything, so that we can begin to institute among comrades of the most diverse tendencies a really fraternal collaboration in discussion and in action.[16]

In October 1933 he was arrested and, after some eighty days in solitary confinement, was deported to Orenburg on the border of Kazakhstan. Struggling to survive in the long freezing winters and scorching summers, and again sometimes seriously ill, Serge spent almost three years there with his son, while his wife, who now suffered from serious mental illness, was often confined in an institution in Leningrad. Because he wrote in French, a campaign in Europe again eventually secured his release, culminating in a personal appeal by the author, Romain Rolland, to Stalin himself. After being ordered to return to Moscow in April 1936, Serge was allowed to leave for Belgium (and subsequently France) with his wife and children, but his manuscripts were confiscated and many of his close relatives were kept in captivity in the Soviet Union and eventually died there.

His return to the West did not resolve his problems, for his denunciations of Stalin were now out of keeping with the Popular Front era, when support for the Soviet Union extended far beyond communist circles. Thus while much of the European Left dismissed claims about the purges and show trials as right-wing propaganda, Serge desperately sought to mobilise opinion against them. However, he was now so 'off-message' that much of the left-wing press would no longer even publish his work.[17] Nor was this all, for by 1938 he had also broken away from Trotsky and the Trotskyist movement. Two key issues now set them apart, despite their common hatred of Stalinism. Serge saw the need for a complete reconceptualisation of strategy and organisation, and he was now prepared to build alliances with forces that rejected the whole Bolshevik tradition—for example, in Spain, where he supported the Partido Obrero de Unificación Marxista (POUM).[18] Trotsky, in contrast, remained adamant about the essential validity of Bolshevism, viewed Serge's notion of alliances with disdain, and had no time for POUM. Moreover, while Trotsky sought to organise a new non-Stalinist Bolshevik movement in a Fourth International, Serge believed that this would be counter-productive, for he no longer thought that a socialist future could be constructed through the revival of the Russian revolutionary model.

Serge spent four years in France, commenting on current developments and reflecting deeply on the course taken in the Soviet Union, both in historical and political texts and in creative works. But after the French surrender to Nazi Germany, the situation became too dangerous for him and he was forced to move again—finally arriving in Mexico in 1941 with his third wife, and son and daughter.[19] He died there six years later.

Writing

Serge always produced political tracts and commentaries, but he had renounced serious writing when joining the Russian revolution:

> Literature seemed quite a secondary matter … in an age like this. My duty was dictated by history itself. Besides, whenever I did any writing, there was such a striking discrepancy between my sensibility and my opinions that I could actually write nothing of any value.[20]

This probably meant that he felt inhibited by the pressures of providing propaganda. However, by 1928 'I felt sufficiently in tune with myself to write.'[21] Although he initially began with the non-fictional work, *Year One of the Russian Revolution*, he did not find historical writing entirely satisfactory:

> [I]t does not allow enough scope for showing men as they really live, dismantling their inner workings and penetrating deep into their souls. A certain degree of light can only be cast on history, I am convinced, by literary creation that is free and disinterested.[22]

He also drew a distinction between political intelligence and the approach of poets and novelists, who are not essentially rational, even if, as in his own case, they identified with 'rising classes':

> The artist ... is always delving for his raw material in the subconscious, in the preconscious, in intuition, in a lyrical inner life that is rather hard to define; he does not know with any certainty either where he is going or what he is creating.[23]

His own conception of writing was

> as a means of expressing to men what most of them live inwardly without being able to express, as a means of communion, a testimony to the vast flow of life through us, whose essential aspects we must try to fix for the benefit of those who come after us. In this respect, I belonged to the tradition of Russian writing.[24]

However, he rejected the conventional form of the novel, for:

> Individual existences were of no interest to me ... except by virtue of the great ensemble of life whose particles, more or less endowed with consciousness, are all that we ever are. And so the form of the classical novel seemed to me impoverished and outmoded, centring as it does upon a few beings artificially detached from the world.[25]

However, he certainly believed in the power of writing, later telling his friend, the revolutionary French poet Marcel Martinet, that 'during our period of tragic passivity and crisis ... everything must be started up again from the bottom up.' In this context he believed that 'a few sincere and truthful books can be extremely useful.'[26] Because of his insecure position, with the constant likelihood of arrest, he had to construct his works in detached fragments that could be completed separately and sent abroad. Nevertheless, between 1928–36 he wrote four novels, two short stories, one volume of poetry, six works of history, politics and literary theory, and translated novels and poems and seven volumes of history, politics, theory and memoirs.[27] Subsequently, while in France from 1936–40, he commented on current developments, reflecting deeply on the course taken in the Soviet Union, both in historical and political texts and in creative works, and in Mexico he wrote his memoirs, three more novels and further historical and political interventions.

Because his political and historical themes are so relevant to the concerns of this book, it is difficult to do justice to his creative writing here.[28] It is therefore worth emphasising the particular qualities of his novels, for Serge manages to convey the hopes and disappointments of the era by evoking the political atmosphere, and simultaneously depicting human relationships and vivid detail. Irving Howe explains this particularly well when he compares Serge's writing in *The Case of Comrade Tulayev* with the similar subject matter in Arthur Koestler's *Darkness at Noon*.[29] Koestler, he suggests, is so keen to make his ideological point that he 'manipulates his characters with a ruthless insistence that they conform to his will, that they illustrate prefabricated themes rather than fulfil their inner possibilities'.[30] Koestler is thus 'like a stricken Midas yearning for the bread of life yet, with every touch, turning experience into the useless gold of ideology'.[31] In contrast, Howe points to two key episodes in *The Case of Comrade Tulayev* where 'the tragedy of politics is counter-posed to the possibilities of experience, the commitment to an idea shown as it brushes against the commitment to compassion'. This, he suggests, is the best possible prescription for a political novel.[32] Of course, Serge's political and ideological engagement were also extremely profound, but he combined this with acute observation of people and their interactions, and he possessed a creative imagination. His fourth novel, *Midnight in the Century*, written while in France, provides a particularly vivid testament to the position he had now reached in his attitude to the contemporary Soviet Union.

The setting for the majority of the book is the labour camp of Chernoe where the ice floes only break up towards the middle of May. Here the prisoners, with various different political viewpoints, discuss the contemporary situation, while informers and spies are also watching them. The central character, Rodion, is portrayed as politically unsophisticated and confused, but with generous basic sentiments and instincts. In his state of perplexity he receives some instruction from another inmate—a lecturer in historical materialism, Mikhael Ivanovich Kostrov. Together they look at a dissident text from another prison (Verhkne-Uralsk), but Kostrov suggests that the problem with this group is that they fail to push the argument through to the very end: "'They don't dare conclude that the old bureaucratised Party is finished for the Revolution and that the moment has come to consider starting everything over again'". Rodion restrained himself from shouting: "I dare!" "That's right", he said'.[33] Meanwhile Stalin, 'the Chief', was preparing for the forthcoming Party congress, which would be 'unanimous in all its manifestations', would 'approve the Chief's remarks 'totally, unconditionally, and from the heart' and 'fifteen hundred frenetic hands will applaud until they wear his smiling patience'. Eventually, he decided to put down the Left, including those associated with the Verhkne–Uralsk minority—that is Rodion and his friends in Chernoe. Rodion escapes from the camp and in the wilderness is rescued by a lone wolf-hunter, who is entirely self-sufficient and is scathing about all notions of revolution and class. Rodion rejects this outlook, leaves him and eventually joins some building workers. However, the only work for them is to construct a new headquarters for the secret police, which will of course reinforce the oppression of the workers. Back in Chernoe, Kostrov had refused to collaborate with the camp commander, who is himself now imprisoned for failing to stamp out the 'Trotskyists' and allowing their 'leader'—Rodion—to escape.

In *Midnight in the Century* Serge depicted the nightmare world of Stalinism, but still concluded with some hope. In the last scene of the book a woman on the building site secretly shares some brandy with Rodion and asks if he feels better. He looks at her:

> Her tall form stood out over the scaffolding, and behind her there was nothing but airy space, plains, and Russian earth, the tortured earth of the Revolution, its black waters, its clouded waters, its clear waters, its frozen waters, its deadly waters, its invigorating waters, its enchanted forests, its mud, its impoverished villages, its countless living prisoners, its countless executed ones in graves, its construction sites, its masses, its solitudes and all the seeds germinating in its womb. Rodion saw it all, ineffably. All— even the germinating seeds, since they too are real. And that the woman drinking brandy from the bottle at that instant was truly, totally, a human being. He was entranced to see it so clearly.[34]

The imagery is unmistakable. At present the Revolution was buried beneath the ice, but the germinating seeds were real and one day it would all begin again—though in a quite different form. By now these were Serge's hopes for Russia but, as Bill Marshall has noted, there was subsequently a further evolution in his fiction, which became more pessimistic. In *The Case of Comrade Tulayev*, there was only a vague hope of a generational renewal, and in his last two novels the protagonists who sought to resist Stalinism were all outside the Party and were faced with hostility or a lack of comprehension by most of society.[35] All this was very different from Serge's position when he had arrived in Petrograd in January 1919.

Revolution and justice: hopes and realities

Some of Serge's early reports of revolutionary Petrograd might, at a first reading, suggest that he had 'seen the light': that he simply saw Bolshevism as the key to a transformation in class relations through the application of a Marxist conception of justice. For example, in a piece entitled 'My road to Russia', originally written in 1920, he explained that the observations and reflections that he had set out in his reports were those of a communist formed in the libertarian tradition of the Latin countries. He had set them down with his former colleagues in mind, for he wanted to counter their objections 'in the hope of enabling them to understand better the proletarian revolution'.[36] The October Revolution, he stated, had been a spectacular revelation for people like himself whose own journey towards communism had lasted some twelve years. This implied a process of gradual revelation towards 'the truth' and a similar trajectory is suggested in his novel, *Birth of our Power*.[37] Yet a closer reading of the texts shows that, from the start, Serge posed some critical questions about political problems: in particular whether the Bolsheviks would pay sufficient regard to the need for free expression of diverse opinions and would guard against dictatorial power.

Authoritarian control versus emancipation and freedom

In his essay, 'The Anarchists and the Experience of the Russian Revolution', written in 1920 and published the next year, he warned that some non-anarchist militants in Russia might get absorbed into bourgeois practices and corrupted by power:

> Anarchist philosophy, which appeals to individuals, imposes on them attitudes in their private life and their inner life, proposes a morality, which is something that Marxism ... does not do to such a great extent. Armed with the spirit of free enquiry, more liberated than anyone else from bourgeois prejudices with regard to the family, honour, propriety, love, from worrying about 'what people will say' and 'what is expected', militants who see anarchism as 'an individual way of life and activity' ... will resist reaction in behaviour with their common sense and their courage in setting an example. While others become officers, functionaries, judges, sometimes joining the privileged elite, they will remain simply men, free workers, who can perform in a stoical fashion all the tasks that are necessary to plough up the old land...[38]

This would, he argued, become still more important in the future—after the revolution had finally triumphed over its enemies—for at this stage the masses would be tempted to believe that the way forward was simply through greater material well-being. At this juncture, the role of anarchists would be decisive: 'In all fields of social activity, it will fall to them to bring their answer to this question: "Towards greater freedom. Towards the fullest development of the human personality"'.[39] Conservative or reactionary tendencies would also appear,

> So we shall need anarchists to go forward, to stimulate the endless quest of the best and the bravest, to ensure the defence of the individual against various intolerant or tyrannical collectivities, to pursue in behaviour and in thought the never-ending revolutionary action which generates all human progress.[40]

He also called for the effective and permanent supervision of the masses over institutions and people, suggesting that while communists knew that this was necessary 'their sense of discipline and their habits of centralisation make those of them who are not libertarians less fit to recommend or indeed exercise this supervision'.[41] Similarly, he warned that some communists might be temperamentally inclined to underestimate the dangers of state power, instead of realising that the goal was to ensure that it withered away.[42] Even more pointedly, while accepting the need for extreme repressive power during the civil war, he was deeply concerned about the militarisation of labour and the use of the state to take full control of the production process:

The confusion between the internal and external defence of the revolution and the organisation of production, resulting from the subordination of the creative apparatus (industry) to the destructive and murderous apparatus (the state) seems to me today to be as serious in the field of ideas as in the field of facts.[43]

He suggested that such tendencies confirmed some of the propositions of anarchism—that the exercise of authority leads to economic corruption (with the possession of power leading to privileged groups) and psychological corruption:

In the one who commands, it arouses arrogance, scorn for the personality of others, and, in times of social war, brutality and general contempt for human life; in the one who has to obey, it produces servility, hypocrisy, dishonesty or, in the best case ... the behaviour of a robot.[44]

The exercise of authority is 'one of the most pernicious forms of the exploitation of man by man' and 'The obsession with commanding, prescribing, decreeing, ordering and bullying, especially when it wins over the uncultivated masses, has been one of the major causes of the cruelties and of the mistakes of the Russian revolution'.[45]

Later, when he looked back on this period, his criticisms became still more pronounced. Thus in *Birth of our Power*'s fictionalised version of the discussions amongst the revolutionaries imprisoned in France in 1918 before departing for Russia, the narrator's descriptions tend to highlight the critical voices rather than those of Bolshevik orthodoxy, represented by one prisoner, Krafft.[46] Such differences become more pronounced on the journey to Russia and, when they finally arrive, it becomes obvious that some are motivated less by idealism than in order to pursue power themselves, while others emerge as iron-fisted organisers who will not tolerate any lack of discipline or petty crime, but regard themselves as 'purifiers' who would use terror not only against the bourgeoisie, but also 'to hit the scoundrels, the rotten apples, the filth carriers, that whole vermin which will infect us with its syphilis if we don't treat it with the hot iron'.[47] Moreover, when they arrive in Petrograd itself they find numerous Commissariats and orders, so that:

Already, in a few hours, we had learned more about the revolution than in many long meditations. And it had appeared to us under aspects very different from those suggested by our imagination, shaped by legend … We had been thinking of the squares transformed into tumultuous forums, of the excited clubs of '92;[48] of the blossoming of many little journals, each crying out its own solution, its system, its fantasy; of the great 'days' of the Soviets, like Conventions. In the language, in the slogans posted every-where, in the only two newspapers published, among the men, we discov-ered one enormous uniformity of a single way of thinking, imperious, almost despotic, but supreme, terribly true, made flesh and blood at each moment through action. We found not the passionate mobs going forward under flags to struggles begun anew each day in tragic and fruitful confu-sions, but a sort of vast administration, an army, a machine in which the most burning energies and the clearest intelligences were coldly inte-grated and which performed its task inexorably. And that task was to strain ceaselessly, for commonplace, often invisible achievements, with forces which, each day, seemed to be the last; to live and to persevere day after day; it was also to make an exhausted country, on the point of falling back into inertia, rise above itself; it was, finally to resist and to conquer every-where, transcending all logic.[49]

Translated into the conceptual categories outlined in Chapter One, Serge's ideas in this early period might be expressed as follows: his overwhelming motivation in his enthusiastic support for the revolution was for a process of structural transformation to bring about a new society—that is, through a Marxist conception of justice. Yet some of his libertarian convictions meant that he was already concerned that authoritarian and coercive tendencies might prevail over other goals that he also identified with the revolution—above all, those of eman-cipation and freedom. Later these traces of his earlier anarchist thought would lead him towards some more liberal conceptions of rights and justice. However, in this period, his belief in the need for structural transformation prevailed, leading him to support the necessity for revolutionary terror.

Violence

In his first published account after his arrival in Russia, 'During the Civil War: Petrograd: May–June 1919 Impressions and Considerations', he explained that it was always difficult to accept revolutionary terror in the abstract and only possible to understand 'if you have seen it growing irresistible out of the surrounding circumstances'.[50] In part, he justified this with the argument that the atrocities of the counter-revolutionary Whites during the previous year were far greater than those of the Reds. But he did not pull his punches in depicting the violence of the latter: 'For our part we don't spare former officers, or non-commissioned officers of any sort. War to the death with no humanitarian hypocrisy; there is no Red Cross and stretcher-bearers are not allowed. Primitive warfare, war of extermination, civil war.'[51] The law was 'kill or be killed', with everyone aware that if the Whites entered Petrograd, they would show no mercy. This meant that '[t]he air is permeated with a vague smell of blood, creating among us a state of mind in which terror cannot fail to grow.'[52]

Noting that an issue of *Pravda* of 31 May carried paragraphs by Lenin and Dzherzhinsky, the head of the Extraordinary Commission for Combating Counter-Revolution and Sabotage (the Cheka), urging 'Death to Spies', he commented that this was a direct order to show no pity.[53] Less than a fortnight later, the front page of *Izvestia* included an instruction from Trotsky, counter-signed by Zinoviev, which stated that all former officers integrated into the command structure of the Red Army must sign a statement acknowledging that they had been informed 'that the consequences of any treachery will fall on their families'.[54] Again he justified such steps partly by referring to merciless counter-revolutionary terror,[55] but also as necessary to save the revolution by terrorising the population as a whole:

> Why does the revolution also have to have recourse to this sickening use of military force? We don't ask about that any more. This is not the time for arguments. The revolution is at war. If it doesn't suppress panic, the physical cowardice of the masses at certain times, the demented, cowardly selfishness of individuals, then it is lost; and its loss will mean that the blood of these same people will flow in huge quantities.[56]

Insisting that it was imperative to crush reactionary forces at whatever cost 'because if it were to triumph even for a moment it would be a calamity for the whole of humanity', he called on those who had not lived through these hours of civil war to 'cast the first stone'.[57] However, he also ended on a sombre note:

> This fight to the death, in Red Russia, has had many victims. ... [T]hese days of hatred are so painful that one feels on the brink of despair, and one loses faith in humanity, and in ideas and in oneself. The horizon seems to

block out all light. The evil madness of humanity seems so great that there is no way out. The Russian revolutionaries have all gone through such doubt ... Some have given in. Most have emerged strengthened in their commitment to the ideal.[58]

But his fears about the long-term impact of such violence were discernible. Thus in an essay, originally published in 1921, he re-affirmed his belief in the necessity for such extreme measures, but continued:

> But it creates nothing; it is powerless to give birth to an idea or a creation. And what is dangerous is the fact that it gives birth to a great illusion. For men are prone to nourish illusions about their own capacities, and to believe that they can construct with the same victorious daring that they used for destruction.

> But this is not the case. The new society can be built only through knowledge, the spirit of organisation and the unceasing development of the consciousness of the masses and of individuals. The guns and bayonets of the Red army, the decrees and measures of compulsion introduced by the dictatorship of the proletariat—these will kill the old regime and defend the new communist society ... but then they must make way for education, propaganda, the initiative of the masses and the organising spirit of leading elements.[59]

Over time, he came to view the price as still higher than he had initially realised, and he was also to become increasingly preoccupied with the nature of the relationship between the measures undertaken in this period and the later repression. This was depicted graphically in his novel, *Conquered City* (first published as *Ville conquise* in 1932), set entirely in Petrograd.[60]

In an early passage a soldier tells the narrator (a member of the party) that everyone was now forced to steal in order to survive and that a man on guard had fired a shot to scare a thief. But this had been a twelve-year-old boy, who was sent out by his mother each night, and he was so frightened that he had fallen through a hole in the ice with a log on his head and was never seen again. As a member of the governing party, the narrator was in a privileged position, but he was uncomfortably aware that a child had been drowned that day for the equivalent of his own ration of warmth and bread.

He continues:

> The Special Commission [the Cheka] works day and night. That is us too. The implacable side of our face we turn to the world. We, the destroyers

of prisons, the liberators, freedmen, yesterday's convicts, often marked indelibly by our chains, we who investigate, search out, arrest; we, judges, jailers, executioners, we! We have conquered everything and everything has slipped out of our grasp. We have conquered bread, and there is famine. We have declared peace to a war-weary world, and war has moved into every house. We have proclaimed the liberation of men, and we need prisons, an 'iron' discipline—yes, to pour our human weakness into brazen moulds in order to accomplish what is perhaps beyond our strength—and we are the bringers of dictatorship. We have proclaimed fraternity, but it is 'fraternity and death' in reality.[61]

The measures portrayed factually in his contemporary account were represented in a still more menacing way in the novel, where he listed elements of the repression:

> Going out after eight in the evening without special permission prohibited. Mandatory guard duty at the doors of dwellings. Mandatory labour. Mandatory surrender of all arms ... within twenty-four hours under pain of death. Telegraphed order from the President of the Revolutionary War Council prescribing the establishment of lists of former officers serving with the Red Army, these families to be considered responsible for the loyalty of the officers. Arrest of hostages. Special surveillance of automobile and motorcycle traffic. House-by-house searches. Identity checks. Arrest of suspects. Division of the city into internal defence sectors. Mobilization of Communist battalions. Death penalty for speculators. Death for spies. Death for traitors. Death for deserters. Death for misappropriators of public funds. Death for spreaders of false reports.[62]

In this atmosphere, two party members with official responsibilities discuss the revolution. One of them suggests that there could be circumstances in which it would be better for the revolution to perish and leave a clear memory than, for example, to turn to a Bonaparte to save it. The other (soon to be a member of the Cheka) tells him to rid himself of such defeatist ideas: 'A philosophy of the whipped. No more of that. We're here to stay, by God. To hold on, to work, to organise, to use everything to the limit including Dung. Dung is also necessary.'[63]

The historical episode that would come to dominate Serge's questioning about the relationship between the early years of the revolution and the later Stalinist dictatorship came after the defeat of the counter-revolution—with the Kronstadt uprising in 1921 and its aftermath. In a situation of extreme economic deprivation in both countryside and towns during the era of 'war communism', a general meeting on 1 March in the garrison of Kronstadt passed a resolution, including fifteen demands. The first three of these were for immediate new elections to the Soviets (local councils or workplace bodies elected by workers, peasants or soldiers), held by secret ballot and preceded by electoral propaganda for all workers and peasants; freedom of speech and of the press for workers and peasants, for the Anarchists, and for the Left Socialist parties; and the right of assembly, and freedom for trade union and peasant associations. Other demands included the liberation of all political prisoners from left-wing parties and of workers and peasants, and the effective abolition of various privileges for the Communist Party and Party-controlled organisations. The Communist Party claimed that the social composition of the sailors had changed fundamentally since 1917 and that the uprising was led by counter-revolutionaries.[64] The government began its attack on 7 March, using approximately 60,000 troops to gain control of the fortress. This led to over 10,000 Bolshevik fatalities, and an unknown number of rebel deaths, followed by thousands being executed and a similar number jailed, with others escaping to Finland.[65]

Although this was a critical moment for Serge, his attitude towards it remained quite convoluted and contradictory. He later recalled that in late February he was informed that Kronstadt had been taken over by the Whites, but was then told by numerous party comrades that this was a lie and that it was the sailors who had mutinied in a naval revolt led by the Soviet. He realised two key points: first that the press was systematically lying about what was going on; secondly, that from the start, when successful negotiations were possible, the leadership was intent on crushing the rebellion through force.[66] Nevertheless, although he claimed that the Kronstadt uprising had right on its side, he backed the leadership in crushing it: 'If the Bolshevik dictatorship fell, it was only a short step to chaos, and through chaos to a peasant rising, the massacre of the Communists, the return of the émigrés, and in the end, through the sheer force of events, another dictatorship, this time anti-proletarian.'[67]

However, this was not the end of the affair. The rising, which also precipitated the introduction of Lenin's 'state capitalism' via his New Economic Policy (NEP), was accompanied by new steps in the creation of the party dictatorship, with a ban on all factions.[68] Serge welcomed the NEP, but also thought that it vindicated many of the demands of the Kronstadt uprising.[69] Furthermore, in his later writings he emphasised his belief that this economic reform should have been coupled with a political relaxation, deploring the fact that Lenin had moved in the opposite direction.[70] Nor did the crushing of the rising end the oppression, for hundreds of Kronstadt prisoners were taken to Petrograd, where they were handed over to the Cheka. According to Serge, 'months later they were still being shot in small batches, a senseless and criminal agony'.[71] All this was a turning point for him, with one of his letters talking of feeling 'heartbroken, desperate, not knowing what is to become of me'.[72] Much later he would claim that it was 'gravely significant' that Trotsky had not bothered to inform himself so as to find out what ordinary party members knew—'that they had just committed through inhumanity *a pointless crime* against the proletariat and the peasants' and that, from the very beginning of the revolution, the Central Committee committed 'the gravest errors', contributing on the one hand to 'the bureaucratization of the party and the state, and on the other to disarming the masses and, more particularly, the revolutionaries'.[73] At the time, the crushing of Kronstadt had not ended his hopes for a change, but it was nevertheless a key turning point in his growing fears that the revolution would become increasingly dominated by its authoritarian and repressive aspects.[74] These were reinforced by his concerns about the absence of law.

Legal injustice

Some of Serge's most powerful convictions and emotions had constantly centred on the death penalty and long prison sentences. In his *Memoirs* he recalled massive protests in pre-war France in 1910 against the death sentence of a twenty-year-old who had wounded four policemen, and claimed that subsequently he had always felt revulsion and contempt for the death penalty and knew of nothing more stupidly inhuman than life imprisonment or very lengthy sentences.[75] The years that he spent in jail reinforced such convictions, and he later said that the experience had been so intolerable that he wrote his first novel, *Men in Prison*, in an effort to free himself from this inward nightmare and to perform a duty towards those who would never so free themselves.[76] Ostensibly, the novel refers solely to prisons in capitalist countries, rather than in post-revolutionary Russia, but Serge clearly intended his meaning to have a universal relevance. Prison regulations, he wrote 'could be summed up in three peremptory words: *Living is forbidden!*', and he inveighed against the cruelty of life sentences 'which death alone ends ... after years of torture'.[77] But, above all, he condemned the death penalty, insisting that the working class must learn

> to abolish a past which has put such arms into its hands, to abolish the refined, senseless, gratuitous cruelty of death inflicted by an 'act of justice' on guilty men who are sometimes brutes, usually unlucky wretches, sometimes rebels (that is to say, the most ardent of men), and always the inevitable products of the normal workings of society, always victims paying a ransom for others ... Nothing, in an opulent and solid society, justifies that abominable thing: the solemn execution, on a set day, at a fixed hour, after complicated formalities, of a miserable wretch who has been kept for sixty or a hundred days in an iron-gray cell in the Maximum Security section, alone with the guillotine blade, that cold line on the back of the neck.[78]

Given such passion on the issue, he was bound to view the system of punishment under post-revolutionary Russia with increasing alarm.

In the immediate aftermath of the revolution, there had been some signs that major reforms would be introduced in the punitive use of the legal system, but all this was quickly reversed by the establishment and increasing role and powers of the Cheka.[79] Serge would subsequently view this as 'one of the gravest and most impermissible errors that the Bolshevik leaders committed in 1918, when plots, blockages, and interventions made them lose their heads'. The Cheka soon became, he argued, 'a State within the State, protected by military secrecy and proceedings *in camera*'.[80]

As he put it:

> what the Cheka was in fact given was the right to apply the death penalty on a mass scale and in secret, without hearing the accused, who were unable to defend themselves and whom in most cases their judges did not even see! By comparison with this inquisitorial process, the 'closed door' status of any court in which the judges and the defendants are face to face, and to which defence counsel are admitted, appears to overflow with safeguards.[81]

The whole legal system was soon tainted by such developments. Serge recalled being constantly telephoned in 1919 by 'panic-stricken women who spoke of arrests, imminent executions, and injustice, and begged me to intervene at once, for the love of God!'[82] Often pardons depended on this kind of personal intercession and he also recounted how in 1922 he defended a distant relative from the death penalty, being 'determined to get him out of there without too much regard for legal fictions'.[83] By 1926, following his return to Russia after his years in central Europe, he was also shocked by a show trial for a collective rape, where there appeared to be no real procedures and the law was simply twisted to allow executions to take place for 'banditry'.[84] He thus became increasingly convinced that crucial errors were made in the early post-revolutionary years. But, as a result of his observations, experience and reflections, what did Serge regard as necessary lessons? And how adequate were they?

Serge's reflections on the Soviet experience

Following his expulsion from the party in 1928, he outlined (though not in his own name) a programme of reform for the Soviet Union, including: a return of internal democracy in the party; a profound reform of the press, guaranteeing the right of response (without reprisal) and the right of expression of all nuances of Soviet and communist opinion; scientific, literary and theoretical freedom; a judicial system that would defend the workers' and peasants' state, without being a tool of counter-revolution, in which the accused must have the right of defence and security, and in which the Cheka must account for its acts in front of the regular justice of the workers' state; and stimulation of the individual interests of the workers and a maximum of workers' democracy in production. This was not a democratic programme, for there was no acceptance here of the existence of other parties, while the right of free expression was reserved for 'all nuances of Soviet and Communist opinion', thereby implicitly limiting the expression of other opinions. Nevertheless, this programme would have constituted a significant step in the direction of greater pluralism and legal justice.

By early 1933, when he wrote the testament that was smuggled out to Paris, his thinking had evolved further. There were, he now maintained, three essential points, 'superior to all tactical considerations', on which he would remain an avowed and unequivocal dissident 'whom only force can silence'. The first was the 'defence of man', which meant respect for everyone's rights, security and value, irrespective of their class background. In this context, 'I hold as an abomination unspeakable, reactionary, sickening, and corrupting, the continued use of the death penalty as a secret and administrative measure (in a time of peace! in a state more powerful than any other!)'. Since life had now fallen so low, 'all capital punishment in the present regime must be condemned', while the suppression—by exile, deportation and imprisonment more or less for life—of all dissent in the working class movement was 'equally abominable and unjustifiable'. Secondly, the 'defence of truth' was a right and he would not consent either to 'the systematic falsification of history or to the suppression of all serious news from the press', for truth was a 'precondition of intellectual and moral health'. Both truth and honesty were rights of man. The third point was the 'defence of thought':

> I hold that Socialism cannot develop in the intellectual sense except by the rivalry, scrutiny, and struggle of ideas; that we should fear not error, which is mended in time by life itself, but rather stagnation and reaction; that respect for man implies his right to know everything and his freedom to think. It is not against freedom of thought and against man that Socialism can triumph, but on the contrary, through freedom of thought, and by improving the condition of man.[85]

This was lacking in detail about any institutional mechanisms to guarantee the protection and enforcement of such rights, but it certainly specified, courageously and clearly, the principles that he now saw as fundamental.

Subsequently, he would constantly search for further lessons from the Russian experience. By 1939 he argued that the Bolsheviks had only dared to be libertarian during the period from October 1917 until the following summer.[86] It was, he continued, easy to explain and even justify the repressive policies in the face of mortal danger, but after the Civil War they should have sought a socialist solution to the problems of the new social organisation in a workers' democracy, building on the initiatives of diverse groups, rather than in the monopoly of power, repression of 'heresies', and the authority and thinking of a single power, which inevitably led to the authority and thinking of a single leader.[87] The spirit of liberty, he concluded, was as necessary for

Marxism as was oxygen for living beings. Subsequently, he also argued that the NEP should have been coupled with a policy of tolerance and reconciliation towards those socialist and libertarian elements prepared to work within the Soviet constitution, and that a coalition government should have been formed. Some possibilities still remained until 1927, but after this date totalitarianism was established over a ten-year period culminating in the show trials, which eliminated the revolutionary generation in 'the bloodiest coup in history'.[88]

Yet this did not lead to any change in his attitude to the revolution itself. In his 1933 'testament', he prefaced his condemnation of Stalin's use of the death penalty and labour camps by saying that he did not wish 'to erase a single line of what I have written on the necessity of terror in revolutions threatened by death'.[89] And in his final published work he still insisted that there had been no possibility of democracy in 1917 and that the choice was between a dictatorship of the Left or a counter-revolutionary dictatorship of the Right.[90] Rather than revising such views, he focused on the subsequent policy decisions that reinforced the trends that would later lead to totalitarianism. In his last years he also emphasised less tangible qualitative aspects, including psychological considerations. Throughout his *Memoirs* he reflected on such issues, culminating in the following comment:

> I immediately discerned within the Russian Revolution the seeds of such serious evils as intolerance and the drive towards the persecution of dissent. These evils originated in an absolute sense of possession of the truth, grafted upon doctrinal rigidity. What followed was contempt for the man who was different, of his arguments and way of life. Undoubtedly, one of the greatest problems which each of us has to solve in the realm of practice is that of accepting the necessity to maintain, in the midst of the intransigence which comes from steadfast beliefs, a critical spirit towards these same beliefs and a respect for the belief that differs. In the struggle, it is the problem of combining the greatest practical efficiency with respect for the man in the enemy—in a word, of war without hate. The Russian Revolution, although led by men who were upright and intelligent, did not resolve this problem because the masses had received, from the experience of despotism, a fatal stamp whose effects were imprinted in the leaders themselves.[91]

This had implications for his attitudes towards retribution, and he also argued that the war and civil war destroyed the notion of human kindness: 'I remain convinced that the Socialist revolution would nevertheless have been much stronger and clearer if those who held supreme power had persevered in defending and applying a principle of humanity towards the defeated enemy with as much energy as they did in overcoming him.'[92] There was also a sense in which his pre-Bolshevik stress on the individual re-asserted itself as his most fundamental value. While re-affirming the scientific spirit and importance of Marxism, it was, he believed, a 'positive disaster ... that a Marxist orthodoxy should ... have taken over the apparatus of power', intruding into education and then exempting itself from criticism. He continued:

> The relationships between error and true understanding are in any case too abstruse for anyone to presume to regulate them by authority. Men have no choice but to make long detours through hypotheses, mistakes, and imaginative guesses, if they are to succeed in extricating assessments which are more exact, if partly provisional: for there are few cases of complete exactness. This means that freedom of thought seems to me, of all values, one of the most essential.[93]

And, as a writer, he was particularly passionate about this in relation to the artistic sphere:

> Order sculptors to sculpt nothing but the effigies of heroes, and Rodin becomes impossible. Assign themes, methods and censorship to writers and poets, and you will get an 'official' literature which may appear narrowly useful for a time—but all the words considered great by the opinion of history because they have influenced social understanding will have become inconceivable. Command the mandarins to construct a philosophy conforming to the intentions of the state, and all philosophy, search for truth and spiritual creation is reduced to dead compilations—unless some of the mandarins disobey the order. The exercise of thought, which is as natural and as imperiously necessary to the human as breathing, is simply not susceptible to complete external control. *Thought that is directed by the church or the state is thought smothered*, is thought which in the past has been fertile only through the rebellions it has inspired.[94]

Writing in the middle of World War II in exile in Mexico he concluded his *Memoirs* by proclaiming that, despite the horrors of the current senseless tyrannies, a new world revolution would be built on new foundations:

> That these foundations must be of social justice, of rational organization, of respect for the individual, of liberty, is for me an obvious fact which,

little by little, is asserting itself out of the very inhumanity of the present time. The future seems to me, despite the clouds on the horizon, to be full of possibilities vaster than any we have glimpsed in the past. The passion, the experience, and even the errors of my fighting generation may perhaps help illumine the way forward, but on one condition, which has become a categorical imperative: never to give up the defense of man against systems whose plans crush the individual.[95]

Wider lessons?

In 1917, casting off his anarchist past, Serge had become an enthusiastic convert to Bolshevism. Passionate about the need for revolution, he was convinced by a Marxist conception of justice. Certainly, he voiced some concerns about potentially authoritarian tendencies from the start, but he believed that the highest priority was to save the revolution and that violence and terror were necessary. From 1928 onwards his stress on the need for a separation of power and forms of legal justice became increasingly evident, with a growing emphasis on individual freedom. In his wartime writings, particularly on the future of socialism outside Russia, he also emphasised notions of social justice more than the Marxist conception. Inevitably he left unresolved contradictions because he was grappling with the most complex questions—many of which need to be confronted in any attempt to consider justice in transitions.[96]

One problem that Serge confronted extremely clearly was that of revolutionary violence. This problem will constantly re-appear in this book, but normally in a less stark and uncompromising way. Many writers, generally with reluctance, have accepted the use of violence in the service of a just cause. But Serge went far beyond this, arguing that it was necessary to practise some indiscriminate terror both against counter-revolutionaries and also against workers and peasants who might otherwise desert the revolutionary cause. In effect, he was arguing that the revolutionary application of a Marxist conception of justice demanded this in a situation when no peaceful solution was possible. Yet even during the civil war he feared that the militarisation of social, economic and political relationships carried the danger that this would also become entrenched in the post-crisis situation. However, when there was increasing evidence that this was happening, his institutional proposals were quite rudimentary and he suggested that, once the emergency had passed, the Bolshevik leaders could and should have stepped back from the command and control model and implemented more democratic, tolerant and libertarian modes of behaviour. This changed when, in later years, he thought about the future of socialism in the light of the Soviet experience, and increasingly stressed the realms of liberty, free speech, artistic creation, democratic representation, and legal justice. All this indicated that he had now incorporated important elements of liberal conceptions of rights and justice into his thinking. He also maintained his vehement opposition to capital punishment and long periods of imprisonment and, in a way that foreshadowed Camus, Serge believed that the death penalty had ramifications far beyond the criminal justice system and, in a sense, encapsulated the values of a repressive society. Finally, although he did not explicitly discuss the way in which former Tsarist officials should be treated, his remarks about winning people over through a more humane approach suggest that he would have tended to favour reparative approaches to transitional justice had they been on the agenda in his era.

The gap between revolutionary aspirations and the eventual tyrannical reality was greater in the Bolshevik case than in any other transition in this book. Having hoped in 1919 that the Bolshevik interpretation of a Marxist conception of justice would be sufficient, Serge learned that other dimensions of justice, and limitations of political power, were necessary for the attainment of a just society. His literary skill ensured that both his intellectual and political journey, and the conclusions themselves, remain highly illuminating.

3

FROM THE VICHY REGIME
TO THE FOURTH FRENCH REPUBLIC

ALBERT CAMUS AND RESISTANCE, JUSTICE AND VIOLENCE

In the early summer of 1940 Nazi Germany rapidly defeated French forces and the government was forced to abandon Paris on 10 June. On 22 June an armistice was agreed, under which Germany occupied approximately three-fifths of France to the north and west of a line through Geneva, Tours and the Spanish border, while a French administration was allowed to take control of the zone south of this area. This would be the domain of the so-called Vichy regime, which was formally established in July 1940 after a National Assembly vote. The division between the two zones remained until November 1942, when the Germans also moved into the southern zone, but the Vichy government remained nominally in charge for almost two more years. Finally, following the allied advance and the liberation of Paris, a new 'national unanimity' government of Resistance forces under General de Gaulle was established on 9 September 1944. For four years France was thus controlled by a combination of Nazism and a semi-autonomous form of domestic repression.

In 1940 Marshal Pétain had assumed the title of 'head of the French state' and was granted full powers. The slogan 'work, family and fatherland' replaced that of 'liberty, equality and fraternity', democratic liberties and guarantees were suspended, and repressive measures were instituted against Jews, immigrants, the Roma, Freemasons, homo-sexuals and the Left. The legitimacy of the regime was immediately contested both by General de Gaulle, initially from London and, after May 1943, from Algeria, and by the domestic Resistance. At first the Resistance was small, partly as a result of divisions between commu-nists and non-communists. Because of the Soviet–German Pact in August 1939, the Parti Communiste Français (PCF) hardly focused on the Germans for the first two years of the war while vehemently denouncing and combating the Vichy regime. This battle was directly related to the experience of the party, which had every reason to regard Pétain's government as the culmination of anti-communist poli-cies initiated before the war. Many of the non-communist *resistants*, in contrast, initially accepted the Pétain government and sought instead to undermine the German occupation. However, during 1941–2 both groups shifted. Hitler's attack on the Soviet Union released the PCF from its shackled position and enabled it to play a leading role in Resistance activities against the Germans, while the non-communist movements increasingly came to realise that their action also required a form of warfare against the Vichy government.[1] Greater militancy was provoked by the increasing impact of the war on the population through greater German pressure on the regime; the abolition of the demarcation line between German occupation forces and the non-occupied zone in November 1942 was also important in this respect. The Gestapo and the French paramilitary force, the Milice, then sought to eliminate the Resistance and all other opponents of the regime.[2] By the end of 1942 the domestic Resistance was generally based on a combination of patriotism and a left-wing republican tradition, even amongst those whose political inclinations were normally on the Centre or Right.[3] Since the PCF also adopted this discourse, rather than specifically revolutionary themes, the differences between com-munists and non-communists in the mainland Resistance, at least in the movements on the ground, were softened. Furthermore, from 1943 onwards the external and domestic Resistance forces were united to the extent that both recognised the ultimate leadership of de Gaulle himself. From then until the Liberation the battle against the Vichy regime intensified.

ALBERT CAMUS AND RESISTANCE, JUSTICE AND VIOLENCE

For several decades after 1945, French attitudes both to the war and the Liberation period tended to be dominated by myths, which were often deliberately cultivated. Both Gaullists on the Right and the PCF on the Left exaggerated the importance of the Resistance, implying that it commanded far greater support than was the case. However, the pro-Vichy mythology was more dangerous, for it repeated the propaganda of Pétain himself in claiming that the regime acted as a shield against Nazi excesses. In this apologia for the collaboration, a sharp distinction was drawn between the allegedly patriotic Pétain, and the prime minister, Pierre Laval, who was executed in October 1945 and was the scapegoat for the regime's pro-Nazi alignment. It was only in 1972 that the American historian Robert Paxton published a ground-breaking work, which decisively rebutted this notion.[4] This revealed Vichy in its true colours: as a vicious, extreme right-wing regime that sought to reverse all the Republican and left-wing traditions in the country. Gradually, this became the mainstream view and further work then also demonstrated the appalling role that the regime had played in the deportations of the Jews.[5]

The controversies about the purge (*l'épuration*) that took place at the time of the Liberation were equally heated. The purge comprised both unofficial executions by local Liberation Committees, and official trials and punishments, including the death penalty, as well as the dismissal of collaborators across the public sector and a range of professions. The merits and effectiveness of the policy are a matter for debate, but it was often subsequently dealt with in a sensationalist way, with right-wing propaganda seeking to undermine the credibility of the whole idea by flagrant exaggeration, claiming that 100,000 had been summarily executed.[6] In fact, the numbers were much lower than this. Henry Rousso has estimated that there were probably 8,000–9,000 such deaths, pointing out that many of these should be regarded as acts of war in the Liberation battle itself. He also suggests that many of the victims would probably have been condemned to death had they stood trial in the official system. Nevertheless, between 1,000–2,000 of the unofficial executions took place after the official legal processes had begun.[7]

This chapter considers the Resistance, the Liberation and the purge through the work of Albert Camus (1913–60).

Camus was one of the most outstanding writers of the twentieth century. His output included philosophy, plays, novels, essays and journalism; and his own reflections about writing, as expressed in his notebooks, provide an insight into his work. He called for 'courage in one's life and talent in one's work' and also declared that 'from the moment when I shall no longer be more than a writer ... I shall cease to write'.[8] He thus saw the need for engagement and a willingness to take a stance, while simultaneously valuing writing of the highest possible quality. His extraordinary achievement in his fiction was to produce texts that appeared simple, but which incorporated his philosophical and political ideas. His reportage raised fundamental ethical issues behind the concrete realities. The war years and the transition from Vichy to the Fourth Republic were of particular intensity and importance for him and would have a major influence on his subsequent life.

It was the appearance of his early works, particularly *L'Etranger* (1942) (*The Outsider*), which established his literary reputation, while his role in the Resistance also made him an important figure on the intellectual Left at the time of the Liberation.[9] Both his writing and his political prominence led him to friendship with Jean-Paul Sartre and his circle, but it was also the reaction of Camus to the transition, and particularly to the purge, that set him on the course that would eventually end that friendship.[10] For, by the end of the war, Camus was already deeply critical of communism and moving towards the position that he would adopt in *L'Homme Révolté* (1951) (*The Rebel*).[11] This work was widely seen as constituting a break with the Left and it certainly shattered the friendship with Sartre. When, in the mid-1950s, Camus also condemned the violence of the Algerian Liberation Movement, the Front de Libération Nationale (FLN), and advocated a compromise settlement for Algeria rather than outright independence, he was widely denounced by the Left and also sometimes regarded as an apologist for French colonialism. In fact, this was a misrepresentation of his position: Camus had condemned French oppression in Algeria much earlier than most of the Left and he continued to do so.[12] Nor did the fact that many on the Right welcomed *The Rebel* mean that Camus had joined their ranks. For he always sought to define his own, independent position.

ALBERT CAMUS AND RESISTANCE, JUSTICE AND VIOLENCE

From non-violence to resistance, 1940–44

Violent resistance as an ethical necessity

Born and educated in Algeria, as a French citizen living in conditions of poverty, Camus's complex identity was always a significant aspect of his life. Having excelled at his Lycée, he was accepted for the School of Philosophy at the University of Algiers, but was forced to defer his entry because at the age of 17 he contracted tuberculosis, which would lead to recurrent severe illness. He eventually re-started his university education in 1930, supporting himself through various forms of part-time work, and married in 1934.[13] In 1935 he joined the Algerian Communist Party and organised a 'Workers' Theatre' with the aim of producing socialist plays for workers. More generally, he was committed to promoting the rights of both French and Algerian workers, but his support for a particular Algerian campaign, regarded as nationalist by the Communist Party, led to his denunciation as a Trotskyist agitator and his expulsion from the party sometime between July 1937 and early 1938.[14] In October 1938, his friend Pascal Pia, who had formerly been editor of the PCF daily in Algeria, took up this role in a new paper, *Alger Républicain*. Camus began writing for it and then became editor of its offshoot, *Le Soir Républicain*, producing the first edition just after the war began.[15] Adopting a non-violent tradition of anti-imperialism, he favoured a peace policy, opposing the war and advocating an immediate peace with Hitler.[16] This was unacceptable to the government and at the beginning of 1940 the authorities closed down *Le Soir Républicain*. He left Algeria and moved to Paris, taking up a post as an editorial secretary for *Paris Soir*, which was then evacuated to Clermont-Ferrand just before the French surrender. When the Vichy government was formed, in a letter to Francine Faure, who would become his second wife in December, he wrote:

> Cowardice and senility, that's all we are being offered. Pro-German policies, a constitution like those of totalitarian regimes, horrible fear of a revolution that will not happen, all this as an excuse for sweet-talking enemies who will crush us anyway and to preserve privileges that are not threatened. Terrible days are in store: famine and general unemployment along with the hate they bring.[17]

And when the new racial laws against Jews were announced in October, he wrote to a Jewish friend, expressing solidarity with her.[18] However, although *Paris Soir* was carrying pro-Vichy propaganda and anti-Jewish articles, Camus did not immediately resign, and only left the paper when made redundant at the end of the year, returning to Algeria in January, where he remained until the summer of 1942.[19] While there he did not take an active stance against the regime: for example, when required to remove a chapter on Kafka (because he was Jewish) in order to secure the publication of *Le Mythe de Sisyphe* (*The Myth of Sisyphus*) by Gallimard in 1942, he appears to have agreed to this.[20] His first novel, *The Outsider*, was also first published that year in Vichy France. Thus he compromised, despite his personal antipathy towards the regime.

His attitude probably evolved as a result of two main factors. First, he remained close to his friend, Pascal Pia, who became actively involved in the Resistance from April 1942. Secondly, he had become seriously ill again and, after returning to France, he began a prolonged period of convalescence on the outskirts of Le Chambon-sur-Lignon, the remote village in the Haute-Loire, that protected up to 3,000 Jews from both the Vichy and Nazi authorities. It is very likely that *La Peste* (*The Plague*), which he was writing at the time, drew on some of his observations of the courage of ordinary people in Chambon. During 1943 his contacts with the Resistance grew through his involvement with the Combat group, which was one of the three major forces in the south, along with Libération-Sud and Franc-Tireurs. His first writing in open opposition to the German occupation was also now published. At the end of the year he was summoned to play a role by the director of the National Resistance Committee, Claude Bourdet, who was himself soon arrested. However, Pia, who now played a key role in underground activities, brought Camus in to establish (with Jacqueline Bernard) *Combat* as a journal, which soon claimed to be the voice of the United Resistance Movements.[21]

This was the most dangerous period of the Occupation years, with increasing atrocities and repression by both Vichy and Nazi forces. Camus was risking his life by editing the paper. Its printer committed suicide just before being arrested; his co-worker, Jacqueline Bernard, was picked up and deported to a concentration camp; and he was deeply affected when another close collaborator and friend, the poet René Leynard, was shot for 'acts of resistance'. In the pages of *Combat*, he constantly drew attention to the massacres, arrests and torture of resistance fighters. But what made him now identify the Nazis and the Vichy regime as a clear enemy that needed to be combated through violence? In order to explain this it is necessary to consider the development of his ideas.

For Camus the key questions were never simply political in a conventional sense, but were also about fundamental life choices. Perhaps partly because of his tuberculosis, which frequently threatened his life, some of his pre-war work had already suggested that the search for happiness should be accompanied by a clear consciousness of death, and this was reinforced by his philosophical notion of the 'absurd'. This suggested that people constantly wanted some transcendent purpose in life, but the world was indifferent to such notions.[22] People were ultimately alone and, as he argued in *The Myth of Sisyphus* (1942), it was only when such absurdity was understood that it was possible to find ways to live. Thus Camus was seeking the essence of the human condition: how should one live in a world without meaning?

The Outsider, his most influential novel, was written before he had made his commitment to the Resistance, but it already contained some relevant themes. The central character, Meursault, is detached from conventional codes of morality, lives in the present, and is completely honest about his own emotions. He becomes friendly with an unsavoury character, Raymond, who beats up his Algerian lover, suspecting her of infidelity. Rather than condemning Raymond, Meursault helps him evade prosecution, and eventually kills the woman's brother who is seeking revenge. Meursault's action is never fully explained, but may have been caused by a combination of fear and acute sensitivity to the heat of the sun. Given the racist attitudes prevalent in French colonialism, he could probably have escaped the guilty verdict and his subsequent execution had he conformed to the expected behaviour of a French citizen. However, he refuses to do so and is therefore seen as devoid of all human feeling, primarily because he had not cried at his mother's funeral and had gone to a comedy film at the cinema with a new girlfriend the next day. As Meursault realises, the prosecutor condemns him because 'I had no soul, there was nothing human about me'.[23] The judge then imposes the death penalty, not because of Meursault's guilt, but because of his general conduct and refusal to show remorse. He thus dies largely because he has not found meaning in the kind of life that society expects of him. But there are also other ideas in the book that would become increasingly important to Camus: those concerning the need to make fundamental choices about justice, violence and punishment in situations of acute personal risk.

The novel makes it clear that Camus certainly did not believe that the court was dispensing justice. Meursault had killed someone, but he could have made a strong case for this being manslaughter, rather than murder, had he been willing to defend himself robustly and had anyone been prepared to listen to him. The description of Meursault's contemplation of the guillotine is also important in relation to Camus's ideas. Much later, in 1957, in an essay opposing capital punishment, he recounted an event involving his father, Lucien (who had died before Camus's first birthday).[24] Lucien had witnessed the execution of a convicted murderer and, having initially supported the punishment, was so revolted by what he saw that he went to bed and vomited. His knowledge of this event seems to have played an important role in Camus's own opposition to capital punishment and in *The Outsider* this tale is recalled in fictional form as Meursault, awaiting execution, recalls his mother telling him of his father's revulsion at such an event. Finally, it is significant that the only time Meursault shows any passion is in his death cell, when a priest tries to persuade him to put his faith in God and repent. Meursault attacks him quite violently and, having fought off this last attempt to control him by conventional norms, he now faces his death in equanimity, laying his 'heart open to the benign indifference of the universe'.[25] *The Outsider* thus emphasised the necessity for making free choices about one's own values and behaviour and rejecting conventional notions of justice and punishment even in the face of execution. Resistance to the Vichy regime would involve much violence and death and Camus was soon forced to confront a whole set of ethical issues that were extremely difficult for him.

Much later he would partially explain his wartime decisions in an essay defending his controversial book, *The Rebel*. During the war, he recounted, he had the experience of facing people whose actions he did not understand—those who could torture while looking at their victim all the time. This meant that he and others of his generation needed to find justifications for resistance. However, existing doctrines were of no help. Religion was powerless to guide him, bourgeois values were totally compromised, and the communists were, in effect, arguing that 'you had to collaborate with the enemy before fighting him'. Nor had he himself any current moral basis for resistance. It was therefore necessary to 'to find reasons to survive and struggle, in ourselves and with others, against murder'.[26] In this situation, it seemed that the only way to derive a rule of conduct and fundamental value was in the act of resistance itself. His thinking here was elaborated more fully in *The Plague*.

There are many themes in this complex book, particularly because he completed it after the war and the final text incorporates ideas belonging to this later period. Nevertheless, at its heart, the act of resistance is explored through the allegorical device of an epidemic (the plague) suddenly arriving in the city of Oran in Algeria. How should one respond to this mortal threat, which also ended all normal life in the community? A minority—as in the Resistance—decided that they must do all they could to overcome it, although some, like Camus himself, hesitated before taking this decision. His own dilemmas are conveyed through three characters. Dr Rieux (who is eventually revealed as the narrator) is world-weary and suspicious of heroism, but also rejects injustice and compromise, and realises that it is imperative to organise teams to rescue victims of the disease. Raymond Rambert, a young journalist, is not a citizen of Oran but is there by chance and is desperate to join his wife in Paris. However, as soon as he has the opportunity to leave he realises that he has become part of the community and must also help the health teams. Finally, Jean Tarrou is reflective about his past and its implications, and expresses Camus's own moral reasoning.

When Rieux asks Tarrou why he has suggested volunteers for rescue work, Tarrou hesitatingly suggests that it is perhaps because of his sense of morality and, when challenged further, he claims that this morality is in fact 'understanding'. Through his narrator, Camus then compares the work of the rescue teams with those of a schoolmaster, who taught that two and two made four:

> But there always comes a time in history when the person who dares to say that two and two make four is punished by death. The schoolmaster

knows this quite well. And the question is not what reward or punishment awaits the demonstration; it is knowing whether or not two and two do make four. For those of the townspeople who risked their lives, they had to decide whether or not they were in a state of plague and whether or not they should try to overcome it.[27]

Those activating the health teams knew that 'one must fight in one way or another, and not go down on one's knees. The truth simply followed as a logical consequence'.[28] Yet his deeply moral tone was certainly predominant in some of his first writings for the Resistance— the four 'Letters to a German friend'.[29]

Here he justified French hesitation in initially not knowing how to respond to the German Occupation. In his first letter (written in July 1943), he suggested that the 'detour' that the French had made had 'safeguarded justice and put truth on the side of those who questioned themselves'.[30] Certainly, he continued, they had paid very dearly for failing to fight earlier: 'with humiliations and silences, with bitter experiences, with prison sentences, with executions at dawn, with desertions and separations, with daily pangs of hunger, with emaciated children, and above all with humiliation of our human dignity'. However:

> It took us all that time to find out if we had the right to kill men, if we were allowed to add to the frightful misery of this world. And because of that time lost and recaptured, our defeat accepted and surmounted, those scruples paid for with blood, we French have the right to think that we entered this war with hands clean—clean as victims and the condemned are—and that we are going to come out of it with hands clean—but clean this time with a great victory won against injustice and against ourselves.[31]

In the final letter, written a year later, he insisted that, unlike his German friend, he chose justice 'in order to remain faithful to the world', and that 'You are the man of injustice and there is nothing in the world that my heart loathes so much'.[32] For Camus, then, the only justification for violence was in the pursuit of justice and, after his own hesitation—projected onto the French people as a whole—he was convinced that resistance against Vichy and the Occupying forces constituted a 'just cause'. Violence was required because the injustice of the enemy had been demonstrated so fully and it could be defeated only by the use of force.

It is thus notable that Camus was posing the questions in an almost entirely ethical way, with little definition of the content of justice. Obviously, there was a rationale for this in terms of seeking the widest possible unity for resistance, but subsequent developments would show that this approach was not based simply on pragmatism, but was fundamental in his outlook. Ultimately, this would expose differences between the thinking of Camus and that of much of the Resistance, which would lead to a major re-orientation in his outlook.

Social justice and freedom: complementary or contradictory?

From 1942 onwards the dominant viewpoint was that there was a need for a transformation of the political, economic and social structures that had existed before the war, and that the Vichy regime was rooted in fundamental failings of the Third Republic. This viewpoint was partly due to the leading role of the Communist Party, but also because of the more general impact of socialist and left-wing ideas in an anti-fascist war. These were reinforced by the increasing privations and suffering of ordinary people, resulting in a widespread belief that the regime was, at least in part, the product of a self-serving elite intent on protecting its own interests at the expense of the population as a whole. There was therefore a broad consensus that post-war renewal would demand radical changes based on a conception of social justice. There was no overall agreed political project, but the clearest statement of general intent came with the programme of the National Council of the Resistance in March 1944. Bringing together eight movements from both northern and southern France, the two Trade Union Confederations, and the representatives of six parties, this set out the policies to be implemented by the departmental committees of the liberation following victory. It called for democratic and liberal freedoms, to be coupled with a form of economic and social democracy. This included the nationalisation of key industries and a degree of central economic planning, with workers securing a role in the direction of economic life, an expansion in social welfare, the promotion of cooperatives, new benefits for farmers, moves towards colonial self-determination, and an egalitarian educational system.[33]

Camus shared these ideas. By now he had probably abandoned his earlier Marxist views, but he certainly believed in a left-oriented conception of social justice. For example, the December 1943 issue of *Combat* contained a ten-point manifesto for the future, rejecting the idea of recreating a parliamentary system that would be powerless when confronted by capitalist powers in the way that the Popular Front government had been 'sabotaged by hostile civil servants and threatened by reigning capitalists who preferred to lose France rather than see it become socialist'.[34] During the battle for the liberation of Paris, he proclaimed that the French now wanted to end the war with revolution:

> [T]his word gives meaning to our preference for energy and honor, to our decision to be done with the spirit of mediocrity and the moneyed interests and with a social state whose ruling class failed ... We want without delay to institute a true people's and workers' democracy. In this alliance, democracy will contribute the principles of freedom and the people will contribute the faith and courage without which freedom is nothing. We believe that any politics that cuts itself off from the working class is futile.[35]

And the same editorial continued by insisting that a new Constitution should restore 'full guarantees of freedom and justice; serious structural reforms, without which any politics of freedom would be a sham; merciless destruction of the trusts and moneyed interests'.

Three days later, as the downfall of the Vichy regime and end of the Nazi Occupation appeared inevitable, Camus greeted the imminent victory enthusiastically:

> No one can hope that men who have fought for four years in silence and for days now in a din of thunder and rifle fire will agree to the return of the forces of resignation and injustice in any form whatsoever. No one can expect those men—the best and the purest that France has to offer—will again be willing to do what the best and purest did for twenty-five years, which was to love their country in silence while silently despising its leaders.

> The Paris that is fighting tonight wants to assume command tomorrow. Not for the sake of power but for the sake of justice, not for political reasons but for moral ones, not to dominate their country but to ensure its grandeur.[36]

Soon, however, Camus alluded to a dilemma to which he would return many times—the need to reconcile justice (by which he now meant social justice) and freedom. History, he asserted, suggested that the two principles were contradictory: 'How could it be otherwise?

Individual freedom means freedom for the banker and the ambitious businessman, hence injustice. Justice for all means that the personality of the individual must be subordinated to the collective good. In such circumstances what does it mean to speak of absolute freedom?'[37] He began to equivocate, arguing for partial rather than definitive revolutions, and he attempted to limit expectations and aspirations. This was particularly because of his incipient, but growing, antipathy towards the PCF. On 1 October 1944, he made this explicit, suggesting that, while *Combat* and the communists generally agreed in relation to collectivist ideas, social programmes, and the conception of justice, the PCF believed in 'political realism' (by which he meant the pursuit of power without morality). Others, no doubt including Camus himself, were looking for a new doctrine: 'The intention is not to reinvent the country's politics from top to bottom. It is to undertake a very limited experiment: to introduce the language of morality into the practice of politics by means of simple, objective criticism.'[38]

This was hardly a guide to political action and was evidence of Camus's growing caution. Certainly, he wanted greater social justice, but his preoccupation with morality was beginning to predominate. It was in this context that the purge would come to occupy a central place in his attitude to transition.

Liberation and l'épuration

The purge

Both de Gaulle and the domestic Resistance groups were committed to *l'épuration* (the purge), but there was a difference of emphasis between them. In 1940 de Gaulle warned that after victory 'justice will be done when the French leaders who have shown themselves unworthy of the name have been sentenced'.[39] He believed that punishments and a purge were necessary in order to undermine the legitimacy of the Vichy regime and to ensure loyalty to himself and the new government that he intended to install in Paris. However, his focus was upon a culpable national leadership and his conception of a purge was always limited. The approach of the domestic Resistance, however, was influenced both by its left-wing political inclinations and, still more, by its

71

direct experience in the brutality of the battle against the Vichy authorities and the Nazis.

In principle, the goals of social justice and political regeneration were intimately connected with a belief in the necessity for a thoroughgoing purge. The programme of the National Council of the Resistance in March 1944 thus demanded the punishment of traitors and the eviction from administrative and professional life of all those who had dealt with the enemy or actively associated themselves with the policy of the Vichy government. This was followed by a call for the confiscation of the property of traitors and black marketeers, the establishment of a progressive tax on war profits and, more generally, on all profits realised at the expense of the people and the nation during the Occupation.[40] However, there were also calls for violent retribution, and some episodes of this kind took place from 1941 onwards.[41] The unofficial purge at the time of the Liberation owed as much to the daily experience of battle, repression and revenge as to the political thinking of the mainland Resistance. When it came to the Milice, there was such ferocity of feeling that most of those who were found were shot without compunction.[42] In addition to this, summary executions (or executions following rudimentary trials by Liberation committees) extended to known or suspected collaborators. And there were, of course, other forms of cruelty, most notably the shaving of women's heads and other forms of humiliation of those accused of 'horizontal collaboration' (sexual relations with members of the German occupying forces).

Much of the groundwork for the subsequent legal purges had been carried out before the Liberation, but there were also a series of decrees and new administrative procedures in the months following August 1944. The most public aspect concerned trial and punishment, but this was only an element in the policy, for the first part of the Provisional Government's programme was the purging of the state, including the judiciary and the police, the armed forces, and employees of semi-public, state-subsidised or state-chartered organisations.[43] The second key aspect was the attempt to ensure that those politically associated with the Vichy regime should now become ineligible for post-war office, and early in 1945 the government presented a revised list of those to be barred.[44] A third aspect of *l'épuration* concerned the economy and several committees were established to confiscate illicit profits.[45] A fourth aspect was a purge of newspapers that had actively favoured the Vichy regime or the Germans and those that continued publication during the Occupation.[46] Finally, the purge extended into key sectors of French society, including education and the Catholic Church.

Underlying the purge was, of course, the threat of criminal trials and punishment. Capital punishment for treasonable activity was the ultimate sanction for the most serious forms of collusion with the enemy. However, all sections of the Resistance had wanted to spread the net more widely than this to include many other forms of collaboration, which would be punished less seriously. This led to an ordinance which instituted national indignity as a crime, applicable to any voluntary aid to the Axis after 16 June 1940 and to offences deemed to be against liberty, equality or fraternity.[47]

The provisional government established new courts of justice throughout liberated France specifically to judge offences related to collaboration; these courts could issue punishments of all kinds, including the death penalty.[48] Finally, an ordinance in November 1944 established the High Court of Justice to try Pétain, Laval, and cabinet and sub-cabinet officers and colonial governors who had participated in the Vichy governments between 17 June 1940 and the Liberation. This court was to be completely sovereign and could assign whatever penalty it thought fit, including execution, to any crime. There was no provision for an appeal, but a presidential pardon was possible.[49]

Much of the implementation of the purge was after the end of the war—and Camus had already defined his attitudes before the fighting finished. But, in addition to his long-term opposition to capital punishment, three points were of particular relevance to his increasing alienation from the process. First, there were serious delays in the trial process, with a large backlog rapidly building up. In the Paris area alone 10,000 people had been interned by early October 1944, but no trials had yet begun. These started at the end of the month, but the *juges d'instruction* could not keep up with the demands on them so that by December 1944 there was a backlog of over 4,200 cases. This was repeated all over the country: by February 1945 only 25,000 cases had been dealt with out of the 60,000 that had been opened and in the following months a further 60,000 were initiated.[50]

Secondly, instead of rapid and proportionate justice, with those at the top being punished the most harshly, the opposite tended to occur.[51] The trials of the Vichy chiefs in the High Court of Justice, which did not even begin until the spring of 1945, started with two military leaders, rather than more notorious figures. Clearly, de Gaulle did not even wish to try Pétain, who actually forced his hand by insisting on returning from Switzerland on 25 April. The trial itself, which began in July, was extremely poorly conducted and, although Pétain was eventually found guilty of sharing intelligence with the enemy, de Gaulle followed the recommendation from the jury not to implement the death penalty because of his age.[52] This leniency towards the leader of Vichy France was in stark contrast with the fate of many lower-level personnel and journalists or propagandists, who were condemned to death.

Thirdly, the PCF was always at the forefront of the demands for faster and more punitive legal procedures. Apart from its memories of being the main recipient of state repression in the early stages of the war, and its belief that radical change might be advanced through tough action of this kind, the PCF also sought political support by seeking to present itself as the reliable channel for popular emotions. In this period the PCF was taking a cautious political line, seeking to demonstrate its patriotism and sense of responsibility. It thus urged workers to concentrate on economic reconstruction and to forego strikes and perhaps this rather conservative position in relation to the so-called 'battle for production' reinforced the temptation to take a populist line in relation to capital punishment and 'rough justice' for collaborators. Thus it maintained the tone set soon after the liberation of Paris when a front-page editorial in *L'Humanité* stated that the summary executions of collaborators and the shearing of 'intolerable street women' were a 'guarantee of order for the population, which could not have survived in contact with these rotten elements'; and it warned that 'the interminable procedures which are holding up the well-deserved punishments of traitors … stirs the legitimate indignation of all moral persons.'[53] In fact, the PCF never directly protested that a particular sentence was too harsh.[54] All this led Camus to view *l'épuration* process with considerable angst, despite his initial support for it.

ALBERT CAMUS AND RESISTANCE, JUSTICE AND VIOLENCE

Camus's agonising re-appraisal

Camus's opposition to the death penalty had been out of keeping with the attitude of the majority of the Resistance. In this situation, he too therefore publicly advocated executions. Thus when de Gaulle authorised and attended the execution of Pierre Pucheu, the former Minister of Interior for Vichy, in March 1944, Camus wrote an article in *Les Lettres Françaises* agreeing that Pucheu should die: 'too many men have died whom we loved and respected', he declared, continuing, 'too many splendours betrayed, too many values humiliated ... even for those of us in the midst of this battle who would otherwise be tempted to pardon him'.[55] But his condemnation was also couched in philosophical terms: Pucheu, he noted, had signed laws in a 'comfortable and anonymous office' and lacked the imagination 'to really see that they would translate into agony for innocent Frenchmen who would be put to death'. He concluded 'the time for abstraction is over'.[56] However, his article was attacked by two communists, who felt that this over-intellectual approach had not been sufficiently categorical about Pucheu, and Camus now responded by explicitly calling for the death penalty for members of the Milice in *Combat* in April 1944:

> [W]hile it is desirable in the case of other traitors that the forms of justice be respected, the Milice has placed itself outside the law. It must be made quite clear that each militiaman, in signing his enlistment papers, is ratifying his own death sentence. By turning against France, these people exclude themselves from France. Rotten branches cannot be left attached to the tree. They have to be lopped off, reduced to sawdust, and scattered on the ground. That is the fate awaiting each of Darnand's murderers. Courts-martial would be pointless, moreover. The Milice is its own tribunal. It has judged itself and sentenced itself to death. Those sentences will be carried out.[57]

He reiterated similar sentiments in several other articles over the next few months. However, his categorical statements masked some inner doubts, particularly once the official purge process began.

He first considered this in relation to its economic aspect—the nationalisation of the Renault car company following the known collaboration of Louis Renault himself. He contrasted the procedures that were being established with those of 'a hasty revolutionary tribunal', which would 'simply find the defendants guilty'. Instead 'we are pre-

75

serving liberty even when it benefits those who always fought against it' and 'if we want to find them guilty, we must therefore substantiate the charges against them'.[58] However Camus was not simply endorsing the legal procedures, but was also grounding his argument in morality. Louis Renault, he claimed, had had a duty to rebel and this meant that even if all the courts in the world absolved him and recognised his defence as irreproachable in legal terms, his actions would still fall within the jurisdiction of a higher law.

Camus was therefore retrospectively characterising 1940 as the moment of existential truth, and as the basis for defining a 'higher law' whose dictates were imperative even if actual law said something quite different. A few weeks later he also highlighted a principle of proportional responsibility, and the need to modify the law for a restricted period, so that it could be reconciled with the 'spirit of democracy'.[59] He was clearly uncomfortable with the idea of the purge, aware that it raised difficulties of legality and practicality, but also convinced of its necessity as a short-term expedient. Already troubled by such questions, he now faced an attack from the celebrated writer, François Mauriac, which would reinforce his self-doubts.

Mauriac's Resistance credentials were impeccable, but he was also a devout Christian whose approach to justice was based on Catholic philosophy. Immediately after the Liberation of Paris, he found the climate of vengeance repugnant and expressed the fear that the new Republic would prove no better than Vichy, warning that 'at no price must the Fourth Republic wear the Gestapo's boots'.[60] His article in Le Figaro on 19 October began an exchange between the two writers. Camus's first reply, in which he re-affirmed his claim that the Resistance was identical with France, and that a revolution was needed, also asserted 'we will be obliged to destroy a living part of this country in order to save its soul'.[61] Mauriac then taunted him by pointing out that the 'inquisitors also burned bodies in order to save souls'.[62] Recalling the French wars of religion, he called instead for a return to the politics of Henry IV, who had introduced the Edict of Nantes to bring about reconciliation between Catholics and Protestants. Camus's reply, just after a collaborationist journalist had been sentenced to death in Paris, was tortuous: 'We have no taste for murder. The human person embodies all that we respect in the world. Our instinctive response to this sentence is therefore one of repugnance.'[63]

However, he explained that this was also an inadequate response because the small minority who had caused the woes of France in 1939 were still doing so. It was therefore their very existence that raised the problem of justice 'and the question was one of destroying them.' He argued that non-believers must either keep silent or become converts to human justice:

> And we have chosen to embrace human justice, with its terrible imperfections, while seeking anxiously to correct it by clinging desperately to honesty. We have never called for blind or precipitous justice.

> We detest arbitrary judgment and criminal stupidity, and we would prefer that France keep her hands clean. But to that end we want justice to be prompt...[64]

He was thus suggesting that even those who found the death penalty repugnant must support it for a limited period in order to ensure that the justice of the Resistance prevailed. However, at the beginning of January 1945 he wrote an editorial that all but reversed his earlier position.

The Courts, he claimed, were carrying out 'absurd sentences and preposterous instances of leniency', and 'in between, prisoners are snatched from their prisons and shot because they were pardoned'. He claimed that 'we should have allowed ourselves to appear unjust in order to do real justice', by creating a 'law of honour' that would have lasted for six months or a year. Now, he suggested, it was too late and he concluded: 'All of this was indeed to be expected, but we cannot say this without bitterness and sadness. A country that fails to purge itself is preparing to fail to remake itself. The face that a nation wears is that of its system of justice.'[65] But Camus's anguished re-appraisal of the purge policy was not yet complete and he would now be tested in the case of Robert Brasillach.

As the editor of *Je suis partout*, Brasillach had adopted an extreme collaborationist position but, despite his advocacy of atrocities against the Resistance and his praise for Nazism, he had not carried out any violent actions himself. After he was sentenced to death, a petition was circulated amongst writers and artists to call on de Gaulle to exercise clemency. Camus decided to sign, returning to his earlier position of categorical opposition to the death penalty, saying that he could not participate in it even by abstention.[66]

This was his turning point and on 2 August 1945 he reversed the position that he had appeared to take in relation to Pétain the previous November. At that time he had welcomed the establishment of the High Court of Justice to judge members of the Vichy government, urging it to move quickly: 'If there are some cases in which our duty is not clear or justice is difficult to define, in this case we take our stand without hesitation. The voices of the tortured and humiliated join with ours in calling for justice of the most pitiless and decisive kind.'[67] This implied that Pétain's guilt had already been established and that the death penalty was necessary, but he now insisted that Pétain's culpability must be proved in a trial and, even if this were established, he should not be executed.[68] A few weeks later, he issued his final judgment on the purge, claiming that it was now totally discredited.

> The word 'purge' itself was already rather distressing. The actual thing became odious. It had only one chance of not ending that way, and that would have required that it be carried out in a way that was neither vengeful nor thoughtless. It seems that the straight path of justice is not easy to find amid the cries of hatred coming from one side and the special pleading of guilty consciences coming from the other. In any case, the failure is complete.[69]

But why did he claim both that the failure of the purge was complete and that 'a country that fails to purge itself is preparing to fail to remake itself'? It would, after all, be quite possible to condemn the penal aspect of the purges without condemning the whole policy, effectively denigrating the transition as whole. Yet to suggest this would be to misunderstand Camus's outlook, particularly given his attitudes to violence and the death penalty.

Justice, violence and politics

Although Camus condemned the implementation of the purge at a very early stage, he undoubtedly pinpointed some of the problems that would become increasingly evident. Apart from the specific and crucial question of summary executions and the extensive use of the death penalty, there were inevitable inconsistencies, degrees of arbitrariness, and injustices. It was evident that many of the most culpable, including Pétain himself, were spared, while others were not. Pierre Laval was certainly guilty, but his trial and execution were nevertheless travesties of justice.[70] It was also clear that the purge was pursued far more vehemently in some sectors than others: de Gaulle was keen to eliminate pro-Vichy and pro-Nazi newspapers and robust action was taken in this sector, but the church was treated with kid gloves despite the role played by the Catholic hierarchy in supporting the Vichy regime, and there was very little purge of the economic elite.[71] Camus was therefore justified in condemning the flaws in the purge that were already revealed and in expecting these to continue, but this does not necessarily validate his verdict, for there is little doubt that, in the circumstances of the time, some form of purge policy was a political necessity. By 1944 the demand for retribution and a purging of collaborators was palpable and unless it was satisfied in some way through official processes, there was a danger of much greater violence.[72] However, the purpose here is not to judge the validity of Camus's contemporary judgment, but to explain it in relation to his own earlier and subsequent thinking, and to explore both the strengths and limitations of his insights. And his attitude to the purge was embedded in his wider notions about justice and violence.

In the early stages of the official purge, Camus was seeking a way of incorporating an element of legal justice into a punitive process that he knew to be imperfect. By maintaining the notion that those most responsible for the Vichy regime and its atrocities had transgressed a higher duty, he was attempting to identify a basis for a law under which they could be judged. His inclination was to favour a very short period of trials for the major transgressors followed by an amnesty for the majority. But he soon found that the approach that he sought was not being implemented. The establishment of the legal procedures was delayed, the judgments were inconsistent, and there was an intolerant political climate. In these circumstances, he despaired of the whole process and uttered his *cri de coeur* about the failure of the purge policy. However, it was his view of the death penalty that was decisive in changing his whole attitude to the purge.

Accepting the necessity for executions even during 1944 had been extremely difficult for him and, when he witnessed both the extent of its use and the often arbitrary decisions about who should die, his rather agonising reversion to his original stance was perhaps not surprising.

Once he took this step, his condemnation of capital punishment became more categorical and public than had ever been the case previously. In 1946, in one of a series of bleak articles in *Combat* entitled 'Neither Victims nor Executioners', he called for an international peace movement, which would link up with communities of labour inside nations to define the values of a new international order. He suggested that they should formulate an international code of justice whose first article would call for the abolition of the death penalty everywhere.[73] His opposition to capital punishment was also an important feature of *The Plague*, which he completed after the end of the war. Here Tarrou explains how his decision to combat the plague had begun when his father, a prosecuting counsel, had called for a man to be sentenced to death. 'From then onwards', he explained, 'I took a horrified interest in justice, in death sentences and in executions', and he continued:

> But what interested me was the death penalty ... Consequently, I went into politics, as they say. I did not want to be a victim of the plague, that's all. I thought the society in which I lived rested on the death penalty and that, if I fought against it, I should be fighting against murder.[74]

Even then Tarrou had thought it might occasionally be necessary to condemn someone to death, for he was told 'that these few deaths were necessary to bring about a world in which no one would kill anyone anymore'.[75] But then he witnessed the horror of an execution and he realised that, even while he believed that he was struggling against the plague, he had indirectly supported the deaths of thousands and 'had even caused their deaths by approving the actions and principles that inevitably led to them'.[76] From then on, Tarrou explained that he had focused on the death penalty and decided: 'I would refuse ever to concede a single argument, a single one, to this disgusting butchery. Yes, I chose that obstinate blindness until I could see more clearly in the matter.'[77]

Through the character of Tarrou, Camus was graphically explaining his own evolution during the Resistance and the purge. And he would maintain this position for the rest of his life. In *The Rebel* he thus proclaimed that 'a revolution is not worth dying for unless it assures the immediate suppression of the death penalty'.[78] Finally, in 1957, the year that he was awarded the Nobel Prize, he wrote the essay 'Reflections on the Guillotine'. This elaborated a range of arguments for its abolition, including its failure as a deterrent, and the state's own contribution to the conditions that brought about murder, such as over-crowded housing and politicians' involvement in the provision of alcohol. But much of the essay concentrates on the horrors of the death penalty itself. Perhaps, as David Carroll suggests, Camus's revulsion from capital punishment was constant, but he had suffered from 'partial amnesia' about this in the early Liberation period.[79] It was surely his guilt about his own temporary support for executions at the time of the purge that subsequently led him to take an important step away from retribution and revenge. There were some other signs of this.

In March 1945, he made a speech which both reflected his despair about the purge and contained, in an embryonic form, this alternative approach. Four years of hatred during the war had, he claimed, left their legacy:

> We were left with the rage that consumes our souls at the memory of certain images and certain faces. The executioners' hatred engendered the victims' hatred. And once the executioners had gone, the French were left with their hatred only partially spent. They still look at one another with a residue of anger.[80]

This, he argued, must be overcome:

> And the most difficult battle to be won against the enemy in the future must be fought within ourselves, with an exceptional effort that will trans-form our appetite for hatred into a desire for justice. Not giving in to hatred, not making any concessions to violence, not allowing our passions to become blind—these are the things we can still do for friendship and against Hitlerism.[81]

Three years later he went further. In a lecture at a monastery in 1948, while re-affirming his inability to accept Christianity, he recalled his debate with Mauriac on the purge, confessing that 'I have come to admit to myself, and now to admit publicly here, that regarding the fundamentals and on the precise point of our controversy, François Mauriac, and not I, was right'.[82] In other words, he apparently now believed that, instead of implementing trials and purges, there should have been an attempt to bring about reconciliation between those (or perhaps at least some of those) who had been on opposing sides during the war years.

By suggesting that reconciliation would be more fruitful than revenge, Camus was intimating the kind of approach that would much later be incorporated into reparative forms of transitional justice. However, he did not develop these ideas and, at the time, there was virtually no possibility that they would have had any great traction had he done so. Yet his insight was surely important: aware of the dangers of an unending climate of retribution, he could envisage a preferable alternative. But this was a short-lived and undeveloped idea because the lessons that he derived from the Liberation period were more negative than positive. His attitude to the purge was crucially important in this, but it was also rooted in wider attitudes to justice and violence.

When taking the decision to join the Resistance he had believed that this embodied 'justice' and that the Vichy regime and its Nazi backers constituted 'injustice'. He would never doubt the ethical justification for the choice that he had made. In his own explanation of the relationship between *The Rebel* and his wartime experiences he thus affirmed that if it were ever necessary to relive 1940, 'I would know both why and against whom I am fighting', and he hoped that *The Rebel* could help other people to survive.[83] However, his attitudes to justice, violence and politics changed very substantially as a result of the nature of the transition in 1944–5.

In 1942 he did not define the term 'justice', but by 1943 and 1944 he gave it more content. He now included in it a form of social justice and democratic political renewal and, when considering the early stages of the purge, he attempted to combine political and ethical considerations with legal justice. But there were also other differences between the two periods. In 1942 Camus had tended to view the struggle between the Resistance and the Vichy regime in overwhelmingly ethical terms—effectively as being between 'good' and 'evil'. With the Liberation, the realities of life and politics were readily apparent. There were power struggles, duplicity and hypocrisy. Many of those who had sided with Vichy suddenly became ardent supporters of de Gaulle. Similarly, some Resistance fighters took the opportunity to settle their personal grudges. All this was no doubt regrettable, but also perhaps understandable. However, Camus tended to abstract a particular feature from a complex situation. Instead of regarding politics as inevitably 'messy', and violence as a feature of the transition from war to peace, he now tended again towards absolutist positions.

These changes of attitude were evident in his writing at the time of the Liberation and in its aftermath. At first he saw (social) justice and freedom as mutually interdependent, but soon he tended to define them in antithetical terms, so that it was necessary to make a choice between them. After some equivocation, he chose freedom. As he expressed it in his notebooks:

> For even if justice is not realised, liberty maintains the power of protest against injustice and keeps communication open. Justice in a silent world, the justice of mute men, destroys complicity, negates revolt, and restores consent, but in the lowest possible form. That's where one sees the priority gradually go to the value of liberty.[84]

The existence of freedom meant that there would always be the possibility of, and necessity for, a struggle against injustice:

> But the difficult thing is never to lose sight of the fact that liberty must *at the same time* insist upon justice ... Once this is established, there is a justice likewise, though quite different, in laying the foundation of the only constant value in the history of men, who have never really died except for liberty.

> Liberty is the ability to defend what I do not think, even in a regime or a world that I approve. It is the ability to admit that the adversary is right.[85]

Reaffirming his own love of liberty, he noted:

> And for any intellectual, liberty is eventually confused with freedom of expression. But I am quite aware that this concern is not the primary one of a very large number of Europeans because justice alone can give them the material minimum they need and rightly or wrongly they would gladly sacrifice liberty to that elementary justice.

> I have known that for a long time. If I found it necessary to defend the reconciliation of justice and liberty it is because I thought the last hope of the west lay in such a reconciliation. But such a reconciliation can be brought about only in a certain climate which today almost strikes me as Utopian. One or the other of these values must be sacrificed? What to think, in that case?[86]

The conclusion that the reconciliation was probably 'utopian' also ended his belief in the possibility of bringing this about in France itself. Thus despite the fact that the war had only just ended, Camus already concluded that there was no likelihood of a democratic form of socialism being established. Whatever kind of transition followed the Vichy regime, he no longer believed that it would conform to the kind of programme that the Resistance had sought. In fact, by November 1946 he was sure that there was no possibility of any kind of structural reform within the confines of the nation-state.[87]

The priority that he now attributed to freedom also led him to oppose Marxism, the Communist Party and the Soviet Union. He had already been the victim of PCF attacks, but his decision to make freedom his highest political priority now led to bitter polemics between himself and the party. By the autumn of 1946 he argued that Marxism justified lies, violence and even murder because it embedded all this in a theory that rejected the possibility of values lying outside history itself.[88] He came to oppose justice as an absolute value on the grounds that those who saw it in this way disregarded other values and were liable to become violent and extreme. This was coupled with the simultaneous belief that violence ultimately negated justice. These were the themes of his post-war play, *Les Justes* (*The Just Assassins*), first performed in 1949.

The play was based on the assassination of the Grand Duke Sergei Alexandrovich of Russia in 1905 by the Social Revolutionary Combat Organisation. In the play, five group members are totally committed to the creation of a just society and believe that the assassination will lead to revolution. Ivan Kaliayev, known as Yanek, who loves poetry, beauty and life, while simultaneously pursuing the group's aims, is chosen to throw the bomb, but calls off the first attempt because the Grand Duke's nephew and niece are with him in the carriage. Stepan Fedorov, the most violent and single-minded member, condemns this refusal, but all the rest endorse the belief that it is unacceptable to kill innocent children. The second attempt is successful, but Yanek is captured, imprisoned and sentenced to death. He looks forward to dying and Dora Dulebov, the bomb maker, who loves him, now also wants to die, convinced that death is the only way to recover innocence. While Camus may not identify himself with any of the characters, the overwhelming 'message' of the play is surely that the pursuit of justice through murder must be self-defeating. Both Yanek and Dora come to believe that the assassination can be redeemed only through their own deaths and, as she tells the leader of the group: 'One throws a bomb and in the next second a whole lifetime flashes by, and all that remains is death'.[89] Fearing that later others will simply kill without paying for it with their lives, she suggests: 'Perhaps that is what justice means—in the long run. And then nobody will want to look justice in the face again'.[90] In other words, the pursuit of justice as an absolute value through violence negated the possibility of civilised life.

In fact, the issue of violence and its relationship with a belief in absolute justice now became central for Camus, as also shown in *The Rebel*. He endorsed the goal of 'relative justice' as necessary to combat injustice and acknowledged that this would sometimes lead to violence.[91] While he did not therefore take the position that violence was never justified, he insisted that it was always wrong and must never be institutionalised in a system that accepted its legitimacy. It should be used only when there was an immediate risk, or to combat another form of violence and, while insurrections would certainly take place against violent and oppressive regimes, the purpose must be to create institutions that would then limit violence.[92] In fact, however, he came to regard violence, and attitudes to it, as an inherent ingredient of some forms of politics, rather than as an outcome of particular situations. Ultimately, this would be a major cause of his unpopular stance on the Algerian war. On this occasion, his tendency to abstract morality from politics led him to an untenable position in opposing Algerian independence.[93] In 1944–5 his position was, I believe, much stronger: he provided important insights into the dangers of retribution and revenge and rightly opposed the death penalty, but was premature in his despair about the transition and the possibility of creating a postwar French state based on greater social justice.

Finally, there is an instructive comparison between Serge and Camus, despite the great differences between them and the situations they depicted. They had similar attitudes to capital punishment, both believing that this had wider implications for any society that resorted to it. But Serge, when supporting the Bolshevik revolution, regarded violence, extending even to revolutionary terror, as both necessary and an integral part of the historical context. At this stage, he thought little about the need for political limitations on the revolutionary process, which would, he hoped, end injustice. The reality of Stalinism convinced him otherwise. Camus, in contrast, tended to view history in terms of moral absolutes. The Resistance embodied justice, but victory brought about a situation in which freedom was threatened by violence and lies. His ethical sensibility would no doubt have led him to appreci-ate the injustices of revolutionary excesses more quickly than Serge. But his own weakness was surely his tendency to view the world through moral absolutes without sufficient appreciation of historical and political realities. Had he been less of a moralist, he might have accepted the idea that justice is a multi-dimensional concept and that it was not necessary to abandon the attempt to combine it with free-dom simply because the transition from the Vichy regime to the Fourth Republic was marred by political manoeuvres and violence.

4

JUSTICE IN THE CONTEXT OF COLONIALISM AND NEO-COLONIALISM

NGŨGĨ WA THIONG'O AND KENYA

The pursuit of justice in a colonial territory, where the central agency of power may be located thousands of miles away, naturally presents a set of distinct challenges. The most obvious form of injustice lies in the very fact that external forces are exploiting local human and material resources for their own interests, and in the first instance the pursuit of justice will normally focus on securing liberation through national independence. However, this is only a beginning, particularly in situations in which colonialism has eliminated many of the pre-existing forms of economic, social, cultural and political life, and where external forces continue to exert substantial control long after formal independence has been achieved. The newly independent state may itself also perpetuate multiple forms of continuing injustice, partly as a result of the colonial heritage and the continuing international constraints. This is the plight of much of the developing world, and this chapter considers the case of Kenya through an examination of the work of Ngũgĩ wa Thiong'o.[1]

Born in January 1938 in Limuru, on the eastern edge of the Great Rift Valley and some thirty miles north-west of Nairobi, Ngũgĩ, a

Gĩkũyũ, has been a leading public intellectual in Kenya since the early 1960s, despite having been exiled from the country since 1982. Currently Distinguished Professor of English and Comparative Literature at the University of California, he has a worldwide reputation and is a novelist, playwright, journalist, author of theoretical and political essays, and activist. Despite much continuity in his work, there have been major shifts, and also some contradictions in his political thinking and literary approach.[2] However, his main preoccupation has been to illuminate the dehumanising impact of colonialism and its negative legacy, and to offer an alternative vision for the future. This chapter considers aspects of his thinking in relation to three periods: colonialism, transition and post-colonial dictatorship.

Colonial Kenya

Kenya was an arbitrary creation of British colonial rule. In the aftermath of the scramble for Africa, following the Congress of Berlin in 1884–5, the area became part of an East African Protectorate, only designated as 'Kenya' after World War I. At first, much of the present country was regarded as too wild and inhospitable for settlement and was viewed primarily as a supply route. This changed with the development of the Uganda railway between 1896–1901, connecting the port of Mombasa with the landlocked territory of Uganda, built largely by Asians transported from the Indian subcontinent as indentured labour. Now white settlement was actively encouraged in order to obtain a return for the outlay on the railway. This involved the dispossession of vast tracts of land from the existing occupants, the extraction of taxation, and the conversion of the African population into a very poorly-paid labour force. The settlers aspired to an aristocratic lifestyle based on notions of white supremacy and this was reinforced after World War I, when the British government promoted a scheme for ex-army officers, who had aspirations to become a landed gentry on their new estates.[3] The settlers' sense of supremacy was particularly blatant in the area they termed the 'White Highlands', situated in the central uplands of the country.

Through force and regulations, colonialism completely overturned the existing systems of law and land ownership. Previously, the communities in East Africa had their own legal systems based on custom and tradition, which were enforced by elders and clan leaders. In general, there was a system of communal land ownership with differential rights, including to access and inheritance. This was based primarily on patrilineal systems, but women normally controlled the houses.[4] While each of the many peoples of Kenya had their own customs, the Gĩkũyũ (called 'Kikuyu' by the British) were the largest of the indigenous communities, with approximately 20 per cent of the population, and would play a central role in the resistance to colonialism.[5] British settlement in the 'White Highlands' forced many Gĩkũyũs to move to other areas, creating subsequent clashes over land that would continue in the post-colonial period. Others became 'tenants at will' for the settlers—sometimes on the land that they had previously owned—and the colonial regime also created a system of indirect rule by recruiting some Gĩkũyũs to work on its behalf in supervisory roles.

Militant African political opposition to the dispossession of land first developed after World War I, but waned as a result of repression and internal disagreements. However, in the mid-1920s the Kikuyu Central Association (KCA) emerged to demand concessions over both land ownership and political representation and Jomo Kenyatta lobbied directly in London. By the outbreak of World War II very little concrete progress had been achieved and in 1939 the settlers ensured that future land grants in the 'White Highlands' would be made only to Europeans.[6] By then the Gĩkũyũ had become the leaders of African resistance and the following year the British government proscribed the KCA and imprisoned its leaders, although Kenyatta remained in London. However, almost 100,000 Kenyan Africans were recruited to the British Army in Africa and this fuelled their militancy, making many less willing to tolerate racist segregation in the post-war era.[7]

During the 1940s the impetus picked up. In 1946 Kenyatta returned to Kenya and quickly acquired new prominence. In the same year, the Gĩkũyũ also initiated their own secret militant resistance movement, calling themselves the Land and Freedom Army, but soon dubbed 'Mau Mau'. Its activity increased, with the main focus of its violence directed towards other Gĩkũyũs who were working for the British. In October 1952 the governor, Sir Evelyn Baring, introduced a state of emergency and arrested several political figures, including Kenyatta. His trial was a flagrant miscarriage of justice, and the immediate aftermath was horrific, for the Kenyan government and the settlers now instituted a reign of terror against the whole Gĩkũyũ people in order to crush Mau Mau. The exact dimensions of the atrocities are still a matter of dispute, but the rebels appear to have killed thirty-two settlers and approximately 200 counter-insurgents, and were responsible for some 1,800 African deaths, with hundreds more disappearing. However, the British and colonial forces probably killed more than 20,000 Mau Mau rebels, of whom 1,090 were hanged. More shocking still were the appalling human rights abuses perpetrated by the British officers and their collaborators, with at least 150,000 Gĩkũyũs detained and over one million forcefully resettled in villages.[8] By 1956 the brutal repression seemed to have succeeded. The capture of the effective leader of the Mau Mau, Dedan Kimathi, in October, followed by his execution early in 1957, led to a shift in the independence movement. The emphasis changed from direct action in the mountain areas to the streets of Nairobi, where popular demands for Black African rule put pressure on the political process. All this occurred while Ngũgĩ was a teenager and the brutality and trauma of the 1950s were of decisive importance in his subsequent outlook.

He came from an extended Gĩkũyũ family, living on the edge of the so-called 'White Highlands'. His father had owned land, but had been deprived of it by the European settlers, retaining only a non-inheritable right of occupancy on a compound. In Ngũgĩ's childhood, food was meagre while the sprawling fertile green fields owned by the white settlers were close by. His early years were rooted in communal life, marked by customary celebrations and rituals, with an emphasis on an oral tradition, including much story telling.[9] The armed resistance to British rule then brought about a near civil war amongst the Gĩkũyũ people, and members of Ngũgĩ's own family were divided in their allegiances.[10]

At the age of seventeen he was the only boy in the town to secure a place at Alliance High School, which was designed to create a new African elite. The circumstances encapsulate the contradictions of his situation. One of his brothers was a Mau Mau fighter, who was arrested and detained, and the colonial forces also killed a deaf and mute half-brother, although he had played no part in the war.[11] Yet a government-appointed headman, who was a ruthless opponent of the Mau Mau, paid Ngũgĩ's school fees because of pride in a local boy achieving a place at Alliance.[12] Once there, the contradictions would only increase, for Ngũgĩ relished both the education itself and the fact that the school was a multi-racial haven in the midst of a war. He also converted to Christianity and, for some time, was passionately committed to his new faith.[13] Between 1959 and 1964 he went to Makere University College in Uganda, where he studied literature. But he continued to be haunted by the earlier period and this, he later claimed, led him to turn to creative writing:

> One event in particular stood out. It was the day, in 1955, that I returned to my village after my first semester at a boarding school. I was looking forward to my reunion with my family, my mother especially; I could even picture her smile. Communication in those days, beyond word of mouth, did not really exist for rural folk. On arrival, I was met by the sight of ashes and burnt debris. Not only our house! The entire village had been razed to the ground by the British forces and the entire community relocated into a concentration village.[14]

While at Makere he wrote articles for the Kenyan press, but found problems in expressing exactly what he wanted to say in this form:

> How could an article really capture the complexity of what I had experienced in colonial Kenya? The blood in the streets; the dead guerrillas hung on trees as a public spectacle; the horror stories of white officers collecting ears, noses, eyes, genitalia, or even heads of the vanquished as trophies![15]

He turned to fiction to help understand 'the encounter with chaos'[16] and his first two novels, *The River Between*, and *Weep not, Child*, which will be discussed below, were completed while he was at Makere.

At this stage, Ngũgĩ had no doubts about the fundamental injustice and racism of British colonialism and, more specifically, the brutality of its counter-insurgency measures. But he was ambivalent in many of his other attitudes. In an article in September 1962 he noted that Kenya had been divided into three groups: European, Asian and African. They were, he suggested, now reconciled to independence under African rule, but the conflicts would continue. The problem was that the three races had never had real cultural contact and could therefore not understand one another and must remain strangers in the same land. Even among Africans there was the curse of separate development, manifested in tribal conflicts and suspicions. No concept of a nation existed, but it was now necessary to move beyond racialism and tribalism. In the long run these would die, 'so one looks hopefully to a time when this vertical rift will vanish'.[17] But Kenya was also faced with a horizontal rift between the elite and the masses and there was a danger that an educated class might assume the position previously held by Europeans. The people of Kenya must find a solution to the problems caused by both the vertical and horizontal rifts, and he noted:

> The traditional African concept of the community should not be forgotten in our rush for western culture and political institutions, which some regard as the ready-made solution to our problems. In the African way, the community serves the individual. And the individual finds the fullest development of his personality when he is working in and for the community as a whole. Land, food and wealth is for the community. In this community, culture belongs to all. For the rich and poor, the foolish and wise are all free to participate in the national life of the community in all its manifestations. Perhaps this is what some have meant when they talk of African socialism. If so, it is a worthy ideal.[18]

This was tentative, with some optimism about independence, coupled with an embryonic socialism, and a continuing focus on distinct cultures. Just after leaving Makere, he also explained his attitude to literature, arguing that the problem for an African writer in Kenya was to be 'able to stand a little bit detached; and see the problem, the human problem, the human relationship, in its proper perspective'.[19] At this stage, he believed that the writer's commitment should not prevent empathy with individuals, whom he regarded as the focus of literature; and he also viewed those individuals as part of an ethnically-defined community. This was his outlook in his first two novels.

Early novels: *The River Between* and *Weep Not, Child*

Ngũgĩ was still a Christian when he wrote *The River Between*. He hoped for some kind of reconciliation between the colonial and African cultures, in which the core of Christian doctrine might be detached from Western culture and grafted onto the central beliefs of the Kenyan peoples.[20] The novel is set during the crisis over female genital mutilation (then termed female circumcision) between the Gĩkũyũ and the Protestant missionaries during the 1920s and 1930s. In Gĩkũyũ tradi-

tion both boys and girls were circumcised in adolescence in a celebration of 'coming of age'. The missionaries forbad this practice for girls.
More generally, they also excluded any possibility of a merging of traditions in which the Gĩkũyũ could absorb some elements of Western
culture, while rejecting others.[21] This led to bitter conflicts both
between colonialist Christianity and the Gĩkũyũ, and within the Gĩkũyũ
community itself.

In *The River Between*, the River Honia divides two rival groups living
on separate ridges. At times, the river, which also joins the ridges on
either side, may bring about healing and unity, but polarising forces
have emerged around two leaders, who allow no compromise. Joshua
is a Christian zealot, while Kabonyi rejects all colonial influence and
has reverted to an equally fundamentalist traditionalism. Those who
seek to steer a way between these two forces are crushed. The key
figure in this attempt is Waiyaki, who has been told by his father to go
to the Mission place and 'learn all the wisdom and all the secrets of the
white man', but not to follow their vices and to 'be true to your people
and the ancient rites'.[22] He finds this task almost impossible, often
regarding education itself as a sufficient goal. His faith in this is infec-
tious and he becomes a head teacher, building new free schools outside
the control of the missionaries:

> And there they stood, symbols of people's thirst for the white man's secret
> magic and power. Few wanted to live the white man's way, but all wanted
> this thing, this magic. This work of building together was a tribute to the
> tribe's way of co-operation. It was a determination to have something of
> their own making, fired by their own imagination.[23]

However, he was challenged by the argument that circumcision was
still more fundamental than education:

> It kept people together, bound the tribe. It was at the core of the social
> structure, and a something that gave meaning to a man's life. End the
> custom and the spiritual basis of the tribe's cohesion and integration would
> be no more.[24]

The conflict over female circumcision leads to the first tragedy in the
book, for Joshua's daughter, Muthoni, wants to be circumcised while
remaining a Christian. When she dies as a result of the mutilation
Joshua, who had renounced her completely, sees this as a warning to

those who rebel against their parents and God. Traditionalists, such as Waiyaki's father, view it as a punishment of Joshua for deserting the ancient wisdom of the land. This tragedy is only the beginning. Waiyaki is treated as a potential leader of the community, and sees himself in this role. But he falls in love with Joshua's other daughter, Nyambura, who has obeyed her father and has not been circumcised. Marriage to a non-circumcised woman is not permitted in the Gĩkũyũ tradition and Kabonyi mobilises the community against Waiyaki for this betrayal. Waiyaki will not renounce Nyambura, but now realises that he had failed to understand the need for political organisation and that 'education for an oppressed people is not all'.[25] He does not view the ways of the white man, including Christianity, as essentially bad:

> Some good, some truth shone through it. But the religion, the faith, needed washing, cleaning away all the dirt, leaving only the eternal. And that eternal that was the truth had to be reconciled to the traditions of the people. A people's traditions could not be swept away overnight. That way lay disintegration. Such a tribe would have no roots, for a people's roots were in their traditions going back to the past, the very beginning ... A religion that took no count of people's way of life, a religion that did not recognise spots of beauty and truths in their way of life, was useless. It would not satisfy. It would not be a living experience, a source of life and vitality. It would only maim a man's soul, making him fanatically cling to whatever promised security, otherwise he would be lost ...

> If the white man's religion made you abandon a custom and then did not give you something else of equal value, you became lost. An attempt at resolution of the conflict would only kill you, as it did Muthoni.[26]

Waiyaki now knows what he would preach if ever given another chance: 'education for unity. Unity for political freedom'.[27] But he never gets that chance, for he and Nayambura are now placed in the hands of the secret movement controlled by Kabonyi for judgment.

By the end of the novel the most intolerant traditionalists appear to have triumphed, but Waiyaki's words shortly before his final defeat almost turned the tide. Calling on the tradition that bound the Gĩkũyũ together, he explained the devastating consequences of disunity between the two ridges:

> And you left the white man alone. Now, instead of learning his ways and coming together so that united we may drive him out, Kabonyi and a few others cry for vengeance against Joshua and his followers. ... [W]e must

fight together in one political movement, or else we perish and the white man will always be on our back. Can a house divided against itself stand?[28]

It was deeply contentious of Ngũgĩ to illustrate his ideas through the conflict over female genital mutilation and, as Elleke Boehmer has emphasised, Muthoni's almost beatific death upholds a patriarchal order in which she is glorified by submitting to the ancient laws of the elders, the fathers of the village.[29] Yet *The River Between* was not endorsing the practice of genital mutilation, but condemning the form of domination that insisted on the wholesale elimination of existing cultural practices. The implication was that political unity amongst the Gĩkũyũ people was essential and that it could and should be based on some kind of cultural synthesis.

Ngũgĩ's second novel, *Weep not, Child*, is more complex, but colonialism, culture and injustice are again central themes. A white landowner, Howlands, is completely immune to the suffering of the dispossessed and is portrayed in wholly negative terms, as are the extreme brutality and arbitrary nature of colonialist anti-insurgency policies. But it is the iniquity of the seizure of Gĩkũyũ ancestral land that lies at the heart of the novel. This has introduced a new form of status and class hierarchy within the community, and dispossession has also destroyed cultural traditions in family life.

Howlands has deprived Ngotho of his land and Jacobo is now the village chief and the overseer of Ngotho's work. But this also means that Ngotho has also lost his traditional authority, particularly in the eyes of one of his sons, Boro, who has joined the Mau Mau. Ngotho, taunted by Boro's lack of respect and resentful about his whole life, attacks Jacobo in the midst of a strike meeting. Although Jacobo is not seriously hurt, Boro subsequently kills him. Ngotho then confesses to the crime in order to save another of his sons, Kamau, who has been arrested in connection with the murder. As a result, Ngotho is tortured and later dies, but on the same day Boro also kills Howlands. All these events, following from the original colonial land seizure, unfold during the childhood and adolescence of Njoroge, who is the central character of the novel (and is based on Ngũgĩ himself).

Njoroge is Ngotho's youngest son and is particularly close to his mother. He shows great educational promise, and eventually passes an exam to get into an elite school, where he is captivated by the liberal school principal and, more generally, by Christianity and the whole educational experience. He wants to pursue his studies and to isolate himself from the chaos and horror that is all around him. He also falls in love with Jacobo's daughter, Mwihaki, thereby transgressing the boundaries of class and family loyalties. But the world that he is seeking is unattainable. In particular, education cannot be detached from the brutal colonial context of which it is a part. Njoroge himself is briefly detained and beaten by the counter-insurgency forces because of the involvement of Boro in Mau Mau. Nor will Mwihaki stay with him after her father's murder. By the end of the novel, Njoroge is therefore desperate. He thinks about his dead father and the fate of his three half-brothers: Boro, soon to be executed; Kamau, in prison for life; and the third brother, Lori, in detention where he might be beaten to death. Njoroge is about to kill himself when his mother and his father's first wife rescue him and take him home.

While the novel evokes some sympathy for Njoroge, it is also critical of him, ending with an emphasis on his feelings of guilt, 'the guilt of a man who had avoided his responsibility for which he had prepared himself since his childhood'.[30] The implication is that he should have supported his family as it was torn apart by colonialism and the Emergency; and, more generally, he should have played some role in resistance rather than seeking to opt out of the conflict in the illusion that the elite high school could be a sanctuary. *Weep not, Child* depicts cultural domination as a particularly powerful form of oppression leading to a general disintegration of the community and seducing the would-be African elite away from earlier loyalties by creating bonds with colonialism through liberal imperialist education and Christianity. These themes would continue to be central in Ngũgĩ's work, but the theoretical approach became more critical and his political perspective moved to the left.

Transition

In the final years of colonialism, the imperative for the British was to search for the most accommodating forces amongst the movement for liberation. The first direct elections for Africans to the Legislative Council took place in 1957 and between then and the establishment of the independent state in 1963, the British colonial administration did everything it could to influence political developments. In 1960 two new parties were established. Kenyatta (who was released from jail in 1961) and the Gĩkũyũ soon dominated the Kenya African National Union (KANU) party. This sought a centralised constitution. The Kenya African Democratic Union (KADU) party attempted to promote the interests of various other peoples and wanted a federal system. The last governor, Malcolm MacDonald, became convinced that Kenyatta should be supported.[31] He also believed it essential that the Gĩkũyũ should predominate in the post-independence regime, on the grounds that they would not accept marginalisation. This decision would have an enduring impact on Kenyan politics.

Under colonialism, the Gĩkũyũ had been dispersed across much of the country. KADU's support for federalism was based largely on a fear of Gĩkũyũ dominance in areas where other peoples had traditionally controlled the land and local power. Immediately after independence, however, the regional assemblies were destroyed amidst tension and violence amongst various ethnic communities. Kenyatta forced through his centralised vision of the constitution and in November 1964 KADU merged with KANU, turning Kenya into a one-party state. Furthermore, while other prominent KANU leaders, including Oginga Odinga, the founder of the party, saw land nationalisation and redistribution as essential, Kenyatta was totally opposed to such policies and was a firm believer in individual ownership and private enterprise.

During this period, Ngũgĩ was in Britain, studying at Leeds University for an MA in Literature. While there he was exposed to new influences—particularly the work of Frantz Fanon, and Marxism. From Fanon he developed a much sharper perspective on the cultural impact of European imperialism on Africa, particularly through its socio-psychological effects on indigenous populations. Marxism, and particularly Lenin's version of it, also led to an emphasis on imperialism as an economic and political system. Such themes were already discernible in his third novel, *A Grain of Wheat*, which he wrote while in Britain, and which will be discussed later. His attitude to literature also changed: 'I believe that a writer must write not only to entertain people, but also to change society for the better. And as far as I am concerned, only if you are working towards a socialist vision, can you be working for the better.'[32] He continued:

Creative writing must mean creative writing—I mean really exploring. But at the same time I do think that beauty must be related to social realities, in the sense that if a man is starving, he has no time for jazz or poetry, or novels or Beethoven. In other words, an African writer should have social responsibilities to society as it is now...[33]

He returned to Kenya in 1967 to take up the position of Special Lecturer in English at University College, Nairobi, but the political climate in Kenya was hardly propitious for his vision of a socialist East Africa.

In 1965 Kenyatta moved against Oginga Odinga, repressing the left-wing forces around him and also mobilising ethnic resentments in order to counter redistribution.[34] Kenyatta was in the process of constructing a personal dictatorship that would not accept dissent and Ngũgĩ therefore faced great difficulties on his return. The focal point of his first clash with the authorities began in September 1968 with his attempt to replace the Department of English with a Department of African Literature and Languages. This proposal encapsulated his conviction about the importance of culture in fostering systems of belief:

> We want to establish the centrality of Africa in the department. This ... is justifiable on various grounds, the most important one being that education is a means of knowledge about ourselves. Therefore, after we have examined ourselves, we radiate outwards and discover peoples and worlds around us. With Africa at the centre of things, not existing as an appendix or a satellite of other countries and literatures, things must be seen from the African perspective. The dominant object in that perspective is African literature, the major branch of African culture.[35]

This campaign was ultimately successful and both the change of name and new syllabus were eventually established, but the political climate affecting university life soon led to his involvement in wider conflicts. In January 1969, at the behest of the government, the university cancelled a public lecture by Odinga. Ngũgĩ drafted a letter, signed by sixteen other lecturers, accusing the Ministry of Education of interfering with academic freedom.[36] Soon afterwards he resigned in protest against such violations and returned to Makere for a year in 1969–70, before leaving Africa for a year in the US as a Visiting Associate Professor at Northwestern University in 1970–71.

Until around 1969, Ngũgĩ's own position, like that of the state itself, was 'transitional'. He was critical of Kenyatta, but he had not abandoned all hope of change. Both criticisms and a degree of optimism were evident in *A Grain of Wheat*, which he wrote while at Leeds University. It is helpful to contextualise this with reference to a particular aspect of Kenyatta's policy—his wish to erase the memory of Mau Mau from the historical record in the struggle for liberation from British rule.

Memory, history and *A Grain of Wheat*

A year before independence Kenyatta denounced the Mau Mau rebellion, maintaining his determination to have peace and not to allow 'hooligans' to rule Kenya. He insisted that Mau Mau had been a disease, which had now been eradicated and must never be remembered again.[37] Similarly, in a speech to white settlers, shortly before independence, he promised that 'We are going to forget the past and look forward to the future'. Telling them that he was 'not going to remember' his suffering in the detention camp during the emergency, he asked them to 'join hands and work for the benefit of Kenya, not for the benefit of one particular community'.[38] Finally, almost a year after independence, Kenyatta demanded a 'forgetting the past', in which Kenyans should commit themselves to erase all hatreds and difficulties of those years from their minds, should never refer to the past and instead unite in concern for the reconstruction of the country and the vitality of the future.[39] However, memory and history were essential aspects of Ngũgĩ's exposure of colonial injustice.

The idea that colonialism was built upon the denial of an indigenous view of the past and the replacement of the existing memory with an alternative colonial version was already present in his first two novels. In fact, even by recounting the cultural clash of the 1930s and the experience of the Emergency years, Ngũgĩ was highlighting the importance of history. The interpretation of the past also affected perspectives on the independent state. The colonial forces had created the dominant image of Mau Mau. This had legitimised the extreme repression of the Gĩkũyũ through a discourse based on the 'othering' of a backward people. It projected a notion of primitive bestiality with emphasis placed upon the secret oath-taking ceremonies.[40] These, it was argued, transformed the Gĩkũyũ people 'from [a] peace-loving though naïve people into "atavistic" savages who could not control their impulse for atrocious killings'.[41] Helping to establish a fundamentally different type of interpretation was central in Ngũgĩ's own attempt to create a counter-colonial version of historical truth and this inevitably brought him into conflict with those who controlled the post-colonial state.

His perspective on Mau Mau was still evolving, but he challenged the official amnesia in his third novel, *A Grain of Wheat*.[42] This is set in a village community preparing a celebration for the day of independence. The fundamental question is whether the recent past, with both its sacrifices and betrayals, will be redeemed by the new state. By dealing with individual histories and memories, Ngũgĩ provides multiple perspectives, which collectively suggest the complexity of the task. All the central characters are guilty of some kind of betrayal, but have also suffered deeply during the Emergency period.

In the background is the local Mau Mau activist, Kihika, who has been betrayed and killed. Although he represents the heroic martyr, he had not in fact fully lived up to this reputation and, amongst other mistakes, had put his faith in Mugo, who had betrayed him. No one knows of this treachery, and Mugo is now treated as a brave liberation fighter and is due to make a speech at the independence ceremony. One figure who views him as a hero is Gikonyo, who himself betrayed the Mau Mau oath while detained by the colonial forces. He had done this in order to return to his wife, Mumbi, who is the sister of the martyred Kihika. Eventually Mugo confesses his betrayal of Kihika to Mumbi, but she does not want him to suffer for the action. She has committed her own betrayal by sleeping with another man, Karanja, and having his child, although he is guilty of the most far-reaching crimes against the liberation, having worked as a home guard for the colonialists. The whole village had been collectively punished for Kihika's actions and it was in this situation that Mumbi had become dependent on Karanja for survival. Yet she had allowed him to sleep with her only when she knew that Gikonyo was returning. Nor is Mugo simply a traitor, for he has also carried out some brave actions, including saving a pregnant women from the brutality of the home guards. His real wish is to remain free from commitment, but this is not possible and ultimately he makes a public confession, recognising that 'he was responsible for whatever he had done in the past, for whatever he would do in the future'.[43]

The implication of the book is that successful independence can be built only in recognition of multiple histories and memories, and an acceptance of new possibilities. Thus when Gikonyo ultimately seeks reconciliation with Mumbi, it is on a new basis. Previously, he had either idealised her or condemned her without seeking to understand her motivations. He knows 'that in future he would reckon with her feelings, her thoughts, her desires—a new Mumbi'.[44] Mumbi herself is an advocate of reconstruction rather than revenge, but on the basis of building something genuinely new. There is a further underlying theme in the book—uncertainty about the future and a fear that the past sacrifices could be betrayed. Gikonyo expresses this by remarking that it is those who ran to the shelter of schools, universities and administration, and some outright traitors and collaborators, whom 'we see riding in long cars and changing them daily as if motor cars were clothes'.[45] And the text includes many references to the ghosts of the colonial past still haunting Kenya and the fear that the tradition of resistance might be betrayed.[46] Furthermore, after insisting that the characters in the book are fictitious, Ngũgĩ's note at the beginning states: 'But the situation and the problems are real—sometimes too painfully real for the peasants who fought the British yet who now see all that they fought for being put on one side'.[47]

In *A Grain of Wheat*, Ngũgĩ was making a serious attempt to wrestle with the problem of historical truth. He had already partially accepted the view that Mau Mau was a national liberation movement fighting for justice. Yet he also implied that no one was a pure hero and depicted Mau Mau violence, including the rape of a white woman, Dr Lynd, for which he was later criticised.[48]

Subsequently, the combination of increasingly dictatorial rule and his own experiences led to his thorough-going condemnation of neo-colonialism.

Neo-colonialism

During his year in the US in 1970–71 he associated with 'Black Power' revolutionary circles and when he returned to the University of

Nairobi (as it became in 1970), he endorsed a militant doctrine, which disavowed the possibility of peaceful change.[49] He now also celebrated the role of Mau Mau in the independence movement; this involved considerable risks in the prevailing political climate.[50] In 1974 he and Michere Githae Mugo began work on a play, *The Trial of Dedan Kimathi*.[51] This was a fictional trial of the Mau Mau leader, and Kimathi was celebrated as a heroic revolutionary. In 1976 the play was performed at the National Theatre in Nairobi to rapturous reception by the audience, although it was only allowed a very short run.[52] The next year Ngũgĩ's novel, *Petals of Blood*, was published and this was an excoriating critique of neo-colonialism, in which all aspects of contemporary Kenyan life—above all the worlds of politics and business, and their interconnections—were subjected both to satire and condemnation.[53] Like *The Trial of Dedan Kimathi*, this drew on an oral and story-telling approach, immediately making it accessible to a wider audience than a conventional novel. The Kenyan state regarded Ngũgĩ s next initiative in 1977 as a still greater threat.

The previous year, Ngũgĩ, who was now Head of the Department of Literature at the University of Nairobi, had been approached to help with the Kamiriithu Community Education and Cultural Centre in Limeru, where he had grown up. This challenged him in a fundamental way—that of language. In Kenya only a small minority spoke and read English, which was inaccessible to most people in Kamiriithu. Writing in Gĩkũyũ would immediately create a far larger audience amongst those that he really wanted to reach, and the aims of the centre could be fulfilled through active community participation. Ngũgĩ became chair of the cultural committee and, with a fellow playwright, Ngũgĩ wa Mirii,[54] wrote a play in Gĩkũyũ, *Ngaahika Ndeenda* (*I Will Marry When I Want*).[55] The play was an attack on neo-colonialism, corruption and the betrayal of the promise to liberate the country, and it ended with the hope that the earlier struggle would now be renewed. When performed, the play attracted people from other parts of the country, who wanted to develop similar community initiatives. The authorities soon withdrew the licence for any further performances and in December 1977 Ngũgĩ was arrested and taken to the Kamiti Maximum Security Prison, where he was detained without charge and held in harsh and humiliating conditions for a year. But he now determined to write his fictional work in Gĩkũyũ, beginning this task in jail, where he wrote his novel, *Caitaani mũtharaba-Inĩ* (*Devil on the Cross*), on toilet paper.[56]

He was released just after the death of Kenyatta at the end of 1978, but the new regime under Daniel arap Moi would soon prove to be still more repressive.[57] In this climate, the University of Nairobi would not re-instate Ngũgĩ, although a petition was signed by 400 academics, and he soon faced further harassment. Despite the intimidating atmosphere, he remained active. In 1981 he again began rehearsals in the Kamiriithu cultural centre for a new play, *Maitu Njugira* (*Mother, Sing for Me*), which also condemned neo-colonialism in forceful terms, and in which the Kamiriithu community re-wrote Ngũgĩ's original draft so as to transform the role of women into a more potent revolutionary force.[58] But, amidst a crackdown on all dissent in 1982, the government closed down the centre and banned all theatre in the region. Following a coup attempt that August, critics and opponents of the regime were arrested and imprisoned, and opposition was pushed underground in an atmosphere of extreme repression. Ngũgĩ was in London at the time and, with his liberty and life in danger should he return, he remained in exile, separated from his wife and children. He remained there until 1989, when he moved to the US.

While in London he and other exiles formed a Committee for the Release of Political Prisoners in Kenya, and in 1987 he also chaired another group of Kenyan dissidents in the United Movement for Democracy in Kenya (Umoja). Finally, in 1990 he became the official spokesperson for the Mwakenya Movement.[59] This called for the overthrow of Moi's government and the end of the military alliance with the US. It denounced 'all foreign imperialist robbery of our wealth' and 'neocolonial puppets', also condemning corruption, the inequity of land access, the slow encroachment of commercial ranching on pastoralist grazing areas, and the endemic social inequality.[60]

From the 1970s he increasingly used the concept of 'neo-colonialism' to condemn the Kenyan state. This paradigm, originated by Kwame Nkrumah in *Neo-Colonialism, The Last Stage of Imperialism* (1965), was particularly powerful as a critique because of its insistence that there was a fundamental continuity between colonialism and the new states, where formal independence masks continuing dependence.[61] Using an

103

approach based in Marxist political economy, Ngũgĩ provided a strident condemnation of neo-colonialism in his non-fictional work, in *Detained*, and elsewhere.[62] Although he did not provide a well-developed theory of the political economy of neo-colonialism, his depiction of life in Moi's Kenya was certainly more accurate than the regime's preferred image.[63] However, his real strength was in developing his cultural critique. In *Decolonising the Mind* (1986) he claimed that the biggest weapon of imperialism was the 'cultural bomb':

> The effect of a cultural bomb is to annihilate a people's belief in their names, in their languages, in their environment, in their heritage of struggle, in their unity, in their capacities and ultimately in themselves. It makes them see their past as one wasteland of non-achievement and it makes them want to distance themselves from that wasteland. It makes them want to identify with that which is furthest removed from themselves; for instance, with other people's languages rather than their own. It makes them identify with that which is decadent and reactionary, all those forces which would stop their own springs of life. It even plants serious doubts about the moral rightness of struggle. Possibilities of triumph or victory are seen as remote, ridiculous dreams. The intended results are despair, despondency and a collective death-wish. Amidst this wasteland which it has created, imperialism presents itself as the cure and demands that the dependant sing hymns of praise with the constant refrain: 'Theft is holy'.[64]

Language, he argued, was the most important vehicle through which imperial power 'fascinated and held the soul prisoner' and was 'the means of spiritual subjugation'.[65] For it carries culture and, particularly through 'orature'[66] and literature, it also carried the entire body of values by which people perceive themselves and their place in the world. Language was therefore 'inseparable from ourselves as a community of human beings with a specific form and character, a specific history, a specific relationship to the world'.[67] Colonialism, he insisted, had made everything about European languages appear superior, while,

> In schools and universities our Kenyan languages ... were associated with negative qualities of backwardness, underdevelopment, humiliation and punishment. We who went through that school system were meant to graduate with a hatred of the people and the culture and values of the language of our daily humiliation and punishment. I do not want to see Kenyan children growing up in that imperialist-imposed tradition of con-

tempt for the tools of communication developed by their communities and their history. I want them to transcend colonial alienation.[68]

Ngũgĩ's writing on language has been controversial and its full implementation would run up against practical difficulties, given the plethora of African languages and the problems of multiple translations. But it was essentially a development of the earlier views about cultural domination and alienation that he had represented so graphically in *The River Between* and *Weep not, Child*.

From the 1970s onwards his view on historical memory also evolved and he became increasingly positive about the Mau Mau.[69] In 1976, he thus stated that the Mau Mau guerrillas 'put up one of the most heroic struggles against imperialism in this century'.[70] This also led him to revise *A Grain of Wheat*, removing some of the cruder acts of violence (for example, the rape of Dr Lynd), and making the book a more robust rebuttal of the colonialist representation of Mau Mau.[71] However, this also raised a question as to whether Ngũgĩ was now using history to promote a view that conformed to a particular national and revolutionary narrative. This has certainly been the view of some of his critics, particularly in the circles of Kenya's professional historians.[72] Yet Ngũgĩ could reply, with justification, that under Kenyatta and Moi, many professional historians helped legitimise the neo-colonial state by their own interpretations of the past, and he would parody this in *Matigari* (see below).[73]

There is certainly more controversy about the notion of Mau Mau as a national liberation movement than is implied in Ngũgĩ's later work.[74] However, even though he arguably presented a simplistic picture of Mau Mau, this has been within a wider intellectual and political context in which discourse about heroes and traitors has been prevalent.[75] His contribution to a form of 'historical justice' therefore needs to be judged in contextual terms. In his critical study, Simon Gikandi argues that the novels have not only provided a radical historiography, but have been 'the vehicles through which two generations of Kenyan readers have been able to access their past or ... to see their history as a key factor in shaping postcolonial cultures and identities'.[76]

More generally, Ngũgĩ provided a critique of the Kenya of Kenyatta and Moi that was certainly full of insight. Daniel Branch argues that the state elite built up great wealth and influence through a combination of legal and illegal means:

> By the 1970s, the elite in control of the state were just as happy smuggling Ugandan coffee or ivory poached from the Maasai Mara as they were legally exporting coffee grown in Kiambu or tea from Kericho. They and their allies owned other interests that were reliant on Kenya's ties to the global economy, such as hotel groups and banks. Acting in their political roles, members of the ruling elite also had it in their power to appoint individuals to run the marketing boards responsible for the different parts of the agricultural economy; to hire executives to sit in the boardrooms of state-owned corporations; and to set legislation and issue the various permissions and permits to allow businesses to operate. A tight web of interdependence was therefore created between the public and the private sectors, and between government and business.[77]

This was the situation that was mercilessly exposed and satirised in several of Ngũgĩ's novels, including *Petals of Blood* and *The Devil on the Cross*. But it is in *Matigari* that he most directly addresses the pursuit of justice in such circumstances.

Matigari and the search for truth and justice

Matigari draws on a traditional oral story about an old man looking for a cure for an illness, and contains both allegory and realism.[78] Matigari is a former fighter in a liberation movement, who believes that victory has now been won. In particular, he has chased the white settler, Williams, away from the house that he, Matigari, had built. He therefore buries his AK47 by a Mugumo tree and puts on his belt of peace, intending to return home. But he decides to find his people and 'build our home together' as 'those who eat alone, die alone'.[79] Almost immediately, he sees distressing sights that are difficult to reconcile with the end of colonialism, so he sets off on a quest for 'truth and justice'. Wherever he goes he finds official proclamations from the voice of 'truth', propagating the view of the government led by 'His Excellency Ole Excellency', which is in total contrast with the actual conditions of extreme repression, squalor and inequality. Matigari repeatedly tells people how he had fought Settler Williams over his house:

> You see, I built the house with my own hands. But Settler Williams slept in it and I would sleep outside on the veranda. I tended the estates that spread

around the house for miles. But it was Settler Williams who took home the harvest. I was left to pick anything he might have left behind. I worked all the machines and in all the industries, but it was Settler Williams who would take the profits to the bank and I would end up with the cent that he flung my way ... I produced everything on that farm with my own labour. But all the gains went to Settler Williams. What a world! A world in which the tailor wears rags, the tiller eats wild berries, the builder begs for shelter. One morning I woke up from the deep sleep of many years, and I said to him: Settler Williams, you who eat what another has sown, hear now the sound of the trumpet and the sound of the horn of justice. The tailor demands his clothes, the tiller his land, the worker the produce of his sweat. The builder wants his house back. Get out of my house.[80]

As he continues his search for truth and justice he acquires ever more power based on the mythical qualities and the spirit of resistance that he embodies. Three themes within the fable have particular relevance.

The first is the merging of the power of the former colonialists and the black elite in the neo-colonial state. When he returns to his old house, Matigari sees a white man and a black man sitting on horseback next to the gate:

Their horses were exactly alike. Both had silky brown bodies. The riders too wore clothes of the same colour. Indeed, the only difference between the two men was their skin colour. Even their postures as they sat in the saddle were exactly the same. The way they held their whips and the reins—no difference. And they spoke in the same manner.[81]

Matigari's claim of ownership and long-term resistance to dispossession is too much for the black man on horseback, who whips him. This man is the son of the servant to Settler Williams and he has studied in Britain, at the London School of Economics. He tells Matigari that the country has remained in darkness because of the ignorance of the people:

They don't know the importance of the word 'individual', as opposed to the word 'masses'. White people are advanced because they respect that word, and therefore honour the *freedom of the individual*, which means the freedom of everyone to follow his own whims without worrying about the others. Survival of the fittest.[82]

The white man is Settler Williams's son, Robert, who is now director of the Anglo-American International Conglomerate of Insurance

(AICI) and Agribusiness Co-ordinating International Organisation (ACIO) and the director of the local branch of Bankers International Union (BIU). This shows a close interlocking of the international (white) and local (black) elites, but the continuing dominance of Western power is suggested by the fact that, in Gĩkũyũ, the three above sets of initials together mean 'the real thieves'.[83] Their combined control is symbolised by the fact that, immediately after this encounter, Matigari is picked up by the brutal police and incarcerated in an overcrowded jail with appalling conditions.

The second theme is the corrupt system of repressive power and its incorporation of other forces through ideology, intimidation and bribery. In jail, most of Matigari's fellow prisoners are there for reasons connected with hunger and poverty. But there are two others: a student who was arrested for asking where democracy was in the country, and a teacher arrested for promoting Marxism and communism by simply saying that the systems of the USSR, China and Cuba were based on the teachings of Marx. When Matigari meets both men again, after they have been released, their earlier defiance has evaporated. The student is extremely scared, having witnessed twenty-five student demonstrators at the university being instantly killed by soldiers and the police. He has stopped asking questions, declaring instead: 'Democracy here means, first fending for oneself'.[84] His plan now is to finish his degree, get a job in a bank and acquire things for himself, or get a scholarship, go to the US and come back to start a private research institute, becoming a consultant for Western companies and governments. The teacher is equally frightened, intending to keep silent so that his wife and children could eat. He suggests that Matigari should ask a priest about truth and justice. But, when he does so, the priest tells him that, in order to find earthly (rather than heavenly) truth and justice, 'you should go to those who rule here on earth'.[85] He explains that His Excellency Ole Excellence loves and believes in Christianity and is very enlightened. The Minister for Truth and Justice, who never missed a church service, is coming to a meeting, to resolve a strike. Matigari attends this.

Ngũgĩ's account of what follows is a witty parody of a menacing situation. The country, he explains ironically, has a good international image because of its rule of 'truth and justice' and the meeting has drawn observers from Western ruling political parties, who sit in front-row seats, 'so that they could properly see how the workers in a Third World Country could be silenced with instant truth and justice!'[86] He follows this with a direct allusion to a demand by Moi that 'all ministers, assistant ministers and every other person' should 'sing like parrots' and 'if I put a full stop, you should also put a full stop', for this is 'how this country will move forward'.[87] The scene continues:

> In the rows immediately behind the minister there sat some white, brown and black men, dressed in judicial robes. Next to them were three others. One was the editor of the newspaper the *Daily Parrotry*. Another was Professor of the History of Parrotology, and the third a university lecturer who had a B.Ed., an MA and a PhD. in the philosophy of Parrotology. The three held a hymn-book, *Songs of a Parrot* which had been composed by a group of specialists in the voices of parrots.[88]

The minister speaks about the virtues of loyalty and observing all laws, specifying that it was those who had obeyed colonial law who had really brought about independence, as shown at a recent history conference of university professors and specialists in Parrotology.[89] He continues:

> I have ordered all those loyalist professors and all holders of PhDs in Parrotology to be promoted and given permanent professorships. For these professors are different from those who are always raising a hue and cry about revolution, revolutionary politics, revolutionary socialism and other *foreign ideologies*. No! These permanent professors are the ones who know how to obey and abide by the law, how to serve the law. You agree with me, Professor, don't you.

> The Permanent Professor in the History of Parrotology shot up at once. So did the PhD in Parrotology and the Editor of the *Daily Parrotry*. They sang three stanzas from *Songs of a Parrot* and then sat down, clinging to the hymn-book as though their lives depended on it.[90]

The minister also explains that because the company has given money to the ruling party, it is now a national company and the system as a whole is '*capitalism with a socialist face—or socialism with a capitalist heart*' and '*true African socialism*'.[91] Thus workers striking against the company are striking against the government. The fate of those who do so is made quite clear, and a trade unionist friend of Matigari's, who argues in support of the justice of the strike, is immediately arrested (and later shot). Matigari himself, who again gives the history of his struggle with Settler Williams, is sent to a mental hospital. Later he and others escape and the government issues instructions to arrest or shoot those who look mad because of their appearance and clothes. However, the US and British governments immediately complain when their citizens are picked up, leading to an immediate exemption for white people, with the chief of police declaring that, in any case, white people do not go mad! Through all this irony Ngũgĩ demonstrates much about the nature of the regime under Moi, including the fact that ultimate power is held externally rather than by the state. For example, in the midst of the repression, the Voice of Truth announces on the radio that Britain, the EEC and the US are giving massive aid for the 'development of the administration of instant justice' and the US is asking the World Bank and the IMF to give aid to the country for the 'development and the defence of the rule of law, truth and justice', and will listen with sympathy to a request to supply the country with Phantom jets, tanks and attack helicopters.[92]

The third theme explicitly addresses the question of how justice can be pursued in such a state. While in the mental hospital, it dawns on Matigari that the enemy cannot be defeated through either arms or words alone: '*Justice for the oppressed comes from a sharpened spear. He removed the belt of peace he had worn earlier and trampled it down on the ground.*'[93] His earlier belief that truth and justice are mightier than any armed power had landed him first in prison and then in the mental hospital. It was necessary to combine truth, justice and armed power to drive the enemy out. After escaping from the mental hospital, Matigari sets off to find the weapons he had buried with his two remaining friends, a woman and a young man named Muriuki. They are pursued, but Matigari is sure that the enemy will not be able to touch them if they can cross the river: 'There in those forests and mountains we shall light the fire of our liberation. Our first independence has been sold back to imperialism by the servants they put in power!'[94] His female friend is shot and it is not clear that they will make it across the river, but Muriuki gets to the mugumo tree where the weapons are buried, and takes them up. And the book ends with him hearing the distant siren as it calls out to the workers and, recalling a strike, he seems to hear the voices of peasants, students and patriots of all the different nationalities of the land, repeatedly singing in harmony, 'Victory shall be ours!'[95]

The message initially seems to be clear: that in a situation of neo-colonial repression, justice can be attained only by force and that the fight must now pass to the younger generation. Yet the underlying argument is more subtle, as Ngũgĩ himself has insisted. The intention of *Matigari*, he has argued, is to pose a challenge. About three-quarters of the novel involves the quest for truth and justice, and *Matigari* is asking: 'Is there a solution to our problems, without violence? There must be another way'.[96] A major theme therefore concerns the possibility of democracy. Because the neo-colonial state refuses the necessary social change, it becomes increasingly repressive, but this alienates the people, leading them to consider all possible ways of fighting against the oppression.[97] Muriuki does not start shooting, but recalls the strike. The implication is therefore that, whatever he does later on, his actions will be linked to wider struggles.[98] And, more generally, the disarming and re-arming in the novel may also be seen as a metaphor for something far more funda-mental—the way in which national independence had also disarmed the people, mentally, spiritually, economically and politically.[99]

Ngũgĩ's position on violence in the pursuit of justice certainly dif-fered from that of Camus, but it was also now far more measured than it had sometimes appeared earlier. *Matigari* incorporates his ideas about injustice and justice through the realms of culture, memory and history in the context of neo-colonialism.

Dreams of a world without prisons and gunpoints

Ngũgĩ's work has incorporated several layers. At root has been his con-stant and passionate denunciation of the injustices arising from colo-nialism, but this condemnation has itself been multi-dimensional. The foundation was perhaps in his bitter protest, arising from personal experience, about the domination exercised through the cultural sphere and its devastating impact on traditional customs and relation-ships. However, this was inextricably tied both to revulsion against the sheer brutality of the repression and to a particular concern about the social and economic conditions of the poor. In time, this dimension of social justice assumed far greater prominence in his thinking and by 1968 he was already warning that the African writer was in danger of becoming too fascinated by 'the yesterday of his people and forgetting the present ... Conflicts between the emergent elitist middle-class and the masses were developing, their seeds being in the colonial pattern of social and economic development'.[100]

By 1986 he had gone further and urged the importance of adopting a class perspective on justice. He cited a poem by a Guatemalan poet, Otto René Castillo, who suggested that one day simple men and women of all countries would rise and ask intellectuals: 'What did you do when the poor/Suffered...?'[101] And he answered with the words of Brecht, that they should be able to say that we helped 'turn the struggles into the spheres of common knowledge and, above all, justice into a passion.'[102] Yet his Marxist conception of justice was still embedded in his preoccupation with the cultural sphere. Furthermore, this was coupled with his insistence on the crucial importance of history and memory as a means both to uncover historical injustice and to rediscover the tradition of resistance. Sometimes, particularly during the 1970s and 1980s, he implied, without any elaboration, that a revolutionary form of socialism would resolve the problems. Yet this was always combined with other layers of thought and conviction.

When Ngũgĩ was incarcerated in jail for a year, some of his deepest feelings about the nature of justice in relation to law and politics also surfaced. As he put it in *Detained*, in relation to the question of whether or not to cooperate with the authorities: 'To say "Yes" or "No" to unfairness, to injustice, to wrong-doing, to oppression, to treacherous betrayal, to the culture of fear, to the aesthetic of submissive acquiescence, one was choosing a particular world and a particular future.'[103] He was, he said, sure that his sanity depended on 'my being able to continually say "No" to any and every manifestation of oppressive injustice and to any and every infringement of my human and democratic rights, a "No" that included detention itself. I would seize any and every occasion to denounce detention without trial.'[104] And in his letters demanding release, he insisted that he was not pleading for mercy, for it was he 'as a Kenyan national, who has been wronged and who now cries aloud for democratic justice'.[105]

As with Serge, his belief in the importance of a more liberal conception of rights and legal justice was brought to the fore partly as a result of his own brutal incarceration. In exile, it was reflected in his role in the Committee for the Release of Political Prisoners in Kenya and Umoja. Similarly, his claim that *Matigari* was an insistence on the necessity for a democratic route for change, rather than an avowal of the armed revolutionary alternative, demonstrated that this was his real wish. In other words, while he was adamant about the absolute need for social justice and pessimistic about the ability or willingness of a neo-colonial state to deliver this, he retained the hope that forms of democracy and legal justice would nevertheless emerge. Put slightly differently, his aspiration was for some kind of political evolution so as to be able to move from a highly repressive and unequal system to one in which there were openings for democratic change. He expressed such sentiments increasingly during the 1990s and in the early twenty-first century.

By 1993, for example, he suggested that it was in the interests of everybody in the world to support democratic trends in Africa even if this resulted in social and economic programmes that did not fit the capital market economies of the West. This was because development was only possible through harnessing the energies of the people, rather than repressing them.[106] And he thought that some movement in the right direction had taken place with the re-introduction of a multi-party system the previous year. This evolution culminated with the election of Mwai Kibaki as President in December 2002, following the victory of his National Rainbow Coalition (NARC). Ngũgĩ welcomed this result and two years later, he returned to Kenya for a visit with his second wife, Njeeri, after twenty-two years in exile. Although many greeted him ecstatically, the trip was deeply traumatic, for he was brutally attacked and Njeeri was raped.[107] Nevertheless, Ngũgĩ strongly supported Kibaki. Njeeri also very courageously returned to Kenya to deliver a message from her husband in his home constituency in Limuru.[108] He made it clear that he stood for more fundamental change than any of the parties, but argued that Kibaki had made some significant improvements.

For a brief period the creation of a multi-party system and some positive memories of Kibaki in the 1960s and 1970s led Ngũgĩ to hope that a new era was beginning. He was also enthusiastic about possibilities for the development of historical justice, for Kibaki reversed previous post-independence policies by withdrawing the order banning Mau

Mau and also unveiled a memorial to Dedan Kimathi, the Mau Mau leader executed by the British. Yet in the current Kenyan context, the commemoration of Mau Mau can also be divisive—viewed by other ethnic communities as a celebration of Gĩkũyũ power. And, more generally, Ngũgĩ's optimism was misplaced. Although there was economic growth, inequality worsened during Kibaki's five years in office; governmental corruption scandals continued; and he ruled repressively, consolidating his power through trusted Gĩkũyũ, Embu and Meru allies and the older generation, with many ties to the Kenyatta era.[109] In 2007–8 Ngũgĩ's hopes for Kenya under Kibaki were shattered with the catastrophic events following the election. This reignited long-term conflicts over land, power and wealth. These focused on ethnicity, and political leaders sought to rig the election results and incited and organised the violent aftermath, with Kibaki orchestrating Gĩkũyũ violence against other communities. At least 1,133 people were killed, thousands of women were raped, property was destroyed, and more than half a million Kenyans were forced from their homes in orchestrated ethnic violence.[110] All this meant that Ngũgĩ returned to a more sober pessimism about the situation, but it also again highlighted some of the key themes in his conceptions of justice and injustice.

After the 2007 election Ngũgĩ quickly realised that the 'ethnic cleansing' was organised by political leaders and he called on the UN to investigate the massacres as crimes against humanity:

> For the sake of justice, healing and peace now and in the future I urge all progressive forces not to be so engrossed with the political wrongs of election tampering that they forget the crimes of hate and ethnic cleansing—crimes that have led to untimely deaths and the displacement of thousands.
>
> The world does not need another Bosnia; Africa certainly does not need another Rwanda.[111]

This raised the question of how his wish to avoid such violence would affect his conceptions of justice. Would he, like Serge in the immediate aftermath of the Bolshevik revolution, regard violence as unavoidable—an inherent aspect of the situation? Or might he emulate Camus in the aftermath of the Liberation, by concentrating on reconciliation and tending to abandon the pursuit of social justice? The question was very relevant in contemporary Kenya, for transitional justice was now on the agenda.

Following the violence in 2007–8, several leading politicians, including the current President, Uhuru Kenyatta, were indicted by the International Criminal Court (ICC) for crimes against humanity, and a Truth, Justice and Reconciliation Commission (TJRC) was established. When this reported in August 2013, it dealt with the fifty years since the declaration of independence in 1963, demonstrating the relationships between the events of 2007–8 and the systematic practices of state-led violence and injustice in the post-colonial state. It also traced the continuities between oppressive forms of power in colonial and independent Kenya.[112] Furthermore, after the British government had failed to obstruct the legal processes by various ploys, in June 2013 the British Foreign Secretary gave a partial and belated apology in the House of Commons for the Emergency period and agreed compensation for some of the elderly victims of the repression carried out between 1952 and 1963.[113] In principle, Ngũgĩ might have regarded these steps both as highly significant and a vindication of his claims about the linkages between colonial and post-colonial injustices. However, he did not make statements to this effect, presumably because he believed that such procedures of transitional justice would be ineffective unless more fundamental causes of the problems were addressed.

In a reflective article in April 2008, setting current events in the context of the history of both the colonial and independent state, he argued that hope for Kenya depended on the social descendants of the real fighters for democracy reaching out to each other, regrouping and energising the nation with a renewed dedication.: 'There has to emerge a third force that is guided by a determination to look into the problems of uneven geographic and social development. A prosperous middle class rooted in mass poverty will always be a prescription for disaster no matter the individual and the party in power.'[114]

Five years later, on the eve of the 2013 general election, he viewed the legacy of Daniel arap Moi as a dominant feature of the political landscape, and doubted whether Uhuru Kenyatta or his running mate William Ruto, who were two of the wealthiest men in Kenya, would revive the economy, reduce poverty and corruption, resettle displaced persons or prioritise the interests of ordinary people. He concluded that a new constitution, adopted in 2010, offered a chance to roll back the entrenchment of Moi's legacy, but he was not optimistic.[115] His scepticism about both this, and the effectiveness of the conventional procedures of transitional justice in the Kenyan context, soon seemed vindicated. For Uhuru Kenyatta mobilised opinion against the 'anti-African imperialism' of the ICC as a means of diverting attention from the charges that he was facing; and the court formally withdrew the charges against him in December 2014 because there was not enough evidence to proceed (primarily because the Kenyan state had not co-operated sufficiently in supplying such evidence). In the same month, Kenyatta called for new anti-terrorist laws to be introduced, which were widely viewed by the opposition as a pretext for reintroducing the kind of repressive legislation of the Moi era.[116]

For more than half a century, Ngũgĩ has been a perceptive com-mentator on political developments in Kenya, where he has continued to be an influential public intellectual. Yet it would be wrong to regard him primarily as a political analyst, for his outstanding contribution to the themes of injustice, justice and transition has been through his cre-ative work. As he once put it, 'I am not in art because of politics; I am in politics because of my artistic calling'.[117] And even during his most revolutionary phase, he was convinced that the success of a novel was dependent on its ability to illuminate human relationships, as in the work of Tolstoy and Balzac, and that people did not turn to fiction to learn about social forces, but because of its human appeal. It was, he suggested, through this appeal that readers began to see the other forces that brought about these forms of relationship between peo-ple.[118] Ngũgĩ set himself the task of producing novels of this kind but, unlike Tolstoy and Balzac, his style of writing was far from realist. Yet he has succeeded in conveying the nature of social realities through characters that are simultaneously compelling and extraordinary. His early novels, *The River Between* and *Weep Not, Child*, focus on the lives of individuals who clearly exemplify both the confrontations between the colonial forces and the Gĩkũyũ, and those within the Gĩkũyũ commu-nity itself. Because the characters carry so much historical weight and tragedy, the books may be viewed as melodramatic, but the reader wants to suspend disbelief because the writing is so engaging. The later novels are often surreal, with much more humour and irony, and a stronger resemblance to traditional oral story-telling. This was one part of Ngũgĩ's wider ambition to engage poor and marginalised peoples through cultural forms in an attempt to bring about social and political change. Matigari, for example, is clearly a super-human figure, incorporating the trans-generational history of Kenya in his own person. His search for truth and justice becomes more powerful because of its mythical form. Ultimately, this is surely also what Ngũgĩ himself has sought through his writing:

> For me, dreaming to change the conditions that confine human life is the mission of art, and it is often in conflict with that of the state as we have known it up to now, in Africa and the world. In such a situation art has the right to take up penpoints, to write down our dreams for a world in which, at the very least, there are no prisons and gunpoints.[119]

This highly optimistic aspiration has underpinned his constant struggle against injustice.

5

JORGE SEMPRÚN AND THE TRANSITION IN SPAIN

JUSTICE, AMNESIA AND MEMORY

Following Franco's death in November 1975, most mainstream Western commentators regarded the subsequent establishment of democracy as a model for a successful transition from dictatorship. This was reinforced once Spain also entered NATO in 1982, and the European Community four years later. Many observers on the Left, however, were more critical, noting the continuity in office of much of the former Francoist elite and the fact that the change was primarily in the political system rather than in the underlying structures of power.[1] Later a further criticism became increasingly prevalent, for the process of democratisation had been accompanied by an all-embracing amnesty. There were no trials, purges, truth commissions or even historical investigations, although the 1936–9 conflict in Spain was one of the most brutal civil wars in twentieth-century Europe, and was followed by extreme repression under the subsequent dictatorship. And for many in Spain, particularly for Republican sympathisers amongst the older generation, it was difficult to distinguish between the Nationalists' actions in the Civil War itself and the subsequent dictatorship of Franco. Both were part of a 'crusade' to crush the democratic reforms of the Second Republic from 1931 to 1936. As Paul Preston has argued, the coup of 1936 had been instigated to defend the central tenets of the Right, as expressed in the slogan of the major Catholic Party, Confederación Española de Derechas Autónomas (CEDA):

> 'Religion, Fatherland, Family, Order, Work, Property', the untouchable elements of social and economic life in Spain before 1931. 'Religion' referred to the Catholic Church's monopoly of education and religious practice. 'Fatherland' meant no challenge to Spanish centralism from the regional nationalisms. 'Family' denoted the subservient position of women and the prohibition of divorce. 'Order' meant no toleration of public protest. 'Work' referred to the duties of the labouring masses. 'Property' meant the privileges of the landowners whose position must remain unchallenged. Sometimes, the word 'hierarchy' was included in the list to emphasize that the existing social order was sacrosanct. To protect all of these tenets, in the areas occupied by the rebels, the immediate victims were not just schoolteachers, Freemasons, liberal doctors and lawyers, intellectuals and trade union leaders ... The killing also extended to all those who might have been influenced by their ideas: the trade unionists, those who didn't attend Mass, those suspected of voting in February 1936 for the left-wing electoral coalition, the Popular Front, and the women who had been given the vote and the right to divorce.[2]

Certainly, the Republican side was also guilty of atrocities during the Civil War. As Preston has shown in meticulous detail, current research suggests that 49,272 people were murdered or executed in the Republican zones, and the figure might be higher.[3] There were also particularly vicious attacks against the Church, including the raiding and burning of monasteries and convents, and the rape of nuns and murder of priests. Yet it would be very misleading to imply that the responsibility for the death and destruction was shared equally between the two sides. First, it was the Francoists who had unleashed the attack on the democratically elected Republic, and their violence was on a far greater scale, with approximately 150,000 murders or executions.[4] Secondly, this was orchestrated from above with the deliberate aim of instituting a programme of terror and extermination, while the brutality on the Republican side was generally from below and, at least initially, in response to the assault on the government, and it largely ended by December 1936.[5] Thirdly, the Francoist forces later sought to eliminate both the personnel and ideology of the defeated forces through a process of terror. Franco could have achieved victory more quickly, but prolonged the war in 1939 so as to crush the Republican forces, with orders to eliminate all those considered leftists in zones where Nationalist forces wrested control from the Republican government.[6] In the last months of 1939 and during 1940, officials of the new regime thus recorded the internment of more than 270,000 prisoners, many of whom died during the next two years through executions and from illness and malnutrition. In addition, there were probably more than 35,000 official executions in the first decade after the war, with perhaps another 15,000 summary executions.[7]

Nor was physical brutality the sole form of retribution, for a law of February 1939 also institutionalised the purging of public officials so as to deprive opponents of their jobs and livelihoods, while guaranteeing employment for those who had been loyal to the Nationalists.[8] The regime then ruled through a climate of intimidation, including the use of informants, and it was a criminal offence to remain silent about the activities of so-called 'Reds'. The role of the Church was also important, for the hierarchy sought a complete restoration of the hegemonic position of Catholicism in Spanish society. In the first decade of the dictatorship it thus supported retribution and punishment against the defeated forces and, through its control of the education system, also accepted the sacking of thousands of teachers in schools and universities, and Opus Dei made sure that professorships were offered only to the faithful. By the 1960s, there was a gradual recognition that Catholicism could not be imposed from above and the excesses of the regime in its final stages were condemned.[9] However, as Casanova puts it: 'During almost the entire dictatorship the Church never wanted to hear anything of forgiveness or reconciliation, contented as it was with the memory of the crusade'.[10] The fear of non-conformity, imposed by both the dictatorship and the Church, was a factor instilling compliance in everyday life. This meant that sympathisers of the Republic were forced into self-censorship through the threat of loss of livelihood or still more extreme threats to their liberty. Francoism was not therefore simply a form of rule that prohibited opposition, prescribed trade unions, and repressed all forms of dissent: it also sought to eliminate all traces of the pre-1936 era by purging the society of an alternative historical memory.

Even during its final years, the dictatorship sometimes resorted to brutal repression, but in general it was able to present a more moderate face, both domestically and internationally. This also enabled it to construct a self-serving narrative about the Civil War which partially moved away from the original official narrative. Instead of presenting the conflict as a 'crusade' against Bolshevism in defence of Christian civilisation, with authoritarianism as a necessary barrier against anarchy, from the 1960s onwards the new emphasis was that the war had been 'fratricidal'—a collective madness that was out of place in a country that was now undergoing rapid economic development and growth.[11] This would easily feed into a call during the transition period for amnesties and amnesia in order to move on and replace the dictatorship with liberal-democracy. Yet this version of history reflected the interests of the victors to a far greater extent than those of the vanquished.

This chapter considers the dictatorship and transition in a long-term perspective. It emphasises memory as an aspect of historical justice, which was finally acknowledged in a limited form more than thirty years after the death of Franco in the Historical Memory Law of 2007 (*Ley de Memoria Histórica*). It considers these issues through the work of Jorge Semprún (1923–2011).

Life and 'autofiction'

Jorge Semprún still tends to be relatively neglected in English-speaking countries although his work is influential elsewhere, particularly in France, Spain and Germany.[12] He is best known for writing about his experiences when incarcerated in Buchenwald during World War II, beginning with his first novel, *Le grand voyage* (1963) (*The Long Voyage*, 1964).[13] He also acquired an international reputation for films, particularly for his screenplays for Costa-Gavras for *Z* (1969), about the murder of a leftist leader in Greece, and *L'Aveu* (1970) (*The Confession*), about the trial of Artur London, one of the defendants in the notorious Slánský trial in Czechoslovakia.[14] Because he wrote mainly in French about themes of general European and international significance, until recently comparatively little attention has been paid to the specifically Spanish aspects of his work, although his identity as a Republican exile was central to his life and writing.[15] As an adolescent he viewed international developments primarily through his Spanish preoccupations, but his extraordinary life experiences later led him to regard the situation in his original homeland through a European lens. This also meant that he had already gone through many transitions himself before the end of the Francoist dictatorship, and these shaped his attitude to the establishment of democracy in Spain. This results in a paradox: in most respects Semprún's life, thought and writing were quite distinct and individual. Yet his work both illuminates and reflects many of the assumptions that underlay the transition after the death of Franco.

He was one of seven children from a privileged family. His maternal grandfather, Antonio Maura (1853–1925), was the prime minister of Spain five times. His mother, Maura's daughter, was Susana Maura Gamazo, who died when he was only eight. His father was José María Semprún Gurrea (1893–1966), a writer, politician and diplomat, who was the civil governor of Toledo during the Second Republic. Semprún Gurrea, who was a very important influence on his son, was a loyal and dedicated supporter of the Republic, whose general position was shaped by the left-liberal Catholic thinking of the French-dominated journal, *L'Esprit*.[16] In 1936, soon after the start of the Civil War, the whole family left Spain and Semprún Gurrea now became the Chargé d'Affaires of the Spanish government in the Netherlands. Less than three years later, they were forced to move to France after the Dutch government recognised Franco.

While at a Lycée in Paris, Jorge Semprún excelled in philosophy and was awarded a prize in 1941 for a thesis on 'intuitive knowledge', with Heidegger and Husserl as key influences, and his later writing would be underpinned by a philosophical approach.[17] But he was now moving to the Left. During the next year he got to know the widow of the French socialist, Lucien Herr, and her house was a centre for refugees from central Europe, many of whom were communists.[18] He became very friendly with her son, Michel, and soon after this they both aligned themselves with the French Communist Party, participating in underground work, including sabotage, for the Resistance. Semprún's willingness to risk his life was now to lead to his most terrible experiences. In 1943 he was arrested near Auxerre and tortured by the Gestapo.[19] He was then held in two prisons before being deported to Buchenwald, where he remained until the end of the war.

He lived in Paris in the early post-war period, working as a translator for Unesco. In 1947 he had a son, Jaime, with the actress Loleh

Bellon, whom he later married, but their marriage was short-lived. At this stage he had some involvement in both the Spanish and French Communist parties, but in 1949 he decided to become a militant with the Spanish party, choosing to work for the clandestine organisation in Spain.[20] In 1952 he became a full-time official in the party, and in 1953 took charge of its activity within Spain. For the next ten years, this involved frequent trips to several parts of the country, using various false names and travelling on a French passport. It was dangerous work, with discovery and arrest leading to certain torture, but he was deeply committed to it.[21] He was in charge of the sector of communist intellectuals, including both university students and academic staff, and he played an influential role in a protest action by students at Madrid University in 1956, which temporarily alarmed the dictatorship.[22] He also organised the party in various industrial sectors and was responsible for coordinating the work of the permanent nucleus of clandestine party workers in Madrid.[23] He soon rose through the party hierarchy, being co-opted to the Central Committee in autumn 1954, and from the summer of 1956 he was a co-opted regular member of the Executive Committee.[24] However, in autumn 1962 the party leader, Santiago Carrillo, suddenly announced that Semprún should stop working in Spain and his last period of clandestine activity was that December. Carrillo claimed that the reason for the move was that it was too dangerous for Semprún to continue, but this was a pretext, for his responsibilities were now reduced, and he moved towards a dissident position on the Executive Committee. Matters came to a head in January 1964, when he and Fernando Claudín were expelled from the Executive Committee, and the next year also from the party.[25]

The success of his first book enabled him to establish himself as a writer and he soon also acquired prominence through his films. This was an interest he shared with his long-term partner, Colette Leloup, the film editor, whom he married in 1963. He later adopted her daughter, and they had four more children together. On the eve of the collapse of the dictatorship, they also worked together in making *Les Deux Mémoires* (1974), a documentary film about interpretations of the Spanish Civil War. After the establishment of democracy, he occupied a governmental role from 1988 as Minister of Culture in the socialist (Partido Socialista Obrero Español [PSOE]) government of Felipe Gonzáles. Subsequently, he continued to write and speak about both national and wider issues and his reflections on Buchenwald and historical memory contributed to the creation of a climate in which it was no longer possible to practise collective amnesia about the past in Spain.

The most striking feature of Semprún's oeuvre was the centrality of memory and his own autobiography within it.[26] This meant that the major experiences and lessons of his life were his primary subject matter, both in works of fiction and non-fiction. In fact there was no clear distinction between the two and his work has been termed 'autofiction'.[27] Thus *Autobiografía de Federico Sánchez* (1977) (*Communism in Spain in the Franco Era: The Autobiography of Federico Sánchez* [1980]) was both an interpretive history of the Partido Comunista de España (PCE) and a personal reflection addressed to his former self, for Federico Sánchez was one of the many pseudonyms Semprún had used as an activist in the party. Similarly, works that were ostensibly novels, such as *The Long Voyage*, were largely autobiographical, with the narrator given the same name, Gérard, by which Semprún had been known in the French Resistance. He also sometimes used autobiography and fiction in still more complex ways. His final novel, *Veinte Años y un Día* (2003) (*Vingt ans et un jour* [2004]), not only included meetings between his father and fictional characters, but Semprún himself appeared in the book, both in his own name and as Federico Sánchez.[28] Another key feature of his writing was his refusal to keep to any chronological order. This was not, he insisted, a rhetorical device, but a fundamental aspect of his mental makeup. In *Vingt ans et un jour* he attempted to explain this through an encounter between himself and a fictional historian, Michael Leidson. Leidson tells him that he will use chronological order because he is an historian and will not follow Semprún's approach—of disorder, by association of ideas, images or events, going back by projecting himself forward.[29] But Semprún replies by explaining that, when first returning to Madrid in secret in 1953 after seventeen years in exile, he had felt like an alien until he saw a haberdashery shop that evoked memories of childhood. Perhaps, he suggests, Leidson can now see

> why it is so difficult for me, despite all my efforts, to write novels that are real novels: for at each step, on each page, I come up against the reality of my own life, of my personal experience, of my memories: why invent situ-

ations when one has had such a Romanesque life, in which one can draw out the narrative material infinitely?[30]

Yet Semprún certainly regarded many of his autobiographical works as novels and, like Serge and Ngũgĩ, believed that it was necessary to approach the most horrific subjects through fiction. His attempt to do this had begun immediately after the war when he first attempted to write about his experiences in Buchenwald. At that stage he had been forced to abandon the book because of the emotional difficulties in undertaking such a project so soon but, as he recalled telling a friend at the time, there were also literary difficulties:

> Because I don't want to do a plain eyewitness account. Right from the start I mean to avoid, to spare myself, any recital of suffering and horror … There's also the fact that I'm not able, at this point, to conceive of a novelistic structure in the third person. I don't even want to consider tackling things from that direction. So I need a narrative 'I' that draws on my experience but goes beyond it, capable of opening the narrative up to fiction, to imagination … Fiction that would be as illuminating as the truth, of course. That would help reality to seem true-to-life, truth to seem convincing.[31]

He eventually achieved this in *The Long Voyage* and subsequently produced a series of 'autofictions'. He aspired to emulate the work of André Malraux who, he believed, had reworked the material of his writings and his life, 'shedding light on reality through fiction, and illuminating the fiction through the extraordinary destiny of his life, thus drawing attention to the constant elements, the contradictions, the fundamental (and often hidden, enigmatic, or ephemeral) meaning of both life and art.'[32]

Memory was thus central to his work, and this often appears to be of a very personal sort in the constant retelling of parts of his own biography. However, there was always more to it than this, and Semprún's changing ideas on injustice, justice and transition emerge from his constant exploration of the meaning of his own past, and particularly the traumas he experienced. Paul Gordon thus makes an important point in suggesting that, despite the vast differences between the two, Semprún is perhaps the writer who most fully embodies the legacy of Serge, for 'they shared a commitment to truth and to witnessing for others, and it was always in the service of these that they wrote'.[33]

The following section attempts to identify some of the most relevant ideas in a partially thematic and partially chronological way in the period between the Civil War and the transition to democracy.

From civil war to transition

A Spanish Republican

One of the deepest layers in Semprún's outlook, instilled in him from childhood, was a commitment to the Republican tradition. His father was a major influence over his early political beliefs and Semprún recalled him saying in 1934 that the most fundamental principle was to support the oppressed and the humiliated.[34] He was only thirteen when the Francoists unleashed the Civil War, but the whole family was united in regarding this as a totally unjustified attack on a legitimate regime which defended the poor against the rich. At this stage they probably all viewed questions of justice and injustice through Semprún Gurrea's combination of liberal, legal and social conceptions. However, the intensity of his convictions is also worth noting. Although Semprún himself rejected Catholicism during adolescence, he later recalled going to church with his religious father in The Hague in 1937, when a parish priest launched into a long sermon against the Spanish 'Reds'. His father, he recalled, turned a deathly pale and explained to the priest

> that he was unworthy of his ministry, that he was not a good servant of God; he explained to him that the war in Spain was essentially a war of rich against poor, and that if the official Spanish Church had chosen to side with the rich and not with the poor, this was not what the Gospels preached; that the Church of silence, the martyred, evangelical Church, the truly Christian community of Spanish Catholics, however few and however persecuted they were, bore witness for Christ and the future of the Church by siding with the poor, the oppressed, the exploited, the starving; and as he cast severe reproach upon his conscience as a priest and his conscience as a believer, my father's voice resounded with accents of pain and anger, and at times grew hoarse with pain and anger, and the Dutch priest, dumbfounded, his face by turns white and beet-red, listened to this diatribe, this other sermon, this long despairing cry from a believer without a Church, aspiring only to the universality of a religious practice faithful to the message of the Gospels, and blushing now, the Dutch priest murmured something about not realizing, said he had not intended to

offend any sincere Catholic, and retreated one step at a time, raising his right hand in a mechanical gesture of benediction, still fleeing however, walking backwards towards a side door of the sacristy through which he suddenly vanished.[35]

Although his own views were already secular, Semprún's commitment to the Republic was equally intense and passionate. As a teenager in Paris, two questions, which would remain important throughout his life, were soon posed for him. The first concerned the relationship between events in Spain and the wider international context. At this stage, he later recalled, his attitude was determined by a single criterion: the bearing of events elsewhere on the fate of the Spanish Republic.[36] However, Franco's victory and the outbreak of World War II inevitably made this far less clear-cut. Secondly, the ending of the Republic, and the likelihood of an extended period of exile, also raised the issue of his own identity. Through an extraordinary act of will and linguistic ability, he now learned to speak French totally fluently and without a trace of a Spanish accent.[37] Yet he insisted that this did not mean that he wanted to become French: on the contrary he would maintain his identity behind the anonymity of correct pronunciation. Paradoxically, he claimed that his fluency in French made him never forget that he was a 'Spanish Red'.[38] He referred to this core identity very frequently and late in life he expressed the wish that, when he died, the Republican flag should be wrapped around his body, even though by then he thought that constitutional monarchy was, in Spanish conditions, the best way to guarantee the continuation of democracy. For this, he believed, signified fidelity to the notion of exile and the mortifying pain experienced by Republicans.[39] His commitment to the ideals he associated with the Republic was the foundation of his subsequent evolution, and always remained fundamental.

Resistance, communism and Buchenwald

Semprún later claimed that his conception of Spanish Republicanism was never a nationalist vision, and he insisted that, when risking his life, it was always for ideas of liberty, justice and solidarity with the humiliated and oppressed rather than for a 'homeland'.[40] When joining communist forces in the Resistance, his *raison d'être* was that of revolutionary internationalism.[41] He later looked back on himself in this period:

> In the beginning you had been a revolutionary intellectual. By that you mean you had assumed and accepted the consequences of your ideas, the praxis implied by your theoretical vision. The reading of Hegel, the discovery of Marx and Lukacs had led you directly to the Maquis in Burgundy, to the handling of explosives, of a Sten gun, and of a stupendous 43-caliber Smith and Wesson revolver. You were eighteen years old and you were happy; you wouldn't dream of hiding that fact.[42]

Many of his other recollections suggest that, in the Resistance, his most fundamental beliefs were a general adherence to a Marxist theory of justice, primarily for ethical reasons, and the belief that Soviet and communist leadership in the anti-fascist war would be the most likely way to bring about the emancipation of Europe as a whole, including Spain.[43]

In Buchenwald, as he would always acknowledge, he was luckier than many others. A German communist, who had first asked him what his job was when he arrived at the camp, effectively saved Semprún's life by ignoring his insistence that he was a student and instead recording his work as a stucco worker (*stukkateur*).[44] This spared him from being sent to work in the most onerous conditions in the Mittelbau-Dora sub-camp, which had the highest death rate. He was again fortunate because he was the only Spanish communist who could speak fluent German and the PCE had designated him to work with the German Communist Party, which played a key role in organising the prisoners within the camp. Semprún thus became a member of the unit that assigned work (*Arbeitsstatistik*), and this also protected him.[45] He drew a sharp distinction between Buchenwald and the extermination camps and stressed that he had been a survivor, rather than a victim, particularly as he continued to view himself as part of the Resistance, as demonstrated by his participation in the uprising in the camp in April 1945.[46] Nevertheless, life in the camp was almost unbearable, with constant brutality by the guards and the starvation, emaciation, illness and death of the prisoners. He also witnessed the plight of Jews who were marched to Buchenwald late in the war, and he was traumatised by the sight of Jewish children being chased by dogs and slaughtered.[47] These experiences would remain with him for the rest of his life. Much later, when asked about his identity, his first inclination was to reply that he was 'before everything else or above it an ex-deportee of the camp of Buchenwald. This is what comes to me first, what is essential to me, what is the most profound there, what shapes my true identity the most.'[48] This meant that, when he subsequently considered the Spanish situation, it was always as part of a wider twentieth-century barbarity.

His first inclination after the war was to try to write about it, but he soon found that this was simply too traumatic. After a possible suicide attempt (he subsequently claimed that he did not know whether he fell out of a train or jumped), he abandoned the project.[49] Unlike Primo Levi, who secured some solace in writing about his experiences, Semprún found the effort agonising and believed he needed to choose life instead of writing.[50] This led to his long period of total immersion in the PCE from 1949. However, towards the end of this period he was finally able to write about Buchenwald in *The Long Voyage*, which won the Formentor prize for literature in 1963. There are several notable features about the book and it would also be immensely significant in his future life and thought.

It is, above all, an extraordinarily powerful account of the journey to Buchenwald, interspersed with passages about life in the camp, the Liberation and the early post-war years. The central character is Gérard, whose experiences were largely his own, but there are also fictional aspects. One of the key themes of the book is the underlying idea that the struggle against Nazism was total and that no compromise of any kind was possible. Secondly, there are frequent allusions to the fact that this was also a war against Franco and that Gérard remained a 'Spanish Red'. Thirdly, the idea of remembrance is fundamental. After the Liberation two French girls tell Gérard that the camps do not look too bad, so he takes them to the absolute horror of bodies piled twelve feet high in the crematorium courtyard. A black flag is flying at half-mast from the control tower and one of the girls asks if that is for the dead: "'No. That's for Roosevelt. The dead don't need a flag." "What do they need?" she asks. "A pure, fraternal look," I reply. "And to be remembered."'[51] Still more poignantly, he aspired to be the voice of the Jewish children: 'And maybe I shall be able to tell about the death of the Jewish children, describe that death in all its details, solely in the hope—perhaps exaggerated, perhaps unrealizable—that these children may hear it.'[52] In fact, much of the purpose of the book was encapsulated in Gérard's thought, as he approached Buchenwald for the first time, fighting

> against the sudden weakness of his own body, trying to keep his eyes open, to let them absorb this icy light on the snowy landscape, these streetlights stretching down the monumental avenue, flanked by tall columns of stone surmounted by the hieratic violence of Hitlerian eagles, this mad landscape in which only the noble, solemn music of some fabulous opera is lacking. Gérard tries to engrave all this in his memory, meanwhile vaguely thinking that it is well within the realm of possibility that the impending death of all the spectators may efface forever the memory of this spectacle, thinking what a shame that would be, he doesn't know why, his brain was a heavy, cottony mass, but it would be a shame, the certainty of this idea takes hold of him and suddenly it seems to him that this noble, solemn music does strike up...[53]

The Long Voyage was thus based on his belief in the crucial importance of providing a testimony to the camps and bringing alive the memory of those who had died there.

The final idea underlying the text was *sotto voce*, but of crucial importance to the author at the time: a message about the relationship between Nazism and capitalism. As Gérard recalls a German soldier whom he had met while imprisoned in Auxerre, he realises that he had been constantly unemployed until the Nazis took power and had therefore never been able to take possession of his own life:

> We're on opposite sides of the bars, and never have I understood more clearly why I was fighting. We had to make this man's being habitable, or rather the being of all men like him, because for him it was no doubt already too late. We had to make the being of this man's sons habitable ... It was no more complicated than that, that is it's really the most complicated thing in the world. For it's quite simply a question of instituting a classless society.[54]

Later, as they left the German village near Buchenwald, he remembered that they used to 'gaze at the life outside, in this village. And then, in a trice, it wasn't the life outside; it was only another way of being inside, of being inside this same world of systematic oppression, consistent to the very end, of which the camp was the expression.'[55]

The unstated implication was that communism was the sole alternative to capitalism and its ultimate consequences—Nazism and Buchenwald.

Traumas, rethinking and self-criticism

Semprún had been increasingly unhappy with aspects of PCE policy for some time, but his break with communism in 1964–5 was devastating for him. In fact, in an interview the year before his death, he claimed that it was more traumatic for him than Buchenwald:

> The memories of Buchenwald were very painful for a long time, but there were also positive experiences, like solidarity and fraternity. Furthermore, I knew why I was there, because of having been a member of the resistance—and I did useful things, there was a moral compensation every day. In contrast, when I was expelled from the PCE, a life project that had started in my adolescence and that had always defined me came crumbling down. The expulsion produced in me an unbearable moral suffering for which there was no possible compensation. My problem is that, after so many years, I had to reconstruct my entire life, on the basis of new and different ideals, and that disillusion, that shattered self, that non-being, had a greater effect on me than the Gestapo's physical torture.[56]

In fact, the two traumas, or at least Semprún's reflections on their significance, became closely interconnected in his subsequent outlook. For a year before his expulsion from the PCE, and before *The Long Voyage* had even been printed, he read Solzhenitsyn's *One Day in the Life of Ivan Denisovich*. This, he later claimed, was overwhelming for him, for the description of the Soviet camp was so similar to Buchenwald. The impact of reading the book meant that he needed to find a way:

> of erasing the guilt I felt at having lived in the blessed innocence of the memory of Buchenwald, the innocent memory of having belonged to the camp of the just, without the slightest doubt, whereas the idea for which I thought I was fighting, the justice for which I thought I was fighting, was serving at the same time to justify the most radical injustice, the most absolute evil: the camp of the just had created and was running the Kolyma camps.[57]

Having read Solzhenitsyn's book, he knew he would have to rewrite his own account so as to destroy that innocence of memory:

> I had written the truth, I suppose, nothing but the truth. If I had not been a Communist, that truth would have been enough. If I had been a

Christian, Social Democrat, nationalist—or simply a patriot, as the peasants in the Othe[58] called me— the truth of my evidence would have been enough. But I was not a Christian or a Social Democrat. I was a Communist. The whole of my account in *The Long Voyage* was tacitly articulated, without making it too obvious, without making a fuss about it, according to a Communist vision of the world. The very truth of my account had as its implicit but constricting reference the horizon of a disalienated society: a society without classes in which the camps would have been inconceivable. The very truth of my account bathed in the holy oils of this latent serene conscience. But the horizon of Communism—its real, historical horizon—was not that of a classless society. The horizon of Communism was, inescapably, that of the Gulag. By the same token, the very truth of my book became a lie…[59]

In fact, Semprún's attitude both to communism and to the interpretation of the camps would evolve over time. From 1965 to 1969 he remained firmly on the Left, co-directing a new magazine on the fringes of the PCE, *Cuadernos de Ruedo Ibérico*, in Paris.[60] Nor did he ever entirely reject some aspects of Marxism. In *Communism in Spain* he distinguished between the essential aspects in the 'critical and practical exposition of Marxism by Marx', and what he now believed to be the completely religious idea that it was better to be wrong in the party than right outside it.[61] And in an interview only a year before his death he still paid tribute to aspects of Marx's analysis of the development of capitalism in *Grundrisse*.[62] Nevertheless, he subsequently became increasingly anti-communist and, as he did so, he also distanced himself from Marxism. Similarly, his later works on Buchenwald were imbued with the notion that the Nazi camps and Soviet gulags were identical. In his autobiographical novel, *What a Beautiful Sunday*, he thus wrote that 'the Nazi concentration-camp society was not, as you had long thought, the concentrated, and hence necessarily deformed, expression of capitalist social relations. This idea was fundamentally false'. And he concluded:

> In fact, the Nazi camps were not the distorting mirror of capitalist society—even if they were the product of the class struggle, or, rather the result of the violent suspension of that struggle by the arbitrary action of the fascists—they were a fairly faithful mirror of Stalinist society.[63]

Neither his anti-communism nor his belief in the identity between the two types of camp meant that he failed to recognise the ethical idea that had inspired much of the communist movement. When he eventually found out that the German communist at Buchenwald had deliberately described him as a '*stukkateur*' rather than a student, he wrote:

> my German Communist had acted like a Communist. What I mean is, in a manner befitting the idea of Communism, whatever its rather bloody, suffocating, morally destructive history has been. He had reacted according to an idea of solidarity, of internationalism. A generous idea of humanity ... [B]ecause he was a Communist, that anonymous German saved my life.[64]

Nevertheless, he came to regard Soviet communism and Nazism as twin (though not identical) forms of 'radical evil'. This notion also led to a reconfiguration of his attitudes towards injustice, justice and transition in Spain.

When Semprún reflected on his past life, he did not spare himself in relation to his past association with Stalinism. In particular, he would subsequently refer several times to a particular episode, which also brought Buchenwald and his communism together: the case of Josef Frank, who had been with him in the camp. Semprún was absolutely certain that Frank was honest and courageous, for they had collaborated on several secret party missions. But in the autumn of 1952 Semprún read in *L'Humanité* that Frank, assistant secretary-general of the Communist Party of Czechoslovakia, had confessed to having worked under Gestapo orders in Buchenwald. Semprún subsequently admitted that as soon as he heard of the confession he knew that it could not possibly be true:

> You said nothing, however. Nowhere did you proclaim Frank's innocence, or the falseness of the accusation brought against him. Had you proclaimed that innocence you would no doubt have ended up being expelled from the party. You decided to remain in the party. You preferred living the lie of the accusation against Frank within the party to living the truth of his innocence outside the party. Frank was sentenced to die and met his death on the gallows.[65]

A sense of guilt about this case perhaps also underpinned his decision to write the screenplay for the Costa Gavros film, *L'Aveu* (1970), based on the account of Artur London, who had also been imprisoned in Czechoslovakia after the same trial, and whom Semprún met in Paris in 1964.[66] More generally, his reflections about the past would form part of his subsequent ideas about the importance of self-criticism, truth and integrity.

These virtues, he believed, were also relevant in relation to collective entities. He recalled a discussion in which he had participated in Paris in 1948 about the relationship between politics and morality. Regarding this as too abstract, he had given the real example of the role of the organised groups at Buchenwald in choosing which 3000 people to send to Dora, the worst camp.[67] Similarly, twelve years later when he re-met and travelled with another communist who had been with him in Buchenwald, Semprún claimed to remember a conversation that they had had in the camp. He had, he recalled, said that they were waging a just war in the most difficult imaginable conditions, 'but we are not innocent for all that, not inevitably so, anyway, since this just war brings us privileges, cushy jobs, power that we can abuse'. Some communists in the Nazi camp, who partly cooperated in the administration, used these privileges to undermine the system and take risks, while others did not, and he concluded:

> For a strategy to become a morality, it isn't enough that it be just in principle. The men who put it into practice must also be just, uncorrupted by the power they have won in order to deploy this strategy, and because they have deployed it. For power snowballs, as we know.[68]

This would have great relevance to his attitude to the transition in Spain because it was closely related to his belief in the importance of integrity and self-criticism, both in personal terms and more generally. This would, once again, also have particular bearing on his attitude to the PCE.

Envisaging democracy in Spain

By 1960, when acting as a clandestine leader of the PCE in Spain, Semprún had become increasingly critical of the leadership's strategy. The key difference centred on the question of how to end the dictatorship.[69] The leadership continued to assume that mass action by the working-class would eventually bring down the regime, probably through a series of strikes escalating into a quasi-revolutionary crisis. The Claudín–Semprún alternative cast doubt on this.[70] Semprún's most compelling depiction of the atmosphere and meaning of the conflict within the PCE was in his film with Alain Resnais, *La Guerre est Finie* (1966), for which he wrote the screenplay soon after his expulsion from the party. The film contains many elements, including a personal story about love and sex, but the political ideas were of central importance.

The main character, Diego/Carlos, based on Semprún himself, lives in Paris amongst a larger group of Spanish exiles. He has been on numerous clandestine trips to Spain, attempting to develop the party's strategy of working for a general strike that will eventually lead to a revolution, and for several years he has been prepared to take enormous risks to help bring this about. However, he has become increasingly aware that the strategy is going nowhere, and he believes that the party leadership is living in the past, still transfixed by their memories of the Civil War. In his view the future now depends on a new generation: 'They are twenty years old and it isn't our past that will make them move, but their future. Spain is no longer the dream of 36, but the truth of 65, even if this is disconcerting. Thirty years have gone by and I'm sick of the war veterans.'[71]

Franco's police have picked up several of Diego's comrades, but this makes no difference to the majority of the party leadership. One stalwart, Roberto, hates hearing news of the arrests, not only because of the fallen comrades, nor even because it takes the party back to square one after months or sometimes years of work, but because 'he hates the fact that reality doesn't conform to his dream'.[72] When Diego tries to point out to the leadership that there is no prospect of the general strike strategy succeeding, and that there is a Francoist crackdown, he is denounced as subjective and pessimistic and having lost his whole political perspective. Even his long-term partner, Marianne, is so desperate to be able to settle down and live with him in Spain that she too wants to believe that the party's strategy will succeed and that Franco's dictatorship will be overthrown soon. At the other extreme, through a brief affair with a young woman (Nadine), Diego also encounters a youthful group who believe that a revolution in Spain can be sparked off by planting bombs that will deter tourists from going to the country. He regards this as ludicrous and is convinced that there are no short cuts to the goal that they all share—the downfall of the dictatorship. But he also maintains his loyalty to the party and solidarity with his comrades. Having initially been instructed to stay in Paris and reflect on his political errors, he is suddenly told to go back to Spain to help another clandestine member. However, he will be in mortal danger there, as the Spanish police have been tipped off, and in the final scene Marianne tries to intercept him.

In *La Guerre est Finie* a crucial political theme, which was central to Semprún's evolving thinking about Spain, was an emphasis on the vital need to face realities. When condemning Diego for his report on the Spanish situation, the senior party official accuses him of counterposing the exiles and the internal movement. Diego insists that he is not doing this—he is just trying to understand the situation on the ground. The implication is that the leadership is putting its clandestine members in danger because it cannot bear the notion of continued exile or the need to revise its ideas about either the past or the future. Yet, ultimately this leads to injustice—and at the end of the film the leadership may be deliberately setting Diego up for the Spanish police because he is now regarded as unreliable.

Semprún soon further developed other ideas that he had suggested in the 1950s. In his campaigning work with students in Madrid in 1956 he had been inclusive in his attitude to protest and had called for reconciliation and common action by the children of Republicans and Francoists.[73] At that stage, Carrillo temporarily seemed to support this strategy, probably in order to discredit the 'old guard' in the PCE leadership.[74] However, in Semprún's case the approach was no doubt based on profound sentiments about the need to move beyond the bitter divisions of the Civil War era in order to establish a new Spain. His 1974 documentary film, *Les Deux Mémoires*, on the eve of the transition, tackled the fixation on the past more directly. This was based on forty hours of interviews, representing an eclectic range of views on the Spanish Civil War and its legacy. He reinforced this message when defending the political point of the documentary:

> To listen to others you need to hide the discourse, the rhetoric that has lived for many years but at the given moment doesn't reflect reality, not the reality of Spain, or the tradition that it follows, that is to say the communist movement. The political choice of *Les Deux Mémoires* consists of letting others speak, this means you hear many silly things, and things that you already know, but at least you hear these things and can try to understand them.[75]

This belief in an open-minded attitude to Spanish history, coupled with the commitment to self-criticism, would be of crucial importance in Semprún's stance during and after the transition from Francoism.

The transition, the amnesty and the 'Pact of Forgetfulness'

By the late 1960s, as Semprún had long recognised, more enlightened forces in the political and economic elites favoured a 'normalisation' of the Spanish system on the basis of liberal-democracy and entry into the European Community. However, there were also more violent and extreme elements on both Left and Right and, at the time of Franco's death, Spain was in a situation of acute crisis with continuing violence on both sides.

Certain features of the subsequent transition need to be highlighted. First, there was a gradual, but only partial, triumph of more pragmatic figures from within the former Francoist forces centred around King Juan Carlos and Adolfo Suárez, whom Juan Carlos engineered to take over as prime minister in July 1976. Secondly, one essential precondition for a non-violent transition appeared to be a reorientation of the major political forces on the Left. This was brought about partly through important shifts in the policies of both the PCE and PSOE and partly by skilful manoeuvres by Suárez.[76] Thirdly, Suárez also constructed a new political party, the Unión de Centro Democrático (UCD), in a successful attempt to ensure that liberal-democracy would be controlled by the more pragmatic post-Francoist forces, rather than the hard-liners. He achieved this with a coalition of various groupings in May 1977, which was able to form a government after elections the next month.

The Suárez government was seeking a political basis within liberal-democracy for the economic and social structure that had previously existed under the dictatorship.[77] The Left effectively renounced a programme of socioeconomic transformation in return for the prospect of political stabilisation and a potential share in government power. The shift was most dramatic in the case of the PCE, which now sought to put itself at the forefront of 'Eurocommunism'.[78] In October 1977, in the so-called Moncloa Pact, both the PSOE and the PCE joined the other parties in establishing a common response to the problems of terrorism, inflation, unemployment and a growing trade deficit. The Left thus accepted a transition through which much of the Francoist elite retained power through an adaptation of the political system. Both the PSOE and the PCE were fully aware of the remaining strength and hostility of the hard-line Francoists and the possibility of a new coup.[79] This was the context in which the Left opted for limited political change and the abandonment of wider social and economic ambitions, at least in the short-term, rather than risking either renewed civil war or, more probably, a new right-wing dictatorship. This was also the context for the amnesties, often known as the *Pacto del Olvido* (Pact of Forgetfulness), the most substantial of which was negotiated in the Moncloa Pact.[80] There are two particularly striking points about the amnesties. First, both the PCE and PSOE were staunch advocates of the agreements, while the army and the Right were the most hesitant about the proposals.[81] Secondly, it was simply assumed that there would be no trials or purges. This was perhaps because, as Leopoldo Calvo-Sotelo, prime minister in 1981–2, would later admit, any proposed action against the military would have put the nascent democracy 'in mortal danger'.[82]

Throughout this period, Semprún favoured the course that the transition was taking. He believed that the amnesty was based on an overwhelming wish by the Spanish population as a whole, rather than being a product of the machinations of the political elites.[83] He was also convinced of the crucial role of the monarchy, both in the initial phase and in the coup attempt in 1981.[84] Yet he had no illusions about the fact that the transition had elevated peace over most forms of justice and he was well aware that the historical continuity 'had enabled magistrates, professors, police, bankers and clerics of all levels of the old regime to keep their posts and powers, their ill-gotten riches and their networks of influence.'[85] As he later recalled, the 'invention of a democratic tradition' was also very much helped by a collective effort, partly conscious and partly unconscious, to forget certain periods of history and reinterpret others.[86] Yet for Semprún, for whom both personal and collective memory were so important, this was perhaps surprising. Why, then, did he accept it?

Part of the reason was certainly his fear that any questioning of the amnesties would re-open the old wounds of the Civil War. This was part of a general conviction that the transition was comparatively fragile and should not be disturbed by awkward questions about the past. In 1991, after the collapse of communism in Eastern Europe, the former Polish dissident Adam Michnik thus told Václav Havel, then president of Czechoslovakia, that he had recently asked Semprún how they had dealt with questions about past police repression and use of informants in Spain and he had answered: 'If you want to lead a normal life, you have to try to forget, otherwise those snakes let out of the box will poison public life for years to come.'[87] Since there was little challenge to the *Pacto del Olvido*, this view was no doubt based on the assumption that the agreement reflected a continuing social consensus. However, some have argued that it was nevertheless primarily an elite bargain that was imposed on the population as a whole. Joan Ramon Resina thus suggests that the amnesty in fact meant 'amnesia by decree' and the 'myth of the consensual pact threw political culture into a deep freeze' and 'proved to be a fetter on the pragmatic evolution of the state'.[88] It was only in the late 1990s that historical studies, novels and documentary and feature films started to focus overwhelmingly on wartime and post-war Francoist repression.[89] However, the question had hardly been addressed at all in 1988, when Semprún received an unexpected invitation to join Gonzáles's government as minister of culture.

The election of the first PSOE government in 1982 had provided no new impetus to question the settlement. In fact, during its fourteen years in office, the socialist government under Felipe González was primarily preoccupied with a 'modernisation' agenda that would demonstrate that the PSOE was a centrist catch-all party.[90] In relation to the memory of the Civil War and the dictatorship, Gonzáles took an ultra-cautious line. He made the most minimal amendment to the triumphalist Francoist memorial at El Valle de los Caídos (Valley of the Fallen) by changing the wording to provide a tribute to all the victims who had died for Spain, but he did nothing to initiate any wider debate about the past. Semprún's words, as reported by Michnik, therefore certainly expressed the general sentiments of the González government and the political elite more generally. However, Semprún subsequently claimed that, as minister of culture, he posed the question of amnesia directly, recalling in a subsequent memoir that he thought the time had come to move beyond it, however necessary it had been:

Isn't democracy precisely a system that sustains itself and develops through its internal conflicts, which are taken on and managed in the transparency of citizen participation?

Hasn't the time come collectively to work through the 'return of the repressed', to shed our wilful amnesia about the stakes involved in the civil war, in order finally to confront them—without resentment, revenge or bitterness—but for the sake of a social advance freed from the revolutionary myths of the past and the silences or omissions of the present?[91]

However, he failed to evoke any interest in such a project in a meeting with Gonzáles in March 1989. On his way he had passed the immense monument in Madrid, which had celebrated Franco's victory and, he recalled, had suddenly felt a malaise in response to its sinister meaning.[92] The previous week he had already evoked the end of the Civil War in a debate in parliament. He had noted that it was the fiftieth anniversary of the death of Antonio Machado, a brave poet with democratic convictions, who remained faithful to the Republic in 1936 and had written for the democratic cause, but had sought refuge in France in February 1939, dying a few days later at Collioure. In the late 1950s his tomb had become a symbolic spot for meetings between intellectuals in exile and those from the interior of Spain, and at the end of his speech Semprún pointed out that Machado's death had been commemorated in a climate of agreement:

> But for all that it is not advisable to forget the past. I think that half a century is a sufficient passage of time for it to be possible to master a vision of the past which is simultaneously peaceful and critical. It is also sufficient to become aware that the past is ours, and to make no mistake about it. We mustn't forget that Machado did not die by chance at Collioure in February 1939. He did not arrive there as a tourist. Machado died at Collioure as a political exile, exiled for a democratic cause for which he had taken a stand, for which he had fought. I think that we can be happy—as a man of the left I am happy—to note that the moral and political attitude of Machado during the civil war is now considered in Spain to go without saying, as a universal value that we can all share.[93]

Semprún reminded Gonzáles that the transition in Spain had been carried out with a continuity that had benefited the existing elites, but that legitimacy should be based on the possibility of a democratic future. One major consequence would be 'the resurgence of the moral and political values held by the republican side in the Civil War', though not by returning to the past or in a spirit of revenge. But the values of those who were defeated now informed the code of morality in Spain:

> The aspirations and objectives for which the democratic forces fought have now not only gained a new currency but have become the potential basis of a political cohesion capable of delivering the permanent reform of institutions and ways of life. In the sometimes intractable density of the historical process—which for the first time this century in Spain has been pluralistic and peaceful—these values are the only ones on which a dynamic social consensus can be built. That is to say, by acknowledging enduring conflicts in order to manage them within the constraints and transparency of democratic reason.[94]

But Semprún could not convince Gonzáles that he should organise a commemoration for the fiftieth anniversary of the death of Manuel Azaña, the president of the Republic in 1936, who had died in 1940.[95] He put a charitable interpretation on this—that Gonzáles, who was born in 1942, was simply too young to see the relevance of the past. In reality, he was not prepared to re-open the controversies that would follow, and Semprún achieved little in terms of recovering the historical memory of the Spanish Republic during his period as a minister. Even his idea of displaying Picasso's *Guernica* in the Prado alongside paintings of Velazquez and Goya, thereby showing it as part of an historical continuity in Spanish art, made no headway.[96] Nevertheless, he remained clear about the need for Spain to address the issue of historical memory.

Yet there was a crucial condition attached to his conception of the use of history: it had to be self-critical and honest, rather than self-serving or manipulated for partisan political goals. Again he condemned the communist approach after reading some interviews by prominent members of the PCE:

> They remember certain things and forget others. And others they banish entirely from their memory. Communist memory in reality is a way of not remembering: it does not consist of recalling the past but of censoring it. The memory of Communist leaders functions pragmatically, in accordance with the political interests and objectives of the moment. It is not a historical memory, a memory that bears witness, but an ideological memory.[97]

He was convinced that it was necessary to move beyond the ideological memories of both communists and Francoists and to look at the past critically and honestly. His critique of the repressive use of history under Franco and its continuing impact was the central theme of his final novel, *Vingt ans et un jour.*

Set mainly in 1956, this highlighted the deliberate manipulation of history to legitimate the use of power. Thus the focal point of the novel is an annual theatrical staging of the assassination of a landowner, José María Avendaño, by a peasant at the beginning of the Civil War. This yearly performance is carried out by order of José Manuel, the authoritarian older brother of the victim, with the local peasants forced to re-enact the events. One of its main purposes is to maintain the peasantry in a condition of servitude, annually portraying a bloodthirsty act that reveals their guilt in breaking the customary bonds of order, thereby initiating general chaos and violence.[98] The re-enactment also has strong religious overtones and the other surviving brother, José Ignacio Avendaño, who has until 1956 played the victim of the assassination, is a priest. The police commissioner is also present, suggesting that the major forces of the Franco regime are assembled to ensure that those who triumphed in 1939 maintain their power. In fact, however, central elements of the history are either false or deliberately oversimplified. For example, the assassinated landowner did not actually believe in the order that he is made to represent: he was a liberal whose beliefs were very close to those of Semprún's father.[99] The point is to re-enact a particular version of history, rather than to seek any kind of historical validity.

But Semprún also offers some additional insights into both the use of history and the actual trajectory of the dictatorship. For, by 1956, there is considerable opposition to the continuation of the re-enactment and José Manuel himself no longer wishes to maintain it. By now he is more interested in opening Spain up to foreign trade and retaining his position through the consolidation of new forms of economic wealth rather than through repeated rituals based on the traditional order, and he is even willing to allow one of the leaders of the peasants who was also killed in 1936 to be recognised in the final re-enactment.[100] The Church's support for repressive Francoism is also eroding. José Ignacio Avendaño himself represents a more moderate form of

Catholicism and a young priest makes an eloquent homily based on a Christian text stressing peace, pity and pardon. This is complete anathema to the police commissioner, who is convinced that it is essential to continue with the annual ceremony without any compromises, and he wants it to be held on a national rather than a simply local level. Unless this explicit public representation of the guilt of those who challenged the established order is constantly re-affirmed, he fears that the whole system of power will soon collapse. Years later, when looking back on the abandonment of the ritual, he believes that this was the moment when the regime began to lose its power.[101] Semprún thus manages to provide insights into different ways of misusing history: from the essentially repressive manipulation of a Francoist version in the first period of the dictatorship to the later period in which the Civil War was represented as fratricidal. By juxtaposing the outlooks of José Manuel and the police commissioner and depicting the evolving position of the Church, he also implied the historical evolution in which the transition to liberal-democracy would eventually be brought about (twenty years later) through a fracturing of the elite support for dictatorship. In addition, he depicts the multi-dimensional nature of society and historical reality, exploring interactions between power, sexual relations, art and transgenerational memory.[102] In 2003, when the book was published, there was already an impetus to address such issues.[103] Nevertheless, the novel itself and Semprún's wider international role in relation to historical memory was certainly part of the movement of opinion that drew attention to their importance in transitions.

He had originally sublimated his unbearable memories of Buchenwald in political activity in the PCE, choosing a 'long cure of aphasia, of voluntary amnesia, in order to survive'.[104] But the publication of *The Long Voyage* then meant that he paid for its subsequent success 'with the brutal return of past despair'.[105] Yet he continued to write about it. Constantly invited to speak and participate in international events commemorating those who suffered in the camps and from extermination policies, Semprún devoted considerable thought to the question of why this kind of collective historical memory was necessary. In time he became particularly impressed with the way in which German society had dealt with its past, arguing that this had been essential for the reconstruction of its national identity, based upon a new 'democratic patriotism'.[106] He argued that the objective was, above all, to ensure that younger generations learned from the past so as to avoid repeating its horrors in new forms.[107] He was insistent that other countries could learn from the German example and this had clear implications for Spain, which *Vingt ans et un jour* expressed through fiction.

The decisive step occurred with the unexpected electoral victory of the PSOE, under José Luis Rodríguez Zapatero, in March 2004, for it was at this stage that condemnation of the long neglect of the issue mounted. As the government hesitated in the face of right-wing opposition, Amnesty International declared that the amnesties of 1975 and 1977 had 'included measures to pardon and forget acts which, under international law, are considered crimes against humanity'.[108] At the same time, the government's draft Historical Memory Law opened up a bitter debate within Spain, with its opponents claiming that it threatened to end the peace and reconciliation that the country had enjoyed for the past thirty years.[109] However, it was passed in autumn 2007.[110]

More than thirty years after the death of Franco, legislation thus introduced a form of historical justice. In comparison with other countries, the Historical Memory Law was modest in its scope. Memory was to remain private, rather than public, so that there was no initiative in relation to history education, no truth or historical commission, and many archives remain closed. By 2015 there had still been no legislation concerning the monument to Francoism in the Valle de los Caídos—for example, on the issue of whether it should include an exhibition showing that 20,000 Republican prisoners had been forced to construct it—and the recommendations of an expert commission set up under the PSOE were set aside by the subsequent right-wing government.[111] Finally, there were, of course, no trials of perpetrators and the attempt in October 2008 by Baltasar Garzón, the judge who had indicted Pinochet of Chile (see Chapter Six), to open an inquiry into alleged crimes against humanity by Franco's forces during and after the Civil War, was blocked, and Garzón was suspended by the Supreme Court in 2010.[112] The Spanish transition therefore remains paradoxical in many respects, initially with a complete amnesty and near amnesia, followed some thirty years later by a limited, though significant, exercise in 'historical memory'.

Semprún welcomed this development in Spain as one part of a wider transnational recovery of the past. However, his attitude also reflected a Spanish mainstream viewpoint. In 2009, he certainly favoured 'historical memory' but was also worried that Garzón might go too far and open up old wounds:

> I think it's a problem that has to be dealt with very carefully because to reconstruct the past, if we do it in a heavy-handed or incorrect way, we'll re-open wounds, even though I believe those injuries have been soothed by the passage of time and the arrival of new generations. I think Spanish society needs to keep remembering, just as it once needed amnesia. That is essential.[113]

Semprún, historical memory and justice

Both the Historical Memory Law and Semprún's own work may be regarded as falling within the framework of 'historical justice' but, as noted in the first chapter, this covers a spectrum of approaches, which may include demands on behalf of individuals, groups and whole peoples. There are also differences in the kind of redress that is called for. While individual and group versions tend towards more limited reparations and commemoration, transformative claims may be made on the basis of prolonged structural injustices, particularly in such situations as colonialism, slavery or the marginalisation of indigenous peoples.[114] Ngũgĩ's approach to the history of Kenya in general and Mau Mau in particular, may be regarded as 'structural' in the sense that he believed that a transformation of historical interpretation would help to bring about major radical changes to challenge neo-colonialism. In contrast, Semprún's advocacy of the recovery of historical memory, and the law of 2007, were within the 'commemorative' part of the spectrum, for they were designed to 'complete' a process of transition by helping to promote reconciliation based on wider recognition of Republican contributions to Spanish democracy. On the other hand, while Ngũgĩ' was prepared to invoke historical myths in order to help promote radical political transformation against neo-colonialism, Semprún feared that partisan interpretations of history themselves tended to be allied to injustice because they avoided self-criticism.

Even when implemented in far more extensive ways than in Spain, historical justice has attracted criticism. In one widely quoted intervention, the historian Charles Maier criticised the 'surfeit of memory'.[115]

One of his fundamental points was that the focus was too much on subjective memories at the expense of the analytical approaches that were central to serious historical analysis. However, in Spain history had been manipulated under the Franco regime for purposes of legitimation and repression, and had remained largely closed during and after the transition. The breakthrough in the early twenty-first century was therefore a prerequisite for the kind of serious analysis that Maier regarded as central to historical scholarship. And although Semprún was not an historian in a conventional sense, his work was an important historical contribution. While his own writing was imbued with memories and autobiography, he nevertheless managed to convey a multi-dimensional treatment of history as both a lived experience and a product of wider social and political forces. Furthermore, as Txetxu Aguado has argued, even his work on Buchenwald was grounded in notions of liberty, justice, and solidarity with the humiliated and oppressed, and was a 'political configuration that recovers the memory of the past ... not so as to paralyse the present but instead to inform action in the future'.[116] Yet there is another aspect of Maier's critique that certainly has relevance: that focusing on particular aspects of the past may divert attention away from structural injustices, and that the obsession with historical justice reflects a trend towards the abandonment of more fundamental projects to transform society.[117] There is truth in this criticism in relation to Semprún.

His outlook on the issue of justice had gone full circle. As an adolescent, greatly influenced by his father's fundamentally liberal conceptions, he had seen justice in terms of legality, but weighted towards the needs of the poor and humiliated. Subsequently, his move to communism led him to a Marxist conception of justice. However, his break with the PCE brought about a preoccupation with the recovery of 'truth' through memory and criticism, as a means to recover a past that was less innocent than he had previously wanted to believe: for anti-fascists could also be guilty of horrific injustices. In his final years he embraced a concept of democratic reason, within which justice was again associated with legality, the use of reason and moderate social reform. Such notions were not dissimilar from ideas espoused by his father and the *Esprit* group, although they were purged of Catholicism. But they were also informed by a sense of horror at the consequences of extremes, which could ultimately lead to the bestiality of Buchenwald or the gulags. Once again, he stressed the interaction between Spain and wider international developments but, while his anti-Franco activities had originally led him into revolutionary internationalism, he now sought moderate social reform on a European level.[118] In fact, he believed that a supranational Europe could also be the basis for democracy, the defence of smaller languages, and federalism. Returning to some elements of the philosophical thinking of his youth, he cited Husserl as an early advocate of the kind of humanitarianism, underpinned by cosmopolitanism, that he sought on a supranational European level.[119]

His break with communism had diluted his belief in social justice. He did not entirely abandon his critical perspective on capitalism as a system in which inequalities and injustice were inevitable.[120] But, like Camus, his growing anti-communism undermined his belief in the possibility of radical social transformation. He praised Gonzáles for his 'realism' and came to believe that liberal-democracy within the European Union, coupled with limited reforms, offered the best possible basis for the creation of a just society.[121] His concept of 'democratic reason' as the path for the present and future was a real attempt to learn lessons from some of the most egregious injustices of the twentieth century and his writing illuminated both the strengths and weaknesses of the Spanish transition from Franco's dictatorship. However, Semprún's thinking was not derived solely from the Spanish experience and his conclusions also had a much wider application. His insistence on such values as integrity and self-criticism, coupled with his constant interrogation of the past, revealed an exceptionally rich search for truth in the complexities of historical memory. The essence of his thinking was that it was only by recognising and acknowledging the multiplicity of ways in which the past was understood and interpreted that it was possible for a society to move on. This provides some essential warnings against simplistic solutions for the establishment of justice.

6

ALLENDE, PINOCHET AND THE TRANSITION
TO DEMOCRACY

ARIEL DORFMAN AND CHILE

Chile had a particular significance for the international Left in the late twentieth and early twenty-first centuries. Between September 1970 and September 1973 many vested their own hopes in the possibility of the government of Salvador Allende effecting a peaceful socialist revolution, but such aspirations were then curtailed with the brutal coup carried out by Augusto Pinochet. From then until the restoration of democratic government in 1990, Chile remained a cause célèbre as Amnesty International and other human rights organisations documented the atrocities and human rights abuses carried out by the dictatorship. Finally, international legal action initiated by the Spanish judge Baltasar Garzón, which led to Pinochet's arrest in London in October 1998, challenged the whole notion of impunity for repressive dictators. And, even though Pinochet was never ultimately tried, the chain of events that began in London played a major role in initiating a new phase in the transition in Chile itself.

The aim of this chapter is to explore these years in the country's turbulent history through the work of Ariel Dorfman, who has combined the international and Chilean dimensions in his own person. An enthusiastic supporter of Allende, he was then forced into exile by the Pinochet coup, before returning to Chile very briefly in 1990, and then deciding after all to remain in the United States. Dorfman resembles some of the other authors in this book in various respects. In a similar way to Serge, Semprún and Ngũgĩ, he was the product of different cultures and languages, partly as a result of exile. Like Camus and Semprún, he abandoned his earlier belief in the Marxist conception of justice, although he arguably retained a stronger commitment to social justice than they did. Like Ngũgĩ, he emphasised the importance of culture in relation to the transmission of political and social attitudes and he shared the concerns of both the Kenyan and Spanish authors with memory and history. But he was the only one who produced a work that focused specifically on transitional justice—his celebrated play, *Death and the Maiden* (1991).[1] This will therefore be examined in some detail in the second part of the chapter. However, this play and Dorfman's subsequent non-fictional work, *Exorcising Terror* (2003), which also illuminated transitional justice, were the products of his own history, politics and cultural background, and the first part of the chapter examines the evolution in his thinking.[2]

Dorfman has been an amazingly prolific writer. As Sophia McClennen puts it:

> He has promiscuously mixed criticism with creativity, refusing the division between the critic and the creative writer. He has written an almost equal number of nonfiction works as literary texts. Moreover, he has written in every major literary genre (novel, short story, poetry, drama) and has adopted the voice of a variety of literary forms, including (among others) the picaresque, the epic, the noir, and the theatre of the absurd. He has also refused common identity categories, understanding himself as a writer, an activist, a Chilean, a North American and more. His works are read alternately and simultaneously as part of the Latin American literary canon; as examples of human rights literature; within the tradition of bilingual, cross-cultural, ethnic writing; and as part of a transnational community of exiled and displaced writers.[3]

The approach here is therefore highly selective, and emphasises certain themes.

The constant exile: identity, politics and writing

Political evolution

Dorfman experienced exile throughout his life. When writing for international audiences he constantly refers to himself as Chilean, but in 1990 he had lived in Chile for only nineteen of his forty-eight years and even during this period he had spent eighteen months in the US. His identity and political outlook have therefore always been complex.

His parents were Jewish, originating in Russia and Eastern Europe before eventually settling in Argentina, where Ariel was born in 1942.[4] However, he was not then known by that name, but as Vladimir or Vlady (after Lenin), for another important part of his heritage was the communist background of his father, Adolfo, who was a prominent left-wing economist. Following a military coup in Argentina in June 1943, Adolfo was stripped of his citizenship, but managed to get to the United States, where the family joined him in February 1945. Although Ariel Dorfman's first language was Spanish, he soon stopped speaking it and was determined to be American.[5] However, this immersion in American language and culture would also be quite shortlived, for the rise of McCarthyism meant that Adolfo was again under threat and the whole family moved to Chile in 1954.[6] Determined to remain 'American', Dorfman now insisted on being called Edward, although his ambition and linguistic skills meant that he also acquired fluency in Spanish.[7] His confusion about his identity was reinforced by his sense that there was a contradiction between his own environment and the Marxism professed by his parents.

The Dorfman family lived in an affluent part of Santiago and he attended an elite private school, but he soon also became aware of the extreme poverty in the country. In his memoirs he recounts a poignant episode in which, at the age of about fourteen, he tried to help a young boy who was begging. At first his mother gave the boy food and some clothes, but this led him to return several times, often accompanied by other poor children. She eventually sent them away, telling Dorfman that they could not deal with the problem in that way. He felt guilty, but the next time the boy arrived he did not answer the door:

> I watched from that house filled with books that analyzed inequality and surplus value and economic underdevelopment and the philosophy of justice and the rights of indigenous peoples. I watched the boy turn away, and the next day he came one last time and I forced myself to contemplate his defeat and my defeat all over again, and that was it. After that, he never rang the bell again. He understood what had happened, the limits of my compassion, he came no more, and whatever guilt I felt was insufficient to make me interrupt the life I had led up until then.[8]

During the 1960s he overcame some of his uncertainty about both his Chilean identity and his political attitudes, and while at university he began to use his middle name, Ariel.[9] Voluntary work following the devastating earthquake in 1960 exposed him to the depths of rural poverty, and as a student of literature at the University of Chile he soon became an activist, participating in a series of protest demonstrations. He began teaching peasants in shantytowns around Santiago on a voluntary basis and in 1963 he set up a mobile university for them. He also became increasingly involved in left-wing social and political activity and began to re-imagine himself as Latin American. When Allende stood for president in 1964, Dorfman was elected president of the Independent Allendista Students at the university.[10] He had also met his future wife Angélica (they married in 1966) and the next year he acquired Chilean nationality. He used Spanish in his revolutionary political speeches and in critical essays, and his first book, on the plays of Harold Pinter, was published in Spanish in 1968.[11] Yet he still resisted the idea of actually writing literature in Spanish.

In 1968 he and Angélica, with their young child Rodrigo, went to Berkeley, California for eighteen months, where Dorfman was a research scholar. Paradoxically, while there he decided to write his literature in Spanish rather than English. According to his own retrospective interpretation, this was because Spanish was the language of insurrection, while English was that of empire.[12] But there was still some fluidity in his political position and he was further destabilised by the eighteen months he spent at Berkeley in 1968–9. He saw 'flower power' as a self-indulgent, individualistic protest by spoiled young people who had no understanding of the kind of grinding poverty and oppression that was experienced daily in Latin America; and he came to despair about the lack of unity and discipline on the American Left, attributing this to the absence of 'a working class that could ground their revolution in reality', and contrasting it with the situation in Chile.[13] But he was also attracted to the American New Left, which was addressing questions about culture, identity and sexuality that were not yet discussed in Chile while also rejecting conventional lifestyles. The family returned to Chile in 1969.

By the late 1960s the situation was increasingly polarised under the Partido Demócrata Cristiano (PDC) president, Eduardo Frei. In 1969 the police killed eight people and wounded fifty others, when attempting to evict some squatters from a plot of land. This was the last straw for many on the left of the PDC. They formed the Movimiento de Acción Popular Unitaria (MAPU), the party that Dorfman would join the following year, and which would later declare itself as Marxist revolutionary.[14] In an atmosphere of political instability in October, the socialists, communists and radicals formed a left-wing alliance with three smaller parties, including MAPU, under the name of Unidad Popular (UP). By mid-December they had agreed a common socialist programme and Allende, from the Partido Socialista de Chile (PS), was adopted as the candidate in January 1970. In the election the following September he defeated his nearest rival by the very narrow margin of 40,000 votes, with 36.2 per cent of the vote. His presidency needed confirmation by Congress, but before this could take place General René Schneider, the Commander-in-Chief of the army, was killed in a kidnapping attempt, with top-level US involvement.[15] This may have been an attempt to provoke a military coup, but the immediate result was to shock Congress into confirming Allende's election.

This victory was also a momentous event for Dorfman himself. He saw Allende as representing the perfect combination of the influences of his own communist father and his more gentle mother: an 'admirer of Cuba and a fervent Marxist', who insisted 'that we could build a more just social order without having to repress our adversaries'.[16] He would constantly recall the three years of Allende's government as the best years of his life and he constructed his identity as primarily political—'fused with Chile and its cause and its people through the revolution that would, we thought, liberate the country'.[17]

In reality, the position of the Left was highly precarious, with strong domestic opposition backed by the US. Certainly, the Allende government rested on strong and enthusiastic support from poorer social classes as it attempted to implement a programme of radical social reform and nationalisations. At first it also achieved considerable economic success, with a growth rate of 8.3 per cent in 1971, greatly increased social spending, higher wages, new initiatives in health and nutrition, land reform, and an ambitious cultural programme. But it was hated and feared by the traditional elites and faced deliberate sabotage by US-backed forces. By-elections in January 1972 indicated growing opposition to the government and by the end of that year there was an economic crisis, with a massive trade deficit.[18] There were also major divisions within the coalition, with Communists, Radicals and Allende's supporters within the Socialist Party preaching moderation, while the Socialist majority and MAPU called for an acceleration of the revolutionary process, and the Movimiento de Izquierda Revolucionaria (MIR), a more militant group inspired by the Cuban revolution, urging a still faster pace from outside the coalition.[19] Any policy that Allende adopted would alienate one of the main forces that had backed him and the atmosphere in the country grew increasingly tense, particularly after the truck drivers' strike in October 1972. Although the UP managed to win 44 per cent of the vote in the elections the following February, there was then a rapid descent into crisis.

Dorfman was fully aware of the threats, but two months before the coup he accepted the position of cultural and media adviser to Fernando Flores, Allende's Chief of Staff, who was also in MAPU. In this capacity he should have been in the Moneda Palace on the night of 10–11 September 1973, but fortuitously was not there.[20] Had he been present when the palace was bombed, he would almost certainly either have been killed outright or taken away and tortured. His life was still in danger, but he escaped and MAPU instructed him to go into exile. After a tense period of moving between safe houses and then sheltering in the Argentine Embassy, he arrived in Argentina in December and was reunited with Angélica and Rodrigo.[21] But he was acutely conscious of what was happening to many of his friends and comrades.

After bombing the Moneda Palace, where Allende committed suicide, Pinochet's forces immediately hunted down UP activists, shooting many of them. At least 7,000 others were taken to the national stadium in Santiago, which was the centre for interrogation, and detention camps were opened throughout the country, with some of the most prominent members of the government sent to the tiny island, Isla Dawson, in the Strait of Magellan. Tens of thousands were arrested, tortured, killed or disappeared, and more than 200,000 went into exile following the coup.[22] At the same time a police state was rapidly constructed. Congress was closed, the UP parties were banned, with the other parties placed 'in recess' before also being banned in 1977. A curfew was imposed, all left-wing newspapers and magazines were closed down, the civil service was purged, and all major institutions were assigned to military officers. The military also played a major role in providing the personnel for the new secret police, the Dirección de Inteligencia Nacional (DINA), which was under Pinochet's own control. By 1977 this had about 10,000 personnel and between 20,000 and 30,000 paid informers, and it was responsible for carrying out torture at home and assassinations abroad, until being replaced in that year by another body, the Central Nacional de Informaciones (CNI).[23] By then the most ruthless phase of repression had passed, but disappearances, torture and murder continued.

Like so many survivors, Dorfman carried a deep and lasting sense of guilt. In fact, he maintained the belief that Flores had saved him because he wanted a witness who could escape the conflagration and tell the world the story. Whether or not this is literally what happened, Dorfman later explained: 'If it is not true that this was why I was saved, I have tried to make it true. In every story I tell. Haunted by the certainty that I have been keeping a promise to the dead.'[24] This would shape his subsequent thought and writing throughout the next seventeen years in exile.

Following a very brief stay in Argentina, the family was forced to move again, this time to Paris via Cuba and Peru. Here, Dorfman passed a miserable two-and-a-half years, living in poverty and suffering from writer's block. In 1976 he accepted a post at the University of Amsterdam where, over the next three years, he again became prolific. Three years later a second son (Joaquín) was born and they planned to move to Mexico, but were refused entry. Instead they moved to the US for what was initially to be a year at Washington D.C. However, this turned into a long stay, and in 1986 they moved to Durham, North Carolina, where Dorfman reached agreement with Duke University to teach one semester each year. While continuing to write in Spanish, he was once again also constantly speaking and writing in English.[25]

Dorfman would remain an active campaigner against Pinochet and he continued to take risks for his beliefs. In 1983, for example, he was finally allowed back into the country and, while there, he condemned the regime in an article that he dictated on a phone, which was bugged by Chilean surveillance.[26] Three years later he returned once more and again denounced the regime in the press, while emphasising the growth of opposition.[27] Ominously the Chilean government announced his death.[28] He returned once again in 1987, with his eight-year-old son Joaquín, and they were arrested at the airport, although international pressure allowed him back two weeks later.[29] But while he campaigned against the dictatorship and worked for the restoration of democracy in Chile, his position had changed in various ways.

Despite his passionate support for the Allende government, he had clearly been conscious of the uncertainty about its future long before the coup, as indicated in his first novel, *Mores en la Costa* (1973) (*Hard Rain*, 1990), which was written at the height of the crisis in 1972.[30] Once in exile, his political views evolved markedly. When taking the university position in Amsterdam, he accepted that he was not 'a minor embodiment of Che Guevara who subordinates everything personal to the cause of revolution'.[31] He also gradually detached himself from MAPU, later claiming that writing led him to question the notion of a Leninist hierarchical structure 'in order to lay the groundwork today for the sort of state we wanted to construct tomorrow—pluralistic, tolerant, humane, without a supposedly superior group of illuminati deciding the ultimate and totalizing truth'.[32] While he still saw Marxist philosophy as 'a superb instrument with which to comprehend and critique capitalism, still a fiery vision of the future to which I continued to subscribe', he grew doubtful as to whether it provided answers to the new dilemmas of the times.[33] As time went on, he saw himself more 'as a public intellectual at the service of all forms of liberation rather than a militant subservient to the web and requirements of a collective' and he increasingly believed that his political work would be through writing and advocacy.[34] This political trajectory was no doubt reinforced by the return to the US, where he joined the Campaign for Peace and Democracy, a group that opposed American foreign policy, but also supported dissidents in Eastern Europe. Since the mid-1970s he had become increasingly uncomfortable about Soviet policies, but it was only in 1982, following the military takeover in Poland, that he was willing to take part in a public protest at the Polish embassy about the clampdown.[35] He was also conscious of changes that were occurring in Chile.

By 1977 Pinochet already felt sufficiently secure to announce that Chile could move towards a 'protected' democracy and in 1980 a referendum was held on a new constitution. With opponents given few opportunities to campaign, it was approved by 67 per cent to 30 per cent, with six million people voting.[36] In March 1981 Pinochet became president.[37] The other fundamental change from the Allende era was in economic policy. Pinochet and the colonels knew nothing about economics and had turned to the neo-liberals of the Chicago school. The immediate impact, reinforced by the increase in oil prices as a result of the Arab-Israeli war, was a rapid rise in both unemployment and the cost of living. In March 1975, Milton Friedman emphasised the need for 'shock treatment' and Pinochet took his advice, removing all controls, slashing public expenditure, and reducing the money supply. Despite unemployment rising to nearly 20 per cent and wages falling to 60 per cent of their 1970 level by the end of the year, neo-liberalism was pursued vigorously over the next seven years, with extensive privatisation of industry. The impact in the countryside was also devastating, with the creation of labour-intensive commercial farms, an increase in rural poverty and a massive exodus of the peasantry to shantytowns. Nevertheless, this neo-liberal restructuring also led to rapid economic growth for five years after 1976, and a significant reduction of dependency on copper exports. In 1982–3, there was a second, and still more serious, recession, with GDP falling by one-seventh, and even higher unemployment than in 1975–6. While the neo-liberal framework was then maintained and strengthened, more pragmatic policies were adopted and there was a further economic revival. Both average life expectancy and infant mortality rates showed significant improvements, but the poorest 40 per cent of the population and sections of the middle classes had static or declining living standards. The most significant impact of the dictatorship's economic policy was that, while poverty and inequality continued, traditional patterns of employment were disrupted and replaced by a very large informal economy. At the other end of the scale there was a growth of internationalised business and the culture of capitalist modernisation, bringing with it increased social atomisation, consumerism and other typical characteristics of 'Western' society.[38]

Dorfman saw how Chile had changed when he returned for his brief visit in 1983 and he became increasingly concerned about the way in which neo-liberalism was creating a new form of internationalised power structure which might remain in place even without the dictatorship. He was also alarmed about the way in which hidden processes penetrated into society, enabling control through the moulding of individual consciousness. This sometimes led him to pessimism.[39] However, he was enthusiastic about the rise of effective opposition to Pinochet.

Culture, dialogue and 'a promise to the dead'

Dorfman's role during the Allende years had been wholly in keeping with his profound belief in the importance of the cultural sphere and its potential social and political influence. At that time, he later recalled, Spanish flowed out of him as if he were a river—and he wrote essays, screenplays, poems, magazine articles, TV programmes, pamphlets, adverts, jingles, political slogans, propaganda tracts, an experimental novel, cultural policy reports, political diatribes, songs and plays.[40] Throughout the three years of the Allende government, he also worked for the state publishing house (Quimantú), where his work included releasing international classics in Spanish in affordable editions. Quimantú distributed five million books and transformed the content of some of the magazines that already existed.[41]

His revolutionary enthusiasm in the early period of the Allende government was conveyed in his book, co-authored with the sociologist Armand Mattelart, *Para leer al Pato Donald* (*How to Read Donald Duck*).[42] The idea was to demonstrate the underlying value system in the American cartoon, the ways in which this dominated the childhood and youth culture of Latin America and developing countries more generally, and the urgent need to create an alternative, autonomous popular culture. Underlying this was an equally strong conviction that the values and ideas that were subconsciously absorbed in childhood were then carried into adult life—the early implantation of particular attitudes shaped the political culture of the whole society. Like Ngũgĩ, Dorfman was thus insisting that resistance to the injustices of imperialism needed to be tackled as much through culture as through political and economic means. However, he took this further, for he was not simply concentrating on the literary form, but also the transmission of ideas through visual images in the most popular media. *How to Read Donald Duck* sought to demonstrate the capitalist, authoritarian, sexist, anti-socialist, racist and imperialist notions underlying the cartoons. Rooted in a generally Marxist framework, emphasising the division between a material base and a cultural superstructure, this was intended as a popular work and, as such, it was outstandingly successful, selling more copies in Chile in one month than all the stories produced locally in the previous 160 years of Chilean independence.[43] It also encapsulated the essence of his influential ideas about the ideological role of mass-produced culture in shaping social consciousness.[44]

His first novel, *Hard Rain*, written during the height of the crisis of the Allende regime in the summer of 1972, was much less optimistic. Its major theme was to explore the relationship between the writer and society and it was full of angst about the role of art in the construction of socialism. As he later moved away from Marxism, his ideas on the cultural sphere also evolved, but he retained his assumptions about its crucial social and political role. He also applied this to his own work. By 1976 he felt that, if he were to play any role in transforming the world, it would be 'by imagining alternatives, by shifting how we feel and think and write about it'.[45] And he clearly continued to believe that cultural production had a general impact upon the consciousness and thinking of a society.

A second key theme was the importance of genuine dialogue. In *Hard Rain* the many voices of the work express different ideas about 'truth' and 'reality'. The forces trying to establish a new form of socialist society are themselves represented as highly diverse, with an element of incoherence partly arising from this. Differences of opinion and contradictions within the socialist project itself were a fact of life, and this meant that discussion and disagreement amongst the proponents of social transformation were necessary. There were some indications that he believed that the UP should have made greater efforts at reaching out to its opponents, and that there was a need for a wider dialogue if catastrophe were to be avoided.[46] One of the most menacing fragments in the book demonstrated the absence of such dialogue and Dorfman's fears for the future. Here, a young Argentine doctor comes into a bar just across the border from Chile, which he intends to cross to rejoin his Chilean wife. However, he meets an extreme right-wing Chilean radio broadcaster and other pro-fascist Chilean exiles (including a colonel), who tell him how wonderful life was in the past and how many lies were now told by the UP government. Their stance becomes increasingly exaggerated and they will not let the doctor leave, asking for his own views. Although they will clearly attack him unless he agrees with them, they insist that they believe in dialogue and would like an exchange of views.[47] The atmosphere is threatening and, as Dorfman would later suggest in relation to the whole book, violence, 'like a hidden wind, blows through the narrative voices'.[48] Despite his passionate commitment to Allende's government at the time, the work demonstrated his long-term conviction about the importance of recognising multiple voices and perspectives, each with their own versions of truth.

Some of these ideas were also present in his second novel, *Viudas* (1981) (*Widows*, 1983), which he began while in the Netherlands. This also introduces another key theme: that of memory and the insistence that part of the struggle for justice involves remembering the dead and 'disappeared'.[49] Despite an attempt to make the plight of missing people seem more universal, the subject matter arose from the movements of women in Chile and Argentina, and emerged from his own 'promise to the dead'. The novel begins with the discovery of an unrecognisable male corpse in the river and an elderly woman, Sofia, asking the captain of the military base for permission to bury him, claiming that this is the body of her father. In fact, almost all the local men have been killed or 'disappeared' and the military authorities do not want to discuss anything that has passed: instead the captain is anxious to talk about reconciliation and pacification, while his more belligerent lieutenant favours a repressive approach. Similarly, there are differences of emphasis between the members of the local economic elite, with the major landowner favouring intransigent brutality at any sign of rebellion, while his wife is more conciliatory. However, more and more bodies appear and the women of the village all insist on the right to bury them—often with disputes over the identity of particular bodies. The novel thus reveals differences of opinion both amongst those who hold autocratic power and amongst those seeking the basic right to bury their dead. Yet the divisions within the two camps are overcome. Faced with the unwillingness of the women to acquiesce, the captain now adopts a brutal approach, giving an order to shoot them unless they call off their vigil by the river. On the other side, Sofia, defiant in the face of death, demands both the return of the bodies and an investigation leading to the punishment of the killers. The book ends with the women finding one more body and waiting to be shot.

The dominant theme is of courageous, and ultimately united, resistance against oppression, and confidence in an eventual triumph. Sofia tells her grandson, Alexis, that their enemies' appearance of power is superficial: 'They're empty, if you opened them a little sad blood might spill out and filth and after a while even their guts would disappear too, and that's why when they died, they died forever'.[50] In contrast, the women's insistence on maintaining the memory of the men would help to sustain the birth of a new society. *Widows* also maintains a clear perspective on the different ethical values represented by the two sides. Finally, there is a significant exchange between Sofia and her grandson about forgiveness for those who had buckled under the repression. She tells him that they must not start to forgive, for this would lead them to 'fall apart' and lose sight of the difference between right and wrong, while he argues that 'in just these kinds of times you had to know how to forgive' and 'give a hand to those who were weaker'. But she remains adamant that 'the most important thing was to survive'.[51]

The themes of multiple voices, dialogue, memory, and the tensions between retribution and forgiveness would all reappear in *Death and the Maiden*.

Another non-fictional work, *The Empire's Old Clothes* (1983), introduced a further related notion.[52] This followed on from the kind of cultural critique of *How to Read Donald Duck*, with much of it originally written in the same era. He rewrote it partly to update it, but also because of the changes in his own thinking, and he included both self-criticism and suggestions for the future. For he now rejected the idea that there was a clear dichotomy between those who had supported Allende and those who would later acquiesce in the dictatorship. His earlier analyses, he now felt, had not appreciated the extent to which myths were deeply rooted in the minds of ordinary people and how tenaciously people cling to their dreams when someone tries to shatter them. He implied that the problem had been about discourse and that it was necessary to win people over through 'the use of a language more refined, perhaps less abrupt, a language which distrusts formulas and dogmas, which avoids the dictionary of the absolute, which has to justify itself with those who do not nod in instant agreement.'[53]

He also introduced another fundamental idea. Through his fiction and poetry, he had, he declared, been discovering 'that jungle which each of us can become'. Violent undergrowths of imaginary characters are successful 'because in our own inner provinces and sewers, they match and accompany certain deep-seated tendencies and fears'.[54] Yet he also argued that we possess within ourselves an intimation of another humanity from which to build, and that such building had constantly been taking place. And it is in the 'prolonged, confused, stuttering attempt' to reach that other humanity that we can find the vision and strength to differentiate ourselves from the views promulgated by those who seek to control our beliefs and emotions.[55] Yet this suggested a very significant change in his outlook: the idea that the 'we' who seek a more just world are also subject to these dominant influences. There was no watertight distinction between 'them' and 'us' because all were affected to an extent by the messages that reflected deep-seated tendencies and fears. This notion of a 'we' that incorporated much of Chilean society was also implicit in many of Dorfman's short stories during the 1980s, where he depicted the ways in which ordinary people and families were affected by the dictatorship.[56] This seemed to imply that there was a possibility of building something new that might transcend the bitter divisions of the past. All these themes were present in *La última canción de Manuel Sendero* (*The Last Song of Manuel Sendero*).[57]

This is a bleak novel in many respects, with Dorfman apparently wondering whether the Allende years were only an illusion of political possibility, with Pinochet having invaded the consciousness of an entire country, stealing people's dreams.[58] Yet the work points to the eventual victory of forces on the side of justice, even though the time-scale is uncertain. The novel is highly complex, with Sophia McClennen suggesting that six sets of narratives interconnect and overlap in a variety of ways, and that there is also a 'gestational structure', relating to the stages of pregnancy.[59] However, two sets of debates within the book have a strong thematic connection with one another and with issues that would resurface at the time of the transition. The first takes place amongst foetuses within the wombs of women. Led by the son of Manuel Sendero, the foetuses refuse to be born because of the lack of justice in the world, but the rebellion is weakening as more foetuses choose birth. Unfortunately, the majority of those who enter the world end up being corrupted by the omnipresent influence of the dictator, Caballero. This leaves the purist, Sendero, engaged in debate with Eduardo, who believes that it is necessary to try to change the world by entering it, rather than clinging to an illusion of perfection. The second set of debates, fragments of which are discovered thousands of years later, are between David and Felipe. They were exiles from Chile during the Pinochet dictatorship and they disagree both about the past under Allende and what should be done now. David was exiled almost immediately and is now revising many of his views, while Felipe, who was imprisoned before being deported, remains unchanged in his outlook.

The repetition of certain ideas indicates some key 'messages'. First, it is important to keep alive both a legend about the magical powers of Manuel Sendero, a singer and committed social activist, and the sense of exhilaration about Allende's attempt to create social justice through peaceful means. However, the novel suggests that the world has changed and it was inappropriate to remain frozen in the past or in myths about it. There is also a change in the identity of the 'enemy'. This is still Pinochet, but it is no longer adequate to view him solely in individual terms: as David insists, and the son of Manuel Sendero reluctantly acknowledges, neo-liberalism has transformed the economy and Chile is now fully incorporated in a system of global capitalism. But this also means that millions of Chileans have been sucked into this new reality, and the destruction of the dictatorship will not destroy the wider system in which it is embedded. Dorfman's answer to the question of whether Pinochet was an integral part of Chile or an aberration was therefore also a paradoxical one. While representing a vicious form of repression, he had constructed a regime with both active support and passive acceptance. And this also related to a further theme—the need for honesty about the past and the present, in acceptance, in David's words, that 'we had to share the responsibility for the disaster we all lived through'.[60] Finally, there was again debate about how to treat the perpetrators of repression, with Eduardo and David both opposing the retribution and capital punishment favoured by 'grandfather' and Felipe.

All these themes were discernible in Dorfman's outlook and writing but they had not been crystallised. The transition itself would bring them to the surface.

Transition: hopes, anger, disappointment... and progress

Effective opposition to Pinochet had first erupted in the early 1980s, with massive street demonstrations and protests, primarily as a result of unemployment and poverty. These also led to a National Accord in 1985 among political parties (though still formally illegal), backed by the Church, demanding a return to democracy. However, continued repression meant that the only peaceful way to bring down the regime was through a plebiscite, which had been agreed under the 1980 constitution. Following the legalisation of 'non-Marxist' parties in 1987, some fifteen parties and movements came together to campaign for a 'no' vote in the October 1988 referendum as to whether Pinochet should extend his rule for another eight years—a result they achieved, with nearly 56 per cent against 44 per cent, with a turnout of over 97 per cent of registered voters. The spokesperson for this coalition was Patricio Aylwin, the leader of the PDC, and he soon emerged as the candidate for the presidential elections that took place at the end of 1989. He won, with 55 per cent of the vote, and was inaugurated as president in March 1990. He was also supported by a very comfortable majority of coalition members in both houses of parliament. However, Pinochet bitterly resented his defeat in the plebiscite, remained president until Aylwin's inauguration, and ensured that both he and the army retained extensive control in the new system.[61] It was in these circumstances that Dorfman and his family returned to Chile in July.

Four years earlier, in an interview, he had suggested that one form of redemption for an exile was 'the opportunity to go back, to return and with what you have learned outside, to renew your original society'.[62] Some early steps taken by Aylwin just before his return probably encouraged him. There was televised coverage of his assumption of office and a mass inauguration the following day at the National Stadium—a highly symbolic site because of its sinister use by Pinochet in the aftermath of the coup. This also included speeches and personal testimonies by those who had long been excluded from national life, as

164

well as a moving performance of the Chilean national dance by wives of the 'disappeared'. In June six government ministers also attended a public funeral for twenty victims of the Pinochet regime, when a shallow unmarked grave was discovered. And Dorfman was back in Chile to witness a very significant symbolic memorial—the reburying of Allende on the anniversary of his inauguration, with Aylwin delivering a moving eulogy.[63]

Dorfman did not intend to speak out politically, noting in his diary that he had sworn not to write a word in public for six months.[64] This was a promise that he failed to keep: within a few months, in deep frustration, he wrote *Death and the Maiden*, and he returned to the US in January 1991. The catalyst for the play would be the Comisión Nacional de Verdad y Reconciliación (National Commission on Truth and Reconciliation), chaired by Raúl Rettig, an elderly Radical Party politician and lawyer, which Aylwin established in April 1990.

The major obstacle to real progress in this sphere was the amnesty law of 1978, introduced by Pinochet to cover the period since the coup—the five years in which the most horrific atrocities had been committed. Aylwin's election manifesto had explicitly promised to repeal the amnesty, and when he came to power there was pressure from the families of victims and from human rights groups to overrule this law.[65] He did not do so, claiming that he had insufficient votes in parliament, but in reality also because of the continuing power of Pinochet. The commission's mandate was to investigate the situations

> of those persons who disappeared after arrest, who were executed, or who were tortured to death in which the moral responsibility of the state is compromised as a result of actions by its agents or persons in its service, as well as kidnappings and attempts on the life of persons committed by private citizens for political purposes.[66]

This excluded torture that did not lead to death and there was no investigation of such cases. Nor was there any reparation for torture survivors. The commission saw its primary role as investigation, but it had no power of subpoena and there was little cooperation from the armed forces. Nevertheless, it would produce an 1800-page report in February 1991—after Dorfman had left Chile—documenting more than 2000 deaths. It strongly criticised the acquiescence by the judiciary in Pinochet's regime, for effectively providing impunity for the violators.[67] And it attributed over 95 per cent of human rights violations to agents of the state.[68]

On 25 August 1990, Dorfman met and talked to his friend José Zalaquett, who was the head lawyer of the commission. Zalaquett had played an important role in the international conferences that had initiated the concept and practice of transitional justice, arguing that taking an absolutist position in relation to human rights norms could jeopardise democratic stabilisations.[69] Dorfman, who was presumably unaware of this, was initially impressed by the commission's passionate commitment and moved by the support being given to widows and orphans of the dictatorship. In his diary, he recorded that the pain of these people was now being granted an official space, making it 'a legitimate component of History... a Truth that can never again be disowned'. He continued, however: 'I'm worried about the victims who survived and have no place on the comisión, in the Official History of Chile, what about their distress?[70] He realised that a commission could not hear all tales of woe or provide recognition and reparation for everybody, for this would 'turn the transition into a wailing wall of laments, stagnate us in an eternal victimhood of regret, destabilise our democracy by repeating the divisions and recriminations that led to this tragedy in the first place.'[71]

But he feared that this legitimate and judicious line of reasoning could let the perpetrators off the hook:

> This fear of the wounds of the past leaves those who have benefited and prospered from that terror to hold their heads up high, creates a haunted country where those who suffered and those who inflicted the suffering have to live side by side, everybody complicit in avoiding the truth of the irreparable harm that was done.[72]

He acknowledged the danger of impatience, but doubted whether genuine reconciliation was possible until there was a measure of justice and 'our enemies have at least recognised the pain they inflicted and swear to never again repeat such actions'.[73]

Just over a week later, he returned to the subject. During the dictatorship, he had assumed

> that there would be some sort of catharsis when Pinochet was gone ... Well, he's gone now ... but instead of using that absence to deal with the dictatorship, the subject has almost disappeared. Now that the war is over,

writers are supposed to go back to roses and birds and beauty ... Except that I can't. I can't turn the page. Everywhere I go, it's enough to scratch the surface of each person, crack open the door to each person with a question or a look—that's enough for the howl of the past to inch out ...[74]

It was, he said, out of that howl that the character of Paulina (in *Death and the Maiden*) emerged, and on 3 September he decided to break his vow of silence so as to allow her to speak.

Death and the Maiden and transitional justice

In fact, he had long thought about a novel on some aspects of the situation and had attempted to write it several times.[75] But it was the transition that brought it all together in his mind. Before turning to the play itself, it is therefore worth emphasising its relationship with the themes noted in the previous section about his earlier thought and writing. First, he intended to make a political impact through a cultural production and decided that it must be in the form of a play. It was

[a] conflict that needs to be enacted by real people on a stage—it is too critical to our sanity as a nation ... to languish between the covers of a novel that would take a year or more to publish. My words have to invade the physical space where the violations occurred.[76]

Secondly, it arose from his conviction that the transition was suppressing the kind of honest dialogue that was so crucial. Thirdly, such a dialogue must include all the relevant voices in a search for a new way forward, and also acknowledge the multiple personalities within each individual. Fourthly, those who had perpetrated the violence under Pinochet must admit what they had done, recognise the suffering that they had caused and, at the least, apologise. All this was part of the 'promise to the dead', and also to the disappeared and tortured. Finally, there was an underlying assumption that, with such conditions fulfilled, some kind of shared future would be possible, which would also then involve addressing other fundamental problems about rights and justice.[77]

The dramatic power of the play lies in its intensity, and its ability to express the contrasting perspectives of each of the three characters persuasively so that the sympathies of the audience shift as the drama develops. Similarly, the ending is left open, so that spectators need to

draw out the meaning themselves in an active way. But the wider reso-
nance of the play is that, through three characters, it pinpoints the
enduring dilemmas of transitional justice: the tensions between truth,
legal and quasi-legal justice and recognition for victims, and the stabilisation of a new political settlement.

The plot is comparatively simple, although little is clear at the beginning. Paulina is alone in a house in a remote location and is extremely
tense. Fifteen years earlier, she was blindfolded, tortured and repeatedly raped by the agents of the dictatorship, and she has never recov-
ered from the trauma. A car arrives and she hears her husband,
Gerardo, a lawyer, thanking someone (Roberto) who had helped him
with a flat tyre. Roberto drives away and Gerardo comes into the
house. He tells her that he has been asked by the president to head a
Truth and Reconciliation Commission, but wants her to agree before
he accepts. He explains that it will only investigate human rights violations that ended in death or the presumption of death. She asks what
will happen to the criminals and Gerardo replies that this depends on
the judges. She exclaims, with increasing hysteria:

> The judges? The same judges who never intervened to save one life in
> seventeen years of dictatorship? Who never accepted a single habeas cor-
> pus ever? Judge Peralta who told that poor woman who had come to ask
> for her missing husband that the man had probably grown tired of her and
> run off with some other woman? That judge? What did you call him? A
> judge? A judge?[78]

At first it seems that Gerardo is concerned about whether she will
be upset if he takes up the position in view of what happened to her in
the past. In fact, as she later forces him to admit, he has already
accepted the job, and his main concern is perhaps that she might have
a breakdown, which could jeopardise his position.

Very soon Roberto, who is a doctor, returns, having heard on the
radio that Gerardo is to head the commission. Saying that he wanted to
congratulate him, he talks as if he had always been against the dictatorship, and he favours retributive measures, including the death penalty,
against the perpetrators of atrocities. Gerardo disagrees, explaining
and defending the limitations of the commission. It is not entirely clear
whether Roberto really believes in what he saying or whether he is
eliciting information—perhaps to find out whether he could be at risk.

168

After some discussion, Gerardo invites him to stay. However, in the middle of the night Paulina drugs Roberto, ties him up, gags him and threatens him with a gun, while speaking in a monologue about aspects of her past. She plays a CD of Schubert's String Quartet No. 14 ('Death and the Maiden'), but says she can no longer listen to his music although he is her favourite composer. When Gerardo appears she also threatens him with the gun, declaring that she recognises Roberto's voice, and claiming that he was the person who tortured her. She tells Gerardo that they are now going to put Roberto on trial. Gerardo implores her not to do so, pointing out that this is revenge, and that he will have to resign from the commission because, in such a position, you needed to show 'exemplary signs of moderation and equanimity'. She retorts, 'We're going to suffocate from so much equanimity!'[79] She is, she says, now feeling alive for the first time in fifteen years, but he warns her that she risks bringing dictators back to power and that she should think of the country and the restoration of democracy. She suggests a 'compromise':

> Compromise, an agreement a negotiation. Everything in this country is done by consensus, isn't it. Isn't that what this transition is all about? They let us have democracy, but they keep control of the economy and of the armed forces? The Commission can investigate the crimes but nobody is punished for them? There's freedom to say anything you want as long as you don't say everything you want?[80]

She tells Gerardo that she has now dropped her original idea of arranging for Roberto to be raped in revenge (perhaps with Gerardo as the perpetrator), and it will now be sufficient if Roberto confesses to everything. However, she will kill him unless he confesses.

When alone with Roberto, Gerardo persuades him to indulge Paulina's fantasies and confess. He then asks her to tell him exactly what happened (for the first time) so that he can recount this to Roberto to give him the details for his confession. Meanwhile, the audience has also learned some other important aspects of the past. Gerardo had been a student leader and Paulina had been tortured to divulge his name, but had refused to do so. However, when finally released, she had found Gerardo with another woman, and she now asks about her. Gerardo insists that Paulina had already forgiven him for this and asks how many times they have to go over this:

We'll die from so much past, so much pain and resentment. Let's finish it—let's finish that conversation from years ago, let's close this book once and for all and never speak about it again, never again, never never again.

PAULINA. Forgive and forget, eh?

GERARDO. Forgive yes, forget, no. But forgive so we can start again...[81]

The audience then hears Paulina beginning to tell Gerardo what happened to her. She only met Roberto after three days and thought he was going to help—he played Schubert to her. This then merges into Roberto's confession: how he had started cooperating with the security forces partly because his father had had a heart attack when peasants took over his land, but also because he wanted to do something humanitarian—to provide some medical attention even to his political enemies. He had begun by looking at how much electrical current people could take and played Schubert to calm them, but he then started enjoying it and participated eagerly.

After Roberto's confession, Paulina persuades Gerardo to get the car, leaving her with Roberto, who tells her that this was not a real confession because he is innocent and he had repeated what Gerardo had told him to say. Paulina replies that she knew that this was what Gerardo would do, but she had made deliberate mistakes and Roberto had corrected them—as she anticipated he would. She gives him ten seconds to repent, threatening that otherwise she will kill him, but he continues to protest his innocence. When the count gets to eight, he exclaims:

So someone did terrible things to you and now you're doing something terrible to me and tomorrow somebody else is going to—on and on and on. ...

PAULINA. Nine.

ROBERTO. Oh Paulina—isn't it time we stopped?

PAULINA. And why does it always have to be people like me who have to sacrifice, why are we always the ones who have to make concessions...? Well, not this time. This time I am going to think about myself, about what I need. If only to do justice in one case, just one. ... What do we lose by killing one of them?[82]

At this point, they freeze in their positions as the lights begin to go down and the audience hears a Mozart quartet. Paulina and Roberto are covered from view by a giant mirror that descends, forcing the members of the audience to look at themselves. The music plays for a few minutes, while the spectators watch themselves in the mirror. Slowly moving spots of light flicker over the audience, picking out two or three at a time, up and down the rows. This then shifts to a final scene at a concert. In the interval Gerardo is talking about being tired but very pleased with the Final Report of the commission. He stresses the fact that people are acting with enormous generosity and without a hint of seeking personal vendettas. He is surprised by this and mentions an old woman, whose husband had disappeared fourteen years previously, and her gratitude to the president of the commission for allowing her to give her evidence sitting down. Paulina is buying sweets and Roberto is also at the event. The concert resumes with the playing of 'Death and the Maiden'. Paulina turns her head and looks at Roberto and their eyes interlock for a moment. Then she turns her head and faces the stage and the mirror before the lights go down with the music still playing.

Some points in the play are quite clear. Paulina had been a courageous woman, who was brutally tortured and raped by the agents of a repressive state, but she would receive no redress or recognition by the Truth and Reconciliation Commission. She had been a victim of the sexual violence of the dictatorship and she would be a victim of the compromise that replaced it, and some sexist asides between Roberto and Gerardo also suggest that this is because she is a woman.[83] It is only by taking matters into her own hands with a gun, and humiliating Roberto in the way that she had been humiliated, that she can exert some power and feel that she is able to live.[84] Gerardo is a flawed character, who had betrayed Paulina with another woman while she was being tortured for his sake. He may genuinely believe in the commission, but is also keen to secure personal advancement by heading it, and he appears a little smug and superficial. He had also collaborated with Roberto in treating Paulina as deranged. But the pain of the past cannot be wished out of existence or ignored. Paulina had never told Gerardo exactly what had happened and he had never previously asked. Nor did he want her to ask about the other woman, telling her 'we'll die from so much past, so much pain and resentment'. Yet there is no prospect either of forgiveness or reconciliation unless what happened in the past is admitted and acknowledged.

There is also much uncertainty in the play. The most obvious question is whether Roberto was guilty. Is it sufficient evidence that Paulina recognises his voice, verbal tics and smell? Or should we be convinced by the fact that he had corrected her deliberate mistakes? Or that both her torturer and Roberto had quoted Nietzche, and that he had a copy of 'Death and the Maiden' amongst his CDs? If he was guilty, as is probably implied, can we accept Paulina's personal retribution as legitimate? She tells him, at gunpoint, to confess or be killed and she even tells Gerardo that if he is innocent he will really be 'screwed' because the only way for him to survive is by confessing. Powerful arguments are used against her. The first is when Gerardo tells her that she is doing exactly what the dictatorship did and it is now necessary to move to a system of law and justice. But, of course, this will not operate against her torturer because of the constraints of the commission. The second argument, this time by Roberto, is that if she kills him she will simply set up a never-ending cycle of revenge and retribution, and this is also related to Gerardo's insistence that the kind of action she is taking could provoke a new coup. These are forceful points, but so is Paulina's heartfelt response: 'why does it always have to be people like me who have to sacrifice, why are we always the ones who have to make concessions when something has to be conceded?'

There is also some ambiguity at the end—in particular, it is not entirely clear whether Roberto is present at the concert or whether he is there as a ghost. But the implication is that he has confessed and, because of this, Paulina is now able to attend a performance of 'Death and the Maiden' and to hear platitudes about the commission in apparent tranquillity. This was surely Dorfman's way of emphasising that this kind of acknowledgement of guilt was a precondition of genuine dialogue and successful transition. And this was also the significance of the mirror and spotlight turned on the audience: all had played some role in the terrible years of the Pinochet dictatorship, and each individual had to recognise his or her own responsibility, in line with Dorfman's view of the 'jungle' in each of us. It was also a way of accusing everyone of trying to cover up the tragedy of the period.[85]

This was a challenging play in the immediate aftermath of the dictatorship and Dorfman knew that the country might not be ready for it. He feared that Chile had no place for Paulina. But he insisted that 'she may be deserted but she isn't dead—and I, for one, with my words am going to bring her out of the darkness'.[86] He also knew that the last scene, in which the mirror was to be projected onto the audience, was regarded as one provocation too far.[87] But he was adamant in wanting to keep it, deploring 'the underlying intellectual failure' of the transition, 'above all, its hypocrisy', and superficial forms of reconciliation.[88] These, he believed, led to 'indifference: a way of shielding oneself from the pain'.[89] Pinochet, he noted, had no illness and remained as strong as steel, while many former political prisoners, relatives of the disappeared, exiles and torture victims had terminal illnesses. It could break people down to live in pain forever and the question was how to allow the pain into your life without becoming destroyed by it. This was Paulina's struggle, and:

> My play might provide some preliminary answer to Chile's search for what to do with the grief, that final scene a way of establishing a zone of liberty, an ethical and aesthetic space that does not compromise, as the politicians must, in order to keep the soldiers in their barracks, keep the past from upsetting the future. But not me. I didn't come back to Chile in order to negotiate away Paulina's story.[90]

Yet he was increasingly aware that the play might not be performed in Chile, particularly as there were rumours of a new coup because Pinochet was angry about investigations into his family:[91]

> I wonder if all these obstacles do not constitute a warning that maybe it is not the time, after all, to force my compatriots to look in the mirror and see what we have become, what we still might avoid becoming if we can all burn with the truth that I have written. What if I am wrong to try to stage the play now, when the wounds are so fresh?[92]

In January 1991, after only six months in Chile, the family went back to the US. They would keep their home in Chile and return frequently, but Dorfman would not be the returning exile, after all.

The impasse faced in staging *Death and the Maiden* certainly triggered his decision to leave, but it was not the sole problem. As a human rights activist, with a wider conception of justice, he was angry and frustrated by a whole range of concerns:

> Under the dictatorship a host of issues not patently political, social issues that galvanised me, had been postponed because of their possible divisive-

ness, but democracy was supposed to be different ... That's why, upon this 1990 return to Chile, I propelled myself into a permanent campaign for all sorts of rights, almost a crusade to change how people feel and think and act.[93]

His experience with the play thus highlighted the inadequacy of the transition and his belief that other forms of injustice would not be rectified unless the past was addressed. This was a very legitimate concern, for the difficulties with his play illuminated the nature and problems of the post-dictatorship regime.

Aylwin himself, as already noted, had made some important symbolic overtures to the victims of the dictatorship. Just after Dorfman left Chile, the Rettig Commission report was published and Aylwin, speaking on national television, begged forgiveness from victims, stressed the need for reconciliation, and asked the armed forces to 'make gestures of recognition for the pain caused'.[94] There were also plans to hold national reconciliation and education events on the issues dealt with in the report. However, the institutions that had perpetrated the atrocities did not accept the report and four weeks after its release an extreme Left group attacked right-wing members of the political elite and assassinated Jaime Guzmán, a key figure of the Pinochet regime.[95] This quickly re-focused attention on 'terrorism', effectively burying the report and all plans for reconciliation events.[96]

In general, political leaders were keen to insist that the transition to democracy had now been concluded. Aylwin himself declared this in August 1991 and, following the election in 1994, his successor, Eduardo Frei, put forward his agenda on the premise that democracy was already consolidated.[97] The attempt to legitimise the new regime was based primarily on this claim, reinforced by rapid economic growth.[98] Of still greater significance, social expenditure rose by around one-third between 1989–93, with a decline in poverty from two-fifths of the population to one-third over the same period.[99] Yet despite the prevailing consensus amongst the political elite that national reconciliation had been achieved, personal relationships remained strained, with an unspoken agreement never to bring up the past or strong differences of opinion.[100] All this was embedded in the particular nature of Chile's transition.

During the 1980s, memory had been a rallying cry for the democratic opposition, with the 'disappeared' a potent symbol of the demand to know what had really happened under the dictatorship.[101] This had merged into the protest movement against austerity and unemployment. However, party politicians had then assumed leadership of the movement. They created the national coalition for the 'no' vote, agreed the platform on which they had stood for election in 1989, and negotiated the terms of Pinochet's exit as president. It was this political elite that forged the agreements amongst themselves as the key to a successful transition, and they maintained this approach until the late 1990s.[102] In general, centre-left politicians tried to avoid provoking the large body of pro-Pinochet opinion by keeping a lid on the past. And, as Cath Collins has argued, very few people cared strongly enough to enter the fray against implacable military and right-wing opposition, while 'those who did still care—mainly relatives and their lawyers—scored the occasional small victory but did not make substantial inroads'.[103] Dorfman had sought to challenge all this in *Death and the Maiden*, but had failed to have any impact. But by the end of the decade, the elite consensus to draw a mask over the past was having negative effects upon the whole society. Alexander Wilde thus noted that, despite substantial economic and political successes, by December 1997 the allegiance of citizens to the regime remained tepid, there appeared to be increased questioning of the transition process itself, and,

> the country's public life since transition has had a certain muffled quality reflective of what might be called a 'conspiracy of consensus' originating among political elites but permeating the whole society. Within the citizenry there appears to be a widespread aversion to open conflict, related to low levels of social trust.[104]

This had been the meaning of Paulina's exasperated cry: 'compromise, an agreement, a negotiation. Everything in this country is done by consensus, isn't it. Isn't that what this transition is all about?' Nor did Dorfman himself change his mind about this, telling an interviewer in 1995 that his own inclinations were towards peace and reconciliation and living in harmony, but 'you cannot do this based upon lies, based upon the suppression of feelings, the suppression of experiences of a part of the population, or a part of your personality' and that 'before we focus on reconciliation we need to face the issue of truth'.[105] However, from 1998 onwards there was a substantial change in the situation.

Pinochet's position had already been weakened in March 1998 when he ceased being Commander-in-Chief of the army and became senator for life, but it was his arrest in London in October of that year that provided the catalyst for re-opening a series of questions about the past.[106] There were also shifts in the public visibility of the issues. One important step was the establishment of the Valech Commission (The National Commission on Political Imprisonment and Torture) in 2003–4, a truth commission on political imprisonment and torture which heard testimonies from tens of thousands of survivors, leading to the official acknowledgement of more than 38,000 victims of torture.[107] There was also broad acceptance of this report in contrast to the refusal of the Right to accept the Rettig Report in 1991, and reparations for torture victims, following the report, signified an important step. The number of public memorial sites increased rapidly, with Michelle Bachelet, the first PS president since Allende, inaugurating a Museum of Memory and Human Rights in Santiago in 2010.[108] In fact, Bachelet herself, who was president from 2006–10 (and was re-elected in 2014, after a right-wing interval), was able to cultivate warmer personal contacts with relatives' and survivors' groups than either of her two immediate predecessors.[109]

None of these changes has, of course, resolved all the problems.[110] Nevertheless, there was a transformation of the situation in comparison with the pre-1998 position. Thus Alexander Wilde, who in 1999 had been very critical of the failure to address the past, subsequently declared that Chile 'is a remarkable example of a nation confronting questions profoundly related to its identity, with considerable success'.[111]

Dorfman had no doubt that it was the arrest of Pinochet that had this effect.[112] He had welcomed his detention in London, had followed the next stages closely, reporting on the issue for several papers, and later collected together these reports and his reflections in *Exorcising Terror*. There are several particularly interesting aspects to this. First, the very strong relationship between Dorfman and his character, Paulina, became still more apparent. For, like Paulina in relation to Roberto, Dorfman did not think it necessary to punish Pinochet: he wanted him to be forced to face his victims—'to look at the black and clear eyes of the women whose sons and husbands and fathers and brothers you kidnapped and disappeared' and to ask forgiveness.[113] Secondly, while most of the text was an indictment of the centre-left political leaders for operating within the consensus in Chile at the expense of the survivors and victims, he also included himself in this. He therefore explained that he had wanted the trial of Pinochet so desperately that he had written *Death and the Maiden* in anticipation of it. Paulina had been aware that the newly elected democratic government could not try him so she decided to act as both judge and executioner:

> I let Paulina loose on that doctor, let her say to him the things I would have said, so many of us would have shouted from the rooftops in Chile ... if we had not been sure that if went too far in our demands, the military would come back and punish us yet one more time for daring to rebel.

> And yet, ... even as I savoured a society ... where the hunted of yesterday became the hunters of today, even in a play where the author supposedly can write whatever he wants, I found myself reluctantly prodding Paulina toward an ending she did not want and I did not want and yet was there, waiting for her and the people of Chile: My protagonist, having tried to bring some personal measure of justice to the world, sits down ... in a concert hall in close and uncanny proximity to the doctor she thinks damaged her irreparably ... In *Death and the Maiden*, I could not, Paulina could not, fantasize another ending. The tragedy of my country ... was that we could not put the murderers and violators on trial. That was the ... consensus we reached. We thought—and we were probably right—that our ambiguous freedom depended on coexisting with the dictator's shadow and ... with his threats, with his oblivion of our memories, with his command that people like Paulina be silenced and ignored and excluded.[114]

This suggests that the play really did emerge from a 'howl' of rage and impotence. As a writer, he believed that literature could never be consensual and there was therefore an unavoidable clash between his mind and Chile's cautious transition. As he later claimed, to remain there silently would have been to disown his responsibility as a writer.[115] Yet the above admission suggests that in political terms he had seen no real alternative to the policies that were being adopted. In this sense, he had also partially made the transition from anti-Pinochet activist to acquiescence in the elite political consensus.

Finally, he was convinced that one of the most significant changes brought about by the arrest was that the mystique of the dictator was finally broken—that people, who for years had been frightened to speak about what had happened or even to show that they had once supported Allende, were now released from the intimidation and, for the first time, felt free.[116] And he was surely right, for the arrest did have this impact: for the first time, open conversations in public and private and between parents and children did take place.[117]

Throughout his years in exile from 1973, Dorfman's aspiration had been for a new society, which would recognise many voices and perspectives, but would create a form of justice for the victims and survivors, and, through genuine dialogue, a sense of collective responsibility for both the past and the future. In the Chilean context, as elsewhere, this has limitations. Recognition of the atrocities carried out by Pinochet, trials of perpetrators, reparations for survivors, and memorials for the dead do not, in themselves, address the fundamental inequalities of the society, and recent protests raise questions about these underlying questions that the post-Pinochet governments scarcely addressed.[118] However, Dorfman never believed that any form of transitional justice was sufficient, for his wider conception of human rights demonstrates his continuing commitment to social justice, both in the traditional sense of socioeconomic redistribution and in the enlarged sense, discussed in Chapter One, through 'recognition' of disadvantaged and marginalised groups. He also continued to believe that culture could play an important role, as for example, in his dramatisation of the voices of human rights activists in *Speak Truth to Power*.[119] He expressed his general outlook particularly eloquently in a ceremony at the American University in Washington in May 2001, when exhorting the new graduates to battle constantly against exploitation and injustice:

> Your energy can be chanelled through your job or it can be channelled outside your job, it can be dedicated to a large and lifelong cause or to a series of small ones, it can engage injustice and discrimination in your neighborhood or in your city, or in your country itself, or in lands whose names you can hardly pronounce but whose misfortunes are all too often the result of the policies of your own government or the consequence of the interests of American companies ...

> Hold fast to the dream that a time can come when people will not slaughter each other due to their national or racial or ethnic differences, hold fast to the certainty that it is unnatural that street children be murdered or that their mothers die of hunger or that someone should be denied a job because of the color of her skin or the sex she was born into, hold fast to the belief that we can imagine a world where certain sicknesses can be

178

conquered and medicine can be reasonably within the grasp of those who need it, where women are free to go out at night without looking over their shoulders, where information or cooperation is not extracted from others with a whip or a threat.[120]

He understood the dangers of seeking to bury the past, and he knew that the solution must be to answer the 'howl' of Paulina. But he also regarded this as a necessary condition for addressing other issues. Such insights illuminate the problems of transition in Chile and elsewhere.

7

NADINE GORDIMER

APARTHEID AND AFTER

In November 1973 the General Assembly of the United Nations passed a resolution which came into force in July 1976 as the 'International Convention on the Suppression and Punishment of the Crime of Apartheid'. Article I declared that

> *apartheid* is a crime against humanity and that inhuman acts resulting from the policies and practices of *apartheid* and similar policies and practices of racial segregation and discrimination ... are crimes violating the principles of international law, in particular the purposes and principles of the Charter of the United Nations, and constituting a serious threat to international peace and security.

> The States Parties to the present Convention declare criminal those organizations, institutions and individuals committing the crime of *apartheid*.[1]

This did not, of course, lead to the end of the apartheid state in South Africa, particularly because leading Western powers effectively ignored the resolution. It was only after the ending of the Cold War, the release of Nelson Mandela from jail in 1990, and prolonged negotiations in a climate of continuing violence, that the first democratic elections took place in April 1994 in South Africa, formally ending apartheid. Nevertheless, for many the resolution in 1973 formalised a position that they had long accepted intellectually, politically and emotionally: that apartheid was not simply a policy implemented by a repressive state, but was an outrage that must be ended. Since then many of those who were engaged in the struggle against apartheid, both inside and outside South Africa, have been deeply disappointed by the continuing immense inequalities, the authoritarian tendencies within the African National Congress (ANC), and corruption by the political elite. Nevertheless, the ending of the apartheid state was of major historical importance, both for South Africa itself and for the world as a whole. This chapter explores these issues through the work of Nadine Gordimer (1923–2014).

Gordimer exposed the injustices of the apartheid system for an international readership for more than four decades, with her first book of stories appearing in 1949.[2] She eventually published numerous works of fiction and also essays on politics and literary criticism, and was awarded the Nobel Prize for literature in 1991. Two of her novels were banned by the South African authorities for considerable periods—*A World of Strangers* (1958) for twelve years and *The Late Bourgeois World* (1966) for ten. *The Conservationist* (1974) was held by the censors for several weeks before they eventually released it and *Burger's Daughter* (1979) was banned briefly, but the authorities soon retreated because of her international reputation.[3] She was also an active supporter of the illegal opposition from the 1960s, becoming increasingly close to the ANC leadership in the last years of the fight against apartheid and in the early years of the transition.

Gordimer began writing at an exceptionally early age.[4] As the second daughter of two Jewish immigrants living in the mining town of Springs, east of Johannesburg, she had an unusual childhood. Her parents' marriage was unhappy and when she was eleven her mother, Nan, withdrew her from school for a year on the false pretext that she had a weak heart. Subsequently, her schooling was intermittent and ceased entirely at the age of fifteen, but she devoted herself to reading voraciously. She also developed acute powers of observation of adult life and relationships. Although she would later spend a year at the University of Witwatersrand, she did not complete a degree and remained essentially self-educated. She was married twice—the first time for only three years (1949–52) to Gerald Gavronsky, and then, until his death in 2001, to Rheinold Cassirer, a well-known art dealer, who was a refugee from Berlin. She had a daughter by her first marriage and a son by her second, but her vocation as a writer was central to her life: she published her first adult story in *Forum*, a liberal South African magazine, at the age of fifteen, and her last novel, *No Time Like the Present*, in 2012 at the age of eighty-eight.[5]

Her interest was in the personal lives and relationships of people of all kinds and the ways in which these were shaped by the wider social context in which they survived, lived and worked. She did not set out to provide a critique of society, let alone the political system, but to depict social reality through imaginary characters and their interactions. Asked about the impact of politics upon her writing, she explained: 'I would have been a writer anyway; I was writing before politics impinged itself upon my consciousness ... But the real influence of politics on my writing is the influence of politics on people.'[6]

This influence was always affected by the specific conditions of South African life. As a child, she was brought up in a lifestyle of almost complete segregation between whites and blacks. Later she recalled that her most powerful conscious recognition of the extreme nature of white racism came at the age of seventeen when she was a Red Cross recruit at a gold mine during World War II. A medical aid worker used no anaesthetic while stitching the gaping wounds of black miners who were accident victims, saying, 'they don't feel like we do'.[7] Gordimer's consciousness of this type of mentality subsequently shaped her understanding of the nature of the society that she was writing about. She began mixing with black people in Johannesburg in the late 1940s, and a few years later formed several friendships with young black musicians, artists and journalists in Sophiatown. From then onwards she would produce her numerous works of fiction, with an enormous variety of central characters, sometimes including those to whom she was completely unsympathetic. In general, she provided very few overt political or didactic 'messages' in her fiction, and her political orientation in the early short stories and novels was moderate liberalism. However, even these works depicted people in situations that were not normally represented in literature and inevitably raised issues that were highly 'political' within the South African context. For example, her early collections of short stories in *Face to Face* (1949) and *The Soft Voice of the Servant and Other Stories* (1952) illuminated the wholly different lives of those divided by a racist society, and her first novel, *The Lying Days* (1953), also raised the enduring theme of whether the central character (based on Gordimer) should commit herself to fighting for a better society or should leave the country.[8] When her second novel, *A World of Strangers* (1958), was banned, this was not for any overt political message, but because of what it showed about the nature of South African society through its depiction of an initially apathetic British journalist (based on her friend, Anthony Sampson) being exposed to the horrific nature of apartheid.

Gordimer did not regard her books as 'political' for two reasons. First, because her primary intention was to portray imaginary people constrained and often humiliated by the society rather than to provide an explicit ideological or political interpretation. Secondly, her own notion of the 'political novel' was one in which the characters were merely ciphers for the author's views. It is easy to appreciate Gordimer's conception of her literature as 'non-political', but ultimately her work transcended her own interpretation of it, particularly with the development of her worldwide reputation as the most outstanding writer to expose the brutality and dehumanisation of apartheid. Furthermore, she was constantly asked to speak about the South African situation, and she published a growing number of essays and commentaries. The way in which Gordimer's work combined both creative and political writing was aptly recognised in the presentation speech for the Nobel Prize:

> Above all, it is people, individual men and women, that have captured her and been captured by her. It is their lives, their heaven and hell, that absorb her. The outer reality is ever present, but it is through her characters that the whole historical process is crystallized. Conveying to the reader a powerful sense of authenticity, and with wide human relevance, she makes visible the extremely complicated and utterly inhuman living conditions in the world of racial segregation. She feels political responsibility, and does not shy away from its consequences, but will not allow it to affect her as a writer: her texts are not agitatorial, not propagandistic. Still, her works and the deep insights she offers contribute to shaping reality.[9]

Despite her protestations and her original intentions, her publications thus assumed an unusually important political role, contributing to the establishment of an international climate in which apartheid was increasingly viewed as an unacceptable evil. Yet she always found it difficult to combine her creative writing and her political commitment.

The apartheid state

Political evolution

In the 1950s Gordimer believed in the possibility of a gradual transformation of apartheid and hoped that much could be changed through interpersonal relations: that equality might be possible if white liberals demonstrated their belief in it by their behaviour. The Sharpeville massacre of 1960, the subsequent decision of the ANC to turn to violent as well as non-violent protest, and the Rivonia trial of 1963–4, effectively ended this era.

Yet despite pessimism as to whether there was any real possibility of a non-racial society in South Africa, some of her writing of the early 1960s was still broadly liberal in its outlook.[10] In an interview in 1965 she explained her own evolution as follows:

> A white South African, brought up on the soft side of the colour-bar, I have gone through the whole packaged-deal evolution that situation has to offer—unquestioning acceptance of the superiority of my white skin, as a small child; acceptance of the paternal attitude that 'they' are only human, after all, as an older child; questioning of these attitudes as I grew up and read and experienced outside the reading and experience that formed my inheritance; and finally, re-birth as a human being among other human beings, with all this means in the face of the discrimination that sorts them into colours and races ... I have no religion, no political dogma—only plenty of doubts about everything except my conviction that the colour-bar is wrong and utterly indefensible.
>
> Thus I have found the basis of a moral code that is valid for me. Reason and emotion meet in it: and perhaps that is as near to faith as I shall ever get.[11]

But this was also a period of change for her, which followed the publication of her novel, *The Late Bourgeois World*, in 1966. In this, the white woman narrator (Liz) is considering some form of political action following the suicide of her ex-husband, who was an undisciplined anti-apartheid activist who made a botched attempt at sabotage and then betrayed his friends under police pressure. In Gordimer's own subsequent interpretation of the novel, she argued that Liz had to

185

realise that she could get no further on the liberal lines that she had been following. Her options were either to turn to something more radical by making a binding and dangerous commitment to the revolutionary movement, or give up her activities completely.[12] In reality, she herself was facing the same dilemma and by 1972 she declared that she was no longer a liberal, but a radical and that she could just as well live under a black government as a white one, but: 'Without justice, there is nothing to commend one above the other. We have never had a just government'.[13] Yet this meant confronting some major intellectual and political challenges.

Gordimer never joined the South African Communist Party (SACP), claiming that she had woken up to the shameful enormity of the colour bar 'through the apparently esoteric speleology of doubt led by Kafka rather than Marx'.[14] However, many acquaintances became party members, including her closest friend, Bettie du Toit, who was arrested following the post-Sharpeville clampdown. Gordimer visited du Toit in jail and this was certainly a radicalising experience for her.[15] Another very important influence was working with and observing Mandela's lead lawyer, Bram Fischer, in the Rivonia trial. Fischer was an Afrikaner from a well-connected family, who had joined the SACP in the 1940s and secretly played a leading role within it. In September 1964 he was arrested and charged with membership of the banned party, but was released on bail to handle a patent case in London. Despite the possibility of remaining in exile, he insisted on returning to South Africa. However, one day he failed to arrive in court, instead sending a letter to his counsel, stating that he was absenting himself 'because I believe that it is the duty of every true opponent of this Government to remain in this country and to oppose its monstrous policy of apartheid with every means in his power. That is what I shall do for as long as I can'.[16] Captured in November 1965, he was tried and sentenced to life imprisonment in March 1966.

Gordimer was deeply impressed by Fischer. She attended his trial and subsequently wrote an essay on him, asking why he had effectively chosen to go to jail. She concluded, 'People of different backgrounds who know Fischer best seem to agree that what brought him back from Europe and what made him turn fugitive were one and the same thing, the touchstone of his personality: absolute faith in human integrity.'[17]

Such integrity was, of course, completely out of keeping with the Western Cold War stereotype of a communist. She was fascinated by Fischer, who died from cancer in 1975 at the age of sixty-seven, and her major novel, *Burger's Daughter* (1979), was an 'an act of homage' to people like him.[18] This did not mean that she embraced his ideas, but they were less problematic for her than the challenge posed by the rise of the Black Consciousness movement in the 1970s.

With so many of the earlier generation of ANC leaders now in exile or prison, this movement became increasingly powerful, particularly after the Soweto uprising in 1976 and the death of Steve Biko in police captivity the following year. Gordimer had discussed Black Consciousness with Steve Biko and sought to understand its position.[19] In 1971 she argued that, whatever feelings of regret there might be, it was necessary to understand the movement in terms of a demand by black people for their own power.[20] However, the new militancy appeared to marginalise any white role by suggesting that even liberals and radicals were an integral part of the structures of white supremacy. In public she continued to defend the inevitability of this black reaction to the failures of most progressive whites to go beyond limited concessions that effectively protected continuing white ascendancy.[21] She allowed the position to 'speak for itself' in *Burger's Daughter*. Nevertheless, Black Consciousness created great difficulties for Gordimer, for it undermined the notion of a 'non-racial' South Africa, striking at the fundamental conceptions of justice and transformation to which she adhered. It was also a major existential challenge because it implied that there might be no place for people like herself in a post-apartheid society. As she had resisted the possibility of leaving the country and had always disavowed the idea that she was a 'European', this was naturally a painful prospect for her. However, by the early 1980s the ANC was again regaining ascendancy in the struggle against apartheid, leading to a revival in the notion of an eventual 'non-racial' South Africa based on some form of socialism.

Gordimer identified herself with these ideas. In 1979 she had already taken it as axiomatic that 'racial problems, both material and spiritual can hope to be solved only in circumstances of economic equality', and in her powerful essay 'Living in the Interregnum' (1982) she stated that in the eyes of the black majority which would rule, the whites of the former South Africa would have to redefine themselves in a new collective life within new structures.[22] This would not just be a matter of blacks taking over white institutions, but of conceiving of institutions that reflected an entirely different social structure. While acknowledging the possibility that a form of capitalism might remain—though wholly changed—she saw this as unlikely:

> The fact is, black South Africans and whites like myself no longer believe in the ability of Western capitalism to bring about social justice where we live. We see no evidence of that possibility ... Whatever the Western democracies have done for themselves, they have failed and are failing, in their great power and influence, to do for us...[23]

Acknowledging the failures of Soviet-style communism, she nevertheless suggested that the essential challenge was 'to pick up the blood-dirtied, shamed cause of the left, and attempt to re-create it in accordance with what it was meant to be, not what sixty-five years of human power-perversion have made of it'.[24] This was the context in which she sought to elaborate her developing insights into the relationships between blacks and whites.

While a post-apartheid state could enforce a more equitable distribution of wealth through laws, she argued that the 'hierarchy of perception that white institutions and living habits implant throughout daily experience in every white, from childhood, can be changed only by whites themselves, from within'.[25] Gordimer identified with Desmond Tutu, whom she quoted as writing in April 1982:

> I am firmly non-racial and so welcome the participation of all, both black and white, in the struggle for the new South Africa ... But ... at this stage the leadership of the struggle must be firmly in black hands. They must determine what will be the priorities and the strategy of the struggle. Whites unfortunately have the habit of taking over and usurping the leadership and taking the crucial decisions—largely, I suppose, because of the head start they had in education and experience ... [H]owever much they want to identify with blacks it is an existential fact ... that they have not really been victims of this baneful oppression and exploitation ... and that must give blacks a primacy in determining the course and goal of the struggle. Whites must be willing to follow.[26]

In Gordimer's view this also meant that whites who supported the liberation struggle needed to go much further than previously:

Between black and white attitudes to struggle there stands the overheard remark of a young black woman: 'I break the law because I am alive'. We whites have still to thrust the spade under the roots of our lives; for most of us, including myself, struggle is still something that has a place. But for blacks it is everywhere or nowhere.[27]

By the late 1980s, with the establishment and rapid growth of the United Democratic Front (UDF), bringing together the ANC and a range of other anti-apartheid movements (but not the Black Consciousness movement), the impetus towards an inclusive, non-racial South Africa developed rapidly, particularly in the changing international context. In 1987 Gordimer became a founding member of, and active campaigner in, the Congress of South African Writers (COSAW), which was closely associated with this wider movement. By now she also accepted that she would be asked as much about South African politics as her literature, and claimed to be happy about this.[28]

One further crucial question needs to be considered: what was her attitude to violence? Her position on this was cautious and nuanced.[29] Clearly, she accepted the necessity for ANC violence in the circumstances, but her reluctance comes through in an interview she gave in 1982: 'I have the obstinate utopian notion—and I'm not alone in this—that we must try to achieve this revolution without the terrible bloodshed that has happened in other places. But whether one can do that or not, I don't know.'[30] In the same year, she also acknowledged that whites like herself have 'felt that we are doing all we can, short of violence—a terrible threshold none of us is willing to cross, though aware that all this may mean is that it will be left to blacks to do so.'[31] This was a pragmatic acceptance of violence as part of the current revolution and she also regarded the armed struggle by anti-apartheid forces primarily as a response to state brutality. But she did not view it with equanimity, perhaps expressing this most poignantly in her creative writing. Thus in *Burger's Daughter* she described the situation in Soweto as follows:

The school riots filled the hospital; the police who answered stones with machine-guns and patrolled Soweto firing revolvers at any street-corner group of people encountered, who ... picked off the targets of youngsters escaping in the stampede, also wounded anyone else who happened to be within the random of their fire. The hospital itself was threatened by a counter-surge of furious sorrow that roused the people of Soweto to burn and pillage everything the whites had 'given' in token for all, through three centuries, they had denied the blacks. The million or more ... residents of Soweto have no municipality of their own; a white official who had done what he could, within the white-run welfare system for blacks, to help them endure their lives, was stoned and kicked to death ... There was no way of identifying one's white face as one that was different from any other, one that should be spared.[32]

In an interview in 1986 she talked not only of the inevitability of the counter-violence, but also of the difference in the way in which atrocities against blacks and whites were treated:

At Christmas-time last year a bomb went off in a supermarket; a white child was killed and someone else was killed. There was a tremendous sense of shock over the death of one white child. The death of a child is tragic and terrible ... But the fact is, the death of that one white child shocked the white population more than the death of thousands of black children...[33]

In November 1988, when three activists were found guilty of treason and seven others of terrorism, Gordimer acted as a defence witness in a plea for the mitigation of their sentences. In court she accepted the necessity for the ANC's armed wing, Umkhonto we Sizwe (MK), as part of the ANC, declaring:

I am against violence but I can see that, in the circumstances brought about in South Africa by the intractability of the establishment to black aspirations, the time had to come when there had to be some sort of military wing ... I think we white people are responsible for it.[34]

Explaining that the ANC had tried all sorts of means between its formation in 1912 and its embrace of armed struggle in 1961, she continued: 'Basically it remains a non-violent organisation in the majority of its manifestations and actions.'[35]

After the end of apartheid, she clarified her views in a discussion of some newly released books by two former participants in the MK, Ronnie Kasrils and Carl Niehaus.[36] Both writers of the books were, she stated, 'declared terrorists by the apartheid regime and accepted as such by many people who were nominally against the regime; liberalism being the middle class of politics, where both the Underdog, revolution, and the Oppressor, the status quo, are equally condemned'.[37]

Gordimer distanced herself from this liberal perspective, but implied some qualms about aspects of the violence. She was relieved that Kasrils condemned the torture by ANC commanders in the detention camp in Tanzania of those believed to be government spies. But she also recognised that those who had lived comparatively comfortable lives could not fully understand the behaviour of those who had experienced terrible suffering at the hands of the South African government.[38] When the ANC was legalised in 1990 and there was supposedly free political activity, Kasrils defied a ban on a march, leading many unarmed protesters to be shot dead without warning by the police. Although he had risked his own life, some now labelled him foolhardy instead of courageous, leading Gordimer to ask:

> [H]ow much do we in South Africa know of the revolutionary personality which was formed by, arose in, and belongs to our society, its inheritance?

> Did we not, through failure to end apartheid by other means, send those people out through the barriers? While not, unlike Kasrils, ourselves baring our breasts to the bullets?[39]

Yet, despite admiring Kasrils's courage, she had greater empathy with Niehaus. Kasrils, she argued, although extremely intelligent, did 'not emerge with the self-doubts and inner conflicts of an intellectual'.[40] The testimony of Niehaus, by contrast, who came from a long-established Christian Afrikaner family, was 'essentially of the moral agony of being at the same time *both* "Us" and "Them"'.[41] Accepting that it was a 'just war', he committed himself to violence but always revealed anxieties—for example over whether cutting off electricity supplies might affect hospitals and intensive care units. But if Gordimer's sympathies lay particularly with Niehaus because of the inner conflicts she well understood, she had no doubt that both men had played an essential role. Speculating as to what they might have done in a peaceful situation, she concluded that, 'In their testimony we learn much of the nature of our society, our Age of Apartheid, which created these men in answer to a terrible, apocalyptic need.'[42]

Certainly, she was worried about some aspects of violence, including the practice of the 'necklacing' of suspected informers[43] and in private correspondence she had earlier expressed the hope that, if released from prison, Mandela would be able to control 'the wild young'.[44] Yet she did not question the use of violence against the apartheid state as a necessary part of the fight for justice.

Combining creative freedom and alignment

Although various different positions were taken within both the ANC and the SACP, by the 1970s there was widespread agreement that the apartheid system combined dual forms of class and race oppression, thereby also meaning that a transformation would necessitate the ending of capitalism and the introduction of a form of socialism.[45] Only in such circumstances, it was argued, could the overwhelming majority of black people overcome the combination of circumstances that had created a system of dual oppression based upon both class and 'race'. This was a Marxist conception of justice/injustice, reinforced by theories about historic ethnic supremacy arising from forms of imperialism and colonialism. As already noted, during the 1980s Gordimer expressed views that were quite close to this position, but it is not clear how comfortable she was, and she sometimes sought to distance herself from her own political writings:

> As a citizen, a South African actively opposed to racism all my life, and a supporter and now member of the African National Congress, in my *conduct*, and my *actions* I have submitted voluntarily and with self-respect to the discipline of the liberation movement. For my *fiction* I have claimed and practised my integrity to the free transformation of reality, in whatever forms and modes of expression I need. There, my commitment has been and is to make sense of life as I know it and observe and experience it. In my ventures into non-fiction, my occasional political essays, my political partisanship has no doubt shown bias, perhaps a selectivity of facts.[46]

The dichotomy that Gordimer sought to establish between her fiction and non-fiction could also be rather convenient in enabling her to take limited responsibility for her own political statements.[47] Perhaps she feared that these were sometimes too propagandist, but she expressed a political commitment and vision with great clarity and could not credibly dissociate herself from her statements. In 1982, she quoted a question posed by Camus: 'Is it possible ... to be in history while still referring to values which go beyond it?'[48] She wrote:

There are two absolutes in my life. One is that racism is evil ... and no compromises, as well as sacrifices, should be too great in the fight against it. The other is that a writer is a being in whose sensibility is fused what Lukács calls 'the duality of inwardness and outside world', and he must never be asked to sunder this union. The coexistence of these absolutes often seems irreconcilable within one life, for me. In another country, another time, they would present no conflict because they would operate in unrelated parts of existence; in South Africa now they have to be co-ordinates for which the coupling must be found. The morality of life and the morality of art have broken out of their categories in social flux. If you cannot reconcile them, they cannot be kept from one another's throats, within you.[49]

It was no longer enough, she argued, even to be a dissident because this would be to remain negatively within the dying white order. It was necessary to make a declaration 'positively as answerable to the order struggling to be born'.[50] And even this was only the beginning, for the white writer:

has to try to find a way to reconcile the irreconcilable within himself, establish himself, establish his relation to the culture of a new kind of posited community, non-racial but conceived with and led by blacks. I have entered into this commitment with trust and a sense of discovering reality, coming alive in a new way—I believe the novels and stories I have written in the last seven or eight years reflect this—for a South Africa in which white middle-class values and *mores* contradict realities has long become the unreality, to me. Yet I admit that I am, indeed, determined to find my place 'in history' while still referring as a writer to the values that are beyond history. I shall never give them up.[51]

Two years later, again referring to Camus, she took this a little further. In his notebooks he had stated, 'It is from the moment when I shall no longer be more than a writer that I shall cease to write', and Gordimer suggested that this meant that he accepted that the writer's greater responsibility was to society and not to art.[52] In South African conditions, she now argued, it followed that, 'whether a writer is black or white, the essential gesture by which he enters the brotherhood of man—which is the only definition of society that has any permanent validity—is a revolutionary gesture'.[53] The idea that she was seeking to express here was complex. On the one hand, she was surely saying that South African writers had a responsibility to align themselves in some way with the coming revolution. On the other hand, she was certainly not suggesting that artistic integrity should be subordinated to this goal and her concept of revolution was itself multidimensional. As she put it in an address to the PEN Congress two years later:

> The Writer ... knows that the only revolution is the permanent one—not in the Trotskyite sense, but in the sense of the imagination, in which no understanding is ever completed, but must keep breaking up and re-forming in different combinations if it is to spread and meet the terrible questions of human existence. [54]

She therefore still maintained that her freedom as a writer, in contrast to the role of a propagandist, meant showing 'human beings as they are, warts and all'. [55] And this also meant that she maintained a view that she had expressed earlier—that even the most politically engaged must be able to write their own 'truth' in their own way: 'Any government, any society—any vision of a future society—that has respect for its writers must set them as free as possible to write in their own various ways in their own choices of form and language, and according to their own discovery of truth'. [56] Turgenev, she suggested, expressed this best: 'without freedom in the widest sense of the word—in relation to oneself ... indeed, to one's people and one's history—a true artist is unthinkable; without that air it is impossible to breathe.' [57] To which she added her own last word: 'In that air alone, commitment and creative freedom become one'. [58] It was this combination that she sought to maintain in quite different ways in three powerful novels in the 1970s and early 1980s.

The first was *The Conservationist* (1974), a poetic and symbolic novel in which much of the text combines the memories and current thoughts of Mehring, the principal character, in a stream of consciousness in which the relationship between reality and imagination is not always clear. Mehring is a wealthy industrialist who has bought a farm after making money from pig iron. His life has revolved around power, possessions and exploitation, including the extreme sexual exploitation of women. Yet despite a wish to continue in this way, he is no longer in control of events. The body of a murdered unknown black man is found in his favourite part of the farm and this unsettles him, particularly after the police cannot be bothered to investigate the murder and simply bury the body where they find it. As Mehring thinks of his own life

in the shadow of this death, it becomes increasingly clear that nobody
and nothing is conforming to his will. His wife has left him and is now
living in the United States and, more recently, his liberal-minded mis-
tress, who opposes the apartheid system, has also abandoned him and
is in London. The farm is assuming increasing importance in his life and
in his notions about his heritage, but all this is also slipping away. He
thought that he was in control of his black farmworkers through
Jacobus, his foreman, but Jacobus has lived on the land throughout his
life and is really ascendant. Mehring has wanted his son, Terry, eventually to take over the farm and keep it for his own children, but Terry,
who is probably gay, is an opponent of the apartheid state and now
joins his mother in New York to evade military service. Finally, in disas-
ters with biblical overtones, the farm and land are destroyed by a
drought, followed by a flood. All this leads Mehring to feel that he is in
danger of annihilation himself and, whether in terror of his own fantasies arising from his guilt over past acts or whether he is actually
entrapped for breaking the apartheid law on interracial sex, he aban-
dons everything. Meanwhile, the floods have caused the body of the
murdered man to rise to the surface and Jacobus wants some money
for wood for a coffin for him. Mehring agrees to this in a phone call,
but is uninterested in details: 'He was leaving that day for one of those
countries white people go to, the whole world is theirs. He gave some
instructions over the phone; Jacobus must look after everything
nicely.'[59] Jacobus does so, with several other local black people, and the
book ends by referring to the murdered black man:

> The one whom the farm received had no name. He had no family but their
> women wept a little for him. There was no child of his present but their
> children were there to live after him. They had put him away to rest, at last;
> he had come back. He took possession of this earth, theirs; one of them.[60]

There is no explicit reference to injustice and justice in *The
Conservationist*, but these are embedded in the structures and relationships
of power and hierarchy that are depicted. The core of the book is surely
allegorical and represents the fragility and impermanence of the apartheid system, despite its apparent control. Mehring represents this by
embodying the system of racial and socioeconomic domination, while
the farm and land stand for South Africa itself, with Jacobus and the other
workers symbolising the continuity of the indigenous people. Mehring

seeks both to dominate others and to incorporate them, simultaneously convincing them and himself that this type of ownership will endure. But he cannot do so: he has lost his power over others and he cannot even maintain a coherent narrative to justify his position to himself. Gordimer herself stated that the novel had a disguised prophetic political message in the burial of the unknown man: though nameless and childless, he was surrounded by the children of other people around him—the future of those who stand for him. This, she explained, meant that he had taken possession of his own earth, with 'a suggestion of something that has been planted, that is going to grow again'.[61] This was thus a tale of redemption in which the unjust and unnatural order could not last, but would eventually be replaced by a new South Africa that would be controlled by the majority of the population.

A second example of this combination of commitment and creativity was in *Burger's Daughter* (1979). Here the central character, Rosa Burger, is the sole surviving child of two communists, both of whom are now dead. They had been wholly committed to the goal of a nonracial South Africa through the liberation struggle against the dual oppression of capitalism and apartheid, and believed that every sacrifice was necessary to bring this about. Rosa's childhood had been in this environment, necessitating frequent visits to one or other of her parents in jail—a deeply painful experience for her, as was the death of her brother. She is now left with this heritage and the question of whether she should continue it herself or live more comfortably in exile in Europe. She spends some time in Nice and soon has a French lover, Bernard, who persuades her to return to Paris with him. Before doing so she goes to London, where she meets Baasie, whom her parents had effectively adopted after his own father had died in prison. But although they had grown up together, Baasie now sees no role for whites in the black struggle for freedom and rejects her. She is devastated by this, but nevertheless makes the decision to abandon Bernard and return to South Africa. She works as a physiotherapist in Soweto and, following the extreme repression after the school students' uprising, she is detained in November 1977.[62] Her lawyer, who had also represented her father, anticipates that she will be charged with furthering the aims of the SACP and the ANC and of aiding and abetting the students' revolt.

The book is far richer than this summary of the surface plot. The narrative is conveyed through various 'voices', including Rosa's semi-conscious thoughts, and it contains extensive discussions of the political situation, including the reproduction of Bram Fischer's speeches in his trial, SACP documents, and the school students' manifesto from Soweto. By presenting Rosa's parents' communist beliefs with such empathy, Gordimer could be interpreted as endorsing their position (and the initial banning of the book was largely for this reason). Yet her stance was one of sympathy and understanding, rather than personal commitment to their position. Gordimer herself disavowed any suggestion that it was an endorsement, arguing that it was a book about commitment, which was 'not merely a political thing', but 'part of the whole ontological problem in life'.[63] However, it was far more aligned than this suggests. Despite the fact that Rosa has been ostracised by Baasie (representing the newly powerful Black Consciousness movement) and that returning to South Africa means abandoning Bernard, she takes this step. The book was not advocating a particular political approach, but Rosa returned to play her own part in continuing the fight for a just and non-racial South Africa. The injustice of the system was so persuasive that she had no real choice, despite the personal and political difficulties.

Finally, Gordimer struck a sombre note in *July's People* (1981).[64] Here a liberal white couple, the Smales, are forced to flee from Johannesburg, which has been taken over by black forces in a violent conflict. They go with their servant, July, to his native village, where they are dependent upon him and his family. While there, a subtle transformation of relationships of power takes place. July's resentment over his past treatment becomes clear and he assumes an increasing dominance, while the continuing white supremacist attitudes of Bam and Maureen Smales are also exposed. The atmosphere becomes increasingly menacing and in the final scene Maureen runs to make her escape in an unmarked helicopter. However, it is unclear who would be her 'friends' or 'enemies' in this new situation or whether she is being rescued or exposed to further danger. In fact, though, the fate of Maureen is probably less relevant than the atmosphere of foreboding and fear depicted in the general situation, and many interpreted the book as Gordimer's gloomy prophecy of what would happen with the

overthrow of apartheid. However, this was almost certainly a misinter-
pretation of its main theme, which was indicated by the quotation from
Gramsci at the beginning of the text about the 'morbid symptoms' of
the interregnum in which 'the old is dying and the new cannot be
born'.[65] This is surely the situation that she sought to portray, later
claiming that those who had seen it as a prophecy of South Africa after
a revolution were guilty of a kind of wish fulfilment born from their
fears of a takeover by blacks. It was, she said, a depiction of a time of
civil war.[66] Once again, the underlying theme was that the existing
system was so unjust that there was no doubt that it must, and would,
end. However, she was making no attempt to hide the fact that the
struggle against apartheid might become increasingly violent. The specific message of *July's People* was surely that the possibilities for the
creation of a reasonably tolerant post-apartheid regime would be
reduced the longer white liberals, like the Smales, avoided making a
genuine commitment to the revolutionary cause.

In these and several other books Gordimer was telling her own truth
about the urgent need to work for the downfall of apartheid—considered an absolute evil—while maintaining the hope that this would
preface the creation of a multi-racial and just society. This core idea,
based on ethical values, permeated her creative writing. Through this
and her speeches and political essays, she was contributing in her own
way to the end that she sought.

Transition and the new state

Apartheid was far more than a racist system of minority white rule
over the majority black population, and the dismantling of the measures that led to daily humiliation could not overcome the deeper levels
of injustice, which only more radical policies could address. This meant
that there was always a real danger that the transition would lead to
widespread disappointment, and several aspects of the situation exac-
erbated the problems. Above all, the transition did not follow from a
victory by the liberation movement, but from a change of regime that
was negotiated with the existing elites, who retained decisive elements
of power. In particular, the ANC accepted the continuation of the capitalist system, abandoning its previous commitment to a socialist econ-

omy, thus reassuring the dominant economic forces, both domestically and internationally.[67] It was equally apparent that there were powerful elements, particularly in the security sector, which were extremely reluctant to accept any change. This meant, for example, that they would certainly have attempted to undermine any settlement that sought to introduce trials and retributive justice on any major scale.[68]

A further important factor lay in the relationship between the ANC and the wider population. The political discourse had reflected the commitment to the establishment of a 'non-racial' society, which would welcome the white minority, but it hardly acknowledged the existence of divisions of class and identity within the black population. The reluctance of the recalcitrant elements within the apartheid state to yield power, their use of the Inkatha Freedom Party to incite Zulu violence against the ANC, and inter-community tensions within some of the townships amongst poor and dispossessed groups, exposed underlying problems that would continue in the longer term.[69] Finally, the Truth and Reconciliation Commission (TRC), which was a central element in the new government's strategy, was simultaneously both highly creative and a reflection of the constraints imposed upon the ANC by the nature of the transition.[70] It was far more ambitious than any previous such commission, both in its range and in its mission to build a new sense of national identity. However, its limitations also stemmed from the general conditions governing the change of regime. The TRC has thus been widely celebrated outside South Africa as a model for transitional justice, where acknowledgement of past injustices and reconciliation and rebuilding have prevailed over revenge and bitterness. However, within South Africa, and subsequently in wider research on transitional justice, considerable attention has also been paid to its weaknesses. In particular, it has been criticised for: concentrating on visible political violence rather than the deeper structural aspects of the apartheid system; focusing on individual atrocities rather than collective historical injustice; effectively insisting on 'forgiveness' rather than acknowledging understandable anger; and failing to address inter-communal conflicts amongst poor and marginalised groups in the townships, and the wider socioeconomic aspects of justice. However, unreasonable expectations were perhaps invested in the TRC, and Tutu himself argued that it was hoped that it would make a substantial contribution to national unity and reconciliation rather than fully to achieve these goals.[71]

'Hanging on a sunrise'

Nadine Gordimer was quite close to some of the ANC leaders, particularly in the early transition period, and was no doubt conscious of many of the problems. However, in general she adopted a very positive attitude. Once Mandela had been released from jail, her main preoccupation was that whites must accept the policies of the ANC as the basis for negotiations.[72] She continued to insist that violence, except by extremist white racist groups, was not based on hatred, but injustice and that so-called 'black on black' violence was also the product of apartheid.[73] She disagreed with those she termed 'subjectivists' who believed that a peaceful resolution of violent conflicts lay in a 'spiritual change of heart' and she argued that 'material justice' was the basis for the elimination of the kind of violence that had 'become a tragic habit' in South Africa.[74] She hoped that a new constitution and new laws to change the economic circumstances of the majority could bring about a situation in which healing could take place, but also emphasised that this required patience and tolerance.

When the first democratic elections took place in April 1994, her mood was one of joyful enthusiasm. She was assigned by her local ANC branch to monitor procedures at a polling booth and she described the experience as follows: 'If to be alive on this day was not Wordsworth's "very heaven" for those who have been crushed to the level of wretchedness by the decades of apartheid and the other structures of racism that preceded it, ... to be living at this hour has been extraordinary.'[75] Later that day she joined a party, and she recalled:

> I thought how what we were celebrating in the garden was the hope that the simple feast of life in peace and in justice before the law might be gained for all the people in that procession; that, at least, at last, 'They shall sit every man under his vine and under his fig-tree' (Micah 4.4).[76]

Despite her stress on the importance of social justice, in her non-fictional work she did not criticise the ANC for abandoning its earlier social and economic policies in return for the ceding of white political power. In 1995, she thus told the World Economic Forum: 'Mandela has done *everything* that foreign capitalists could wish for: reassured them on nationalisation, pushed ahead with privatising, avoided borrowing, been tough with trade unions—and still they are not investing in South Africa.'[77] Two years later she justified black South Africans 'climbing the corporate ladder', arguing that this was a way of pushing the frontier of black ownership in a system that still entrenched white economic power.[78] This evolution led one critic to argue that Gordimer, who had previously been a resistance writer, had become the 'state writer' of the ANC.[79] Certainly, she generally remained loyal to the new government, but it seems a little harsh to treat her as an apologist for the new regime. First, she continued to question whether capitalism could resolve the problems of South Africa. In 1999 she pointedly stated that black dignitaries in the professions, business, communications and arts seemed to favour the same kind of landscaped town house complexes with security services as the privileged whites, but also noted that some better housing was being built in old townships. She continued:

> This kind of levelling of material conditions is my primary criterion of justice in my country ... I know it could not possibly be brought about in five years, or ever can be completely achieved, on the evidence of the chasms between the life of rich and poor in developed capitalist countries that have declared themselves dedicated to it for several hundred years, and the failure of socialist countries (of socialism—so far in human history, but not for ever, in my belief) to avoid making freedom a prisoner of its own dictates. South Africa ... has had to choose pragmatically to be a hybrid: a mixed economy, with every bias it can afford towards making the legal equality, now achieved, meaningful in economic, material form for the impoverished majority.[80]

But, while she was no doubt sincere in continuing to maintain a commitment to a form of socialism, her real concerns had centred on the ambition to create a 'non-racial' South Africa and her broadly positive attitude to the transition was based on the hopes that this might be realised through the leadership of Mandela.

In 1994 she quoted the poetry of Mongane Wally Serote:

> One morning
> my people will hang on a sunrise ... we shall stand face to face with the sun ... leaving behind us

so many dead

. . .

we shall have buried apartheid—how shall we shake hands
how shall we hug each other that day? . . . What first words will we utter?[81]

This expressed her own sentiments in the year of South Africa's first
democratic elections: 'We are', she said, 'searching for those words.
Wounded, precarious; yet hanging on a sunrise'.[82]

Her enthusiasm for Mandela was hardly surprising and she was also
a keen supporter of the central elements in the new system of legal and
transitional justice. In 1995 she welcomed the abolition of the death
penalty, despite the fact that 80 per cent of whites and 49 per cent of
blacks had wanted to retain it: 'Those who kill will go to prison for life;
the state will not become a murderer'.[83] Crucially, she also welcomed
the establishment of the TRC as a route to reconciliation, which was
superior to the Nuremberg trials or Chile's blanket amnesty:

> It's going to be a process full of doubts and difficulties, both for the per-
> petrators of ghastly deeds and for the families of those they killed or
> maimed. But it is surely the way to deal with the past of a people who have
> to live with it, together; and a dedicated move towards making South
> Africa a human place to live in, today.[84]

And despite the criticisms that would be made of the TRC, she
defended it.[85] In 2006, in a warm tribute to Desmond Tutu, she saw
this as his supreme achievement to date, declaring that his own bold-
ness was never punitive and that he always had the power 'to make it
impossible for any group, any formation, any persons not to recognise
their responsibility for what they do to demean and brutalise others.'
She continued:

> Was this not the principle of the Commission? Its faith? It did not offer
> dispensation for confession but reconciliation with the victim by total
> public admittance of responsibility for terrible acts committed. A much
> more difficult attempt at resolution of crimes against humanity than a
> Nuremberg. The truth is harsh, shocking, terribly wonderful: Desmond
> has never accepted the evasion that truth is relative, for himself. At the
> Commission I understood that he extended that ultimate condition to
> our people and our country as the vital necessity for living together in
> survival of the past. The acceptance of that, he has taught, has to come
> from within.[86]

This general support for the principles and philosophy enunciated by Mandela and Tutu may have been a little uncritical, but it was surely both sincere and embedded in her fundamental loyalty to the ANC. Yet, once again, her creative insights in relation to the transition processes seemed to incorporate her more profound notion of 'truth'. Two of her novels in this period—*None to Accompany Me* (1994) and *The House Gun* (1998)—were particularly important in this context.

None to Accompany Me deals quite directly with the politics of the transition and was written between 1990–93, while the settlement was being negotiated. The central character is Vera Stark, a white activist lawyer whose main work has been to try to protect black people from forcible evictions from land designated for whites. Throughout the novel, Vera reflects on her own past in relation to the changes in South Africa. Her name, derived from the Latin 'veritas' (truth) and the German 'stark' (strong), may be intended to suggest that she is a powerful seeker of truth.[87]

However, for Gordimer such truth was always multi-dimensional and experienced in different ways. This is demonstrated through two other key characters, Didymus Maqoma and his wife, Sibongile—black revolutionaries who have recently returned after twenty years of exile. The novel is not simply a representation of the political transition, for it also explores gender relations, with both Didymus and Vera's husband, Ben, becoming secondary figures in relation to their wives, and it deals with class tensions within the black community. One of the key themes is the transformation of the ANC (though not named specifically) into a negotiating partner to end apartheid. Didymus had been a fighter for liberation who had 'interrogated' agents of the state who had infiltrated the opposition. Although he had eventually protested against the methods used to extract information, the ANC now wanted no association with torture and he was relegated to the background. Meanwhile Sibongile, who was attractive and charming, became a rising star of the movement, destined for eventual Cabinet office. Didymus is shocked when none of the new executive committee engage with the warning by an elderly veteran, who accepts the necessity of compromises made in the past, but then continues:

> [I]f we really want to serve our people, if we really want to convince them, in every hut and shack and hostel, if we want to convince them that when

they make their cross on a bit of paper in our first one-man-one-vote elections they really have the chance to be led by and represented by honesty, by men and women who are not seeking power to sleep in silken sheets, to grant themselves huge salaries, to take and give bribes, to embezzle and to cover up for others who steal, to disperse secret funds of public money buying contracts that are never to be fulfilled—if we're going to ask our people to put trust in a new constitution we have first to put our lives on the table to vow integrity, we have to swear publicly ... that we will not take up with power what the previous regime has taken.[88]

Without explicitly endorsing the critique, Gordimer lets it stand, already suggesting some critical distance from the ANC. But perhaps the most pervasive themes of the novel are the sense of continuing violence—Vera is shot and Sibongile receives a death threat—and uncertainty about the future. Ultimately, Vera becomes a member of the euphemistically termed 'technical committee' designed to reconcile divergent interests in a new Constitution. While sceptical of contemporary discourse and the power of politics to end ongoing cycles of violence, she believes that there is a purpose in attempting to break that cycle on the premise that the resolution will be justice 'even if it is renamed empowerment'.[89] But Gordimer's key point was to demonstrate the complex legacies from the past. The task was to try to put things right, in the awareness that 'it's all broken up' and 'it's some sort of historical process in reverse we're in. The future becomes undoing the past'.[90] There was no certainty that this would be achieved, and she was demonstrating the multifaceted nature of the liberation struggle—in line with her general wish to show flaws in both individuals and political movements.

Such themes are also present in *The House Gun* (1998), her first novel written entirely in the post-apartheid era. Here Gordimer revealed the complexity of her attitude to the transition, highlighting the interconnected themes of violence, justice and reconciliation, and the relationships between past, present and future.[91] The central characters are the white middle-class liberals, Harald and Claudia Lindgard, whose son, Duncan, has committed a murder, killing his former male lover after he slept with Duncan's girlfriend, Natalie, who is now pregnant. Duncan is represented by a black lawyer, Hamilton Motsamai, but is found guilty of the murder. In a perhaps conscious reference to Meursault in Camus's *The Outsider*, Gordimer highlights the fact that the judge notes that Duncan shows no remorse. Nevertheless, he benefits from the fact that the death penalty is abolished during the trial, and he is sentenced to seven years in jail. Through this work of fiction Gordimer deals with some key questions about the transition.

The TRC made a distinction between political and non-political violence, with only the former subject to the amnesty procedures. Many have questioned this restriction, arguing that it served the interests of the agents of the apartheid state and the ANC, while arbitrarily narrowing the definition of 'political violence' and failing to tackle the historical injustice and socioeconomic circumstances that made violence an endemic and continuing feature of South African society.[92] Gordimer was acutely aware of the depth and dimensions of continuing violence, but typically attention was subsequently paid to the so-called 'black-on-black' violence in the townships and in the 'taxi-wars'. She certainly saw this as part of the legacy of apartheid, but in *The House Gun* her focus was on the illusions of liberal whites, who sought to isolate themselves both mentally and physically from the brutality of the apartheid system and the pervasive effects of that violence. Thus both parents had taught their son the overwhelming value of life— Harald through religion and Claudia through humanism. Yet they had also moved to a gated community with security protection, and guns were easily available and ubiquitous. Their shallow liberalism, expressed in moral disapproval of the most overt features of the apartheid state, was thus quite insufficient to insulate them from its real impact and nature, as Duncan's murderous act revealed. But nor did their own behaviour conform to their professed beliefs. Claudia was a doctor, but kept herself aloof from the suffering of her patients. Harald had never thought about the death penalty until the decision of the ANC government to abolish it fortuitously spared the life of his own son, and both parents found it extremely difficult to accept their dependence on a black lawyer. Gordimer was thus simultaneously drawing attention both to the fact that liberal whites had benefited from the apartheid system while only opposing it superficially, and to their continuing reluctance to support the new regime. Yet her cautious optimism was also evident.

Duncan's refusal to express remorse at his trial may have shocked the judge, but this reflected Gordimer's own view that it was far too easy to make a formal apology that meant little and repaired nothing. On such grounds, she had refused to sign the 'Home for All' petition in which white people, as a kind of symbolic atonement, acknowledged the benefits that they had derived from apartheid, and she may also have thought that the TRC's own amnesty conditions were too lenient.[93] Duncan will not therefore apologise even to his parents for the murder he has committed. But his confinement in prison leads him to consider the future. Natalie's son may or may not be his but, once he gets out of prison, he can at least help him to make a reasonable life. There are several 'messages' here. The judge accepts that all are victims of the violent legacy of apartheid and gives Duncan a comparatively light sentence, noting that the gun 'happened to be there, on the table' and that 'this is the tragedy of our present time, a tragedy repeated daily, nightly, in this city, in our country.'[94] However, Gordimer was also suggesting that white South Africans must accept their responsibility for the past by building a better future. Because Duncan seems more able to accept Natalie's child than his parents are, she implies that a greater hope lies with the younger generation. Finally, there is an implicit warning to black professionals. Motsamai's enthusiasm for his new position is understandable, but should he not be building a wider community amongst the majority population, rather than emulating the wealth, power and prestige of the white elite and living in a gated community in a showy house? This encapsulated Gordimer's attitude to the transition: no shallow complacency about the difficulties, but a belief that, with a united effort, it might be possible to construct a non-racial future based on substantial justice for all. The TRC may have constituted an important element in this, but she also believed that justice transcended any legal or quasi-legal institutional processes and would depend upon both wider social structures and relationships.

There is one final sense in which both novels and her fictional writing in general added an important dimension to our understanding of transition that was lacking in the TRC.

Gordimer never doubted that the negotiated settlement with the previous regime and the political discourse of Mandela and Tutu were of central historical importance in creating the possibility of a relatively harmonious new 'rainbow nation'. She also wanted to contribute to this—partly by refraining from public criticism of ANC policies.

However, her observations of daily life and her creative imagination meant that she would never confuse rhetoric for reality and this was important in two respects. First, *The House Gun*, in particular, expressed the 'truth' that Tutu's insistence on forgiveness as necessary for a successful transition did not mean that this was, in fact, the prevailing emotion in the population as a whole, and this has been confirmed by empirical evidence.[95] Secondly, and more generally, the novels provided an important form of truth that was missing in the TRC. Because it was keen to acknowledge and value the horrific experiences of survivors of violence, the Commission adopted a complex concept of truth, emphasising individual stories in hearings and written evidence.[96] However, critics have made the important point that this kind of testimony can never provide a collective, structural account of the reality of apartheid, and that this deeper kind of historical truth was downplayed in the TRC in comparison with historical commissions in other countries.[97] Of course, Gordimer did not attempt to provide this kind of truth herself, but nor were her fictional depictions of life during the transition simply partial and individual. As in her literary oeuvre as a whole, they sought to encapsulate major features of wider social and political life through individual characters and their interactions with others. The social attitudes and gender and class relationships in both *None to Accompany Me* and *The House Gun* thus provide crucial insights into both the continuities and contrasts between the apartheid state and the embryonic new society.

Having dealt with issues of transition in both her fiction and non-fiction, Gordimer now wanted to move on, both by dealing with issues outside South Africa and by maintaining a comparatively low profile at home. Her next major novel, *The Pickup* (2001), was as much concerned with conditions in an unnamed Arab country as with South Africa, and she now often spoke and wrote about world literature.[98] She was irritated when people implied that the end of apartheid meant that South African authors would lose the focal point of their preoccupations and she no doubt hoped that it could now be treated as a 'normal' country. In general, she remained loyal to the new regime so that when, for example, she publicly criticised Thabo Mbeki's attitude to HIV/AIDs in 2000, she made it clear this was not a critique of the wider policies of the government.[99] The next year she was upset when

July's People was removed from the school curriculum by a panel of teachers in Gauteng on the grounds that it was 'deeply racist, sexist, patronising, one-sided and outdated'.[100] However, the education minister quickly reversed the decision and it was only after 2010, with the state assault on press freedom in the proposed Protection of State Information Bill, that Gordimer expressed a more wide-ranging attack on the system. Two years later she publicly stated that the 'rainbow nation' had been lost and that a non-racial South Africa based on equality had not been created.[101] In the same year, she told an interviewer that the problem in 1994 had been: 'We were naive, because we focused on removing the apartheid government and never thought deeply enough about what would follow.'[102]

This was the theme of her final novel, *No Time Like the Present* (2012), which was far more critical of contemporary South Africa than her previous works. The enduring problems of the society are reflected through the relationship between the central characters, a married couple, Steve Reed and Jabu Gumede. He is white, the son of a Christian father and secular Jewish mother, and she is from a Zulu family, the daughter of a headmaster and granddaughter of a Methodist pastor. Steve and Jabu had been active combatants in the armed resistance against apartheid, united in their commitment to the ANC. Yet although they had been in constant danger, their beliefs had not been challenged in the way that they are in the post-apartheid society. Gordimer depicts the multiple contemporary problems—pervasive inequality, new cleavages in class, ethnicity, gender and generation, environmental threats, violence against migrants—and exposes some of the superficial palliatives to deal with the legacies of apartheid in the legal and educational spheres. The novel also portrays Jacob Zuma and his close associates as corrupt populists who have betrayed the legacy of Mandela.

The depth of the book is in posing fundamental questions about how former ANC activists should respond to this political degeneration. Steve is tempted to abandon the attempt to seek change and instead to emigrate to Australia, but Jabu's roots in the society now seem much deeper than his and it is never clear that she and the children will join him. In fact, she is never forced to make the decision because Steve changes his mind and stays in South Africa. Gordimer seems to be suggesting that the forces that built the new state are just about maintaining a fragile unity, with her overall attitude expressed in an epigram she quotes from the poet Keorapetse Kgositsile:

> Though the present remains
> A dangerous place to live,
> Cynicism would be a reckless luxury.[103]

She was certainly disillusioned and now prepared to speak out and attack the post-apartheid regime, both in her fiction and non-fiction. Nevertheless, she maintained considerable loyalty to the ANC and the transition that had taken place.[104]

The moral outrage of a sceptic

Nadine Gordimer regarded creative writing as her vocation and the most fundamental part of her identity. But she also had passionate beliefs about justice and injustice, as expressed forcefully in two statements that have already been quoted: her declaration in 1965 that she had doubts about everything except that 'the colour-bar is wrong and utterly indefensible', and her insistence, seventeen years later, that 'racism is evil—human damnation in the Old Testament sense, and no compromises, as well as sacrifices, should be too great in the fight against it'. Throughout her long career, she sought to combine her commitment to free expression and artistic imagination with the political implications of her beliefs. She often feared that there was an irreconcilable tension between them and she had an ambivalent attitude towards her own political interventions, although these were sometimes very forceful and effective. Yet it was because of her equally deep convictions about both the value of literature and the evils of apartheid that she was able to convey her ideas about injustice so effectively through her fictional works.

Gordimer always insisted that, as a writer, the lives, emotions, relationships and interactions of people in society were her subject matter. In the South African context it was, she argued, impossible to represent these in a fictional form without also showing the way in which people's lives and possibilities were shaped by the apartheid system. She thus claimed that she was forced into a consideration of the political realm simply because of the impact of apartheid upon society and individuals. Yet this was not a sufficient explanation of the way in which she explored and exposed this impact. For it was her absolute moral rejection of the idea of racist hierarchy and domination that enabled her to depict its negative effects upon people's lives in all sections of South African society. Her underlying sense of moral outrage was embedded in the ways in which she showed the corrupting effects of the system on its beneficiaries, the daily humiliation and subjugation of its victims, and the futile vacillations and rationalisations of liberal reformers. She did this with little overt commentary, embedding her value judgments within the characters, relationships and structures that she depicted. Her ability to achieve this effect through her writing rested on her acute powers of observation and her artistic imagination. Just after her death, Ilse Wilson, the daughter of Bram Fischer, on whom Rosa in *Burger's Daughter* was based, provided an interesting insight into the way in which Gordimer did this.

Wilson recalled her first clear memory of Gordimer in 1960 during the State of Emergency, when she came to the women's prison to visit her friend, Bettie du Toit. Wilson, then aged sixteen, was there too, visiting her mother. She also remembered Gordimer subsequently sitting throughout her father's trial. More than a decade later, before the publication of *Burger's Daughter*, Gordimer sent Wilson the manuscript to read because she knew that people would make the connection to the family and thought she should see it first. But Gordimer also explained that 'she had specifically not wanted to get to know me better before the writing of the book, because it was a novel'.[105] This demonstrates the way in which she sought to understand the lives and thinking of the characters that inspired her fiction, but then deliberately re-cast them through her imagination. Wilson told her, when returning the manuscript, that Gordimer had 'captured the life that was ours' and, on her death, noted more generally that 'she had the extraordinary ability to describe a situation and capture the lives of people she was not necessarily a part of'.[106] She was also able to enter the mindset of characters with whom she had much less sympathy, such as Mehring in *The Conservationist*. Her fiction was so powerful in exposing and exploring the monstrous nature of apartheid because the characters and situations through which she exposed its injustices were so lifelike.

NADINE GORDIMER

Of course, her thinking evolved. Her earliest works embraced a liberal conception of justice, emphasising ideas of equal rights, non-discrimination and tolerance as her aspirations, and this then merged seamlessly into a belief in greater social justice. It was only from the mid-sixties onwards that the liberal approach, as represented by Liz in *The Late Bourgeois World*, was portrayed as futile. Subsequently, as in *The Conservationist* and *Burger's Daughter*, there was a much stronger sense of the absolute necessity to choose sides, and in *July's People*, a bleak message about the likelihood of an increasingly violent outcome if white liberals failed to join the revolution. During these years, Gordimer seemed partially to accept socialist and even Marxist conceptions of justice in her political essays, incorporating ideas about class, which also included notions about historic injustice based on colonialism. During the early stages of the transition, she emphasised the virtues of compromise, endorsed the TRC as a form of transitional justice, and provided a generally positive view about the prospects for the post-apartheid era.

Her aspirations at this time involved a transformation of the social, economic and historical structures that had created the system of apartheid: above all, she hoped that it would now be possible to create a single 'nation', rather than one that was marked by the separation of whites and blacks through the legacy of colonialism. Yet her transition novels, *None to Accompany Me* and *The House Gun*, were already more nuanced about the situation than many of her political statements. While certainly suggesting some optimism, both books also implied a necessity for caution as to whether the impact of the past could be overcome in the short-term. Her fiction did not seek to resolve the question of whether a 'rainbow nation' would be constructed or whether instead the whites (like the Lindgards in *The House Gun*) would refuse to recognise the transformation that had taken place and the new black political and economic elite (like Hamilton Mosamai in *The House Gun* and Sibongile Maqoma in *None to Accompany Me*) might be too inclined to seek the trappings of power and privilege. In fact, she did not believe that writers could provide answers: at best, they might have a long-term influence by making people think. However, she did believe that they could sometimes be prophetic and could appeal to the imagination. In this context, she cited Dorfman's play, *Death and the*

211

Maiden, as moving people in a way that reports of the South African TRC never could.[107]

Her fundamental interest was always in individuals and their personal and social relationships. Because she believed that people, political parties and society itself were all flawed, she never believed that a utopia could be created. From an idealistic point of view, this might have been a limitation, but it also gave her great openness and flexibility. She obviously knew—long before she spoke out—that post-apartheid South Africa was no 'new Jerusalem', but she had no doubt that it was incomparably better than the evil that had previously existed. Similarly, she did not like violence, greed or an obsession with power, but she did not expect them to cease to exist: in her view, they were part of the human condition. Perhaps because her aspirations for justice were never as elevated as those of Camus or Semprún in their most optimistic periods, she was also far less inclined to adopt the kind of moral absolutism that they did in their disappointment. She had no doubt that the fight against apartheid was just and she pragmatically accepted the necessity for violence, but she never believed that everyone in the liberation movement was 'pure' or heroic. Certainly she could have taken a more critical attitude in the early years of the transition, but her reluctance to speak out publicly is understandable and she continued to express some latent concerns in her creative writing. When she finally criticised the government openly in 2010 and in her final novel, *No Time Like the Present*, she was no longer jeopardising a period of transition. Rather, she was voicing her fears about the degeneration of a political movement that she still supported.

Nadine Gordimer remains a paradoxical figure. She was a rather unwilling contributor to the world of politics, but made a political contribution from her earliest writing. Ultimately, her passion about racist injustice, including its legacy in the post-apartheid era, was an integral part of her literature. Ngũgĩ wa Thiong'o recognised this in his warm obituary tribute: 'She remained true to her art but she also knew that the politics of struggle gave energy to her art; she was born on the other side of the colour line, but she built bridges across it. Speaking truth to power was the real power of her art.'[108]

8

MULTIDIMENSIONAL JUSTICE

This book has considered major political upheavals in six countries through the work of six authors. All the authors were committed to ending injustice and courageously pursued their beliefs in the hope of contributing in some way to the establishment of just societies. As they all lived through political transitions, it has also been possible to explore their evolving judgments and perceptions, which constitute important elements in situations of transformation. The study has taken an eclectic approach to the authors' writing, drawing on a variety of genres, including journalism, political commentary, autobiography and hybrid works, as well as novels, plays and films. For the works of the six authors transcend the normal distinctions between categories of writing, providing insights through various combinations of observation, reportage, analysis, empathy, narrative, drama and characterisation. Their creative writing has depicted the issues at the heart of this study with particular force, but even in their non-fictional works they provide vivid insights into the situations that they discuss because of the nature their writing. Camus's journalism thus highlights the fundamental ethical issues at stake for both the Resistance and the post-war regime; the memoirs of Serge, Ngũgĩ and Dorfman never simply recount their own histories, but recreate the meaning, motivation and atmosphere of their lives and struggles. Semprún's combination of autobiography, reflections and creative writing is so distinct that it has been aptly characterised as 'autofiction'. And, while Gordimer herself appeared to attach comparatively little importance to her essays, many of them conveyed the menace of apartheid and the aspirations for emancipation in a very compelling and imaginative way.

This chapter summarises the positions of the six authors on injustice and justice, including the main elements in the evolution of their thinking, before drawing out some general conclusions about their ideas. It then considers their attitudes to transition more specifically, and concludes with some final observations on their specific contribution to our understanding of the issues.

In Chapter One, six overlapping forms of justice were identified and discussed. Four of these—liberal, social, Marxist and legal justice— might be regarded as general notions, with application to any society. The other two—historical and transitional justice—have particular relevance in situations following acute collective traumas and the fall of repressive regimes. It was also suggested, following Amartya Sen and Eric Heinze, that the relationship between the concepts of justice and injustice is often over-simplified, and the discussion of the authors generally confirmed that they tended to be more motivated by a sense of injustice than a precise notion of justice. Nevertheless, the primary ways in which they understood injustice were rooted in their ideas about justice. Their conceptions of injustice also evolved, both in response to external events and because of shifts in their thinking. In no case, therefore, did an author begin with a clear conception of injustice under one regime and later simply compare the new one with a kind of 'check list' in order to evaluate progress or regression. This was partly because they were influenced by the changing social and political context, which brought new questions to the fore. But it was also because, as writers with a strong sense of commitment, they were constantly observing such changes and reflecting on their significance.

Each author was surely right, on general grounds of justice, to support the overthrow of the regime that initially moved them to this kind of political engagement: Tsarist Russia, Vichy France, colonial Kenya, Francoist Spain, Pinochet's Chile, and apartheid South Africa. But each author identified the fundamental nature of the injustice in a different way, and the regimes themselves differed considerably. When supporting the Bolsheviks, Serge was clear that the injustice of Tsarism had been the product of capitalism and could not be eradicated without a revolutionary overthrow of the whole system and the establishment of a completely new form of state. However, through observation of post-revolutionary developments and his own experiences, he came to accept the need for elements of legal justice and autonomous political institutions to curb the power of the dictatorship that had been created. The evolution of Camus was quite different. He entered the Resistance with a belief that the injustices of Nazism and the Vichy regime constituted an absolute evil that must be opposed by violence. However, after the Liberation his alienation from the atmosphere of retribution and revenge reinforced his earlier revulsion against capital punishment. This, coupled with his growing anti-communism, led to a shift in his whole conception of injustice, which he increasingly identified with a lack of freedom, and with violence and 'extreme' ideologies. Ngũgĩ's evolution, over a much longer period, was more complex. Initially he identified the primary injustice as colonialism and white power, but after independence he saw the continuation of similar forms of injustice and sought to explain this through the concept of 'neo-colonialism', stressing cultural domination as well as the more overt forms of economic and political repression. He now paid particular attention to historical injustice and the control of language and identity. Semprún also shifted from a relatively simple concept to a complex one. Initially, he saw Franco's regime as constituting injustice from a Spanish republican perspective and, from about 1942, viewed this through a Marxist lens. However, two traumas led to a very substantial change in his outlook. The first was his incarceration in Buchenwald and the second, two decades later, was his expulsion from the PCE and his break with communism. The combined impact of all this was his adoption of the view that both Nazism and communism constituted different forms of 'radical evil', which led to shifts in his perceptions of injustice. Dorfman's evolution was also marked by a shift from Marxism. During the Allende years, he emphasised the total injustice of the imperialist system, paying particular attention to the way in which this was transmitted through American popular culture. The coup in 1973, and the subsequent Pinochet dictatorship, represented total injustice for him, and he was particularly affected by the fate of the victims of the repression. In exile his position became more nuanced. He continued to regard the Chilean dictatorship as embodying extreme injustice, but his perspective transmuted into that of a human rights activist. There was some evolution in Gordimer's ideas too. She initially viewed apartheid, defined in terms of racist discrimination, as the embodiment of injustice in South Africa and hoped for the creation of a non-racial democratic regime through a negotiated change of government. But from the mid-1960s onwards she increasingly came to accept that racist discrimination was built into the economic and political structures of apartheid and that the injustice could not be defeated through liberalism. At least in the period up to the change of regime, she accepted the ANC theses on the colonial and class aspects of the regime and also the justification for the use of violence to dislodge the apartheid system.

Each writer explored the issues of justice and injustice in ways that transcended the tangible, concrete and material realms of much legal, historical and political analysis. Both in his novels and commentary, the approach of Camus was to encapsulate fundamental moral dilemmas through his depiction of characters in situations that required them to make essential choices and decisions. Serge focused on the ways in which existing literary forms, particularly the traditional novel, inculcated bourgeois values, both through subject matter and the idea of individuals and characters insulated from wider social and historical processes; and he sought to counteract this in his own writing. Here he projected a collective view, generally with working-class characters in quite different social settings—for example, a prison, a revolutionary struggle, and a labour camp. When attempting to counter the Stalinist autocracy, with its bureaucratic tentacles seeking overall control of all aspects of society, Serge also sought to highlight nature and spontaneity—the beauty of the landscape, or the enjoyment of old Bolsheviks throwing snowballs at each other. At the same time, he sought to recapture the kind of thinking that predated the closure of debate: his novels voiced the expression of diverse views about forms of revolution and strategic and tactical issues, emphasising the differing possibilities that Stalinist discourse eliminated. Both his fiction and non-fiction sought to depict a realm of freedom that was, or could be, autonomous from the monumental injustice of the Stalinist system. Gordimer, in contrast, showed the ways in which the separate communities, enforced by apartheid, moulded and controlled behaviour and beliefs within these boundaries. Much of her work demonstrated how these different life-styles fostered the beliefs of superiority and inferiority at the heart of the racist injustice. Several of the authors emphasised the cultural dimensions of injustice and these aspects were explored the most fully and explicitly in the work of Ngũgĩ, Dorfman and Semprún, who also highlighted memory and history in this context.

A common theme in much of Ngũgĩ's writing was the impact of the colonial appropriation of history and identity on poor, dispossessed indigenous peoples. Through the imposition of Christianity, Western literature, cultural images and a dominant European language, colonial rulers used these powerful forms of control to effect a general dispos-session of the native peoples of Kenya. While he also emphasised the economic, political and repressive dimensions of injustice, the most important element of Ngũgĩ's contribution in both fiction and non-fiction has been to insist that liberation can come only through 'decolo-nising the mind'. Countering injustice effectively depends upon an understanding of its true dimensions—an understanding that he has sought to promulgate in all the forms of his writing.

When he was a cultural adviser in the Allende government, Dorfman's views had many points of similarity with Ngũgĩ's, for he attached particular importance to the imperialist message in US popu-lar culture and he urged the necessity to provide alternatives in order to facilitate emancipation in Chile. His shift from Marxism led to a change in his discourse, but he maintained his absolute commitment to the role of culture, both in perpetuating injustice and in countering it. As Pinochet's regime became more entrenched, Dorfman feared that it was 'stealing the minds' of the population through the media and in its attempt to suppress dissident historical memory. Both his literary output and non-fiction were designed to sustain an alternative view-point during the years of exile.

Memory was also of crucial importance for Semprún. His view of the Francoist attempt to suppress the Left by erasing alternative memories of the Republic and controlling the historical account of the Civil War and dictatorship, had some striking similarities with the ideas of both Ngũgĩ and Dorfman. However, he also insisted that collective history must seek as much objectivity as possible and avoid substituting one set of myths for another, as he believed was the case with communist views of the past. As his position shifted, he increasingly viewed both the communist and Francoist attempts to control historical memory as closely linked to the injustices they had perpetrated. He believed that German society had achieved honesty about the past, which was also necessary in Spain if historical injustice was to be transcended.

What emerges from all these evolving perceptions and interpretations? The complexity of justice was already recognised in Chapter One, but consideration of the work of the six authors reinforces and amplifies this point. It also shows that it is misconceived to view injustice as either static or one-dimensional, and the attempt to eliminate a particular form of injustice can produce new forms of injustice. To argue in this way does not entail the entirely relativist view that all forms of injustice are equally pernicious or that each concept of justice is equally valid. But it does suggest the need for caution in allowing any one dimension to acquire absolute supremacy over all others: to assume that only one concept of justice matters or that the eradication of any single form of injustice will bring about a just society. This point may be illustrated with reference to the six authors' ideas of injustice.

Some of these conceptions of injustice emphasised structural aspects, and some were primarily about values. For example, in the immediate aftermath of the Bolshevik revolution, Serge appeared to accept that Marxist theory provided a full explanation for oppression. Another form of structural theory to explain overall injustice, though with a strong emphasis on its non-material dimensions, was evident in Ngũgĩ's explanation of neo-colonialism. In contrast, Camus and Semprún increasingly came to emphasise values that were largely detached from structural explanations of injustice. They were, in different ways, arguing that the injustice lay in, and was defined by, its manifestations in such forms as dishonesty, capital punishment, violence and vengeance. In my view, both structural exclusivity and value exclusivity fail to capture injustice as a multidimensional phenomenon. As Serge saw and experienced the excesses of Stalinist autocracy, he came to accept the need to counter-balance state power through elements of legal justice and liberal concepts of rights and constitutionalism. Similarly, after his imprisonment and exile, Ngũgĩ campaigned for the rights of prisoners and subsequently talked of the need for democracy in Kenya. In introducing these ideas, Serge and Ngũgĩ were in fact incorporating values from other traditions into their structural approaches, thereby recognising both injustice and justice as multidimensional. In contrast, while Camus and Semprún certainly espoused important values, these tended to become near absolutes, sometimes leading to a neglect of structural dimensions of injustice. True, both writers continued to believe that social inequality was a form of injustice, but this was subordinated to other concerns, for it was no longer central to their world outlooks. In different ways, however, both Dorfman and Gordimer avoided this kind of impasse, maintaining multidimensional conceptions.

As he abandoned Marxism, Dorfman certainly increasingly emphasised values rather than structures, but not in the 'absolute' way of Camus and Semprún. He had been attracted by elements of American New Left thinking even before he joined Allende's socialist project, and in exile he reverted to a similar position as a human rights activist. Certainly, the Pinochet dictatorship continued to occupy a central place in his thinking and emotions, but he also came to see injustice in several other spheres, including violations of human and civil rights, ecological threats, expansionist wars, gender inequality and the massive disparities between the Global North and South. Because of his passionate wish to honour 'the memory of the dead', he was able to make an important contribution by identifying a particular kind of injustice that needed to be rectified after the collapse of the dictatorship. But this did not mean that he regarded the addressing of past atrocities as the only important question, either in Chile or more generally, and his outlook on justice and injustice remained multidimensional. Gordimer's constructive role was different, perhaps because she maintained one crucially important value in a consistent way while adopting a generally sceptical attitude to politics and society. Her core value was in the equality of all peoples, which was the basis for her insistence on the necessity to abolish apartheid, it being the epitome of injustice. She consistently exposed the iniquity and inhumanity of this system, but she maintained a multidimensional conception of justice and injustice because she never allowed her core value to become abstracted from social, political and historical realities.

Taken overall, this exploration of the work of the six authors has added layers of non-material aspects to the six concepts of justice discussed earlier by focusing on the spheres of culture, memory and societal trauma. Similarly, it has uncovered aspects of injustice that go beyond visible, physical oppression or even economic and social exploitation. But the authors also help us to think of justice and injustice less in terms of enumerating their facets than in recognising that both are multidimensional and constantly evolving.

Having discussed the authors' ideas of injustice and justice generally, let us turn to the more specific question of transition. In Chapter One, it was argued that the original concept of transitional justice was over-simplified and ideologically skewed towards the idea of a transition from dictatorship to liberal-democracy. It was, however, also suggested that the focus on the need for new regimes to address past atrocities is important and that the notion of transitional justice is helpful when used in a flexible and critical way. This has been confirmed by the exploration of the thinking of the authors.

Of the six cases, only the aftermath of the Bolshevik conquest of power in 1917 constituted a revolutionary transformation in the sense that there was an attempt to bring about a complete reconstruction of economic, political, social, legal and cultural life. While each transition was distinct, Serge experienced problems that were quantitatively and qualitatively different from every other case. In 1919 he believed that the revolution was wholly justified and that it must be defended and advanced by all available means; by the mid-twenties he feared that it was going in the wrong direction; and during the 1930s he was convinced that Stalin was establishing a new system of monumental injustice. The fundamental questions for him were: when and why had the promise of justice been turned on its head; what should and could have been done differently; and what lessons might all this hold for future attempts to establish socialism? Serge faced enormous difficulties in seeking to understand and analyse the on-going barbarism while reaffirming key elements in his initial beliefs, and his thinking was embedded in the historical specificities of the Russian Revolution and subsequent Stalinist dictatorship. Nevertheless, he came to accept the need for the following: legal justice, including the abolition of capital punishment, rather than arbitrary judgment; political pluralism rather than autocracy; conciliation rather than constant violence; and acceptance of an autonomous sphere of civil society, rather than control from above. These crucial lessons about guarding against new injustices were the result of living through Stalinism and lie outside the conventional paradigm of transitional justice. But Serge provided powerful warnings about the necessity for a multidimensional approach to justice in revolutionary transitions.

The other five authors were confronting and experiencing situations in which there were compromises of various kinds during the transition, but they exhibited a wide range of reactions. Camus took a position that was not at all typical for a left-inclined intellectual who had been committed to the Resistance. For he neither explicitly supported nor condemned the compromises taken in relation to the socialist position that he had previously advocated. Instead he concentrated on the purge and capital punishment, coming to regard the implementation of these measures as totally unjust, and he moved towards a preference for conciliation. These convictions then dominated his attitude to the transition and played a major role in his subsequent political evolution. The conclusions that he drew from this aspect of the transition may have been excessive, but it was living through the many instances of injustice in the trials and purges that enabled Camus to make important points about the disadvantages and dangers of this form of retribution. Though only embryonic, his ideas foreshadowed the direction that would be taken later by many advocates of transitional justice.

Such issues were also important for Dorfman. He understood the main parameters of the transition in Chile, chafing at the extent to which democracy was constrained by the continuing power of Pinochet, and questioning whether it had been necessary to make as many concessions to him as were made. He was also unhappy about the way in which the seventeen years of dictatorship had pushed the country back towards conservatism and Catholicism, fearing that there was too much passivity at the time of the transition. However, the key issues for him were recognition of, and justice for, the survivors and victims of the dictatorship. Like Camus, he too opposed revenge and the death penalty, but he saw the shallowness of reconciliation unless it addressed the issue of accountability for past human rights violations. Given his passion on the subject and his view of the importance of culture, it is therefore not surprising that he wrote *Death and the Maiden* in the hope that the play could help to counter the attempt to bury the 'memory of the dead'. In fact it failed to do so because circumstances were not propitious in the immediate aftermath of the dictatorship. Yet after the detention of Pinochet in London in 1998, Chile gradually took steps in the direction that Dorfman had foreshadowed. And his attitude to this kind of transitional justice has a wider relevance. Addressing the crimes of former repressive regimes certainly does not mean the end of injustices. Nor is this always possible immediately, and it may not suit all cultures and circumstances. But in many transitions an appropriate way of recognising past atrocities surely makes a contribution to building a new society. In recent years, detailed attention has been paid to the many forms in which the violations of the previous regime may be addressed, but Dorfman certainly identified the general principles and problems particularly forcefully.

In partial contrast, Semprún accepted the initial failure to confront the past in Spain during the transition. He was well aware that the terms of the negotiated transfer of power offered great continuity to the economic, political, judicial and military elites, but he believed that compromise was necessary in order to guarantee the establishment of democracy because the transition was fragile. He accepted centre-right leadership in the process and also later welcomed the 'modernisation' agenda of the PSOE under Gonzales, knowing that this meant the abandonment of socialism. The stabilisation of the new regime was his main priority. This was a widely shared viewpoint and was also in line with the shift in Semprún's thinking from the mid-1960s onwards, but the attitude that he took towards the amnesty was particularly significant. On the one hand, support for it was so overwhelming and so crucial in terms of securing right-wing support for the transition that his commitment to it might be expected. It is also true that, even while in the PCE, he had favoured reconciliation between the former Civil War enemies, particularly amongst the younger generation, and he saw the amnesty as a means of containing an eruption of bitterness about the past and providing conditions in which new social and political relationships might be established. On the other hand, amnesia was the antithesis of historical memory, to which he attached so much importance. There were therefore no doubt contradictions in his own mind about the relationship between amnesty and amnesia long before he tentatively approached Gonzales on the issue as minister of culture in the PSOE government. His position was that it was right to maintain the amnesty, but that a precondition for full democracy in Spain was recognition of the fact that the Republic had embodied the values and goals of the new regime. He believed that historical justice involved recognition of the crimes committed by the Francoists, but that this should be brought about without bitterness or vengeance. In other words, his position was very close to that eventually adopted in the Historical Memory Law. Semprún's arguments also raise questions of wider relevance about transitions. Because of his anti-communism he paid too little attention to questions about social justice and inequality, but it is striking that he was convinced of the necessity to wait for some years before addressing history. Whether or not he was justified in accepting amnesia for so long, his thinking serves as a valuable corrective to those who argue or assume that whenever a civil war ends or a repressive regime collapses, one of the first tasks must always be to confront the past.

The concerns of transitional justice were less central for Ngũgĩ and Gordimer. Ngũgĩ was totally opposed to the way in which Kenyatta (and later Moi) drew a veil over the past, including any recognition of or discussion about the role of Mau Mau. But he did not elaborate on how past atrocities should be addressed, either at the time of transition or when the question was re-activated in the twenty-first century.

Gordimer's position was different, for she fully supported the Truth and Reconciliation Commission as part of the transition. She was convinced that this would be far more humane than trials on the Nuremberg pattern, and she paid a special tribute to Desmond Tutu for his role. She also agreed with the abolition of capital punishment. However, she was not forced to consider these questions in any depth, as she readily supported the decisions that had been made. Nevertheless, Gordimer's attitude to the transition in South Africa certainly raises wider questions. Like Semprún, she was worried about the vulnerability of the new democracy. However, while the Spanish transition depended upon the construction of a new coalition, the South African one effectively involved a transfer of political rule to a dominant party, and this was potentially problematic for Gordimer. She had great loyalty to the ANC and its leading personnel, and probably also accepted, on pragmatic grounds, the need for its hegemony in order to bring about such a major transformation. Yet there was evidence that the ANC was exacerbating inequality and stifling internal dissent within the party long before she spoke out against Mbeki's policies on HIV/AIDS in 2000, and the degeneration was very marked when she finally denounced the clampdown on the freedom of the press in 2010.[1] Gordimer's restraint throughout this period was no doubt partly because she did not want to appear to align herself with right-wing white critics of the regime and jeopardise the creation of a 'rainbow nation'. She also continued to exhibit greater scepticism in her fiction than in her political statements. Nevertheless, her position illustrates a more general question about the extent to which loyalty to a particular party or state should supersede a commitment to liberal, legal and social justice. Eventually, she decided that it should not do so, but her dilemma highlights the enduring contradictions that so often exist between political loyalty and the pursuit of justice.

The issues raised by Ngũgĩ were quite different. He initially regarded white colonial power as the overwhelming question about justice, but the main focus of his loyalty was always to the poor, indigenous communities of Kenya. He quickly became sceptical about the extent to which these concerns were genuinely shared by Kenyatta, and later denounced the whole nature of the post-colonial regime. In effect, he therefore soon held that there had not been a transition at all: there was a change in the skin colour of the local rulers, but the fundamental nature and causes of the injustices remained, with neo-colonialism a new incarnation of colonialism. He thus differed quite substantially from Camus, Dorfman, Semprún and Gordimer, all of whom believed that a genuine change had taken place, even if, to various extents, they remained critical of its limitations. In this respect Ngũgĩ was far closer to Serge, for both emphasised betrayal as the main feature of the situation. For Serge this lay in the fact that the revolution had created the horrors of Stalinism rather than true socialism, while for Ngũgĩ it was because the ending of British colonial rule had led to a new form of arbitrary, repressive dictatorship, rather than genuine self-rule, with a path out of poverty and inequality. There was similarity too in that both attempted to give voice to theories and values demonstrating alternative paths to justice, without being able to point to the political agency that might implement them in practice. This also has a much wider relevance.

If, then, we consider the positions of all six authors, it is evident that each transition led to specific concerns, partly as a result of their own varied outlooks, but also because of the diverse historical situations that they experienced. Only Camus and Dorfman were preoccupied with issues that lie at the heart of transitional justice, with the main emphasis of the other authors being on other aspects of the evolution to a new regime. This leads to more general conclusion. There are, in my view, good normative reasons for preferring reconciliation to retribution and for advocating a reparative approach to addressing atrocities committed by the repressive agents of a deposed regime. Yet such ideas must surely grow organically in each society and, even when they do, they are only an element both in multidimensional justice and in the policies that may be necessary to effect a satisfactory transition.

This exploration of the lives and work of the six authors has confirmed and amplified Chapter One's observations about the complexity of the concepts of injustice, justice and transition, and the relations between them. Each author has illuminated key questions with reference to a particular country, but their collective insights have relevance for numerous other cases. Of course, their work is no substitute for academic studies. They were not theorists who formulated clear principles underlying their concepts of justice and injustice, or historians who explained specific national evolutions in depth, or social scientists who aspired to derive reliable generalisations from their analyses of several transitions. When the six authors approach political and social issues, their analyses may sometimes mirror those of others but, particularly in their fiction, they also provide a different perspective specifically because they depict and encapsulate collective situations through the subjective sphere, the lived experiences of individuals and groups, and their own creative imaginations. Two contemporary authors have recently pinpointed this power of fiction particularly well.

In a recent essay Aminatta Forna wrote:

> A novel is a work of imagination, it is not a dissertation. When a writer writes a book, he or she makes a pact with the reader. For a writer of non-fiction the contract is clear. The author pertains to objectivity. The reader may rely on the facts contained therein, the writer promises (to the best of their ability) to provide a factual truth. A writer of fiction makes no such promises. Fiction is subjective: it comes from within the writer, and not only

that, the story itself is composed of a sequence of lies. The writer of fiction says to the reader only this: come with me on a journey of the imagination and I will try to show you something you have not seen before.[2]

And yet, as Chimamanda Ngozi Adichie has argued, some works of literature can make a crucial contribution to understanding the world. Such fiction, she explains, is not the same as the real world, but 'close enough, alive enough, to illuminate it'. It 'seeks to infuse the world with meaning' and 'is the process of turning facts into truth'. She had thus known the facts of Nigerian history before reading Chinua Achebe's *Things Fall Apart* and *Arrow of God*, but it was from these books that she learnt the truth.[3] Such literature was a search for humanity, involving a leap of imagination that brought about a co-existence between grim facts about the world and human stories. Stories could also uncover the losses brought about by unjust governments, such as colonial rule, which go far beyond those that can be measured in concrete ways. Logic, she suggested, could convince, but it is the emotions that lead us to act and it is in this realm that we are moved by literature.

Both Forna and Adichie have written novels that illuminate brutal and tragic situations by 'a sequence of lies' that turn 'facts into truth'.[4] The paradoxes that they highlight about fiction apply to the six authors, all of whom expose injustice, justice and transition through their creative writing. Furthermore, they raise matters of universal significance, while apparently concentrating on particular countries and situations, and this too is a feature of literature.[5] These writers have attempted to open their readers' minds in ways that provoke further questions. It is hoped that, by highlighting their ideas, this book will also carry some of the major debates about injustice, justice and transition beyond the rather esoteric circles to which they are often confined.

NOTES

1. LITERATURE, JUSTICE AND TRANSITION

1. Hardi, Choman in 'How Literature can respond to the past', broadcast on BBC Radio 4, *Open Book*, 11 May 2014, http://www.bbc.co.uk/programmes/b042z66b (last accessed Feb. 2015).
2. Tabucchi, Antonio, *Pereira Maintains*, Edinburgh: Canongate Books, 2010, p. 25.
3. Full biographical detail and references will be provided in the individual chapters.
4. Dorfman, Ariel, *Death and the Maiden*, London: Nick Hern books, 1991, revised edition 1994.
5. Interview with Stephen Sackur, BBC World News, Hard Talk, first shown 13 May 2011 and re-broadcast, 15 July 2014 http://www.bbc.co.uk/iplayer/episode/b0112dnf/hardtalk-nadine-gordimer-south-african-writer (last accessed Feb. 2015).
6. Quoted in Allott, Miriam, *Novelists on the Novel*, London: Routledge and Kegan Paul, 1959, p. 99.
7. Sartre, Jean-Paul, *What is Literature?* New York: Philosophical Library, 1949, p. 25. (Originally published as *Qu'est-ce que la littérature?* Paris: Gallimard, 1948).
8. Howe, Irving, *Politics and the Novel*, London: Stevens and Sons, 1961, pp. 203–5.
9. Soueif, Ahdaf, *Cairo: Memoir of a City Transformed*, London: Bloomsbury, 2014.
10. Allott, *Novelists*, pp. 103, 99, 102, 98, 104.
11. Conolly, Oliver and Bashshar Hayder, 'Literature, Politics, and Character', *Philosophy and Literature*, 32 (2008), p. 100; Octavio Paz, quoted in van Delden, Maarten and Yvon Grenier, *Gunshots at the Fiesta, Literature and Politics in Latin America*, Nashville: Vanderbilt University Press, 2009, p. 239.

12. Sartre, *What is Literature?*, p. 10.
13. Ibid., p. 62.
14. Allott, *Novelists*, p. 92.
15. Van Delden and Grenier, *Gunshots*, p. 9.
16. Ibid., p. 12.
17. Orwell, George, 'Why I Write', in *The Collected Essays, Journalism and Letters of George Orwell, Vol. 1 An Age Like This, 1920–1940*, Harmondsworth: Penguin, 1979, pp. 28–9. (Originally published in *Gangrel* 4, Summer 1946).
18. Shehadeh, Raja, *Palestinian Walks: Notes on a Vanishing Landscape*, London, Profile Books, 2nd edition, 2008, pp. 154–5; 171–2.
19. *The Devil that Danced on the Water: A Daughter's Memoir of Her Father, Her Family, Her Country and a Continent*, London: Harper Collins, 2002; *The Memory of Love*, London: Bloomsbury 2010.
20. Wolf, Christa, *Parting from Phantoms: Selected Writings, 1990–1994*, Chicago: University of Chicago Press, 1997, p. 122. Wolf had already been attacked for delaying until 1990 the publication of her short novel, *What Remains*, which depicted the intimidating surveillance of a writer in East Germany, although she had written it in 1979 (*What Remains and other Stories*, London: Virago, 1993); she was soon to be excoriated when it was discovered that she had briefly informed the Stasi about other writers between 1959 and 1962. Günter Grass, who believed that Wolf should have expressed clearer and stronger criticism of the party in the GDR, nevertheless told her on 9 February 1993 that this was 'recognizably an attempt to use this episode … to discredit the critical attitude which you demonstrated over decades, and to discredit your literary work along with it'. Ibid., pp. 207–10.
21. Marchant, Peter, Judith Kitchen, and Sanvel Rubin, 'A Voice from a Troubled Land: A Conversation with Nadine Gordimer' in Bazin, Nancy Topping and Marilyn Dallman Seymour (eds), *Conversations with Nadine Gordimer*, Jackson, Mississippi: University Press of Mississippi, 1990, p. 260.
22. There is clearly a potential problem when we are not sure how to read the author and what kind of truth is being depicted. This has arisen in an acute form in recent years with a form of writing specifically concerned with issues of justice and injustice known as the *testimonio*, particularly in Latin America. In this case testimonies about extreme injustice that were generally taken to be historically true have subsequently been disputed, leading to claims, counter-claims and controversies. The controversy was triggered particularly with the *testimonio* of Rigoberta Menchú who, in 1982 narrated a book about her life to Elizabeth Burgos, *Me llamo Rigoberta Menchú y así me nació la conciencia* (translated as *I, Rigoberta Menchú: An*

Indian Woman in Guatemala (New York and London: Verso, 1984). She received the Nobel Peace Prize in 1992, but subsequently an anthropologist cast doubts on aspects of the book's authenticity (Stoll, David, *Rigoberta Menchú and the Story of all Poor Guatemalans*, Boulder, Colorado: Westview Press, 1999). Stoll approved of her Nobel Prize and thought that her story enabled her to focus international attention on the Guatemalan army, which deserved condemnation, but he believed that that she gave a misleading interpretation of the relationship of the Mayan peasants to the revolutionary movement. A further issue is that when the words of the *testimonio* are heavily edited and re-structured by an editor, the 'literary truth' or authenticity of the text may be compromised. On the controversy itself, see Grandin, Greg, 'It Was Heaven That They Burned: Who is Rigoberta Menchú?', *The Nation*, 27 Sept. 2010, http://www.thenation.com/article/154582/it-was-heaven-they-burned (last accessed Feb. 2015) For discussions of the wider issues about this form of literature, see Nance, Kimberly A., *Can Literature Promote Justice? Trauma Narrative and Social Action in Latin American* Testimonio, Nashville: Vanderbilt University Press, 2006.

23. Sen, Amartya, *The Idea of Justice*, London: Penguin Books, 2010.

24. Heinze, Eric, *The Concept of Injustice*, Abingdon, Oxon. and New York: Routledge, 2013.

25. Galston, William A., 'Liberalism' in Gibbons, Michael T. (ed.), *Encyclopedia of Political Thought*, Hoboken, New Jersey: John Wiley & Sons, 2015, p. 2150.

26. Nozick, Robert, *Anarchy, State, and Utopia*, New York: Basic Books, 1974.

27. Rawls, John, *A Theory of Justice*, Cambridge, MA: Harvard University Press, 1971.

28. Kelly, Paul, *Liberalism*, Cambridge: Polity, 2004.

29. Hudson, Barbara, *Justice in the Risk Society: Challenging and Re-Affirming 'Justice' in Late Modernity*, London: Sage, 2004, p. 38.

30. Jackson, Ben, 'The Conceptual History of Social Justice', *Political Studies Review*, 3, (2005), pp. 356–73.

31. Rawls, *Theory of Justice*; Sen, *Idea of Justice*; Sandel, Michael, J., *Justice: What's the right thing to do?*, New York: Farrar, Straus and Giroux, 2010.

32. United Nations, *Social Justice in an Open World: The Role of the United Nations*, New York: United Nations, Department of Economic Social Affairs, The International Forum for Social Development, 2006, p. 2.

33. Ibid., p. 3. However, David Miller, one of the major theorists of social justice, has stressed the nation-state as the necessary political framework for social justice. Miller, David, *On Nationality*, Oxford: Oxford University Press, 1995; and *Principles of Social Justice*, Cambridge, MA.: Harvard University Press, 1999.

34. Ibid., pp. 6–10.
35. Fraser, Nancy, 'Rethinking Recognition', *New Left Review* 3, May/June, 2000.
36. Newman, Ines, *Reclaiming Local Democracy: A Progressive Future for Local Government*, Bristol: Policy Press, 2014, pp. 90–1, citing Fraser, Nancy, 'Recognition and multiculturalism', Multicultural Bites, Open University, http://itunes.apple.com/us/itunes-u/multiculturalism-bites-audio/id449122394?mt=10 (last accessed, Feb. 2015).
37. Wilson, E. and J. Piper, *Spatial planning and Climate Change*, London: Routledge, 2010, cited in Newman, *Reclaiming Local Democracy*, pp. 97–8; *Social Justice in an OpenWorld*, pp. 6–10.
38. For a succinct discussion of the debate, which concludes that Marx did not have a theory of justice, see Lukes, Steven, *Marxism and Morality*, Oxford: Clarendon Press, 1985, pp. 48–59.
39. For this argument, see Wood, Allen W., 'Justice and Class Interests', *Philosophica* 33, 1 (1984), pp. 9–32; Geras, Norman, 'The Controversy about Marx and Justice', *New Left Review* 150, Mar/Apr. 1985, pp. 49–55.
40. Ibid., pp. 55–6
41. Ibid., pp. 62–85.
42. Quoted in Luban, D. J., 'Justice and Law', Smelser, Neil J. and Paul B. Baltes, (eds), *International Encyclopedia of the Social and Behavioral Sciences*, Vol. 12, Oxford: Elsevier, 2001, p. 8043.
43. Caputo, John D., *Deconstruction in a Nutshell. A Conversation with Jacques Derrida*, New York: Fordham University Press, 1997, pp. 16–17, quoted in Moosa, Ebrahim, 'Truth and Reconciliation as performance: spectres of Eucharistic redemption', in Villa-Vicencio, Charles and Wilhelm Werwoerd (eds), *Looking Back, Reaching Forward: Reflections on the Truth and Reconciliation Commission of South Africa*, Cape Town: University of Cape Town Press, 2000, p. 119.
44. Mani, Rama *Beyond Retribution: Seeking Justice in the Shadows of War*, Cambridge: Polity, 2002, pp. 55–86.
45. West, Robin, 'Re-Imagining Justice', *Yale Journal of Law and Feminism* 333 (2003), Georgetown Public Law and Legal Theory Research Paper No. 11–107, http://scholarship.law.georgetown.edu/facpub/685 (last accessed Feb. 2015).
46. Luban, 'Justice and Law' in Smelser and Baltes (eds), *International Encyclopedia*, pp. 8047–48.
47. Fuller, L. L., *The Morality of Law*, New Haven, Ct: Yale University Press, 1969, summarised in ibid., p. 8044.
48. Gordimer, Nadine, *Burger's Daughter*, Harmondsworth: Penguin, 1979.
49. Ivison, Duncan, 'Historical Injustice', in Dryzek, Jon, Bonnie Honnig, Anne Phillips (eds), *Oxford Handbook to Political Theory*, Oxford: Oxford

University Press, 2006; Herstein, Ori J., 'Historic Injustice, Group Membership and Harm to Individuals: Defending Claims for Historic Justice from the Non-Identity Problem', *Harvard BlackLetter Law Journal*, 25 (2009); Marrus, Michael R., 'Official Apologies and the Quest for Historical Justice', *Journal of Human Rights*, 6, 1 (2007).

50. The *Nakba* (or 'catastrophe') refers to the expulsion and displacement of Palestinian Arabs from their homes with the creation of Israel and the 1948 Arab-Israeli war.

51. Berg, Manfred and Bernd Schaefer, *Introduction* in Berg, Manfred and Bernd Schaefer (eds), *Historical Justice in International Perspective: How Societies are Trying to Right the Wrongs of the Past*, Cambridge: Cambridge University Press, 2008, pp. 2–3.

52. International Center for Transitional Justice (ICTJ), 'What is Transitional Justice?', http://ictj.org/about/transitional-justice (last accessed Feb. 2015).

53. Ibid.

54. The term originated in relation to the collapse of dictatorships, particularly in Latin America, and was subsequently applied more broadly in relation to peacebuilding following violent conflicts and external interventions. In this book the original context remains more relevant.

55. Arthur, Paige, 'How "Transitions" Reshaped Human Rights: A Conceptual History of Transitional Justice', *Human Rights Quarterly*, 31, 2 (May 2009).

56. The periodical, *International Journal of Transitional Justice*, established in 2007, has always included several articles that have contested many of the normative assumptions underlying the original framework and Vol. 2, 3 in December 2008 was a special issue on 'Transitional Justice and Development'. There are also various organisations that have emphasised such perspectives, including *FriEnt*, a German Working Group on Peace and Development, the Centre for the Study of Violence and Reconciliation in South Africa, and *Centro de Estudios Legales y Sociales* in Argentina.

57. Andrieu, Kora, 'Transitional Justice: A New Discipline in Human Rights', *Online Encyclopedia of Mass Violence*, Jan. 2010, http://www.massviolence. org/Transitional-Justice-A-New-Discipline-in-Human-Rights (last accessed Feb. 2015).

58. Some have suggested that a different terminology should be used. Rama Mani has advocated the term 'reparative justice' (Mani, Rama, 'Rebuilding an Inclusive Political Community after War', *Security Dialogue*, 36, 4, 2005) and a critical network has advocated the term 'transformative justice' (Worldwide Universities Network: Transformative Justice Network, http://www.wun.ac.uk/research/transformative-justice-network). An important rationale for this was provided in Boesten, Jelke et.al, 'Transformative Justice—A Concept Note', Oct. 2010, http://www.wun.

ac.uk/sites/default/files/transformative_justice_-_concept_note_web_version.pdf (last accessed Feb. 2015).

2. VICTOR SERGE, THE BOLSHEVIK REVOLUTION AND STALINISM

1. For a general discussion, see Caute, David, *Politics and the Novel during the Cold War*, New Brunswick and London: Transaction Publishers, 2010.
2. On this particular debate, he once stated: 'It is often said that "the germ of all Stalinism was in Bolshevism at its beginning". Well, I have no objection. Only, Bolshevism also contained many other germs, a mass of other germs and those who lived through the enthusiasm of the first years of the first victorious socialist revolution ought not to forget it. To judge the living man by the death germs which the autopsy reveals in a corpse—and which he may have carried since his birth—is that very sensible?', Serge, Victor 'A Letter and Some Notes: Reply to Ciliga', *New International*, Feb. 1939, in Marxists' Internet Archive: Victor Serge, https://www.marxists.org/archive/serge/1939/02/letter.htm (last accessed Feb. 2015).
3. He adopted the name Serge in 1917, but had used, and would subsequently again use, various other names in his writing.
4. Serge, Victor, *Memoirs of a Revolutionary*, New York: The New York Review of Books, 2012, pp. 11–14.
5. Marshall, Bill, *Victor Serge: The Uses of Dissent*, New York/Oxford: Berg, 1992, p. 5. (Rirette Maitrejean was a pseudonym of Anna Estorges.)
6. 'The Bandits', *L'Anarchie*, No. 352, 4 Jan. 1912, https://www.marxists.org/archive/serge/1912/01/bandits.htm (last accessed Feb. 2015).
7. The other survivors of the gang were initially sentenced to death, but one sentence was commuted to life imprisonment and two others commuted to life imprisonment with hard labour, though one of these later committed suicide and the other was sent to a penal colony. Garnier had already been killed in a police siege the previous year and Serge's other childhood friend, Callemin, was executed with two others.
8. Letter to Emile Arnaud, 19 Mar. 1917, https://www.marxists.org/archive/serge/1917/03/letter-armand.htm (last accessed Feb. 2015).
9. Salvador Seguí was a Catalan anarcho-syndicalist, who constantly sought power through working-class organisation, rather than paramilitary action. He was assassinated in 1923.
10. Weissman, Susan, *Victor Serge: The course is set on hope*, London and New York: Verso, 2001, p. 19.
11. He had previously been married to Rirette.
12. Marshall, *Victor Serge*, p. 7.
13. The Left Opposition was a faction within the Bolshevik Party from 1923

with Trotsky as its main leader. After Trotsky was marginalised, losing his ministerial post in 1925, two other Bolshevik leaders, Kamenev and Zinoviev, broke with Stalin and formed the so-called 'New Opposition'. After their defeat, they allied with the Left Opposition in a United Opposition. However, in October 1927 all its members were expelled from the Central Committee and, following the Party Congress in December, all the leading oppositionists were expelled from the Party. Zinoviev and Kamenev subsequently surrendered and were re-admitted, but both were later executed after a show trial in 1936.

14. Weissman, *Victor Serge*, pp. 100–1.

15. Ibid., p. 107.

16. Quoted in ibid., p. 143.

17. Marshall, *Victor Serge*, pp. 15–17.

18. POUM was formed in 1935 from a merger between the Communist Left of Spain (mainly from Catalonia) and a Workers and Peasants' bloc. It opposed the official Communist Party of Spain, the Partido Comunista Español (PCE), and was bitterly attacked by it, and also by the Comintern, which sought to eliminate it. One of its most prominent leaders was Andrés Nin, who was a close friend of Serge's. Nin disappeared in 1937 and may have been killed by Stalin's agents.

19. Liuba was now confined permanently to a mental hospital in France. Serge's third wife was Laurette Séjourné.

20. Serge, *Memoirs*, p. 303.

21. Ibid.

22. Ibid., p. 304.

23. Ibid., p. 307.

24. Ibid.

25. Ibid., p. 305.

26. Greeman, Richard, 'The Novel of the Revolution', in Weissman, S. (ed.), *The Ideas of Victor Serge: A Life as a Work of Art*, London: Critique Books/Merlin Press, 1997, p. 68.

27. Weissman, *Victor Serge*, p. 111.

28. For insights into his creative writing, with many examples, see Gordon, Paul, *Vagabond Witness: Victor Serge and the Politics of Hope*, Winchester/Washington, D.C.: Zero Books, 2013.

29. Serge, Victor, *The Case of Comrade Tulayev*, New York: New York Review Books, 2003 (originally published as *L'Affaire Toulaév*, Paris: Editions du Seuil, 1948); Koestler, Arthur, *Darkness at Noon*, New York: The Modern Library, 1941.

30. Howe, Irving, *Politics and the Novel*, London: Stevens & Stevens, 1961, p. 227.

31. Ibid, p. 231.

32. Ibid, p. 234.
33. Serge, Victor, *Midnight in the Century*, London: Writers and Readers Publishing Co-op.,1982, p. 139. (originally published as *S'il est minuit dans le siècle*, Paris: Grasset, 1939).
34. Ibid., p. 217.
35. Marshall, *Victor Serge*, pp. 187–8.
36. 'The Endangered City: Petrograd Year: Year Two of the Revolution' in Serge, Victor, *Revolution in Danger: Writings from Russia, 1919–1921*, London: Redwoods, 1997, p. 35.
37. Serge, Victor, *Birth of Our Power*, London: Victor Gollancz, 1968 (originally published as *Naissance de notre force*, Paris: Rieder, 1931).
38. 'The Anarchists and the Experience of the Russian Revolution' in Serge, *Revolution in Danger*, p. 118.
39. Ibid., p. 119.
40. Ibid.
41. Ibid., p. 96.
42. Ibid., pp. 109–10.
43. Ibid., p. 112.
44. Ibid., p. 115.
45. Ibid.
46. Serge, *Birth*, pp. 205–7. In his *Memoirs* he made it clear that this was based on real episodes. There was, he said, only one Bolshevik, 'the chemical engineer Krauterkrafft, whose constant antagonist I was, since he advocated a merciless dictatorship, suppression of press freedom, authoritarian revolution, and education on Marxist lines', while 'we desired a libertarian, democratic revolution, without the hypocrisy and flabbiness of the bourgeois democracies—egalitarian and tolerant towards ideas and people, which would employ terror if it was necessary but would abolish the death penalty'. Serge, *Memoirs*, p. 74.
47. Serge, *Birth*, p. 250.
48. This refers to the proliferation of political clubs during the French revolution.
49. Serge, *Birth*, pp. 266–7.
50. 'During the Civil War: Petrograd: May–June 1919 Impressions and Considerations' in Serge, *Revolution in Danger*, p. 3.
51. Ibid., p. 8
52. Ibid., p. 11.
53. Ibid. The Cheka was established in December 1917. In theory, its activities were initially confined to making preliminary investigations only— 'enough to break up [the counter-revolutionary act]' (Decree of the Sovnarkom, 20 Dec. 1917). However, its jurisdiction covered a variety of ill-defined crimes and the paper restrictions on its activity were never

effective, perhaps because the Bolshevik leadership wanted to make its rights as uncertain as possible in order to facilitate its work of ruthless suppression (Kucherov, Samuel, *The Organs of Soviet Administration of Justice: Their History and Operation*, Leiden: Brill, 1970, pp. 60–1). This grew in intensity when the Germans resumed their advance, leading to the proclamation on 22 February 1918 that 'the socialist fatherland is in danger', and an order by the Cheka to 'seek out, arrest and shoot immediately all enemy agents, counter-revolutionary agitators and speculators' (quoted in Carr, E. H., *The Bolshevik Revolution*, Vol. 1, 1917–1923, Harmondsworth: Penguin, 1966, p. 168). Two months later this was extended and the Cheka began its evolution into a large and independent department of state. Ibid., p. 169.

54. 'During the Civil War' in Serge, *Revolution in Danger*, p. 15.

55. Ibid., pp. 23–4.

56. Ibid., p. 12.

57. Ibid., pp. 24–7.

58. Ibid., p. 32.

59. 'The Anarchists and the Experience of the Russian Revolution' in Serge, *Revolution in Danger*, p. 116.

60. Serge, Victor, *Ville conquise*, Paris: Rieder, 1932.

61. Serge, Victor, *Conquered City*, London: Gollancz, 1976, pp. 30–1.

62. Ibid., p. 108.

63. Ibid., p. 131.

64. This claim is refuted in a thorough study of the political and social history of Kronstadt (Getzler, Israel, *Kronstadt 1917–1921: The Fate of a Soviet Democracy*, Cambridge: Cambridge University Press, 2002).

65. Figes, Orlando, *A People's Tragedy: The Russian Revolution 1891–1924*, New York: Viking Press, 1997, pp. 760–67.

66. Serge, *Memoirs*, pp. 146–9.

67. Ibid., pp. 150–1.

68. The NEP represented a substantial departure from outright nationalisation, allowing private individuals to own small enterprises. It also abolished forced grain requisition—a source of major peasant discontent—replacing this with a tax system. It appeared to be economically successful, leading to a growth in production, but it also slowed industrialisation and led to a partial restoration of capitalism in the countryside, bringing new inequalities. It was replaced in 1928 by Stalin's Five-Year Plan, which involved forced collectivisation of agriculture and rapid industrialisation. Since the NEP constituted an obvious retreat from socialism, this (along with the suppression of the Kronstadt uprising) was liable to increase dissent within the party. Lenin was not prepared to accept this and at the 10th Party Congress in March 1921 a ban on factions was imposed. This

led to a great increase in the disciplinary power of a small inner group of leaders and in a purge in the autumn up to 25 per cent of the membership was expelled. Carr, *Bolshevik Revolution*, pp. 208–19; Service, Robert, *Lenin: A Biography*, London: Macmillan, 2000, pp. 383–427.

69. Serge, *Memoirs*, p. 153; 'Once More: Kronstadt', *New International*, 4, 7, (July 1938), pp. 211–12 in https://www.marxists.org/archive/serge/1938/04/kronstadt.htm (last accessed Feb. 2015).

70. Serge, Victor, 'Thirty Years after the Russian Revolution' (originally published in *La Révolution Prolétarienne*, 1947), in Weissman, *Ideas*, pp. 248–9.

71. Serge, *Memoirs*, p. 153.

72. Letter to Michael Kneller, 29 May 1921, Serge Archives, quoted in Marshall, *Victor Serge*, p. 10.

73. 'Kronstadt 1921, Trotsky's Defense. Response to Trotsky', *La Révolution Prolétarienne*, 25 Oct. 1938, https://www.marxists.org/archive/serge/1938/10/25.htm (last accessed Feb. 2015).

74. Marshall, *Victor Serge*, p. 10.

75. Serge, *Memoirs*, p. 36.

76. Ibid., p. 53.

77. Serge, Victor, *Men in Prison*, London: Gollancz, 1970, p. 53, p. 84 (originally published as *Les Hommes dans la prison*, Paris: Rieder, 1930).

78. Ibid., p. 85.

79. Beirne, Piers and Alan Hunt, 'Lenin, Crime and Penal Politics, 1917–1924', in Beirne, Piers (ed.), *Revolution in Law: Contributions to the Development of Soviet Legal Theory, 1917–1938*, London and New York: Sharpe, 1990, pp. 99–126.

80. Serge, *Memoirs*, p. 94. He attributes the increasing role of the Cheka to the beginning of the Civil War in the summer of 1918, and it was certainly in this climate that the 'mass red terror against the bourgeoisie and its agents' was launched (quoted in Carr, *Bolshevik Revolution*, p. 176), with the Cheka accumulating far greater power. In fact its role now increased so substantially that defendants' rights in criminal cases had virtually ceased to exist by the end of 1919. Huskey, Eugene, 'From Legal Nihilism to Pravovoe Gosudarstvo: Soviet legal Development 1917–1990', in Barry, Donald D., (ed.), *Toward the "Rule of Law" in Russia? Political and Legal Reform in the Transition Period*, New York: Sharpe, 1992, pp. 24–5. Although it was formally closed in December 1921—to be replaced by the GPU in 1922 and OGPU in 1923—these changes were largely cosmetic, and Serge continued to refer to it as 'the Cheka'.

81. Serge, Victor, 'Secrecy and Revolution: A Reply to Trotsky' (1938), first published in *Peace News*, 27 Dec. 1963, https://www.marxists.org/archive/serge/1938/xx/secrecy.htm (last accessed Feb. 2015).

82. Serge, *Memoirs*, p. 93.
83. Ibid., p. 185.
84. Ibid., pp. 241–2.
85. Quoted in ibid., pp. 326–8.
86. Serge, Victor, 'Puissance et limites du marxisme' 3 (nouvelle série), March 1939, reproduced in *La Bataille Socialiste*, http://bataillesocialiste.word-press.com/documents-historiques/1939-03-puissance-et-limites-du-marxisme-serge/ (last accessed Feb. 2015).
87. Ibid.
88. Serge, 'Thirty Years after the Russian Revolution', pp. 248–54.
89. Serge, *Memoirs*, p. 327.
90. Serge, 'Thirty Years after the Russian Revolution', pp. 240–3.
91. Serge, *Memoirs*, p. 440; see also p. 156.
92. Ibid., p. 118, see also p. 179.
93. Ibid., p. 441.
94. Serge, Victor, 'Planned Economies and Democracy' (1944/45), first published in *Revolutionary History*, 5, Autumn 1994, https://www.marxists.org/archive/serge/1944/xx/planecon.html (last accessed Feb. 2015).
95. Serge, *Memoirs*, p. 447.
96. A recently discovered set of unpublished writings from his final years adds to the ambiguity about Serge's eventual position. See Serge, Victor, 'Mexican Notebooks 1940–1947, *New Left Review* 82, July–Aug. 2013.

3. FROM THE VICHY REGIME TO THE FOURTH FRENCH REPUBLIC: ALBERT CAMUS AND RESISTANCE, JUSTICE AND VIOLENCE

1. Kedward, H. R., *Resistance in Vichy France: A Study of Ideas and Motivation in the Southern Zone 1940–1942*, Oxford: Oxford University Press, 1978, p. 137.
2. The Service d'ordre légionnaire, an extreme right-wing collaborationist militia, under Joseph Darnard, was already operating in the Southern Zone before 1942, but was transformed into the Milice Française in January 1943.
3. Kedward, *Resistance in Vichy France*, p. 230.
4. Paxton, Robert O., *Vichy France: Old Guard and New Order 1940–44*, New York: Alfred A. Knopf, 1972.
5. Paxton also played an important role in this research. See Marrus, Michael R., and Robert O. Paxton, *Vichy France and the Jews*, New York: Basic Books, 1981. It is estimated that the Vichy government actively abetted the deportation of 76,000 French and foreign Jews, fewer than 3% of whom survived. More generally, by the time of the Liberation, the regime had been directly responsible for the imprisonment of 135,000 people, the internment of

70,000 suspects (including numerous political refugees from central Europe) and the dismissal of 35,000 civil servants; it had sent 650,000 workers to Germany as conscript labour, and had harassed Freemasons, sending 989 to camps, where 549 of them died. Rousso, Henry, *Vichy Syndrome: History and Memory in France Since 1944*, Cambridge: Harvard University Press, 1991, p. 7.

6. Rousso, *Vichy Syndrome*, pp. 21–25.

7. In the official purge 1,500 and 1,600 death sentences were actually carried out, which was the highest rate of death penalties per capita in comparison with Germany, Austria, Italy, the Netherlands, Norway, Belgium and Denmark. In addition, 124,613 people were judged by the courts, with 76.5 per cent condemned in some way; more than 44,000 people were given prison sentences, and more than 50,000 were condemned to national degradation. In addition, 350,000 individuals were initially threatened with a legal process, although two-thirds of these never came to a trial; and at least 60,000 and 70,000 people were interned for some period in the early post-Liberation period. Rousso, Henry, 'L'épuration en France: une histoire inachevée', *Vingtième Siècle. Revue d'Histoire*, No. 33, Jan.–March 1992, pp. 78–105, http://www.persee.fr/web/revues/home/prescript/article/xxs_0294–1759_1992_num_33_1_2491 (last accessed Feb. 2015).

8. From Camus, Albert, *Carnets, 1942–51*, London: Hamish Hamilton, 1966, quoted by Gordimer, Nadine, *The Essential Gesture: Writing, Politics and Places*, London: Jonathan Cape, 1988, p. 134, p. 412.

9. Camus, Albert, *The Outsider*, London: Hamish Hamilton, 2nd Edition, 1957 (originally published as *L'Etranger*, Paris: Gallimard, 1942).

10. Aronson, Ronald, *Camus and Sartre: The Story of a Friendship and the Quarrel that Ended It*, Chicago: University of Chicago Press, 2004, pp. 66–93.

11. Camus, Albert, *The Rebel*, New York: Alfred A. Knopf, 1954 (Originally published as *L'homme révolté*, Paris: Gallimard, 1951).

12. Carroll, David, *Albert Camus, the Algerian: Colonialism, Terrorism, Justice*, New York: Columbia University Press, 2007.

13. His first wife was Simone Hié, the daughter of a wealthy ophthalmologist, but they were divorced in 1936.

14. Todd, Olivier, *Albert Camus—A Life*, New York: Carroll & Graf, 2000, p. 62. (These dates of party membership appear reliable, although Camus himself later claimed that he joined in 1934 and left in 1935).

15. Ibid., pp. 73–87.

16. Ibid., pp. 87–93.

17. Quoted in ibid., p. 115.

18. Ibid., p. 117.

19. Ibid., p. 119.

20. Aronson, *Camus and Sartre*, p. 27. (Camus, Albert, *Le Mythe de Sisyphe*, Paris: Gallimard, 1942; *The Myth of Sisyphus*, London: Hamish Hamilton, 1955).

21. Todd, *Albert Camus*, pp. 177–9.

22. Sprintzen, David, *Camus: A Critical Examination*, Philadelphia: Temple University Press, 1988, pp. 1–64.

23. Camus, *Outsider*, p. 106.

24. 'Reflections on the Guillotine' in Camus, Albert, *Resistance, Rebellion and Death*, New York: The Modern Library, 1963, pp. 130–1; available at www.deakinphilosophicalsociety.com/texts/camus/reflections.pdf (last accessed Feb. 2015) (originally published as 'Réflexions sur la Guillotine' in Koestler, Arthur and Albert Camus, *Réflexions sur la peine capitale*, Paris: Calmann-Lévy, 1957).

25. Camus, *Outsider*, p. 127.

26. 'Défense de "L'Homme Révolté"' in Camus, Albert, *Essais*, Paris: Bibliothèque de la Pléiade, 1965, 1703–04.

27. Albert Camus, *The Plague*, London: Allen Lane, 2001, pp. 101–102 (originally published as *La Peste*, Paris: Gallimard, 1947).

28. Ibid., p. 102.

29. Camus, Albert, *Resistance, Rebellion and Death*, London: Hamish Hamilton, 1964 (first published together as *Lettres à un ami allemand*, Paris: Gallimard, 1945).

30. Ibid., p. 7.

31. Ibid.

32. Ibid., pp. 21–2.

33. Conseil national de la Résistance, 'Le programme d'action de la Résistance' (adopted on 15 March 1944), Musée de la résistance en ligne, http://www.museedelaresistanceenligne.org/media.php?media=2839&expo=75&popin=true#zoom-tab (last accessed Feb. 2015).

34. Quoted in Todd, *Camus*, pp. 179–80. The Popular Government was elected in May 1936, comprising the Socialist Party, left-wing radicals and republicans, under the premiership of Léon Blum, the Socialist Party leader. It was supported by the PCF, but the party did not form part of the government coalition. The left-wing victory was greeted by a general strike, leading to the negotiation of various social reforms, including paid holidays and increased trade union rights. This led to a backlash by employers, an economic slow-down and the vilification of Blum by the Right. The Popular Front dissolved itself in autumn 1938.

35. 'From Resistance to Revolution' in Lévy-Valensi, Jacqueline (ed.) *Camus at Combat, Writing 1944–1947*, Princeton and Oxford: Princeton University Press, 2006, p. 13.

36. 'The Blood of Freedom', 24 Aug. 1944 in ibid., p. 17.

37. 'Justice and Freedom', 8 Sep. 1944 in ibid., p. 31.
38. Editorial, 7 Oct.1944 in ibid., p. 64.
39. Quoted in Novick, Peter, *The Resistance Versus Vichy:The Purge of Collaborators in Liberated France*, London: Chatto and Windus, 1968, pp. 23–4.
40. Le programme d'action de la Résistance.
41. Novick, *Resistance Versus Vichy*, pp. 24–6.
42. Kedward, H. R., *Occupied France: Collaboration and Resistance 1940–1944*, Oxford: Basil Blackwell, 1985, p. 74.
43. Novick, *Resistance Versus Vichy*, pp. 80–1.
44. Among the criteria for inclusion were: having been a Vichy minister, having been removed from office by the administrative purge, having been fined for illicit profits under the Occupation, having been named a National or Departmental Councillor by Vichy, having voted for full powers to Pétain on 10 July 1940, and having retained a Vichy appointment to an executive position after Laval's return to office in April 1942 (since this was when the pro-Nazi orientation became more overt). Ineligibility could be suspended for an individual who had carried out Resistance activity and a Jury of Honour was established to make judgements about such cases. Novick, *Resistance Versus Vichy*, pp. 100–101.
45. These could either impose professional penalties, such as exclusion from positions of authority, or national degradation if an individual had not already been summoned to appear before the Cours de Justice or the *chambres civiques*. Rousso, '*L'épuration*', p. 24.
46. Newspaper owners and editors of such papers could be tried under the penal aspects of the purge, and a decree in May 1945 also allowed for the prosecution of the newspapers themselves. Lottman, Herbert R., *The People's Anger: Justice and Revenge in Post-Liberation France*, London: Hutchinson, 1986, pp. 229–34.
47. Specifically, amongst the actions that would carry a presumption of guilt were:
    1. having been a member of any of Pétain's cabinets;
    2. having held an executive position in either Vichy's propaganda services or in the Commissariat for Jewish Affairs;
    3. having been a member, even without active participation, of collaborationist organisations;
    4. having helped organise meetings or demonstrations in favour of collaboration;
    5. having published writings or given lectures in favour of the enemy, collaboration with the enemy, racism or totalitarian doctrines. Novick, *Resistance Versus Vichy*, pp. 147–8.
48. The Cours de Justice were to judge the majority of those accused of collaboration, but military tribunals continued and could also issue the death

sentence. They remained active in the early phase, before the Cours de Justice had been properly established. Furthermore, a different ordinance established the *chambres civiques*. These could judge only in relation to the offence of *indignité nationale* (national unworthiness), with the choice between acquittal or a sentence of *dégradation nationale* (national stripping of rank), which could be for life or a specific term. The penalty could also be suspended if there was evidence that a condemned individual had helped the Resistance.

49. Novick, *Resistance Versus Vichy*, pp. 155–6.
50. Ibid., pp. 158–60.
51. This was reinforced by very sharp regional disparities in sentencing. Ibid., pp. 160–166.
52. Novick, *Resistance Versus Vichy*, pp. 172–6.
53. Cachin, Marcel, *L'Humanité* (Paris edition), 28 Sept. 1944, quoted in Lottman, *The People's Anger*, pp. 88–9.
54. Novick, *Resistance Versus Vichy*, p. 167, p. 179.
55. Quoted in Zaretsky, Robert, *Albert Camus, Elements of a Life*, Ithaca and London: Cornell University Press, 2010, p. 66.
56. Quoted in Todd, *Camus*, p. 181.
57. 'Outlaws', April 1944 (attributed to Camus) in Lévy-Valensi, *Camus at Combat*, p. 4. (Joseph Darnand, the founder of the Milice, was executed in Oct. 1945.)
58. Editorial, 26 Sept. 1944 in ibid., pp. 47–8. (Renault was accused of collaboration, but died while awaiting trial. The company was nationalised.)
59. Editorial, 18 Oct. 1944 in ibid., p. 77.
60. Quoted in Zaretsky, *Albert Camus*, pp. 65–6.
61. Editorial, 20 Oct. 1944 in Lévy-Valensi, *Camus at Combat*, p. 81.
62. Quoted in Zaretsky, *Albert Camus*, p. 68.
63. Editorial, 25 Oct. 1944 in Lévy-Valensi, *Camus at Combat*, pp. 89–90
64. Ibid.
65. Editorial, 5 Jan. 1945 in ibid., pp. 163–5.
66. Zaretsky, *Albert Camus*, p. 73.
67. Editorial, 2 Nov. 1944 in Lévy-Valensi, *Camus at Combat*, p. 97.
68. Editorial (attributed to Camus), 2 Aug. 1945, in ibid., pp. 232–3.
69. Editorial, 30 Aug. 1945, in ibid., pp. 249–50.
70. It was effectively a show trial and even Léon Blum (whom the Vichy regime had attempted to convict of treason in an abortive show trial in 1942 and who was sent to Buchenwald by the Germans the following year) unsuccessfully appealed to de Gaulle not to carry out the execution because it undermined the idea of legal justice (Lacouture, Jean, *Léon Blum*, Paris: Seuil, 1977, pp. 512–13). Before the execution, Laval tried

to commit suicide, but he was restored to the degree of consciousness required by French law so that he could be shot by a firing squad.

71. Novick, *Resistance Versus Vichy*, pp. 3–1; Lottman, *The People's Anger*, pp. 216–17; pp. 223–8; Rousso, '*l'épuration*', pp. 100–1.

72. Several historians also emphasise the positive aspects of the purge. For example, in the mid-1980s Lottman concluded that the official France was on the side of 'law and order' and that 'the French need not be ashamed of their purge, as they often seem to be, even today' (*The People's Anger*, pp. 290–1). Without minimising the injustices and violence of the unofficial purge, Kedward also stresses that this was a time in southern France when ordinary people tried 'to relaunch their communities on a more equal, just and fraternal footing' (*Occupied France*, p. 77). He has also stressed the extent to which the rural *Maquis* was subsequently allotted minor historical status, ostensibly because of the association with retribution, but, in reality, also because it included groups outside official France—agricultural and industrial workers, immigrants and youth. Kedward, H. R., *In Search of the Maquis, Rural Resistance in Southern France, 1942–44*, Oxford: Clarendon Press, 1993, pp. 228–9.

73. Nov. 29 1946 in Lévy-Valensi, *Camus at Combat*, p. 273.

74. Camus, *The Plague*, p. 192.

75. Ibid., p. 193.

76. Ibid., p. 194.

77. Ibid.

78. Camus, *Rebel*, p. 259.

79. Carroll, *Albert Camus*, pp. 91–8.

80. 'A Defence of Intelligence', 15 Mar. 1945, in Camus, *Resistance, Rebellion and Death*, p. 45.

81. Ibid.

82. 'The Unbeliever and Christians', ibid., p. 50.

83. Camus, 'Défense de l'homme revolté', p. 1714.

84. July 1945 in Notebook IV: Jan.1942–Sep. 1945 in Camus, Albert, *Notebooks, 1942–1951*, New York: The Modern Library, 1970, pp. 104–5.

85. Ibid.

86. Sep. 1945, Notebook V September 1945–April 1948, ibid, p. 110.

87. 'A New Social Contract', 29 Nov. 1946 in Lévy-Valensi, *Camus at Combat*, p. 271.

88. 'Socialism Mystified', 21 Nov. 1946 in ibid., pp. 262–4; Camus, Notebeook V 29 Oct. 1946, p. 148.

89. *The Just Assassins* in Camus, Albert, *Caligula and Three Other Plays*, New York: Vintage Books, 1962, p. 296.

90. Ibid.

91. Camus, *Rebel*, pp. 252–6.
92. Ibid., pp. 258–9.
93. Carroll does not believe that the approach was based on either an ideology or an abstract ethical principle, but on Camus's revulsion at the spectacle of capital punishment, and on his wider belief that this, with political assassination, terrorism and counter-terrorism, were all attempts to legitimise murder. Carroll, *Albert Camus*, pp. 102–4.

4. JUSTICE IN THE CONTEXT OF COLONIALISM AND NEO-COLONIALISM: NGŨGĨ WA THIONG'O AND KENYA

1. He was given the name James Ngugi when converting to Christianity as a teenager and wrote his first books under this name. In 1977 he officially re-changed his name to Ngũgĩ wa Thiong'o.
2. Gikandi, Simon, *Ngũgĩ wa Thiong'o*, Cambridge: Cambridge University Press, 2000, pp. 1–38.
3. Cain, P. J. and Anthony G. Hopkins, *British Imperialism: Crisis and Deconstruction, 1914–1990*, London: Longman, 1993, p. 221, cited in Judd, Denis, *Empire: The British Imperial Experience from 1765 to the Present*, London: HarperCollins, 1996, p. 348.
4. Benschop, Marjolein, *Rights and Reality: Are women's equal rights to land, housing and property implemented in East Africa?*, Kenya: United Nations Human Settlements Programme, 2002, p. 41.
5. The current Kenyan usage is followed except when 'Kikuyu' was used in the original.
6. Judd, *Empire*, p. 350.
7. Killingray, David, *Fighting for Britain: African Soldiers in the Second World War*, Martelsham, Suffolk: Boydell and Brewer, 2010, pp. 220–1.
8. Anderson, David, *Histories of the Hanged: Britain's Dirty War in Kenya and the End of Empire*, London: Orion, 2005; and Elkins, Caroline, *Britain's Gulag: The Brutal End of Empire in Kenya*, London: Pimlico, 2005, give differing estimates, with Elkins suggesting higher figures for atrocities by the British.
9. Ngũgĩ wa Thiong'o, *Homecoming*, London: Heinemann, 1972, p. 48; Ngũgĩ wa Thiong'o, *Dreams in a Time of War: A Childhood Memoir*, London: Harvill Secker, 2010, pp. 208–15.
10. Ngũgĩ, *Dreams*, pp. 205–8.
11. Ibid., p. 208–11.
12. Ibid., p. 244.
13. Ibid., p. 85.
14. Ngũgĩ wa Thiong'o, 'The English Master and the Colonial Bondsman' in *Globalectics: Theory and the Politics of Knowing*, New York: Columbia

University Press, 2012, pp. 17–18. The policy of 'Villagisation' was initiated in 1954. It was a policy of forced internal displacement, with the colonial forces bulldozing people's homes or torching them when the owners resisted. The mass relocation was followed by forced land consolidation. More than a million Gĩkũyũs were relocated into settlements behind barbed-wire fences and watchtowers. Elkins, *Britain's Gulag*, pp. 234–5.

15. Ngũgĩ, 'The English Master', p. 17.
16. Ibid.
17. Ngũgĩ wa Thiong'o, 'Kenya: The Two Rifts' (Sep. 1962), in *Homecoming*, London: Heinemann, 1972, p. 24.
18. Ibid., p. 25.
19. Interview with Aminu Abdullahi (1964) in Sander, Reinhard and Bernth Lindfors (with assistance of Lynette Cintrón), *Ngũgĩ wa Thiong'o Speaks: Interviews with the Kenyan Writer*, Oxford: James Currey, Nairobi: EAEP, 2006, p. 15.
20. James Ngugi interviewed by fellow students at Leeds University (1967) in ibid., p. 27.
21. Rosberg, Carl Gustav and John Cato Nottingham, *The Myth of "Mau Mau" Nationalism in Kenya*, New York: Praeger, 1966, cited in Robson, James Stephen, 'Ngũgĩ wa Thiong'o's fight against colonialism and neo-colonialism: An explanation of the theme of betrayal', MA thesis, Simon Fraser University, 1987, pp. 51–2.
22. Ngũgĩ wa Thiong'o, *The River Between*, London: Heinemann, 1988 (original publication, London: Heinemann, 1965), p. 23. (Although this was published after *Weep not, Child*, it was written earlier).
23. Ibid., p. 68. After three missionary schools banned female genital mutilation, the Gĩkũyũ in Central Province began to boycott missionary schools and demanded an end to the monopoly of education. When the government refused to open secular schools, the Gĩkũyũ began to open their own and in 1934 formed the Kikuyu Independent Schools Association (KISA), which was followed by the establishment of a rival organisation, the Kikuyu Karing'a Education Association (KKEA), which sought complete independence from European influence. Both KISA and KKEA schools were closed with the state of emergency in 1952.
24. Ibid.
25. Ibid., p. 138.
26. Ibid., pp. 141–2.
27. Ibid., p. 143.
28. Ibid., p. 149.
29. Boehmer, Elleke, 'Master's Dance to the Master's Voice: Revolutionary Nationalism and the Representation of Women in the Writing of Ngũgĩ

wa Thiong'o', *The Journal of Commonwealth Literature*, 26 (1) (1991), p. 193. Subsequently, women would normally be much more powerful figures in Ngũgĩ's novels, although some have still criticised him for representing them through male-dominated values (ibid; and for a full critical evaluation, see Nicholls, Brendon, *Ngũgĩ wa Thiong'o. Gender, and the Ethics of Postcolonial Reading*, Farnham, Surrey: Ashgate, 2010).

30. Ngũgĩ wa Thiong'o, *Weep Not, Child*, Johannesburg: Penguin Books, 2009, p. 148. Amoko is far harsher in his judgment of Njoroge, concluding that this ending exposes 'the absurdity of his self-deluding messianic fantasies'. Amoko, Apollo Obonyo, *Postcolonialism in the Wake of the Nairobo Revolution. Ngũgĩ wa Thiong'o and the Idea of African Literature*, New York: Palgrave Macmillan, 2010, p. 66. Ngũgĩ appears to have had more sympathy for, and empathy with, Njoroge and some other characters, than Amoko suggests.

31. Branch, Daniel, *Kenya Between Hope and Despair, 1963–2011*, New Haven and London: Yale University Press, 2011, p. 4.

32. Discussion (1966) in Sander and Lindfors, *Ngũgĩ wa Thiong'o Speaks*, p. 23.

33. Ibid., p. 24.

34. Branch, *Kenya*, p. 45; pp. 52–63.

35. Ngugi, James, Henry Owuor-Anyumba and Taban Lo Liyong, 'On the Abolition of the English Department' (Oct. 1968) in Ngũgĩ, *Homecoming*, pp. 149–50.

36. Branch, *Kenya*, p. 124.

37. Clough, Marshall S, 'Mau Mau and the Contest for Memory', in Atieno Odhiambo, E. S., and John Lonsdale (eds), *Mau Mau and Nationhood: Arms, Authority and Narration*, Oxford: James Currey, 2003, p. 255, quoted in Wu, Sharon, 'Mau Mau Historiography, Ngũgĩ wa Thiong'o's *A Grain of Wheat* and M.G. Vassanji's *The In-Between World of Vikram Lall*', MA thesis, National Central University, Taiwan, 2007, p. 14.

38. Wu, 'Mau Mau Historiography', p. 51, quoting Elkins, *Britain's Gulag*, p. 362.

39. Ibid., p. 14, quoting Elkins, *Britain's Gulag*, p. 360.

40. Sicherman, Carol, *Ngũgĩ wa Thiong'o, The Making of a Rebel: A Source Book in Kenyan Literature and Resistance*, Borough Green, Sevenoaks: Hans Zell, 1990, pp. 358–88.

41. Wu, 'Mau Mau Historiography, p. 10.

42. In a review of Madjalany, Fred, *A State of Emergency: The Full Story of Mau Mau*, Boston: Houghton Mifflin, 1963, he wrote: 'Violence in order to change an intolerable, unjust social order is not savagery: it purifies man. Violence to protect and preserve an unjust, oppressive social order is criminal, and diminishes man. To gloat in the latter form of violence … is revolting'. Ngũgĩ, '"Mau Mau", Violence and Culture' (1963) in

Homecoming, p. 28. He was probably influenced by the first 'revisionist' memoir by a former leader of the detainees in the camps, which argued that the organisation had been an effectively led and well-disciplined force. Kariuki, J. M., *"Mau Mau"Detainee*, Harmondsworth: Penguin, 1963.

43. Ngũgĩ wa Thiong'o, *A Grain of Wheat*, London: Heinemann revised edition, 1988, p. 236. (Original publication, London: Heinemann, 1967).

44. Ibid., p. 247.

45. Ibid., p. 68.

46. Ibid., pp. 221–2; see also Gikandi, *Ngũgĩ wa Thiong'o*, pp. 115–27.

47. Ngũgĩ, *Grain of Wheat*, Note by author, Nov. 1966.

48. Maughan-Brown, David, '"Mau Mau" and Violence in Ngũgĩ's Novels', *English in Africa*, 8, 2 (1981), p. 10.

49. 'Literature and Society' (1973) and 'The Robber and the Robbed' (1976) in Ngũgĩ wa Thiong'o, *Writers in Politics*, London: Heinemann, 1981.

50. For example, one of his endorsements of Mau Mau was in a postscript to the re-issue of the book, *"Mau Mau"Detainee* (1963), by Mwangi Kariuki. By the early 1970s Kariuki had become the most prominent critic of Kenyatta's policies and in 1975 he was assassinated, and a parliamentary inquiry into the events surrounding his death was blocked from above. Branch, *Kenya*, pp. 105–117.

51. Micere Githae Mugo is another Kenyan playwright, author, activist, teacher and poet. She is currently Professor of Literature at the Department of African American Studies at Syracuse University.

52. '"Handcuffs" for a Play (or the difficulties of staging a Kenyan play on Kenyatta day)', *Daily Nation*, 15 Oct. 1976 in Ngũgĩ, *Writers in Politics*, p. 51.

53. Ngũgĩ wa Thiong'o, *Petals of Blood*, London: Heinemann, 1977.

54. Ngũgĩ wa Mirii also came from Limuru. He worked at the Institute of Development Studies at Nairobi University, but was forced into exile in Zimbabwe in 1982. He was killed in a car crash in 2008.

55. Ngũgĩ wa Thiong'o and Ngũgĩ wa Mirii, *I Will Marry When I Want*, London: Heinemann, 1982.

56. Ngũgĩ wa Thiong'o, *Devil on the Cross*, London: Heinemann, 1982 (originally published as *Caitaani mũtharaba-Inĩ*, London: Heinemann, 1980).

57. Kenyatta had favoured the Gĩkũyũ, both in high-level political appointments and in the settlement of land, while also exacerbating the structural inequalities (Branch, pp. 95–9). Moi, who was from the Kalenjin community, soon set about replacing the existing privileged group with his own inner circle. With a downturn in the economy, there was also increased unemployment and hardship, with continued corruption by the political and economic elites and, in 1981, the introduction of an IMF austerity plan. Ibid., pp. 142–4.

58. Delgado, Celeste Fraser, 'MotherTongues and Childless Women', in Nnaemeka, Obioma, *Politics of (M)othering*, London: Routledge, 1997, pp. 135–8.

59. Schwerdt, Dianne, Interview with Ngũgĩ (1990) in Sander and Lindfors, *Ngũgĩ wa Thiong'o Speaks*, p. 287.

60. 'Draft Minimum Programme, 1987', quoted in Branch, *Kenya*, p. 163.

61. Nkrumah, Kwame, *Neo-Colonialism, The Last Stage of Imperialism*, London: Thomas Nelson, 1965. For a brief discussion of the concept, see Ashcroft, Bill, Gareth Griffiths and Helen Tiffin, *Post Colonial Studies: The Key Concepts* (3ʳᵈ edition), London and New York: Routledge, 2014, pp. 177–80.

62. KANU, he argued, had originally been an anti-imperialist movement, but this was reversed soon after independence. By 1966 all the most repressive colonial laws had been restored and the comprador bourgeois line had triumphed. The faction led by Kenyatta, 'using the inherited colonial state machinery ousted the patriotic elements from the party leadership, silencing those who remained and hounding others to death'. He claimed that, abandoning any commitment to nationalisation, the KANU government then became a mouthpiece of Anglo-American interests. At home those who had very dubious or treacherous records in the independence struggle were transformed into nationalists, and the teaching of colonial history was left to those who glorified the role of traitors and collaborators. By 1977 KANU had thus become the organ of the home guards and comprador bourgeoisie. Ngũgĩ wa Thiong'o, *Detained: A Writer's Prison Diary*, London: Heinemann, 1981, pp. 54–6. See also interviews with Raoul Granqvist (1982) and with Raina Whatiri and John Timmins (1984) in Sander and Lindfors, *Ngũgĩ Speaks*, p. 168 and pp. 229–30.

63. Branch, *Kenya*, p. 163, referring to the Mwakenya programme.

64. Ngũgĩ wa Thiong'o, *Decolonising the Mind: The Politics of Language in African Literature*, Oxford: James Currey, 2005, p. 3 (original publication, London: Heinemann, 1986).

65. Ibid., p. 9.

66. Ngũgĩ uses this term to describe oral literature and practice and traditions.

67. Ngũgĩ, *Decolonising the Mind.*, p. 16.

68. Ibid., p. 28. For other aspects of his critique, see 'The Allegory of the Cave: Language, Democracy, and a New World Order' in Ngũgĩ wa Thiong'o, *Penpoints, Gunpoints, and Dreams: Towards a Critical Theory of the Arts and the State in Africa*, Oxford: Oxford University Press, 1998, pp. 81–100.

69. 'Literature and Society' (1973) in Ngũgĩ, *Writers in Politics*, p. 27; 'Born Again: Mau Mau Unchanged' (1975) in ibid., p. 92.

70. '"Handcuffs" for a Play' in ibid., p. 51.

71. Schwerdt, Dianne, 'Caught in the Crossfire: Writing Conflict in Two African Novels', *The Australasian Review of African Studies*, 30 (1) 2009, pp. 101–17.

72. It was expressed in an extreme form by William Ochieng, who claimed that, rather than educating and raising issues for debate, Ngũgĩ was 'terrorising us' (Ochieng, William, 'Dignitaries not spared', *Weekly Review* (Nairobi), 24 July 1981, in Sicherman, *Ngũgĩ*, p. 39). Ochieng's particular vitriol was no doubt connected to the fact that Ngugi had attacked his own work, regarding it as a neo-colonial interpretation of Kenyan history (Ngũgi, *Detained*, p. 132). But Ngugi's view of Kenya's past does tend to be one of heroes and traitors (Sicherman, Carol, 'Ngũgĩ wa Thiong'o and the Writing of Kenyan History', *Research in African Literatures*, 20, 3 [1989], pp. 358–9). Once he came to regard Mau Mau as a revolutionary movement for national liberation he also sought to construct a particular view of the past (Gikandi, *Ngũgĩ*, pp. 181–5). Furthermore, because of his interest in the power of stories and conveying history through fiction, he was less concerned about the evidential base for his judgments than professional historians. Thus at a Kenya Historical Association event devoted to the historiography of Kenya, one historian, Henry Mwanzi, dismissed 'Ngũgĩ's fans' for having 'an emotional attachment to the man' that blinded them to 'his falsification of history' (quoted in Sicherman, 'Ngũgĩ and Writing' pp. 361–2).

73. Ngũgĩ wa Thiong'o, *Matigari*, London: Heinemann, 1989 (originally published in Gĩkũyũ by Nairobi: Heinemann, 1987).

74. There has been a sharp debate as to whether it can be regarded as a genuinely national movement, given the fact that it was primarily Gĩkũyũ (and Embu, and Meru) and did not include the other larger communities in Kenya. Some, including William Ochieng, have not only disputed its national credentials, but have also claimed that its ethnic exclusiveness was linked to Gĩkũyũ dominance in the post-independence state (Atieno-Odhiambo, E. S., 'The Production of History in Kenya: The Mau Mau Debate', *Canadian Journal of African Studies* 25, 2 (1991), especially pp. 300–302, cited in Wu, 'Mau Mau Historiography', p. 24). This has been bitterly disputed by others and John Lonsdale has sought to re-orientate the debate with the argument that, while primarily Gĩkũyũ and regionally limited, the folk memory of Mau Mau as a movement arising from poor people being goaded beyond endurance is the 'the nearest Kenya has to a national memory and a watchful political culture'. 'The Moral Economy of Mau Mau', Part II in Berman, Bruce and John Lonsdale, *Unhappy Valley: Conflict in Kenya and Africa, Book Two: Violence and Ethnicity*, Oxford: James Currey, 2002, p. 467 quoted in Wu, p. 27.

75. Sicherman, 'Ngũgĩ and Writing', pp. 358–9.

76. Gikandi, *Ngũgĩ*, p. 290.

77. Branch, *Kenya*, pp. 122–3.

78. Gikandi, *Ngũgĩ*, pp. 223–46; Hooper, Glenn, 'Ngũgĩ's *Matigari* and the Politics of Literature', *Alternation*, 5,1 (1998), pp. 13–31, http://alternation.ukzn.ac.za/pages/volume-5/volume-5-number-1–1998.aspx (last accessed Feb. 2015).

79. Ngũgĩ, *Matigari*, p. 6.

80. Ibid., p. 21.

81. Ibid., p. 44.

82. Ibid., pp. 48–9.

83. Ibid., p. 50 (note).

84. Ibid., p. 90.

85. Ibid., p. 99.

86. Ibid., p. 100.

87. Speech of 13 Sept. 1984, quoted in Ngũgĩ, *Decolonising the Mind*, note 5, p. 86.

88. Ngũgĩ, *Matigari*, p. 101.

89. Parodying the meeting of historians mentioned in note 72.

90. Ngũgĩ, *Matigari*, p. 103.

91. Ibid., p. 108.

92. Ibid., p. 132.

93. Ibid., p. 131.

94. Ibid., p. 172.

95. Ibid., p. 175.

96. Jaggi, Maya, interview (1989) in Sander and Lindfors, *Ngũgĩ Speaks*, p. 265.

97. Schwerdt, interview (1990) in ibid., p. 287.

98. Adisa, Oji and Langerster Anderson, 'Ngũgĩ wa Thiong'o's quest for justice', *The Varsity* (University of Toronto's Student Newspaper), 24 Dec. 2005 (modified, 11 Jan. 2012) http://thevarsity.ca/2005/12/24/ngugi-wa-thiongos-quest-for-justice/ (last accessed, Feb. 2015).

99. Jaggi, interview (1989) in Sander and Lindfors, *Ngũgĩ Speaks*, p. 266.

100. 'The Writer and His Past' in Ngũgĩ, *Homecoming*, p. 44.

101. Poem in Marquez, Robert, *Latin American Revolutionary Poetry: A Bilingual Anthology*, New York: Monthly Review Press, 1974, quoted in Ngũgĩ, *Decolonising the Mind*, p. 106.

102. 'Speech to Danish Working-Class Actors on the Art of Observation', quoted in ibid.

103. Ngũgĩ, *Detained*, p. 97.

104. Ibid., pp. 98–9.

105. Letter of 23 June 1978 to Chairman of the Detainees' Review Tribunal in ibid., p. 187.

106. Cantalupo, Charles, interview (1993) in Sander and Lindfors, *Ngũgĩ Speaks*, pp. 338–9.

107. The circumstances of the crime remain controversial, with Ngũgĩ suspecting his political enemies. His nephew, John Kiragu Chege, was initially accused of involvement, but was subsequently acquitted. In 2006 three guards were convicted and sentenced to death, but Ngũgĩ opposed this (*Daily Nation*, 18 December 2006, http://allafrica.com/stories/200612180137.html [last accessed February 2015]). In 2012 the High Court upheld the convictions of three men, turning down their appeal. *The Star*, 15 Feb. 2012, http://www.the-star.co.ke/news/article-30060/judges-reject-appeal-wa-thiongo-attackers (last accessed Feb. 2015).

108. Branch, *Kenya*, pp. 297–8.

109. Ibid., pp. 252–79.

110. Branch, *Kenya*, pp. 271–5.

111. 'Ngũgĩ laments Kenya violence', BBC news channel, 10 Jan. 2008 http://news.bbc.co.uk/1/hi/world/africa/7180946.stm (last accessed February 2015).

112. Kenya Transitional Justice Network, 'Summary: Truth, Justice and Reconciliation Commission Report', Aug. 2013, http://www.acordinternational.org/silo/files/kenya-tjrc-summary-report-aug-2013.pdf (last accessed, Feb. 2015).

113. Foreign and Commonwealth Office, 'Statement to Parliament on Settlement of Mau Mau Claims', 6 June 2013, https://www.gov.uk/government/news/statement-to-parliament-on-settlement-of-mau-mau-claims (last accessed, Feb. 2015).

114. Ngũgĩ wa Thiong'o, 'Opinion: Kenya', *Granta*, 15 Apr. 2008, http://www.granta.com/New-Writing/Opinion-Kenya (last accessed Feb. 2015).

115. Ngũgĩ wa Thiong'o', 'A Dictator's Last Laugh', *New York Times*, 14 Mar. 2013, http://www.nytimes.com/2013/03/15/opinion/a-dictators-last-laugh.html?_r=0 (last accessed February 2015).

116. Following a legal challenge from the Opposition and rights groups, in February 2015 the High Court ruled that eight sections of the new law were unconstitutional. *Jurist*, 23 February 2015, http://jurist.org/paperchase/2015/02/kenya-high-court-declares-portions-of-anti-terrorism-law-unconstitutional.php (last accessed July 2015).

117. Ngũgĩ, *Penpoints, Gunpoints*, p. 5.

118. Bardolph, Jacqueline and Jean-Pierre Durix, interview (1983) in Sander and Lindfors, *Ngũgĩ Speaks*, p. 164.

119. Ngũgĩ, *Penpoints, Gunpoints*, p. 132.

5. JORGE SEMPRÚN AND THE TRANSITION IN SPAIN: JUSTICE, AMNESIA AND MEMORY

1. For a variety of interpretations, see Muro, Diego and Alonso Gregorio, *The Politics and Memory of Democratic Transition: The Spanish Model*, New York and Abingdon, 2011.

2. Preston, Paul, *The Spanish Holocaust: Inquisition and Extermination in Twentieth-Century Spain*, London: HarperPress, 2011, pp.xv–xvi.

3. Ibid., p.xvi. He cites several sources, in particular Ledesma, José Luis, 'Una retaguardia al rojo: las violencias en la zona republicana', in Maestre, Francisco Espinosa, *Violencia roja y azul: España, 1936–1950*, Barcelona: Editorial Crítica, 2010.

4. Preston, *Spanish Holocaust*, p.xviii. The most reliable current number is 130,199 but Preston provides convincing reasons for suggesting the higher figure.

5. Ibid., pp.xiii–xiv.

6. De Mata, Ignacio Fernádez, 'The Rupture of the World and the Conflicts of Memory' in Jerez-Farrán, Carlos and Samuel Amago (eds), *Unearthing Franco's Legacy: Mass Graves and the Recovery of Historical Memory in Spain*, Notre Dame, Indiana: University of Notre Dame Press, 2010, p. 289.

7. Casanova, Julián, 'The Faces of Terror: Violence during the Franco Dictatorship' in ibid., pp. 90–1.

8. Ibid., pp. 103–4.

9. Preston, Paul, *The Triumph of Democracy in Spain*, London: Routledge, 1990, p. 33; p. 74.

10. Casanova, *Faces of Terror*, p. 116.

11. Richards, Michael, 'Grand Narratives, Collective Memory, and Social History: Public Uses of the Past in Postwar Spain' in Jerez-Farrán and Amago, *Unearthing*, pp. 133–4.

12. However, three new books in English demonstrate his range and importance: Ferrán, Ofelia and Gina Herrmann (eds), *A Critical Companion to Jorge Semprún: Buchenwald, Before and After*, New York: Palgrave Macmillan, 2014; Tidd, Ursula, *Jorge Semprún: Writing the European Other*, Oxford: Legenda, 2014; Omlor, Daniela, *Jorge Semprún: Memory's Long Voyage*, Oxford: Peter Lang, 2014.

13. Semprún, Jorge, *Le grand voyage*, Paris: Gallimard, 1963; *The Long Voyage*, London: Weidenfeld and Nicolson, 1964. It was also republished as *The Cattle Truck*, London: Serif, 2005.

14. *Z* was based on a novel by Vassilis Vassilikos and was a fictional account of the assassination of the politician Grigoris Lambrakis in 1963. *L'Aveu* was based on Artur London's own account of his forced confession and subsequent imprisonment as one of the defendants in the Slánský trial of

1952. Fourteen prominent communists (of whom eleven were Jewish) were falsely accused and convicted of participating in a Trotskyite-Titoist-Zionist conspiracy. Eleven were executed and three (including London) were sentenced to life imprisonment.

15. Fox, Soledad, 'Exile and Return: The Many Madrids of Jorge Semprún' in *Ciberletras: Revista de Critica Literaria y de Cultura*, Dec. 2003, http://www.lehman.cuny.edu/ciberletras/v10/fox.htm (last accessed Feb. 2015); Hopkins, Stephen, 'Still a "Spanish Red"? The communist past and national identity in the writing of Jorge Semprún', *Twentieth Century Communism*, 3 May 2011, pp. 71–91; Kiss, Csilla, 'La guerre est toujours là: Defeat, Exile and Resistance in the Works of Jorge Semprún', *Bulletin of Spanish Studies: Hispanic Studies and Researches on Spain, Portugal and Latin America*, 89, 7–8 (2012) pp. 95–108; Omlor, Daniela, 'Exile and Trauma in Jorge Semprún', *Journal of Iberian and Latin American Research*, 17, 1 (2011) pp. 69–79; Omlor, *Semprún: Memory's Long Voyage*; Ferrán, Ofelia, *Working Through Memory: Writing and Remembrance in Contemporary Spain*, Lewisburg, PA: Bucknell University Press, 2007, pp. 66–101.

16. Kiss, 'La guerre est toujours là', pp. 101–103. *Esprit* was a French literary magazine founded in October 1932 by Emmanuel Mounier (1905–1950), who promoted the philosophy of 'personalism', which he saw as an alternative to both liberalism and Marxism. Semprún Gurrea also wrote for the Spanish Catholic journal, *Cruz y Raya*.

17. Ibid., p. 191.

18. Semprún, Jorge, *What a Beautiful Sunday*, London: Secker and Warburg, 1983, p. 306. (Originally published as *Quel beau dimanche*, Paris: Gallimard, 1980). Lucien Herr (1864–1926) was an intellectual who played a key role in the campaign to clear Dreyfus and influenced many socialist politicians and writers.

19. Ibid., p. 306, p. 380; Semprún, Jorge, *Literature or Life*, New York: Viking Penguin, 1997 p. 71, p. 131 (originally published as *L'écriture ou la vie*, Paris: Gallimard, 1994).

20. Semprún, Jorge, *Adieu Vive Clarté*, Paris: Gallimard, 1998, p. 216; Pradera, Francisco Javier, 'Jorge Semprún and his heteronym, Federico Sánchez' in Ferrán and Herrmann, *Critical Companion*, p. 54.

21. Semprún, *Literature or Life*, pp. 15–16.

22. Gabriel, Ian B., '*Toma La Calle*: An Analysis of The Influences Behind the Anti-Franco Student Protests of February 1956 at the University of Madrid', Honors Thesis, Rutgers University, 2012, pp. 39–48.

23. Semprún, Jorge, *Communism in Spain in the Franco Era: The Autobiography of Federico Sánchez*, Brighton: Harvester Press, 1980, pp. 187–8 (originally published as *Autobiografía de Federico Sánchez*, Barcelona: Planeta, 1977).

24. Semprún, *Communism in Spain*, pp. 3–10, p. 97, p. 163. His own accounts

of his role in the party are largely corroborated in Preston, Paul, *The Last Stalinist:The Life of Santiago Carrillo*, London:William Collins, 2014.

25. Fernando Claudín (1915–90) was a senior figure in the PCE, having been a member of the Political Bureau since 1947. He subsequently wrote several books, including *La crisis del movimiento comunista: de la Komintern al Kominform*, Paris: Éditions Ruedo Ibérico, 1970, which was published in English as *The Communist Movement: From Comintern to Cominform*, Harmondsworth: Penguin, 1975. For a detailed explanation of the issues involved in the expulsion, see Preston, *Last Stalinist*, pp. 205–54.

26. Omlor, *Jorge Semprún*, pp. 205–11.

27. Munté, Rosa-Auria, 'The Convergence of Historical Facts and Literary Fiction: Jorge Semprún's Autofiction on the Holocaust', *Forum Qualitative Sozialforschung / Forum: Qualitative Social Research*, 12, 3 Art. 14, (Sept. 2011), http://www.qualitative-research.net/index.php/fqs/article/view/1754/3261 (last accessed Feb. 2015).

28. Semprún, Jorge, *Vingt ans et un jour*, Paris: Gallimard, 2004 (originally published as *Veinte Años y un Día*, Barcelona:Tusquets, 2003).

29. Ibid., p. 348.

30. Ibid., p. 356.

31. Semprún, *Literature or Life*, p. 165.

32. Ibid., p. 52.

33. Gordon, *VagabondWitness*, p. 93.

34. Semprún Gurrea also believed it was wrong for trade unions or parties of the Left to use insurrectional strikes or violence. Semprún, Jorge, *Federico Sánchez vous salue bien*, Paris: Grasset, 1993, p. 31.

35. Semprún, *Communism in Spain*, pp. 172–3.

36. Semprún, *Adieu*, p. 30.

37. Ibid., p. 79.

38. Ibid.

39. Ibid., p. 220.

40. Semprún, *Literature or Life*, p. 114; '"…Une Tombe au Creux des Nuages…"' (1994) in Semprún, Jorge, *Une tombe au creux des nuages: Essais sur l'Europe d'hier et d'aujourd'hui*, Paris: Climats-Flammarion, 2010, p. 135.

41. Semprún, Jorge, 'Une communauté de valeurs' in Semprún, Jorge et Dominique de Villepin, *L'Homme Européen*, Paris: Plon, 2005, p. 219.

42. Semprún, *Communism in Spain*, p. 97.

43. He later claimed he had not read a single line Stalin had written when he was in Buchenwald, and he hardly knew who he was, for he had no bearing whatsoever on his Marxism at the time (Semprún, *Literature or Life*, p. 66). Other retrospective judgments provide further insight into his early Marxism. In general, he claimed, his interest in politics was always

related to major issues, rather than detailed policies, and was embedded in an essentially moral framework; and that his Marxist commitment was not based in economic theory, but in a belief that emancipation would be brought about by a universal class. Semprún, *Communism in Spain*, pp. 3–10; Semprún, *Adieu*, pp. 31–2; Semprún, *Beautiful Sunday*, p. 169.

44. Semprún, *Literature or Life*, p. 298.
45. Semprún, *Beautiful Sunday*, pp. 29–30.
46. The underground resistance saved many lives by obstructing Nazi orders to evacuate the camp, with emaciated prisoners taking control on 11 April and marching out with arms that they had captured. Semprún recalled this as a triumph, witnessed by two American personnel, in his posthumously published memoir, *Exercises de Survie*, Paris: Gallimard 2012, pp. 99–110.
47. Ibid., p. 288; Semprún, *Long Voyage*, pp. 162–6.
48. Semprún, 'Mère Blafarde, Tendre Soeur—L'avenir de l'Allemagne' (1995) in *Une tombe*, p. 167.
49. Semprún, *Literature or Life*, pp. 194–212.
50. Semprún, *Federico Sánchez vous salue*, p. 27. For many insights into Semprún's writing on Buchenwald, trauma and memory, see Omlor, *Jorge Semprún*, pp. 106–37.
51. Semprún, *Long Voyage*, p. 76.
52. Ibid., p. 162.
53. Ibid., p. 236.
54. Ibid., pp. 46–7.
55. Ibid., p. 122. For a full discussion of the Marxist and communist themes, see Bargel, Antoine, 'Semprún and Lukács: For a Marxist Reading of *Le Grand Voyage* in Ferrán and Herrmann, *Critical Companion*.
56. Azancot, Nuria, 'La Literatura me facilitó la ruptura política', Interview with Jorge Semprún, *El Mundo*, 12 Nov. 2012, quoted in 'Introduction', Ferrán and Herrmann, *Critical Companion*, p. 10.
57. Semprún, *Beautiful Sunday*, pp. 150–1. Kolyma is the far north-eastern region of Russia, with a sub-arctic climate, and became the most notorious site for Stalin's gulags.
58. The region in northern France where he had fought with the Resistance.
59. Ibid., pp. 426–7.
60. Pradera, 'Semprún and his heteronym', p. 67.
61. Semprún, *Communism in Spain*, pp. 258–63.
62. Semprún, Jorge, '"J'ai perdu mes certitudes, j'ai gardé mes illusions", Entretien avec Jorge Semprun', nonfiction.fr, 'Le quotidian des livres et des idées', 10 May 2010, http://www.nonfiction.fr/article-3391-jai_perdu_mes_certitudes_jai_garde_mes_illusions_entretien_avec_jorge_semprun.htm (last accessed Feb. 2015).

63. Semprún., *Beautiful Sunday*, p. 416.
64. Semprún, *Literature or Life*, pp. 301–2.
65. Semprún, *Communism in Spain*, p. 96; See also ibid., pp. 102–6 and *Beautiful Sunday*, pp. 40–3.
66. Ibid., p. 179. In some cases, however, he certainly defended himself. In particular, much later he was accused of having acted as a collaborator (Kapo) within the camp. He refuted this charge, arguing both that normal morality could not apply in such conditions and that he sometimes falsified identification sheets to save people, thereby risking execution had he been discovered. Céspedes, Jaime, 'Jorge Semprún's Speeches' in Ferrán and Herrmann, *Critical Companion*, pp. 228–30.
67. Semprún, *Beautiful Sunday*, pp. 228–35.
68. Ibid., pp. 251–2.
69. Semprún, *Communism in Spain*, pp. 175–6; pp. 206–7.
70. First, they no longer believed that the Spanish working-class had either the ability or the militancy to bring down the regime by itself. Instead of an ever-increasing accumulation of strikes, these were often defeated by repression, which led to an erosion of morale. Secondly, and still more fundamentally, Claudín and Semprún argued that the Spanish economy had changed very substantially since the 1930s: some of the working-classes had shared in increased material benefits and, equally importantly, sectors of the bourgeoisie no longer regarded the maintenance of the dictatorship as essential for their interests. This also meant that Claudín and Semprún believed that a Spanish pluralist democracy could be constructed through forging alliances with sections of the middle-classes. In other words, their alternative policy was close to the 'Eurocommunism' of the 1970s. See Pradera, 'Semprún and his heteronym'.
71. Semprún, Jorge, *La Guerre est finie: scenario du film d'Alain Resnais*, Paris: Gallimard, 1966, p. 89.
72. Ibid., p. 57.
73. Gabriel, '*Toma La Calle*', pp. 3–48; Semprún, *Communism in Spain*, p. 32; Semprún, *Vingt ans*, pp. 146–51; p. 381.
74. Preston, *Last Stalinist*, pp. 188–90.
75. Quoted in Riambau, Esteve, 'The Clandestine Militant Who Would be Minister: Semprún and Cinema' in Ferrán Herrmann, *Critical Companion*, pp. 85–6.
76. Preston, *Triumph of Democracy*, pp. 102–4.
77. This was evident within the UCD itself, with the overwhelming majority of ministers having occupied second or third level executive positions during the last years of Franco's regime. Linz, Juan, Miguel Jerez and Susana Corzo, 'Ministers and Regimes in Spain: From First to Second Restoration, 1874–2001', *Center for European Studies*, Working Paper

No. 101, 2001, p. 29, cited in Encarnación, Omar G., 'Justice in Times of Transition: Lessons from the Iberian Experience', *Center for European Studies*, Working Paper Series 173, 2009, p. 25.

78. This attempt to woo the centre ground involved a rapid jettisoning of the former position of the party. The previous year it had advocated a nation-wide strike to bring about a so-called 'democratic rupture', which would also involve the departure of Juan Carlos, but in February 1977 in an agreement with Suárez, Carrillo recognised the monarch and offered support for a future social contract in return for legalisation of the party. Preston, *Triumph of Democracy*, p. 85, pp. 106–8, pp. 114–19.

79. This was attempted on 23 February 1981, when a group of civil guards under Colonel Tejero burst into parliament and tried to hold the whole political elite hostage. After the king denounced this action and supported the democratically elected government, the hostage takers surrendered. Tejero was imprisoned until 1996. For the role of King Juan Carlos, see Preston, Paul, *Juan Carlos, A People's King*, London: HarperCollins, 2004, pp. 450–85.

80. The first stage came with a limited pardon at the time of Juan Carlos's coronation in November 1975, when 528 political prisoners were released. Following further mass mobilisation, a Royal Decree Amnesty Law was passed in July 1976, covering many political crimes, but there were demands for a far more extensive amnesty at the time of the Moncloa Pact discussions in October 1977, leading to a new law, which was passed almost unanimously in parliament. Between 1978 and the early 1990s, there were a series of complementary measures for former Republicans, including the restoration of citizenship rights and rights to benefits and compensation for those who had previously been denied these because they had been in prison. Aguilar, Paloma, 'Transitional Justice in the Spanish, Argentinian and Chilean Case', International Conference, Building a Future on Peace and Justice, Nuremberg, 25–27 June 2007, pp. 4–8, http://www.peace-justice-conference.info/download/WS%20 10%20Aguilar%20report.pdf (last accessed February 2015).

81. Encarnación, 'Justice in Times of Transition', pp. 27–8; Preston, *Triumph of Democracy*, p. 134; Aguilar, 'Transitional Justice', p. 6.

82. Interview, 21 Mar. 1994, quoted in Encarnación, 'Justice in Times of Transition', p. 25.

83. Semprún, *Federico Sánchez vous salue*, pp. 114–18.

84. He interviewed King Carlos early in 1981, and became convinced that the king was resolute in his support of the democratic transition and that there was no possibility of any military action succeeding in these cir-cumstances. Ibid., pp. 205–7. When Tejero subsequently made his coup attempt, he repeated this view in an interview on French television

Interview on *Antenne 2*, 24 Feb. 1981, http://www.youtube.com/watch?v=DXrV9irzOTw (last accessed Feb. 2015).

85. Semprún, *Federico Sánchez vous salue*, p. 247.
86. Ibid., p. 117.
87. 'The Uncanny Era of Post-Communism' (Prague, Nov. 1991) in Havel, Václav, *An Uncanny Era: Conversations Between Václav Havel and Adam Michnik* (edited, translated and with an introduction by Elzbieta Matynia), New Haven, CT: Yale University Press, 2014, p. 38.
88. Resina, Joan Ramon, 'The Weight of Memory and the Lightness of Oblivion' in Jerez-Farrán and Amago, *Unearthing*, p. 229.
89. Labanyi, Jo, 'The Politics of Memory in Contemporary Spain', *Journal of Spanish Cultural Studies*, 9, 2 (2008), p. 124.
90. It simultaneously used highly repressive extra-judicial methods against the Basque militant nationalist group, ETA. Woodworth, Paddy, *Dirty War, Clean Hands: ETA, the Gal and Spanish Democracy*, 2nd Edition, Connecticut: Yale Nota Bene, 2003.
91. Semprún, *Federico Sánchez vous salue*, pp. 118–19.
92. Ibid., pp. 240–1.
93. Ibid., p. 246. Semprún distanced himself from the celebration organised by Alfonso Guerra, the Deputy Prime Minister, with whom his relations were particularly poor.
94. Ibid., pp. 248–9.
95. Ibid., p. 250.
96. Ibid., p. 192. He subsequently claimed that during the Franco era he had heard Picasso say, on numerous occasions, that he wanted this. 'Bilbao et Marx' (1997) in Semprún, *Une tombe*, p. 192.
97. Semprún, *Communism in Spain*, p. 182.
98. Semprún, *Vingt ans*, pp. 243–50.
99. Ibid., pp. 380–2.
100. Ibid., pp. 53–4.
101. Ibid., pp. 47–50.
102. Omlor, Daniela, 'Reassessing history, rediscovering memory: Jorge Semprún's *Veinte años y un día*', *Nomenclatura: aproximaciones a los estudios hispánicos*, 1: 1, Art. 1, 2011, pp. 1–15. http://uknowledge.uky.edu/naeh/vol1/iss1/1 (last accessed Feb. 2015).
103. The impact of Spanish campaigning for the indictment of Pinochet for human rights atrocities in Chile without having addressed such issues at home, and the pressure of the Association for the Recovery of Historical Memory, were particularly important. Davis, Madeleine, 'Is Spain Recovering its Memory? Breaking the "Pacto del Olvido"', *Human Rights Quarterly*, 27 (3), 2005, pp. 869–73.
104. Semprún, *Literature or Life*, p. 196.

105. Ibid., p. 226.
106. Semprún, 'Les victimes du National-Socialisme' (2003) in Semprún, *Une tombe*, pp. 295–303.
107. Semprún, 'Ni héros, ni victimes' (1995) in ibid., pp. 150–1.
108. Amnesty International, 'España: poner fin al silencio y la injusticia. La deuda pendiente con las victimas de la guerra civil' ('Spain: Putting an End to Silence and Injustice'), 18 July 2005, quoted in Tremlett, Giles, 'Grandsons of Grandfathers', in Jerez-Farrán and Amago, *Unearthing*, p. 332.
109. Following the publication of the draft law on Historical Memory, the Plenary Assembly of the Spanish Bishops' Conference, the most senior body of the Church in Spain, issued a warning that 'Reconciliation is Under Threat', and the same line was taken by the right-wing party, the People's Party (Partido Popular, PP, renamed from the Alianza Popular, AP, the Francoist successor party), and the parliamentary debates on the proposed legislation were bitter and heated (Tremlett, Grandsons, pp. 342–3). In contrast, both the United Left (Izquierda Unida, IU) and the Republican Left of Catalonia (Esquerra Republicana de Catalunya, ERC) withdrew from co-sponsorship in the late autumn of 2006, decrying the draft law's acceptance of impunity for perpetrators of atrocities. The IU then accepted a concession. Golob, Stephanie R, 'Volver: The Return of Transitional Justice Politics in Spain', *Journal of Spanish Cultural Studies*, 9, 2 (2008), p. 136.
110. Article 1 of the law stated its purpose was to: 'Recognise and expand the rights of those victimised by the prosecution or violence of the Civil War and the Dictatorship, for political or ideological reasons; to promote the recuperation of personal and family memory; and to adopt measures destined to suppress elements of division among the citizenry with the goal of promoting cohesion and solidarity across the different generations of Spaniards around constitutional principles, values and liberties' (quoted in Encarnción, Omar, G., 'Reconciliation after Democratization: Coping with the Past in Spain', *Political Science Quarterly*, 123, 3 (2008), p. 452). This led to significant progress in the removal of Francoist monuments and symbols in public places, in the award of pensions to those who had been orphaned or sent into exile, in the granting of Spanish nationality to the descendants of exiles, and in the identification of mass graves from the Civil War.
111. Buck, Tobias, 'Facing up to Franco: Spain 40 years on', *FT Magazine*, 8 May 2015, http://www.ft.com/cms/s/2/5e4e6aac-f42f-11e4-99de-00144feab7de.html#slide0 (last accessed, July 2015).
112. For a discussion of the significance of the action against Garzón see Chinchón Álvarez, J, 'The Challenges posed to the recent investigation

of crimes committed during the Spanish Civil War and Francoism' in Almquist, Jessica and Carlos Espósito, *The Role of Courts in Transitional Justice.Voices from Latin America and Spain*, New York: Routledge, 2013.

113. Semprún, Jorge, 'Apathy a danger to Europe', Euronews, 1 July 2009, http://www.euronews.com/2009/07/01/jorge-semprun-apathy-a-danger-to-europe/ (last accessed February 2015).

114. Torpey, John, *Making Whole What Has Been Smashed: On Reparations Politics*, Cambridge: Harvard University Press, 2006, p. 337, cited in Berg, Manfred and Bernd Schaefer (eds), *Historical Justice in International Perspective: How Societies Are Trying to Right the Wrongs of the Past*, Cambridge: Cambridge University Press, 2008, p. 3.

115. Maier, Charles S., 'A Surfeit of Memory? Reflections on History, Melancholy and Denial', *History and Memory*, 5 (2) 1993, pp. 136–52.

116. Aguado, Txetxu, 'Memory, Politics and Post-national Citizenship in Jorge Semprún's *L'Écriture ou la vie*', *Hispanic Research Journal*, 6, 3 (2005), p. 250.

117. Maier, 'A Surfeit of Memory', pp. 150–1.

118. Semprún and de Villepin, *L'Homme européen*; Semprún, 'la gauche en Europe après les utopias' (1992) in Semprún, *Une tombe*, pp. 106–9.

119. Ibid, p. 108; 'la diversité culturelle et l'europe' (1992) in ibid., pp. 112–8. However, he believed that Husserl was too restrictive in emphasising Greek thought as the major source for the European idea. Ibid., pp. 120–28.

120. 'Bilbao et Marx', pp. 212–3; 'la gauche en Europe après les utopias', p. 107.

121. Semprún, *Federico Sánchez vous salue*, pp. 48–5 and pp. 75–6; Semprún, 'Une Tombe au Creux des Nuages' (1994) in *Une Tombe*, p. 135.

6. ALLENDE, PINOCHET AND THE TRANSITION TO DEMOCRACY: ARIEL DORFMAN AND CHILE

1. Dorfman, Ariel, *Death and the Maiden*, London: Nick Hern Books, 1991 (first published in Spanish as *La Muerte y la doncella*, Buenos Aires: Ediciones de la Flor, 1992). It has been argued that the play 'might be considered a "pre-text" of transitional justice, foreshadowing some of the issues that would later become central to theoretical understandings of the field'. McAuliffe, Padraig, 'Ariel Dorfman's *Death and the Maiden* as a Mirror Reflecting the Dilemmas of Transitional Justice Policy' in Rush, Peter D. and Olivera Simić (eds), *The Arts of Transitional Justice: Culture, Activism, and Memory after Atrocity*, New York: Springer, 2014, pp. 82–3.

2. Dorfman, Ariel, *Exorcising Terror: The Incredible Unending Trial of General Augusto Pinochet*, London: Pluto Press, 2003.

3. McClennen, Sophia A., *Ariel Dorfman: An Aesthetics of Hope*, Durham and London: Duke University Press, 2010, p.x.

4. Dorfman, Ariel, *Heading South, Looking North: A Bilingual Journey*, London: Hodder & Stoughton, 1998, pp. 11–25.

5. Ibid., pp. 28–48.

6. Ibid., pp. 66–76.

7. Ibid., pp. 79–81.

8. Ibid., p. 125.

9. Ibid., p. 159. His mother had adopted the name Ariel from an essay by the Uruguayan, José Enrique Rodó, in 1900.

10. Ibid., pp. 163–72.

11. Dorfman, Ariel, *El absurdo entre cuatro paredes: El teatro de Harold Pinter*, Santiago: Editorial Universitaria, 1968.

12. Dorfman, Ariel, *Feeding on Dreams: Confessions of an Unrepentent Exile*, Boston and New York: Mariner Books, 2012, p. 238.

13. Dorfman, *Heading South*, p. 225.

14. MAPU initially based itself on Marxism as a 'source of inspiration', and in 1970 declared its intention of liquidating the 'fundamental enemies of the Chilean people', defined as imperialism, monopolies and *latifundio*. The leader and founder was Rodrigo Ambrosio, but he died in May 1972 and internal division and splits then developed. At its second congress in December 1972 it defined itself as Marxist-Leninist, with the leadership passing to the extreme left of the party under Oscar Guillermo Garretón. This led to a further division in March 1973, with Jaime Gazmuri Mujica, who was closer to the Communist Party and the government coalition, establishing MAPU Obrero Campesino or MAPU/OC Historia Política Legislativa del Congreso National de Chile, 'Movimiento de Acción Popular Unitaria', http://historiapolitica.bcn.cl/partidos_politicos/wiki/Movimiento_de_Acción_Popular_Unitaria (last accessed Feb. 2015). Although Dorfman always claimed to be a member of MAPU, he appears to have joined MAPU/OC at the time of the split. Vidal, Hernán, 'Ariel Dorfman: The Residue of Hope After Public Personae Construction', *Exile, Intellectuals, and the Memory Wars. Hispanic Issues On Line Debates* 5 (Fall 2012), p. 18, http://hispanicissues.umn.edu/assets/doc/01_VIDAL_EIMW.pdf (last accessed Feb. 2015).

15. The CIA has admitted that both the US government and the CIA itself 'were aware of and agreed with' Chilean officers' assessment that the abduction of the Commander-in-Chief was an essential step in any coup plan. They also admitted meetings with various coup plotters, including supplying arms to one group, but claimed that they had not authorised the specific abduction attempt, which led to Schneider's death. Nevertheless, the CIA admits subsequently providing the group with

$35,000. 'CIA Activities in Chile, September 18, 2000' in https://www.cia.gov/library/reports/general-reports-1/chile/# (last accessed Feb. 2015). Another document of 16 September 1970, on 'Project Fubelt', shows the Director of the CIA, William Colby, reporting that 'President Nixon had decided that an Allende regime in Chile was not acceptable to the United States ... The President asked the Agency to prevent Allende from coming to power or to unseat him. The President authorised ten million dollars for this purpose, if needed. Further, the Agency is to carry out this mission without coordination with the Departments of State or Defense'. Colby also reported that he had been asked by Henry Kissinger, the National Security Assistant, to meet him on 18 September to give him the CIA's views on how the mission could be accomplished. See http://www2.gwu.edu/~nsarchiv/NSAEBB/NSAEBB8/docs/doc03.pdf in Kornbluh, Peter, *Chile and the United States: Declassified Documents Relating to the Military Coup, September 11, 1973* on http://www2.gwu.edu/~nsarchiv/NSAEBB/NSAEBB8/nsaebb8i.htm (last accessed, Feb. 2015). See also Gustafson, Kristian, *Hostile Intent: US Covert Operations in Chile, 1964–1974*, Dulles: Potomac Books, 2007, Chapter Two.

16. Dorfman, *Feeding*, p. 231.
17. Ibid., p. 39.
18. Collier, Simon and William F. Sater, *A History of Chile, 1808–2002* (2nd edition) Cambridge: Cambridge University Press, 2004, pp. 343–4.
19. MIR was founded in 1965 and at its height had around 10,000 members. It was a Marxist-Leninist organisation that supported direct revolutionary action, but generally offered critical support for the Allende government while also seeking to mobilise support amongst the peasantry and dispossessed Mapuche with a 'revolutionary peasant movement', which seized more than 1700 properties. Ibid., pp. 337–8.
20. Dorfman, *Heading South*, pp. 34–8.
21. Ibid., pp. 139–44; pp. 176–7; pp. 201–4; p. 254.
22. Exact numbers have never been agreed, but the total number of people officially recognised as disappeared or killed between 1973 and 1990 stands at 3,216, and survivors of political imprisonment and/or torture at 38,254. Amnesty International, *Chile: 40 years on from Pinochet's coup, impunity must end*, http://www.amnesty.org/en/news/chile-40-years-pinochet-s-coup-impunity-must-end-2013–09–10 (last accessed Feb. 2015).
23. Collier and Sater, *History of Chile*, pp. 359–62.
24. Dorfman, *Heading South*, p. 39.
25. These events are recounted non-chronologically throughout Dorfman, *Feeding* and summarised in a timeline, pp. 329–30.
26. Dorfman, Ariel, 'An Exile Finds Chile "Struck by a Plague"', *New York*

Times, 11 Sep. 1983, http://www.nytimes.com/1983/09/11/opinion/an-exile-finds-chile-struck-by-a-plague.html (last accessed, Feb. 2015). *Feeding*, pp. 212–15.

27. Dorman, Ariel, 'The Challenge in Chile' *New York Times Magazine*, 29 June 1986, http://www.nytimes.com/1986/06/29/magazine/the-challenge-in-chile.html (last accessed, Feb. 2015).

28. Dorfman, *Feeding*, p.xi–xi. He was also threatened with a machine gun, kicked and hit with a rifle butt during a demonstration. Ibid., pp. 217–19.

29. Ibid., p. 330.

30. Dorfman, Ariel, *Mores en la Costa*, Buenos Aires: Editorial Sudamericana, 1973; *Hard Rain*, Columbia, Louisiana: Readers International, 1990. Dorfman's own translation, *Hard Rain*, appeared only in 1990 and was considerably shorter than the original version. The most important difference was that in the original version there was a notion that the creative writer might eventually be absorbed wholly in the process of politics; by 1990 Dorfman saw this as a fantasy, realising that his life would always be dedicated at least in part to literature, and he therefore expressed this as something that he dreamed about but did not happen. Some specific contemporary references to Chile were cut out and the use of Bob Dylan's song *Hard Rain* in the title and epigraph allowed the message to expand to a wider realm of social critique. McClennen, *Aesthetics of Hope*, pp. 104–8.

31. Dorfman, *Feeding*, p. 97.

32. Ibid., p. 238.

33. Ibid.

34. Ibid., p. 239.

35. Ibid., p. 240.

36. The constitution provided for a powerful eight-year presidency, a congress with limited powers, with a third of the senate nominated rather than elected, and mechanisms to entrench military influence over future governments. After Pinochet's first term as president, there would be a plebiscite to endorse or reject the military's candidate for a second term and only then could elections be called in the event of a negative vote.

37. Collier and Sater, *History of Chile*, pp. 362–4.

38. Ibid., pp. 364–76.

39. This was particularly evident in his novel, *Mascara*, New York: Viking, 1988. This was a tale of an authoritarian society with absolute surveillance and control represented by two figures: a photographer without a face, whose photographs captured the deepest secrets of his subjects, and a plastic surgeon, who could create whole new faces with new histories. In this dark dystopian world, ultimate power appeared to lie with the sur-

geon who could create new images and eliminate memories of the past, and there was little sign of rebellion or even alternative voices. Instead the focus was on the psychology of those who sought to inflict pain on others. The sole sign of optimism lay in the Acknowledgements, where Dorfman wrote: 'In this novel of deception and betrayal, the reader will be hard pressed to find human beings who show a hint of loyalty to one another. It is particularly gratifying, therefore, to acknowledge in real living people a quality that the characters, in *Mascara* at least, do not possess'.

40. Dorfman, *Heading South*, p. 245.
41. McClennen, *Aesthetics of Hope*, p. 14.
42. *Para leer al Pato Donald: Comunicación de masa y colonialismo*, Valparaíso: Ediciones Universitarias de Valparaíso, 1971; *How to Read Donald Duck: Imperialist Ideology in the Disney Comic*, New York: International General Editions, 1975.
43. Dorfman, *Heading South*, pp. 250–1. Thousands of copies of *How to Read Donald Duck* were immediately publicly burnt by the new regime after the coup against Allende. Ibid., p. 139.
44. McClennen, Sophia, 'Beyond "Death and the Maiden": Ariel Dorfman's Media Criticism and Journalism', *Latin American Research Review*, 45, (2010), p. 175.
45. Dorfman, *Feeding*, p. 97.
46. Dorfman, *Hard Rain*, pp. 166–9; pp. 260–62.
47. Ibid., pp. 201–26.
48. Ibid., p.vii.
49. *Viudas*, Mexico City: Siglo XXI, 1981; *Widows*, London: Pluto Press, 1983. In an attempt to avoid censorship he set the novel in an unnamed country (apparently Greece) during World War II. The author had supposedly been a Danish resistance fighter killed in a concentration camp, with the manuscript discovered by his son forty years later. The plan was to pretend that the text had been translated into Spanish and then to secure its publication in Chile. This elaborate ploy failed, as the Chilean publisher would not risk producing a work about resistance against fascist occupation, and Dorfman eventually published it under his own name, keeping the original text.
50. Dorfman, *Widows*, p. 135.
51. Ibid., p. 130.
52. Dorfman, Ariel, *The Empire's Old Clothes: What the Lone Ranger, Barbar, and Other Innocent Heroes Do to Our minds*, New York: Pantheon Books, 1983.
53. Ibid., pp. 11–12.
54. Ibid., p. 12.
55. Ibid., p. 208.

56. See, for example, 'Family Circle' in Dorfman, Ariel, *My House is on Fire*, New York: Viking Penguin, 1990.

57. Dorfman, Ariel, *The Last Song of Manuel Sendero*, New York: Viking Penguin, 1987 (originally published as *La última canción de Manuel Sendero*, Mexico City: Siglo XXI, 1982).

58. McClennen, Sophia A., 'Ariel Dorfman', *Review of Contemporary Fiction*, 20, 3 (2000), p. 91. In an interview in December 1986, Dorfman admitted that he began the novel in despair. Boyers, Peggy, Juan Carlos Lertora and Ariel Dorfman, 'Ideology, Exile, Language: An Interview with Ariel Dorfman', *Salmagundi*, No. 82/83, (1989), p. 155.

59. McClennen, *Aesthetics of Hope*, pp. 133–4.

60. Dorfman, *Last Song*, p. 389.

61. The constraints imposed by Pinochet included guarantee of tenure to public sector employees, packing the Supreme Court and Constitutional Tribunal, consolidating his own power within the different military commands (with direct authority over the army until 1998), incorporating the 19,000 operatives of the CNI secret police into military intelligence under his line command, and destroying secret police archives. Congress also included nine 'designated senators', and the electoral system overrepresented the political Right, ensuring a blocking coalition against most systemic reforms. Wilde, Alexander, 'Irruptions of Memory: Expressive Politics in Chile's Transition to Democracy', *Journal of Latin American Studies*, 31, 2 (1999), p. 480.

62. Boyers, Lertora and Dorfman, 'Ideology, Exile, Language', p. 155.

63. Wilde, 'Irruptions'; Diary, 5 Sep. 1990 in Dorfman, *Feeding*, pp. 241–2 (extracts from his diary, entitled 'Diary of my return to Chile in 1990', are included in *Feeding*).

64. Diary, 23 July 1990 in Dorfman, *Feeding*, pp. 20–21.

65. Collins, Cath, 'Human Rights Trials in Chile during and after the "Pinochet Years"', *International Journal of Transitional Justice*, 4, 2010, p. 70.

66. Article 1, Supreme Decree No. 355 establishing the National Commission for Truth and Reconciliation, 25 April 1990, *Report of the Chilean National Commission on Truth and Reconciliation*, Notre Dame, Indiana: University of Notre Dame Press, vol. 1, 1993, http://www.usip.org/sites/default/files/file/resources/collections/commissions/Chile90-Charter.pdf (last accessed Feb. 2015).

67. Ibid., p. 148.

68. Hayner, Priscilla, B., *Unspeakable Truths: facing the challenge of truth commissions*, New York and London: Routledge, 2002, p. 36.

69. Arthur, Paige, 'How "Transitions" Reshaped Human Rights: A Conceptual History of Transitional Justice', *Human Rights Quarterly* 31, (2) 2009, pp. 335–6, p. 354, p. 358.

70. Diary, 25 Aug. 1990, Dorfman, *Feeding*, pp. 150–1.
71. Ibid., p. 152.
72. Ibid.
73. Ibid., p. 153.
74. Diary, 3 Sep. 1990, in ibid., p. 223.
75. Diary, 25 Aug. 1990, ibid., p. 154.
76. Diary, 3 Sep. 1990, in ibid., p. 224.
77. He hoped that it would be seen to have a universal significance, but he wrote it in reaction to the transition in Chile and, in particular, his frustration with the Rettig Commission. His stage directions stated that the place 'is probably Chile but could be any country that has given itself a democratic government just after a long period of dictatorship'. The play has been performed across the world, and analysed in numerous critical essays, emphasising a whole range of different concerns—from the impact of torture to the role of music, to the cultural specificity of its performance in different locations. McClennen, *Aesthetics of Hope*, pp. 160–76.
78. Dorfman, *Death and the Maiden* (1994), p. 6.
79. Ibid., p. 24.
80. Ibid., pp. 26–7.
81. Ibid., p. 36.
82. Ibid., p. 44.
83. For a discussion highlighting the significance of the sexual violence, see Luban, David, 'On Dorfman's Death and the Maiden', *Yale Journal of Law and the Humanities*, 10, 1 (1998), Iss.1, Art 3, http://digitalcommons. law.yale.edu/yjlh/vol10/iss1/3/ (last accessed Feb. 2015).
84. For a critique of Dorfman's representation of women, see Novak, Amy, 'Gendering Trauma: Ariel Dorfman's Narratives of crisis and Reconciliation', *Critique: Studies in Contemporary Fiction*, 48, 3 (2007).
85. Diary, 20 Dec. 1990 in Dorfman, *Feeding* p. 281.
86. Diary 8 Oct. 1990, Ibid., p. 256. He retained some elevated ideas about the importance of the play: 'Because what better sign that you are back from exile than to have written a play that requires a community to receive it and a community to support it, a play written and spoken in Spanish and simmered in the same language of rage and hope that is being suffocated in the streets of our city…?' (ibid, pp. 256–57). However, he immediately translated it into English for its first reading in London where, according to the actress Juliet Stevenson, who played Paulina in the premiere the next year, Chilean refugees were 'thrilled that someone was telling their story', Jaggi, Maya, 'Speaking for the Dead', *Guardian*, 14 June 2003, http://www.theguardian.com/stage/2003/jun/14/theatre.fiction (last accessed Feb. 2015).
87. Diary, 20 Dec 1990, *Feeding*, p. 280.

88. Ibid., p. 281.

89. Ibid., p. 282.

90. Ibid.

91. Ibid., p. 283; on the coup threats, see Loveman, Brian, 'Misión Cumplida? Civil Military Relations and the Chilean Political Transition', *Journal of Interamerican Studies and World Affairs*, 33, 3, (1991), pp. 36–7, p. 40.

92. Diary, 20 Dec.1990, Dorfman, *Feeding*, p. 284.

93. Diary, 6 Jan. 1991, Ibid., pp. 303–304.

94. Statement on 4 Mar. 1991, quoted in Hayner, *Unspeakable Truths*, p. 37.

95. Guzmán was a Professor of Constitutional Law and right-wing ideologue, who played a key role in drafting the 1980 Constitution for Pinochet. He was assassinated by the *Frente Patriótico Manuel Rodríguez* (FPMR), a far-left urban guerrilla movement.

96. Nevertheless, behind the scenes Aylwin (and his successor, President Frei) ensured that individuals associated with the worst human rights violations under the dictatorship were not promoted in either the armed forces or the judiciary. Wilde, Alexander, 'A Season of Memory: Human Rights in Chile's Long Transition' in Collins, Cath, Katherine Hite, and Alfredo Joignant, *The Politics of Memory in Chile: From Pinochet to Bachelet*, Boulder, Co: Lynne Rienner, 2013, pp. 37–8.

97. Wilde, 'Irruptions', p. 494.

98. From 1989–1998 annual GDP growth averaged 7.5 per cent and then fell to an average of 3.8 per cent between 1999–2008. From 2009–2012 the annual average was 4.1 per cent. Averages derived from World Bank data on http://data.worldbank.org/indicator/NY.GDP.MKTP. KD.ZG (last accessed Feb. 2015).

99. Collier and Sater, *History of Chile*, pp. 385–6. Chile is now ranked fortieth in the world in the Human Development Index—the highest in Latin America, advancing five places between 2007 and 2012. This places it above several European countries, including Portugal, Latvia, Lithuania and Croatia. Its annual HDI percentage growth was 0.78 between 1990 and 2000 and 0.64 between 2000 and 2012. *Human Development Report 2013. The Rise of the South: Human Progress in a Diverse World*, Statistical Tables. http://www.undp.org/content/dam/philippines/docs/HDR/HDR2013%20Report%20English.pdf (last accessed Feb. 2015).

100. Hayner, *Unspeakable Truths*, pp. 159–60.

101. Wilde, 'A season of memory', p. 36. For a full discussion, see Sterne, Steve J., *Battling for Hearts and Minds: Memory Struggles in Pinochet's Chile, 1973–1988*, Durham, CO: Duke University Press, 2006.

102. Wilde, 'Irruptions', p. 494.

103. Collins, 'Human Rights Trials', p. 75.

104. Wilde, 'Irruptions', p. 476.

105. Berman, Jenifer, 'Ariel Dorfman', *Bomb Magazine*, Winter 1995, http://bombmagazine.org/article/1833/ariel-dorfman (last accessed Feb. 2015).

106. Some analysts stress the increasing momentum on the issue within Chile itself, pointing out that the case in London could not have had the impact that it did without the accumulation of changes that had already taken place. Collins, 'Human Rights Trials', p. 79. The main stages in the prolonged legal action against Pinochet began in October 1998, when the Spanish judge, Baltasar Garzón, filed an official warrant with the UK authorities to question Pinochet, who was placed in police custody in London. Garzón then issued an international arrest warrant to prepare a request for extradition. The UK High Court ruled that, as a former head of state, Pinochet was immune from extradition, but the UK prosecution authorities appealed and the following month the Judicial Committee of the House of Lords reversed this judgment. In December 1998 this ruling was set aside, following a challenge that one of the Law Lords was linked to Amnesty International, but in March 1999 the Law Lords confirmed the previous decision that Pinochet could be extradited because a former head of state did not have immunity from prosecution for torture. In October 1999 a magistrate ordered the extradition, but in November the Chilean government asked the UK authorities to undertake medical tests in order to consider his release on humanitarian grounds for dementia. In March 2000 the UK Home Secretary halted proceedings for extradition, on health grounds, and Pinochet returned to Chile. Although the Chilean Congress then granted Pinochet immunity from prosecution and a financial allowance, he was also required to resign his seat as senator-for-life. Two months later, the Court of Appeal lifted his immunity and a series of indictments, claims of ill health, and reversals of decisions continued until his death on 10 December 2006, just after a judge had ordered a further period of house arrest. By then he had also been discredited for tax fraud and money laundering.

107. Collins, Cath, Katherine Hite, and Alfredo Joignant, 'The Politics of Memory in Chile' in Collins, Hite and Joignant, *Politics of Memory*, p. 13, p. 19.

108. Wilde, 'Season of Memory', 2013, pp. 45–9.

109. This was facilitated by the fact that she was the daughter of a constitutionalist air force general who died in prison after the coup, and she had been imprisoned and then exiled. Collins, 'Human Rights Trials', p. 85.

110. Following a visit to Chile in August 2013, the UN Working Group on Enforced or Involuntary Disappearances welcomed progress in investigations of human rights violations under Pinochet, but expressed con-

cern that few of the convicted perpetrators were serving a sentence because of the short penalties imposed. It called for the 1978 Amnesty Law to be repealed; for a national plan to search for the disappeared; and for the allocation of additional resources in order to expedite judicial proceedings. According to official data, as of August 2012 court proceedings in 150 cases of past human rights violations had been completed since 2002; 133 of these had resulted in convictions. *Amnesty International Annual Report 2013, Chile*, http://www.amnesty.org/en/region/chile/report-2013 (last accessed Feb. 2015).

111. Wilde, 'Season of Memory', p. 52.
112. Dorfman, Ariel, *Exorcising Terror*, pp. 157–8; pp. 198–9.
113. Open Letter, originally published in *El Pais*, 28 Oct. 1998, in ibid., p. 29.
114. Ibid., pp. 48–9.
115. Ibid., p. 317. He has been criticised for endorsing a commercially successful Broadway production of the play that deliberately sought to eliminate most of its political messages and ensured that the audience was not asked any difficult questions. Morace, Robert A., 'The Life and Times of Death and the Maiden', *Texas Studies in Literature and Language*, 42, 2, (2000), pp. 145–50; Weaver, James and Jeanne Colleran, '"Whose Memory? Whose Justice?" Personal and Political trauma in Ariel Dorfman's Death and the Maiden', *Performance Research* 16,1, (2011), pp. 37–8.
116. Dorfman, *Exorcising Terror*, p. 83; Dorfman, *Feeding*, pp. 210–11.
117. Hite, Collins, and Joignant, 'Politics of Memory in Chile', p. 19.
118. Hite, Collins, and Joignant, 'Afterword' in Collins, Hite and Joignant, *Politics of Memory.*, pp. 239–50.
119. Dorfman, Ariel, *Speak Truth to Power: Voices from Beyond the Dark*, New York: Umbrage Editions (in collaboration with Amnesty International), 2000.
120. 'The Children are Watching' (May 2001) in Dorfman, Ariel, *Other Septembers, Many Americas: Selected Provocations, 1980–2004*, London: Pluto, 2004, pp. 239–40.

7. NADINE GORDIMER: APARTHEID AND AFTER

1. United Nations Treaty Collection, No. 1486, *International Convention on the Suppression and Punishment of the Crime of Apartheid*, Adopted by the General Assembly of the United Nations on 30 November 1973, https://treaties.un.org/doc/Publication/UNTS/Volume%201015/volume-1015-I-14861-English.pdf (last accessed February 2015).
2. Gordimer, Nadine, *Face to Face: Short Stories*, Johannesburg: Silver Leaf Books, 1949.
3. *A World of Strangers*, London: Gollancz, 1958; *The Late Bourgeois World*,

London: Gollancz, 1966; *The Conservationist*, London: Jonathan Cape, 1974; *Burger's Daughter*, London: Jonathan Cape, 1979. The formal process in relation to *Burger's Daughter* was very unusual. The book was banned in July 1979, with the Censorship Board arguing that it was an outspoken promotion of communism and that its effect on the public attitude of mind was dangerous in all respects. However, the Director of Publications then appealed against the banning by his own committee, and appointed a panel of literary experts to evaluate the merit of the novel. They argued that it was difficult to read and would not become popular and because of its limited readership and its one-sidedness, the effect of the book would be counterproductive rather than subversive. The ban was lifted in October 1979. Barrett, Susan '"What I say will not be understood": Intertextuality as a subversive force in Nadine Gordimer's *Burger's Daughter*', E-rea (En Ligne), 2.1, 2004, http:erea.revues.org/491 (last accessed Feb. 2015), citing Dugard, John and Nadine Gordimer, *What Happened to Burger's Daughter: Or How South African Censorship Works*, Emmarentia: Taurus, 1980.

4. The biographical information is derived from various sources, including the interviews in Bazin, Nancy Topping and Marilyn Dallman Seymour (eds), *Conversations with Nadine Gordimer*, Jackson and London: University Press of Mississippi, 1990, and several of her own essays in her collections: Gordimer, Nadine, *Writing and Being*, Cambridge and London: Harvard University Press, 1995; *Living in Hope and History: Notes from our Century*, London: Bloomsbury, 1999; *Telling Times: Writing and Living, 1954–2008*, London: Bloomsbury, 2010; *The Essential Gesture: Writing, Politics and Places*, London: Jonathan Cape, 1988. Roberts, Ronald Suresh, *No Cold Kitchen—A Biography of Nadine Gordimer*, Johannesburg: STE Publishers, 2005, is also informative.

5. Gordimer, Nadine, *No Time Like the Present*, London: Bloomsbury, 2012.

6. Gordimer, Nadine (interviewed by Jannika Hurwitt), 'The Art of Fiction No. 77', *The Paris Review*, No. 88, Summer 1983, http://www.theparisreview.org/interviews/3060/the-art-of-fiction-no-77-nadine-gordimer (last accessed Feb. 2015).

7. 'Our Century' (1991), in Gordimer, *Living in Hope*, p. 226.

8. *The Soft Voice of the Servant and Other Stories*, New York: Simon & Schuster, 1952; *The Lying Days*, London: Gollancz, 1953.

9. Nobel Prize in Literature 1991 Nadine Gordimer, Presentation Speech by Professor Sture Allén, http://www.nobelprize.org/nobel_prizes/literature/laureates/1991/presentation-speech.html (last accessed Feb. 2015).

10. For her pessimism, see her interview with Studs Terkel (1962) in Bazin and Seymour, *Conversations*, pp. 30–1.

11. Alan Ross, 'Nadine Gordimer: A Writer in South Africa' (1965) in ibid., pp. 34–5.
12. 'Nadine Gordimer: Interview with Johannes Riis' (1979) in ibid., p. 101.
13. Diane Cassere, 'Diamonds are Polished—So is Nadine Gordimer' (1972) in ibid., p. 56.
14. 'A Bolter and the Invincible Summer' (1963), in Gordimer, *Essential Gesture*, p. 26.
15. Bettie du Toit (1910–2002) was a trade union activist in the Textile Workers Union from the late 1920s and was banned from further trade union activity in 1952 under the Suppression of Communism Act. Despite this she continued her political activities and was arrested several times, but finally went into exile
16. South African Communist Party, Letter sent by Bram Fischer to his Counsel in February 1965 when he went underground, and read to the court', http://www.sacp.org.za/main.php?ID=2369 (last accessed, Feb. 2015).
17. 'Why did Bram Fischer Choose Jail?' (1966), in Gordimer, *Essential Gesture*, p. 78.
18. Marilyn Powell, 'Nadine Gordimer: An Interview' (1984) in Bazin and Seymour, *Conversations*, p. 230.
19. Recollections of Mongane Wally Serote in Steele, Jonathan 'The Guardian Profile: Nadine Gordimer', *Guardian*, 27 Oct. 2001, http://www.the-guardian.com/books/2001/oct/27/fiction.artsandhumanities (last accessed February 2015).
20. 'Speak Out: the Necessity for Protest' (1971) in Gordimer, *Essential Gesture*.
21. 'Letter from Johannesburg' (1976) in Ibid.
22. 'Relevance and Commitment' (1979) in ibid., p. 134; 'Living in the Interregnum' (1982) in ibid., pp. 264–5.
23. Ibid., p. 282.
24. Ibid., p. 283.
25. Ibid., p. 265.
26. Ibid., p. 267.
27. Ibid., p. 271.
28. Hermione Lee, 'Talking to Writers: Nadine Gordimer' (1986) in Bazin and Seymour, *Conversations*, p. 244.
29. Roberts quotes a private letter from Gordimer in February 1957 following a bus boycott by black workers: 'The thing that appals me is this proof that they have no voice but violence' (Letter to Anthony Sampson, 22 Feb. 1957, quoted in Roberts, *No Cold Kitchen* p. 214). He concludes that this meant that Gordimer effectively separated herself from South African liberals at this time, but this surely over-estimates the significance of the letter.

30. 'A Conversation with Nadine Gordimer, Robert Boyers, Clark Blaise, Terence Diggory, Robert Elgrably' (1982), in Bazin and Seymour, *Conversations*, p. 198.

31. Gordimer, 'Living in the Interregnum', p. 271.

32. Gordimer, Nadine, *Burger's Daughter*, Harmondsworth: Penguin 1984, p. 342.

33. Lee (1986) in Bazin and Seymour, *Conversations*, p. 240.

34. Quoted in Roberts, *No Cold Kitchen*, p. 456.

35. Ibid.

36. Kasrils, Ronnie, *'Armed and Dangerous': My Undercover Struggle Against Apartheid*, London: Heinemann, 1993; Niehaus, Carl, *Fighting for Hope*, Cape Town: Human & Rousseau, 1994.

37. 'Hanging on a Sunrise: Testimony and the Imagination in Revolutionary Writings', in Gordimer, *Writing and Being*, p. 25.

38. Ibid., p. 29.

39. Ibid., p. 30.

40. Ibid., p. 27.

41. Ibid., p. 31.

42. Ibid., p. 35.

43. 'Necklacing' was a form of extra-legal punishment in which a tyre soaked in petrol was placed around the victim's neck and set alight.

44. Letter to Elizabeth Hardwick, 9 February 1986, quoted in Roberts, *No Cold Kitchen*, p. 447.

45. Wolpe, Harold, *Race, Class and the Apartheid State*, London: James Currey, 1987; Van Diepen, Maria, *The National Question in South Africa*, London: Zed Books, 1988; Drew, Allison, *Discordant Comrades: Identities and Loyalties on the South African Left*, Aldershot: Ashgate, 2000.

46. 'Three in a Bed' (1988), Gordimer, *Living in Hope*, p. 14.

47. For a critical interpretation of Gordimer's position, see Auga, Ulrika, 'Intellectuals between Resistance and Legitimation: The Cases of Nadine Gordimer and Christa Wolf', *Current Writing: Text and Reception in Southern Africa*, 2003, pp. 7–11.

48. Camus, Albert, *Carnets, 1942–51*, London: Hamish Hamilton, 1966, p. 104, quoted in Gordimer, 'Living in the Interregnum', p. 276.

49. Ibid., pp. 276–7.

50. Ibid., p. 278.

51. Ibid.

52. 'The Essential Gesture' (1984), in Gordimer, *Telling Times*, pp. 412–13.

53. Ibid., p. 420.

54. 'The Writer's Imagination and the Imagination of the State' (1986), in Gordimer, *Living in Hope*, p. 193.

55. Fullerton-Smith, Jill, 'Off the Page: Nadine Gordimer' (1988) in Bazin and Seymour, *Conversations*, p. 299.

56. 'A Writer's Freedom' (1975), in Gordimer, *Essential Gesture*, p. 110.

57. Quoted in ibid., p. 110.

58. Ibid.

59. Gordimer, Nadine, *The Conservationist*, Harmondsworth: Penguin, 1978, p. 266.

60. Ibid., p. 267.

61. Gordimer, 'Art of Fiction'.

62. The catalysts for the Soweto uprising had been the introduction of Afrikaans as a compulsory language (alongside English) in education in 1974, and the rise of the Black Consciousness movement, which mobilised the students. On 16 June 1976 several thousand students marched to demonstrate against the directive, but were met by heavily armed police, who fired teargas and later bullets at the protesters. This resulted in the uprising, which was countered by extreme police brutality, shocking much opinion abroad, and thereby contributing to the growth of international opposition to apartheid.

63. Ibid.

64. Gordimer, Nadine, *July's People*, London: Cape, 1981.

65. Quoting Gramsci, Antonio, *Selections from Prison Notebooks* (edited and translated by Quintin Hoare and Geoffrey Nowell-Smith), London: Lawrence & Wishart, 1971, p. 276.

66. Margaret Walters, 'Writers in Conversation: Nadine Gordimer' (1987) in Bazin and Seymour, *Conversations*, p. 294.

67. Bond, Patrick, *Elite Transition: From Apartheid to Neoliberalism in South Africa*, London: Pluto Press, New Edition, 2014; Habib, Adam and Vishnu Padayachee, 'Economic Policy and Power Relations in South Africa's Transition to Democracy', *World Development* 28, 2 (2000), pp. 245–63.

68. Boraine, Alex, 'Truth and Reconciliation in South Africa: The Third Way', in Rotberg, Robert and Dennis Thompson (eds), *Truth Versus Justice: The Morality of Truth Commissions*, Princeton: Princeton University Press, 2000, pp. 143–4

69. During the early 1990s there was an escalation of violence within and between black communities, and the Truth and Reconciliation Commission estimated that approximately 14,000 deaths occurred between 1990–4. Chapman, Audrey, 'The TRC's Approach to Promoting Reconciliation in Human Rights Violations Hearings' in Chapman, Audrey R. and Hugo Van der Merwe, *Truth and Reconciliation in South Africa: Did the TRC Deliver?*, Philadelphia: University of Pennsylvania Press, 2008, pp. 63–4.

70. There is a vast literature on the TRC. For appraisals of its strengths and weaknesses and long-term impact, see Chapman and Van der Merwe, *Truth and Reconciliation* and Gready, Paul, *The Era of Transitional Justice: The Aftermath of the Truth and Reconciliation Commission in South Africa and Beyond*,

London: Routledge, 2011. See also Jakopovich, Daniel, 'A Humanist Defence and Critique of the South African Truth and Reconciliation Commission', *Peace Studies Journal*, 4, 1 (2011), pp. 51–65.

71. Tutu, Desmond, *No Future without Forgiveness*, London: Rider, 1999, p. 126.

72. 'Sorting the Images from the Man: Nelson Mandela' (1990) in Gordimer, *Telling Times*, p. 462.

73. 'How shall we look at each other then?' in Gordimer, *Living in Hope*, pp. 139–45.

74. Ibid.

75. Gordimer, Nadine, 'The First Time' in Gordimer, Nadine, *Living in Hope*, p. 157.

76. Ibid., p. 160.

77. Quoted in Roberts, *No Cold Kitchen*, p. 562.

78. 'As others see us' (1997), in Gordimer, *Living in Hope*, p. 177.

79. Auga, 'Intellectuals between Resistance', p. 11.

80. 'Five Years into Freedom: My New South African Identity' (1999), in Gordimer, *Telling Times*, pp. 562–3.

81. From Serote, Mongane Wally, *A Tough Tale: South Africa*, London: Kliptown Books, 1987, quoted in Gordimer, 'Hanging on a Sunrise: Testimony and Imagination in Revolutionary Writings' in *Writing and Being*, 1995, pp. 41–2.

82. Ibid., p. 42.

83. 'One Year Later' (1995) in Gordimer, *Living in Hope*, p. 167.

84. Ibid.

85. Paul, Donald, 'The Other Side of the Story', *Boston Phoenix*, 5 Jan. 1998, http://www.weeklywire.com/ww/01–05–98/boston_books_3.html (last accessed Feb. 2015).

86. 'Desmond Tutu as I Know Him' (2006) in Gordimer, *Telling Times*, p. 699.

87. Chalamanda, Fiona Michaela Johnson, 'Interpretations in Transition: Literature and political transition in Malawi and South Africa in the 1990s', University of Stirling: PhD., 2002, pp. 26–7.

88. Gordimer, Nadine, *None to Accompany Me*, London: Bloomsbury, 1994, p. 234.

89. Ibid., 305.

90. Ibid., p. 261.

91. Gordimer, Nadine, *The House-Gun*, London: Bloomsbury, 1998. See also Diala, Isidore, 'Nadine Gordimer, J. M. Coetzee, and Andre Brink, 'Guilt, Expiation, and the Reconciliation Process in Post-Apartheid South Africa', *Journal of Modern Literature*, 25, 2 (2001–2), pp. 50–68.

92. Mallinder, Louise, *Indemnity, Amnesty, Pardon and Prosecution Guidelines in South Africa*, Working Paper No. 3 from *Beyond Legalism: Amnesties, Transition and Conflict Transformation*, Institute of Criminology and Criminal Justice,

Queen's University Belfast, 2009, https://www.qub.ac.uk/schools/
SchoolofLaw/Research/InstituteofCriminologyandCriminalJustice/
Research/BeyondLegalism/filestore/Filetoupload,152146,en.pdf (last
accessed, 18 November 2015).

93. Roberts, *No Cold Kitchen*, p. 549. Under the TRC an Amnesty Committee
was established, chaired by a judge. Those seeking an amnesty needed to
submit an application and, in order to be successful, this needed to meet
the following criteria: 1. A violation of human rights must have occurred;
2. The act had to take place between 1960 and 1994; 3. The violation had
to be 'associated with a political "objective"'. (In establishing whether the
act was political, the Committee could consider the motive, objective,
whether it was directed against the state or an individual, and the proportional relationship between the act and the political objective); 4. The
applicant had to admit fault (possibly with an excuse or justification, such
as self-defence); 5. The applicant had to make a full disclosure of all the
relevant facts.

94. Gordimer, *The House-Gun*, p. 267.

95. Van der Merwe, Hugo, 'What Survivors Say about Justice: An Analysis of
the TRC Victim Hearings' in Chapman and Van der Merwe, *Truth and
Reconciliation*, pp. 28–42; and Chapman, Audrey R., 'Perspectives on the
Role of Forgiveness in the Human Rights Violations Hearings' in ibid.,
pp. 67–89.

96. The TRC adopted a complex notion of truth, distinguishing between four
types: factual or forensic truth; personal or narrative truth; social (or
'dialogue') truth; healing and restorative truth (Truth and Reconciliation
Commission of South Africa, *Report—Volume 1*, 1998, pp. 110–114,
http://www.justice.gov.za/trc/report/finalreport/Volume%201.pdf
[last accessed Feb. 2015]). Personal truth evoked the cathartic benefits of
storytelling, which was supposed also to contribute to psychological healing after trauma. By social or dialogue truth, the TRC meant engagement
of the public in discussion and reflection about the past through open
hearings and media. Restorative truth was to come from validating experience of people and thus restoring the dignity of survivors. While previous Truth Commissions sought objective truth that might be accepted
by all, the TRC emphasised hearing processes that seemed more focused
on the subjective dimensions of truth. This played down the significance
of objective truth-finding functions. Chapman, Audrey R., and Hugo Van
der Merwe, 'Introduction' in Chapman and Van der Merwe, *Truth and
Reconciliation*, pp. 13–14.

97. Chapman, Audrey R. and Patrick Ball, 'Levels of Truth: Macro-Truth and
the TRC'; and Chapman, Audrey R., 'Truth Recovery through the TRC's
Institutional Hearings Process' in Ibid.

98. Gordimer, Nadine, *The Pickup*, London: Bloomsbury, 2001.

99. Gordimer, Nadine and Anthony Sampson, 'President Mbeki's Career' in *New York Review of Books*, 16 Nov. 2000, http://www.nybooks.com/articles/archives/2000/nov/16/president-mbekis-career/ (last accessed, Feb. 2015).

100. Steele, 'Guardian Profile: Nadine Gordimer'.

101. 'Nadine Gordimer: 'The Culture of Corruption' on *Al Jazeera*, 29 Sep. 2012, http://www.aljazeera.com/programmes/talktojazeera/2012/09/201292913438182241.html (last accessed, Feb. 2015).

102. Interview with Justin Cartwright in Apr. 2012, re-published in *The Telegraph*, 14 July 2014, http://www.telegraph.co.uk/culture/books/authorinterviews/9163672/Nobel-laureate-Nadine-Gordimer-I-have-failed-at-many-things-but-I-have-never-been-afraid.html (last accessed, Feb. 2015).

103. 'Wounded Dreams' by Keorapetse Kgositsile, quoted at the beginning of Gordimer, *No Time Like the Present*.

104. For her simultaneous disillusionment and loyalty shortly before her death, see Gordimer, Nadine, 'The disillusion and corruption of post-Mandela South Africa', *Christian Science Monitor*, 16 Apr. 2014, http://www.csmonitor.com/Commentary/Global-Viewpoint/2014/0416/Nadine-Gordimer-The-disillusion-and-corruption-of-post-Mandela-South-Africa (last accessed, Feb. 2015).

105. Wilson, Ilse, 'At home with Nadine Gordimer, a very private individual', *Mail and Guardian*, 18 July 2014, http://mg.co.za/article/2014–07–17-at-home-with-nadine-gordimer-a-very-private-individual (last accessed Feb. 2015).

106. Ibid.

107. Gordimer, Nadine and Ariel Dorfman, 'Writing and Political Oppression', *In Our Time* (Melvyn Bragg), 8 Apr. 1999, http://www.bbc.co.uk/programmes/p00545g8 (last accessed February 2015).

108. Tribute to Nadine Gordimer by Ngũgĩ wa Thiong'o, *Mail and Guardian* (South Africa), 18 July 2014, http://mg.co.za/article/2014–07–17-nadine-gordimer-farewell-to-a-great-spirit (last accessed Nov. 2015).

8. MULTIDIMENSIONAL JUSTICE

1. Lesufi, Isbmael, 'Six years of neoliberal socioeconomic policies in South Africa', *Journal of Asian and African Studies*, 37, 3–5, (2002), pp. 286–98; Gumede, William Mervin, *Thabo Mkeki and the Battle for the Soul of the ANC*, London: Zed Books, 2007.

2. Forna, Aminatta, 'Don't judge a book by its author', *Guardian Review*, 14 Feb. 2015.

3. In the lecture, she termed this literature 'realist', but this mainly served to distinguish it from fantasy and science fiction. Adichie, Chimamanda Ngozi, 'To Instruct and Delight: a Case for Realist Literature', Commonwealth Lecture 2012, published 16 Mar. 2012, https://www.youtube.com/watch?v=vmsYJDP8g2U (last accessed Feb. 2015).

4. Adichie, Chimamanda Ngozi, *Purple Hibiscus*, London: Fourth Estate, 2004; *Half of a Yellow Sun*, London: Fourth Estate, 2006; Forna, Aminatta, *The Memory of Love*, London, Bloomsbury, 2010; *The Hired Man*, London: Bloomsbury, 2013.

5. Forna, 'Don't judge a book by its author'.

BIBLIOGRAPHY

Works by the Six Authors, Including Interviews and Edited Collections

Albert Camus

The Outsider, London: Hamish Hamilton, 2nd edition, 1957 (first published in English by Hamish Hamilton, 1946 and in the US as *The Stranger*, New York: Alfred A. Knopf, 1946) (originally published as *L'Etranger*, Paris: Gallimard, 1942).

'Letters to a German Friend' in *Resistance, Rebellion and Death*, London: Hamish Hamilton, 1964 (first published together as *Lettres à un ami allemand*, Paris: Gallimard, 1945).

The Rebel, New York: Alfred A. Knopf, 1954 (originally published as *L'Homme Révolté*, Paris: Gallimard, 1951).

The Myth of Sisyphus, London: Hamish Hamilton, 1955 (originally published as *Le Mythe de Sisyphe*, Paris: Gallimard, 1942).

The Just Assassins in *Caligula and Three Other Plays*, New York: Vintage Books, 1962 (originally published as *Les Justes: pièce en cinq actes*, Paris: Gallimard, 1950).

'Reflections on the Guillotine' in *Resistance, Rebellion and Death*, New York: The Modern Library, 1963, available on www.deakinphilosophicalsociety. com/texts/camus/reflections.pdf (originally published as 'Réflexions sur la Guillotine' in Koestler, Arthur and Albert Camus, *Réflexions sur la peine capitale*, Paris: Calmann-Lévy, 1957).

'Défense de "L'Homme Révolté"' in *Essais*, Paris: Bibliothèque de la Pléiade, 1965.

Notebooks, 1942–1951, New York: The Modern Library, 1970 (published in the UK as *Carnets, 1942–51*, London: Hamish Hamilton, 1966) (originally published as *Carnets 1942–51*, Paris: Gallimard, 1964).

The Plague, London: Allen Lane, The Penguin Press, 2001 (originally published as *La Peste*, Paris: Gallimard, 1947).

BIBLIOGRAPHY

Lévy-Valensi, Jacqueline (ed.), *Camus at Combat, Writing 1944–1947*, Princeton and Oxford: Princeton University Press, 2006.

Ariel Dorfman

El absurdo entre cuatro paredes: El teatro de Harold Pinter, Santiago: Editorial Universitaria, 1968.

How to Read Donald Duck: Imperialist Ideology in the Disney Comic (co-authored with Armand Mattelart), New York: International General Editions, 1975 (originally published as *Para leer al Pato Donald: Comunicación de masa y colonialismo*, Valparaíso: Ediciones Universitarias de Valparaíso, 1971).

Widows, London: Pluto Press, 1983 (originally published as *Viudas*, Mexico City: Siglo XXI, 1981).

The Empire's Old Clothes: What the Lone Ranger, Babar, and Other Innocent Heroes Do to Our minds, New York: Pantheon Books, 1983.

The Last Song of Manuel Sendero, New York: Viking Penguin, 1987 (originally published as *La última canción de Manuel Sendero*, Mexico City: Siglo XXI, 1982).

Mascara, New York: Viking, 1988.

Hard Rain, Columbia, Louisiana: Readers International, 1990 (originally published as *Mores en la Costa*, Buenos Aires: Editorial Sudamericana, 1973).

My House is on Fire, New York: Viking Penguin, 1990.

Death and the Maiden, London: Nick Hern books, 1991, revised edition 1994 (first published in Spanish as *La Muerte y la doncella*, Buenos Aires: Ediciones de la Flor, 1992).

Heading South, Looking North: A Bilingual Journey, London: Hodder & Stoughton, 1998.

Speak Truth to Power: Voices from Beyond the Dark, New York: Umbrage Editions (in collaboration with Amnesty International), 2000.

Exorcising Terror: The Incredible Unending Trial of General Augusto Pinochet, London: Pluto Press, 2003.

Other Septembers, Many Americas: Selected Provocations, 1980–2004, London: Pluto, 2004.

Feeding on Dreams: Confessions of an Unrepentent Exile, Boston and New York: Mariner Books, 2012.

'An Exile Finds Chile "Struck by a Plague"', *New York Times*, 11 Sept. 1983, http://www.nytimes.com/1983/09/11/opinion/an-exile-finds-chile-struck-by-a-plague.html

'The Challenge in Chile', *New York Times Magazine*, 29 June 1986, http://www.nytimes.com/1986/06/29/magazine/the-challenge-in-chile.html

Boyers, Peggy, Juan Carlos Lertora and Ariel Dorman, 'Ideology, Exile, Language: An Interview with Ariel Dorfman', *Salmagundi*, No. 82/83, (1989), pp. 142–63.

BIBLIOGRAPHY

Berman, Jenifer, 'Ariel Dorfman', *Bomb Magazine*, Winter 1995, http://bombmagazine.org/article/1833/ariel-dorfman

Nadine Gordimer

Face to Face: Short Stories, Johannesburg: Silver Leaf Books, 1949.
The Soft Voice of the Servant and Other Stories, New York: Simon & Schuster, 1952.
The Lying Days, London: Gollancz, 1953.
A World of Strangers, London: Gollancz, 1958.
The Late Bourgeois World, London: Gollancz, 1966.
The Conservationist, Harmondsworth: Penguin, 1978 (originally published, London: Jonathan Cape, 1974).
July's People, London: Cape, 1981.
Burger's Daughter, Harmondsworth: Penguin Books, 1984 (originally published, London: Jonathan Cape, 1979).
The Essential Gesture: Writing, Politics and Places, London: Jonathan Cape, 1988.
None to Accompany Me, London: Bloomsbury, 1994.
Writing and Being, Cambridge and London: Harvard University Press, 1995.
The House-Gun, London: Bloomsbury, 1998.
Living in Hope and History: Notes from our Century, London: Bloomsbury, 1999.
The Pickup, London: Bloomsbury, 2001.
Telling Times: Writing and Living, 1954–2008, London: Bloomsbury, 2010.
No Time Like the Present, London: Bloomsbury, 2012.
Bazin, Nancy Topping and Marilyn Dallman Seymour (eds), *Conversations with Nadine Gordimer*, Jackson and London: University Press of Mississippi, 1990.
Gordimer, Nadine (interviewed by Jannika Hurwitt), 'The Art of Fiction No. 77', *The Paris Review*, No. 88, Summer 1983, http://www.theparisreview.org/interviews/3060/the-art-of-fiction-no-77-nadine-gordimer
Paul, Donald, 'The Other Side of the Story', *Boston Phoenix*, 5 Jan. 1998, http://www.weeklywire.com/ww/01–05–98/boston_books_3.html
(with Ariel Dorfman), 'Writing and Political Oppression', *In our Time* (Melvyn Bragg), 8 Apr. 1999 http://www.bbc.co.uk/programmes/p00545g8
(with Anthony Sampson) 'President Mbeki's Career' in *New York Review of Books*, 16 Nov. 2000, http://www.nybooks.com/articles/archives/2000/nov/16/president-mbekis-career/
Interview with Stephen Sackur, BBC World News, *Hard Talk*, first shown 13 May 2011 and re-broadcast, 15 July 2014 http://www.bbc.co.uk/iplayer/episode/b0112dnf/hardtalk-nadine-gordimer-south-african-writer
'The Culture of Corruption' on *Al Jazeera*, 29 Sep. 2012, http://www.aljazeera.com/programmes/talktojazeera/2012/09/201292913438182241.html

BIBLIOGRAPHY

'The disillusion and corruption of post-Mandela South Africa', *Christian Science Monitor*, 16 Apr. 2014, http://www.csmonitor.com/Commentary/Global-Viewpoint/2014/0416/Nadine-Gordimer-The-disillusion-and-corruption-of-post-Mandela-South-Africa

Interview with Justin Cartwright in Apr. 2012, re-published in *The Telegraph*, 14 July 2014, http://www.telegraph.co.uk/culture/books/authorinterviews/9163672/Nobel-laureate-Nadine-Gordimer-I-have-failed-at-many-things-but-I-have-never-been-afraid.html

Ngũgĩ wa Thiong'o

Homecoming, London: Heinemann, 1972.

Petals of Blood, London: Heinemann, 1977.

Writers in Politics, London: Heinemann, 1981.

Detained: A Writer's Prison Diary, London: Heinemann, 1981.

(With Ngũgĩ wa Mirii), *I Will Marry When I Want*, London: Heinemann, 1982 (originally published as *Ngaahika Ndeenda: ithaako ria ngerekano*, London: Heinemann, 1980).

Devil on the Cross, London: Heinemann, 1982 (originally published as *Caitaani mũtharaba-Inĩ*, London: Heinemann, 1980).

The River Between, London: Heinemann, 1988 (original publication, London: Heinemann, 1965).

A Grain of Wheat, London: Heinemann revised edition, 1988 (original publication, London: Heinemann, 1967).

Matigari, London: Heinemann, 1989 (originally published in Gĩkũyũ, by Nairobi: Heinemann, Kenya, 1987).

Penpoints, Gunpoints, and Dreams: Towards a Critical Theory of the Arts and the State in Africa, Oxford: Oxford University Press, 1998.

Decolonising the Mind: The Politics of Language in African Literature, Oxford: James Currey, 2005 (original publication, London: Heinemann, 1986).

Weep Not, Child, Johannesburg: Penguin Books, 2009 (original publication, London: Heinemann, 1964).

Dreams in a Time of War: A Childhood Memoir, London: Harvill Secker, 2010.

Globalectics: Theory and the Politics of Knowing, New York City: Columbia University Press, 2012.

Sander, Reinhard and Bernth Lindfors (with assistance of Lynette Cintrón), *Ngũgĩ wa Thiong'o Speaks: Interviews with the Kenyan Writer*, Oxford: James Currey, Nairobi: EAEP, 2006.

'Ngũgĩ laments Kenya violence', BBC news channel, 10 Jan. 2008, http://news.bbc.co.uk/1/hi/world/africa/7180946.stm

'Opinion: Kenya', *Granta*, 15 Apr. 2008, http://www.granta.com/New-Writing/Opinion-Kenya

'A Dictator's Last Laugh', *New York Times*, 14 Mar. 2013, http://www.nytimes.com/2013/03/15/opinion/a-dictators-last-laugh.html?_r=0

BIBLIOGRAPHY

'Tribute to Nadine Gordimer by Ngũgĩ wa Thiong'o', *Mail and Guardian* (South Africa), 18 July 2014, http://mg.co.za/article/2014-07-17-nadine-gordimer-farewell-to-a-great-spirit

Jorge Semprún

The Long Voyage, London: Weidenfeld and Nicolson, 1964 (originally published as *Le grand voyage*, Paris: Gallimard, 1963; also re-published as *The Cattle Truck*, London: Serif, 2005).

La Guerre est finie: scenario du film d'Alain Resnais, Paris: Gallimard, 1966.

Communism in Spain in the Franco Era: The Autobiography of Federico Sánchez, Brighton: Harvester Press, 1980 (originally published as *Autobiografía de Federico Sánchez*, Barcelona: Planeta, 1977).

What a Beautiful Sunday, London, Secker and Warburg, 1983 (originally published as *Quel beau dimanche*, Paris: Gallimard, 1980).

Federico Sánchez vous salue bien, Paris: Grasset 1993.

Literature or Life, New York: Viking Penguin, 1997 (originally published as *L'écriture ou la vie*, Paris: Gallimard, 1994).

Adieu Vive Clarté, Paris: Gallimard, 1998.

Vingt ans et un jour, Paris: Gallimard, 2004 (originally published as *Veinte Años y un Día*, Barcelona: Tusquets, 2003).

L'Homme Européen (co-authored with Dominique de Villepin), Paris: Plon, 2005.

Une tombe au creux des nuages: Essais sur l'Europe d'hier et d'aujourd'hui, Paris: Climats-Flammarion, 2010.

Exercises de Survie, Paris: Gallimard, 2012.

Interview on 1981 coup attempt in Spain, *Antenne 2*, 24 Feb. 1981, http://www.youtube.com/watch?v=DXrV9irzOTw

'Apathy a danger to Europe', *Euronews*, 1 July 2009, http://www.euronews.com/2009/07/01/jorge-semprun-apathy-a-danger-to-europe/

'"J'ai perdu mes certitudes, j'ai gardé mes illusions". Entretien avec Jorge Semprun', *nonfiction.fr, Le quotidian des livres et des idées*, 10 May 2010, http://www.nonfiction.fr/article-3391-jai_perdu_mes_certitudes_jai_garde_mes_illusions_entretien_avec_jorge_semprun.htm

Victor Serge

a) Publications in the Marxists' Internet Archive: Victor Serge, http://www.marxists.org/archive/serge

'The Bandits', *L'Anarchie*, No. 352, 4 Jan. 1912, https://www.marxists.org/archive/serge/1912/01/bandits.htm

Letter to Emile Arnaud, 19 Mar. 1917, https://www.marxists.org/archive/serge/1917/03/letter-armand.htm

BIBLIOGRAPHY

'Once More: Kronstadt', *New International*, 4, 7 (July 1938), pp. 211–12 in
https://www.marxists.org/archive/serge/1938/04/kronstadt.htm

'Kronstadt 1921, Trotsky's Defense. Response to Trotsky', *La Révolution Prolétarienne*,

25 Oct. 1938, https://www.marxists.org/archive/serge/1938/10/25.htm

'Secrecy and Revolution: A Reply to Trotsky' (1938), first published in *Peace News*, 27 Dec. 1963, https://www.marxists.org/archive/serge/1938/xx/secrecy.htm

'A Letter and Some Notes: Reply to Ciliga', *New International*, Feb. 1939, https://www.marxists.org/archive/serge/1939/02/letter.htm

'Planned Economies and Democracy' (1944/45), first published in *Revolutionary History*, 5, Autumn 1994, https://www.marxists.org/archive/serge/1944/xx/planecon.html

b) Other publications

Istrati, Panaït (in reality, Victor Serge), *Soviets 1929*, Paris: Rieder, 1929.

'Puissance et limites du marxisme' 3 (nouvelle série), March 1939, reproduced in *La Bataille Socialiste*, http://bataillesocialiste.wordpress.com/documents-historiques/1939-03-puissance-et-limites-du-marxisme-serge/

Birth of Our Power, London: Victor Gollancz, 1968 (originally published as *Naissance de notre force, Paris:* Rieder, 1931).

Men in Prison, London: Gollancz, 1970 (originally published as *Les Hommes dans la prison*, Paris: Rieder, 1930).

Conquered City, London: Gollancz, 1976 (originally published as *Ville conquise*, Paris: Rieder, 1932).

Midnight in the Century, London, Writers and Readers Publishing Co-op, 1982 (originally published as *S'il est minuit dans le siècle*, Paris: Grasset, 1939).

Revolution in Danger: Writings from Russia, 1919–1921, London: Redwoods, 1997.

'Thirty Years after the Russian Revolution' (originally published in *La Révolution Prolétarienne*, 1947) in Weissman, Susan (ed.) *The Ideas of Victor Serge: A Life as a Work of Art*, London: Critique Books/ Merlin Press, 1997.

The Case of Comrade Tulayev, New York: New York Review Books, 2003 (originally published as *L'Affaire Toulaév*, Paris: Editions du Seuil, 1948).

Memoirs of a Revolutionary, New York: New York Review Books, 2012 (originally published as *Mémoires d'un révolutionnaire*, Paris: Editions du Seuil, 1951).

'Mexican Notebooks 1940–1947, *New Left Review* 82, July–Aug. 2013.

Other Works

Adichie, Chimamanda Ngozi, *Purple Hibiscus*, London: Fourth Estate, 2004.

BIBLIOGRAPHY

————— *Half of a Yellow Sun*, London: Fourth Estate, 2006.

————— 'To Instruct and Delight: a Case for Realist Literature', Commonwealth Lecture 2012, published 16 Mar. 2012, https://www.youtube.com/watch?v=vmsYJDP8g2U

Adisa, Oji and Langerster Anderson, 'Ngũgĩ wa Thiong'o's quest for justice', *The Varsity* (University of Toronto's Student Newspaper), 24 Dec. 2005 (modified, 11 Jan. 2012), http://thevarsity.ca/2005/12/24/ngugi-wa-thiongos-quest-for-justice/

Aguado, Txetxu, 'Memory, Politics and Post-national Citizenship in Jorge Semprún's *L'Écriture ou la vie*', *Hispanic Research Journal*, 6, 3 (2005), pp. 237–51.

Aguilar, Paloma, 'Transitional Justice in the Spanish, Argentinian and Chilean Case', International Conference, Building a Future on Peace and Justice, Nuremberg, 25–27 June, 2007, pp. 4–8, http://www.peace-justice-conference.info/download/WS%2010%20Aguilar%20report.pdf

Allott, Miriam, *Novelists on the Novel*, London: Routledge and Kegan Paul, 1959.

Almquist, Jessica and Carlos Espósito, *The Role of Courts in Transitional Justice. Voices from Latin America and Spain*, New York: Routledge, 2013.

Amnesty International, *Chile: 40 years on from Pinochet's coup, impunity must end*, http://www.amnesty.org/en/news/chile-40-years-pinochet-s-coup-impunity-must-end-2013–09–10

Amnesty International, Annual Report 2013, Chile, http://www.amnesty.org/en/region/chile/report-2013

Amoko, Apollo Obonyo, *Postcolonialism in the Wake of the Nairobo Revolution. Ngũgĩ wa Thiong'o and the Idea of African Literature*, New York: Palgrave Macmillan, 2010.

Anderson, David, *Histories of the Hanged: Britain's Dirty War in Kenya and the End of Empire*, London: Orion, 2005.

Andrieu, Kora, 'Transitional Justice: A New Discipline in Human Rights', *Online Encyclopedia of Mass Violence*, Jan. 2010, http://www.massviolence.org/Transitional-Justice-A-New-Discipline-in-Human-Rights

Aronson, Ronald, *Camus and Sartre: The Story of a Friendship and the Quarrel that Ended It*, Chicago: University of Chicago Press, 2004.

Arthur, Paige, 'How "Transitions" Reshaped Human Rights: A Conceptual History of Transitional Justice', *Human Rights Quarterly*, 31, 2 (May 2009), pp. 321–67.

Ashcroft, Bill, Gareth Griffiths and Helen Tiffin, *Post Colonial Studies: The Key Concepts* (3rd edition), London and New York: Routledge, 2014.

Atieno-Odhiambo, E.S., 'The Production of History in Kenya: The Mau Mau Debate', *Canadian Journal of African Studies*, 25, 2, (1991), pp. 300–307.

————— and John Lonsdale, *Mau Mau and Nationhood: Arms, Authority and Narration*, Oxford: James Currey, 2003.

BIBLIOGRAPHY

Auga, Ulrika, 'Intellectuals between Resistance and Legitimation: The Cases of Nadine Gordimer and Christa Wolf', *Current Writing: Text and Reception in Southern Africa*, 15, 1 (2003), pp. 1–16.

Azancot, Nuria, 'La Literatura me facilitó la ruptura política', Interview with Jorge Semprún, *El Mundo*, 12 Nov. 2012.

Bargel, Antoine, 'Semprún and Lukács: For a Marxist Reading of *Le Grand Voyage*' in Ferrán, Ofelia and Gina Herrmann (eds), *A Critical Companion to Jorge Semprún: Buchenwald, Before and After*, New York: Palgrave Macmillan, 2014.

Barrett, Susan '"What I say will not be understood": Intertextuality as a subversive force in Nadine Gordimer's *Burger's Daughter*', E-rea (En Ligne), 2,1, (2004) http:erea.revues.org/491

Barry, Donald D. (ed.), *Toward the "Rule of Law" in Russia? Political and Legal Reform in the Transition Period*, New York: Sharpe, 1992.

BBC Radio 4, *Open Book*, 'How Literature can respond to the past', broadcast 11 May 2014, http://www.bbc.co.uk/programmes/b042z66b

Beirne, Piers (ed.), *Revolution in Law: Contributions to the Development of Soviet Legal Theory, 1917–1938*, London and New York: Sharpe, 1990.

———— and Alan Hunt, 'Lenin, Crime and Penal Politics, 1917–1924 in Beirne, Piers (ed.), *Revolution in Law: Contributions to the Development of Soviet Legal Theory, 1917–1938*, London and New York: Sharpe, 1990.

Benschop, Marjolein, *Rights and Reality: Are women's equal rights to land, housing and property implemented in East Africa?*, Kenya: United Nations Human Settlements Programme, 2002.

Berg, Manfred and Bernd Schaefer (eds), *Historical Justice in International Perspective: How Societies are Trying to Right the Wrongs of the Past*, Cambridge: Cambridge University Press, 2008.

Berman, Bruce and John Lonsdale, *Unhappy Valley: Conflict in Kenya and Africa, Book Two: Violence and Ethnicity*, Oxford: James Currey, 2002.

Boehmer, Elleke, 'Master's Dance to the Master's Voice: Revolutionary Nationalism and the Representation of Women in the Writing of Ngũgĩ wa Thiong'o', *The Journal of Commonwealth Literature*, 26, 1 (1991), pp. 188–97.

Boesten, Jelke et. al., 'Transformative Justice—A Concept Note', Oct. 2010, http://www.wun.ac.uk/sites/default/files/transformative_justice_-_concept_note_web_version.pdf

Bond, Patrick, *Elite Transition: From Apartheid to Neoliberalism in South Africa*, London: Pluto Press, 2014.

Boyers, Peggy, Juan Carlos Lertora and Ariel Dorfman, 'Ideology, Exile, Language: An Interview with Ariel Dorfman', *Salmagundi*, No. 82/83, (1989), pp. 142–63.

Branch, Daniel, *Kenya Between Hope and Despair, 1963–2011*, New Haven and London: Yale University Press, 2011.

BIBLIOGRAPHY

Buck, Tobias, 'Facing up to Franco: Spain 40 years on', *FT Magazine*, 8 May 2015, http://www.ft.com/cms/s/2/5e4e6aac-f42f-11e499de-00144 feab7de.html#slide0

Cain, P. J. and Anthony G. Hopkins, *British Imperialism: Crisis and Deconstruction, 1914–1990*, London: Longman, 1993.

Caputo, John D., *Deconstruction in a Nutshell. A Conversation with Jacques Derrida*, New York: Fordham University Press, 1997.

Carr, E. H., *The Bolshevik Revolution*, Vol. 1, 1917–1923, Harmondsworth: Penguin, 1966.

Carroll, David, *Albert Camus, the Algerian: Colonialism, Terrorism, Justice*, New York: Columbia University Press, 2007.

Casanova, Julián, 'The Faces of Terror: Violence during the Franco Dictatorship' in Jerez-Farrán, Carlos and Samuel Amago (eds), *Unearthing Franco's Legacy: Mass Graves and the Recovery of Historical Memory in Spain*, Notre Dame, Indiana: University of Notre Dame Press, 2010.

Caute, David, *Politics and the Novel during the Cold War*, New Brunswick and London: Transaction Publishers, 2010.

Céspedes, Jaime, 'Jorge Semprún's Speeches' in Ferrán, Ofelia and Gina Herrmann (eds), *A Critical Companion to Jorge Semprún: Buchenwald, Before and After*, New York: Palgrave Macmillan, 2014.

Chalamanda, Fiona Michaela Johnson, 'Interpretations in Transition: Literature and Political transition in Malawi and South Africa in the 1990s', PhD thesis, University of Stirling, 2002.

Chapman, Audrey and Hugo Van der Merwe, *Truth and Reconciliation in South Africa: Did the TRC Deliver?*, Philadelphia: University of Pennsylvania Press, 2008.

Chinchón Álvarez, J., 'The Challenges posed to the recent investigation of crimes committed during the Spanish Civil War and Francoism' in Almquist, Jessica and Carlos Espósito, *The Role of Courts in Transitional Justice. Voices from Latin America and Spain*, New York: Routledge, 2013.

Claudín, Fernando, *The Communist Movement: From Comintern To Cominform*, Harmondsworth: Penguin, 1975 (originally published as *La crisis del movimiento comunista: de la Komintern al Kominform*, Paris: Éditions Ruedo Ibérico, 1970).

Clough, Marshall S., 'Mau Mau and the Contest for Memory' in Atieno Odhiambo, E.S., and John Lonsdale (eds), *Mau Mau and Nationhood: Arms, Authority and Narration*, Oxford: James Currey, 2003.

Collier, Simon and William F. Sater, *A History of Chile, 1808–2002* (2nd edition) Cambridge: Cambridge University Press, 2004.

Collins, Cath, 'Human Rights Trials in Chile during and after the "Pinochet Years", *International Journal of Transitional Justice*, 4, 2010, pp. 67–86.

———, Katherine Hite, and Alfredo Joignant (eds), *The Politics of Memory in Chile: From Pinochet to Bachelet*, Boulder, Co: Lynne Rienner, 2013.

BIBLIOGRAPHY

Conolly, Oliver and Bashshar Hayder, 'Literature, Politics, and Character', *Philosophy and Literature*, 32 (2008), pp. 87–101.

Conseil national de la Résistance, 'Le programme d'action de la Résistance' (adopted by the CNR on 15 March 1944), Musée de la résistance en ligne, http://www.museedelaresistanceenligne.org/media.php?media=2839&expo=75&popin=true#zoom-tab

Davis, Madeleine, 'Is Spain Recovering its Memory? Breaking the "Pacto del Olvido"', *Human Rights Quarterly*, 27, 3, (2005) pp. 869–73.

Delgado, Celeste Fraser, 'Mother Tongues and Childless Women' in Nnaemeka, Obioma, *Politics of (M)othering*, London: Routledge, 1997.

De Mata, Ignacio Fernádez, 'The Rupture of the World and the Conflicts of Memory' in Jerez-Farrán, Carlos and Samuel Amago (eds), *Unearthing Franco's Legacy: Mass Graves and the Recovery of Historical Memory in Spain*, Notre Dame, Indiana: University of Notre Dame Press, 2010.

Diala, Isidore 'Nadine Gordimer, J. M. Coetzee, and Andre Brink: Guilt, Expiation, and the Reconciliation Process in Post-Apartheid South Africa', *Journal of Modern Literature*, 25, 2 (2001–2002), pp. 50–68.

Drew, Allison, *Discordant Comrades: Identities and Loyalties on the South African Left*, Aldershot: Ashgate, 2000.

Dryzek, Jon, Bonnie Honnig, Anne Phillips (eds), *Oxford Handbook to Political Theory*, Oxford: Oxford University Press, 2006.

Dugard, John and Nadine Gordimer, *What Happened to Burger's Daughter: Or How South African Censorship Works*, Emmarentia: Taurus, 1980.

Elkins, Caroline, *Britain's Gulag: The Brutal End of Empire in Kenya*, London: Pimlico, 2005.

Encarnación, Omar G., 'Reconciliation after Democratization: Coping with the Past in Spain', *Political Science Quarterly*, 123, 3 (2008), pp. 435–59.

——— 'Justice in Times of Transition: Lessons from the Iberian Experience', *Center for European Studies*, Working Paper Series 173, 2009.

Ferrán, Ofelia, *Working Through Memory: Writing and Remembrance in Contemporary Spain*, Lewisburg, PA: Bucknell University Press, 2007.

——— and Gina Herrmann (eds), *A Critical Companion to Jorge Semprún: Buchenwald, Before and After*, New York: Palgrave Macmillan, 2014.

Figes, Orlando *A People's Tragedy: The Russian Revolution 1891–1924*, New York: Viking Press, 1997.

Foreign and Commonwealth Office, 'Statement to Parliament on Settlement of Mau Mau Claims', 6 June 2013, https://www.gov.uk/government/news/statement-to-parliament-on-settlement-of-mau-mau-claims

Forna, Aminatta, *The Devil that Danced on the Water: A Daughter's Memoir of Her Father, Her Family, Her Country and a Continent*, London: Harper Collins, 2002.

——— *The Memory of Love*, London, Bloomsbury, 2010.

BIBLIOGRAPHY

———— *The Hired Man*, London: Bloomsbury, 2013.

———— 'Don't judge a book by its author', *Guardian Review*, 14 Feb. 2015.

Fox, Soledad, 'Exile and Return: The Many Madrids of Jorge Semprún' in *Ciberletras: Revista de Crítica Literaria y de Cultura*, Dec. 2003, http://www.lehman.cuny.edu/ciberletras/v10/fox.htm

Fraser, Nancy, 'Recognition and multiculturalism', Multicultural Bites, Open University, http://itunes.apple.com/us/itunes-u/multiculturalism-bites-audio/id449122394?mt=10

Fraser, Nancy, 'Rethinking Recognition', *New Left Review* 3, May–June, 2000.

Fuller, L. L., *The Morality of Law*, New Haven, Ct: Yale University Press, 1969.

Gabriel, Ian B., '*Toma La Calle*: An Analysis of the Influences Behind the Anti-Franco Student Protests of February 1956 at the University of Madrid', Honors Thesis, Rutgers University, 2012, http://history.rutgers.edu/honors-papers-2012?start=15

Galston, William A., 'Liberalism' in Gibbons, Michael T. (ed.), *Encylopedia of Political Thought*, Hoboken, New Jersey: John Wiley & Sons, 2015.

Geras, Norman, 'The Controversy about Marx and Justice', *New Left Review* 150, Mar/Apr.1985, pp. 47–85.

Getzler, Israel, *Kronstadt 1917–1921: The Fate of a Soviet Democracy*, Cambridge: Cambridge University Press, 2002.

Gibbons, Michael T. (ed.) *Encylopedia of Political Thought*, Hoboken, New Jersey: John Wiley & Sons, 2015.

Gikandi, Simon, *Ngũgĩ wa Thiong'o*, Cambridge: Cambridge University Press, 2000.

Golob, Stephanie R., 'Volver: The Return of Transitional Justice Politics in Spain', *Journal of Spanish Cultural Studies*, 9, 2 (2008), pp. 127–41.

Gordon, Paul, *Vagabond Witness: Victor Serge and the Politics of Hope*, Winchester, UK/Washington, USA: Zero Books, 2013.

Gramsci, Antonio, *Selections from Prison Notebooks* (edited and translated by Quintin Hoare and Geoffrey Nowell-Smith), London: Lawrence & Wishart, 1971.

Grandin, Greg, 'It Was Heaven That They Burned: Who is Rigoberta Menchú?', *The Nation*, 27 Sept. 2010, http://www.thenation.com/article/154582/it-was-heaven-they-burned

Gready, Paul, *The Era of Transitional Justice: The Aftermath of the Truth and Reconciliation Commission in South Africa and Beyond*, London: Routledge, 2011.

Gumede, William Mervin, *Thabo Mkeki and the Battle for the Soul of the ANC*, London: Zed Books, 2007.

Gustafson, Kristian, *Hostile Intent: US Covert Operations in Chile, 1964–1974*, Dulles: Potomac Books, 2007.

Habib, Adam and Vishnu Padayachee, 'Economic Policy and Power Relations

BIBLIOGRAPHY

in South Africa's Transition to Democracy', *World Development* 28, 2 (2000), pp. 245–63.

Hardi, Choman in 'How Literature can respond to the past', broadcast on BBC Radio 4, *Open Book*, 11 May 2014, http://www.bbc.co.uk/programmes/b042z66b

Havel, Václav, *An Uncanny Era: Conversations Between Václav Havel and Adam Michnik* (Edited, translated and with an introduction by Elzbieta Matynia), New Haven, CT: Yale University Press, 2014.

Hayner, Priscilla, B., *Unspeakable Truths: Facing the Challenge of Truth Commissions*, New York and London: Routledge, 2002.

Heinze, Eric, *The Concept of Injustice*, Abingdon and New York: Routledge, 2013.

Herstein, Ori J., 'Historic Injustice, Group Membership and Harm to Individuals: Defending Claims for Historic Justice from the Non-Identity Problem', *Harvard BlackLetter Law Journal*, 25 (2009), pp. 230–76.

Historia Política Legislativa del Congreso National de Chile, 'Movimiento de Acción Popular Unitaria', http://historiapolitica.bcn.cl/partidos_politicos/wiki/Movimiento_de_Acción_Popular_Unitaria

Hooper, Glenn, 'Ngũgĩ's *Matigari* and the Politics of Literature', *Alternation*, 5, 1 (1998), pp. 13–31, http://alternation.ukzn.ac.za/pages/volume-5/volume-5-number-1-1998.aspx

Hopkins, Stephen, 'Still a "Spanish Red"? The communist past and national identity in the writing of Jorge Semprún', *Twentieth Century Communism*, 3, May 2011, pp. 71–91.

Howe, Irving, *Politics and the Novel*, London: Stevens and Sons, 1961.

Hudson, Barbara, *Justice in the Risk Society: Challenging and Re-Affirming 'Justice' in Late Modernity*, London: Sage, 2004.

Human Development Report 2013. The Rise of the South: Human Progress in a Diverse World, *Statistical Tables*, http://www.undp.org/content/dam/philippines/docs/HDR/HDR2013%20Report%20English.pdf.

Huskey, Eugene, 'From Legal Nihilism to Pravovoe Gosudarstvo: Soviet legal Development 1917–1990' in Barry, Donald D., (ed.) *Toward the "Rule of Law" in Russia? Political and Legal Reform in the Transition Period*, New York: Sharpe, 1992.

International Center for Transitional Justice (ICTJ), 'What is Transitional Justice?', http://ictj.org/about/transitional-justice

Ivison, Duncan, 'Historical Injustice' in Dryzek, Jon, Bonnie Honnig, Anne Phillips (eds), *Oxford Handbook to Political Theory*, Oxford: Oxford University Press, 2006.

Jackson, Ben, 'The Conceptual History of Social Justice', *Political Studies Review*, 3, (2005), pp. 356–73.

Jaggi, Maya, 'Speaking for the Dead', *Guardian*, 14 June 2003, http://www.theguardian.com/stage/2003/jun/14/theatre.fiction

BIBLIOGRAPHY

Jakopovich, Daniel, 'A Humanist Defence and Critique of the South African Truth and Reconciliation Commission', *Peace Studies Journal*, 4, 1 (2011), pp. 51–65.

Jerez-Farrán, Carlos and Samuel Amago (eds), *Unearthing Franco's Legacy: Mass Graves and the Recovery of Historical Memory in Spain*, Notre Dame, Indiana: University of Notre Dame Press, 2010.

Judd, Denis, *Empire: The British Imperial Experience from 1765 to the Present*, London: HarperCollins, 1996.

Kariuki, J. M., *"Mau Mau" Detainee*, Harmondsworth: Penguin, 1963.

Kasrils, Ronnie, *'Armed and Dangerous': My Undercover Struggle Against Apartheid*, London: Heinemann, 1993.

Kedward, H. R., *Resistance in Vichy France: A Study of Ideas and Motivation in the Southern Zone 1940–1942*, Oxford: Oxford University Press, 1978.

————— *Occupied France: Collaboration and Resistance 1940–1944*, Oxford: Basil Blackwell, 1985.

————— *In Search of the Maquis, Rural Resistance in Southern France, 1942–44*, Oxford: Clarendon Press, 1993.

Kelly, Paul, *Liberalism*, Cambridge: Polity, 2004.

Kenya Transitional Justice Network, 'Summary: Truth, Justice and Reconciliation Commission Report', Aug. 2013, http://www.acordinternational.org/silo/files/kenya-tjrc-summary-report-aug-2013.pdf

Killingray, David, *Fighting for Britain: African Soldiers in World War II*, Martelsham, Suffolk: Boydell and Brewer, 2010.

Kiss, Csilla, 'La guerre est toujours là: Defeat, Exile and Resistance in the Works of Jorge Semprún', *Bulletin of Spanish Studies: Hispanic Studies and Researches on Spain, Portugal and Latin America*, 89, 7–8 (2012), pp. 95–108.

Koestler, Arthur, *Darkness at Noon*, New York: The Modern Library, 1941.

Kornbluh, Peter, *Chile and the United States: Declassified Documents Relating to the Military Coup, September 11, 1973*, http://www2.gwu.edu/~nsarchiv/NSAEBB/NSAEBB8/nsaebb8i.htm

Kucherov, Samuel, *The Organs of Soviet Administration of Justice: Their History and Operation*, Leiden: Brill, 1970.

Labanyi, Jo, 'The Politics of Memory in Contemporary Spain', *Journal of Spanish Cultural Studies*, 9, 2 (2008), pp. 119–25.

Lacouture, Jean, *Léon Blum*, Paris: Seuil, 1977.

Ledesma, José Luis, 'Una retaguardia al rojo: las violencias en la zona republicana' in Maestre, Francisco Espinosa, *Violencia roja y azul: España, 1936–1950*, Barcelona: Editorial Crítica, 2010.

Lesufi, Isbmael, 'Six years of neoliberal socioeconomic policies in South Africa', *Journal of Asian and African Studies*, 37, 3–5, (2002), pp. 286–98.

Lévy-Valensi, Jacqueline (ed.), *Camus at Combat, Writing 1944–1947*, Princeton and Oxford: Princeton University Press, 2006.

BIBLIOGRAPHY

Linz, Juan, Miguel Jerez and Susana Corzo, 'Ministers and Regimes in Spain: From First to Second Restoration, 1874–2001', *Center for European Studies*, Working Paper No. 101, 2001.

Lottman, Herbert R., *The People's Anger: Justice and Revenge in Post-Liberation France*, London: Hutchinson, 1986.

Loveman, Brian, 'Misión Cumplida? Civil Military Relations and the Chilean Political Transition', *Journal of Interamerican Studies and World Affairs* 33, 3 (1991), pp. 35–74.

Luban, David, 'On Dorfman's Death and the Maiden', *Yale Journal of Law and the Humanities*, 10, 1 (1998) Iss.1, Art. 3. Available at http://digitalcommons.law.yale.edu/yjlh/vol10/iss1/3/

———— 'Justice and Law' in Smelser, Neil J. and Paul B. Baltes, *International Encyclopedia of the Social and Behavioral Sciences*, Vol. 12, Oxford: Elsevier 2001.

Lukes, Steven, *Marxism and Morality*, Oxford: Clarendon Press, 1985.

McAuliffe, Padraig, 'Ariel Dorfman's *Death and the Maiden* as a Mirror Reflecting the Dilemmas of Transitional Justice Policy' in Rush, Peter D. and Olivera Simić (eds), *The Arts of Transitional Justice: Culture, Activism, and Memory after Atrocity*, New York: Springer, 2014.

McClennen, Sophia A., 'Ariel Dorfman', *Review of Contemporary Fiction*, 20, 3 (2000), pp. 81–133.

———— *Ariel Dorfman: An Aesthetics of Hope*, Durham and London: Duke University Press, 2010.

———— 'Beyond "Death and the Maiden": Ariel Dorfman's Media Criticism and Journalism', *Latin American Research Review*, 45, (2010), pp. 173–88.

Madjalany, Fred, *A State of Emergency: The Full Story of Mau Mau*, Boston: Houghton Mifflin, 1963.

Maestre, Francisco Espinosa, *Violencia roja y azul: España, 1936–1950*, Barcelona: Editorial Crítica, 2010.

Maier, Charles S., 'A Surfeit of Memory? Reflections on History, Melancholy and Denial', *History and Memory*, 5 (2) 1993, pp. 136–52.

Mallinder, Louise, *Indemnity, Amnesty, Pardon and Prosecution Guidelines in South Africa*, Working Paper No. 3 from *Beyond Legalism: Amnesties, Transition and Conflict Transformation*, Institute of Criminology and Criminal Justice, Queen's University Belfast, 2009, https://www.qub.ac.uk/schools/SchoolofLaw/Research/InstituteofCriminologyandCriminalJustice/Research/BeyondLegalism/filestore/Filetoupload,152146,en.pdf

Mani, Rama, *Beyond Retribution: Seeking Justice in the Shadows of War*, Cambridge: Polity, 2002.

———— 'Rebuilding an Inclusive Political Community after War', *Security Dialogue*, 36, 4 (2005), pp. 511–26.

Marquez, Robert, *Latin American Revolutionary Poetry: A Bilingual Anthology*, New York: Monthly Review Press, 1974.

BIBLIOGRAPHY

Marrus, Michael R., and Robert O. Paxton, *Vichy France and the Jews*, New York: Basic Books, 1981.

————— 'Official Apologies and the Quest for Historical Justice', *Journal of Human Rights*, 6, 1 (2007), pp. 75–105.

Marshall, Bill, *Victor Serge: The Uses of Dissent*, New York/Oxford: Berg, 1992.

Maughan-Brown, David, '"Mau Mau" and Violence in Ngũgĩ's Novels', *English in Africa*, 8, 2 (1981), pp. 1–22.

Menchú, Rigoberta (ed. Elisabeth Burgos-Debray) *I, Rigoberta Menchú: An Indian Woman in Guatemala*, New York and London: Verso, 1984.

Miller, David, *On Nationality*, Oxford: Oxford University Press, 1995.

————— *Principles of Social Justice*, Cambridge, Mass: Harvard University Press, 1999.

Moosa, Ebrahim, 'Truth and Reconciliation as Performance: Spectres of Eucharistic Redemption' in Villa-Vicencio, Charles and Wilhelm Werwoerd (eds), *Looking Back, Reaching Forward: Reflections on the Truth and Reconciliation Commission of South Africa*, Cape Town: University of Cape Town Press, 2000.

Morace, Robert A., 'The Life and Times of Death and the Maiden', *Texas Studies in Literature and Language*, 42, 2, (2000), pp. 135–53.

Munté, Rosa-Auria, 'The Convergence of Historical Facts and Literary Fiction: Jorge Semprún's Autofiction on the Holocaust', *Forum Qualitative Sozialforschung/Forum: Qualitative Social Research*, 12, 3 Art. 14, (Sept. 2011), http://www.qualitative-research.net/index.php/fqs/article/view/1754/3261

Muro, Diego and Alonso Gregorio, *The Politics and Memory of Democratic Transition: The Spanish Model*, New York and Abingdon, 2011.

Nance, Kimberly A., *Can Literature Promote Justice? Trauma Narrative and Social Action in Latin American Testimonio*, Nashville: Vanderbilt University Press, 2006.

Newman, Ines, *Reclaiming Local Democracy: A Progressive Future for Local Government*, Bristol: Policy Press, 2014.

Nicholls, Brendon, *Ngũgĩ wa Thiong'o. Gender, and the Ethics of Postcolonial Reading*, Farnham, Surrey: Ashgate, 2010.

Niehaus, Carl, *Fighting for Hope*, Cape Town: Human & Rousseau, 1994.

Nkrumah, Kwame, *Neo-Colonialism, The Last Stage of Imperialism*, London: Thomas Nelson, 1965.

Nnaemeka, Obioma, *Politics of (M)othering*, London: Routledge, 1997.

Nobel Prize in Literature 1991. Nadine Gordimer, Presentation Speech by Professor Sture Allén, http://www.nobelprize.org/nobel_prizes/literature/laureates/1991/presentation-speech.html

Novak, Amy, 'Gendering Trauma: Ariel Dorfman's Narratives of crisis and Reconciliation', *Critique: Studies in Contemporary Fiction*, 48, 3 (2007), pp. 295–317.

BIBLIOGRAPHY

Novick, Peter, *The Resistance Versus Vichy: The Purge of Collaborators in Liberated France*, London: Chatto and Windus, 1968.

Nozick, Robert, *Anarchy, State, and Utopia*, New York: Basic Books, 1974.

Omlor, Daniela, 'Reassessing history, rediscovering memory: Jorge Semprún's *Veinte años y un día*', *Nomenclatura: aproximaciones a los estudios hispánicos*, 1: 1, Art. 1, 2011, pp. 1–15, http://uknowledge.uky.edu/naeh/vol1/iss1/1

———— 'Exile and Trauma in Jorge Semprún', *Journal of Iberian and Latin American Research*, 17, 1 (2011) pp. 69–79.

———— *Jorge Semprún: Memory's Long Voyage*, Oxford: Peter Lang, 2014.

Orwell, George, 'Why I Write', in *The Collected Essays, Journalism and Letters of George Orwell, Vol. 1, An Age Like This, 1920–1940*, Harmondsworth: Penguin, 1979.

Paxton, Robert O., *Vichy France: Old Guard and New Order 1940–44*, New York: Alfred A. Knopf, 1972.

Pradera, Francisco Javier, 'Jorge Semprún and his heteronym, Federico Sánchez' in Ferrán, Ofelia and Gina Herrmann (eds), *A Critical Companion to Jorge Semprún: Buchenwald, Before and After*, New York: Palgrave Macmillan, 2014.

Preston, Paul, *The Triumph of Democracy in Spain*, London: Routledge, 1990.

———— *Juan Carlos, A People's King*, London: HarperCollins, 2004.

———— *The Spanish Holocaust: Inquisition and Extermination in Twentieth-Century Spain*, London: HarperPress, 2011.

———— *The Last Stalinist: The Life of Santiago Carrillo*, London: William Collins, 2014.

Rawls, John, *A Theory of Justice*, Cambridge, MA: Harvard University Press, 1971.

Report of the Chilean National Commission on Truth and Reconciliation, Notre Dame, Indiana: University of Notre Dame Press, vol. 1, 1993, http://www.usip.org/sites/default/files/file/resources/collections/commissions/Chile90-Charter.pdf

Resina, Joan Ramon, 'The Weight of Memory and the Lightness of Oblivion' in Jerez-Farrán, Carlos and Samuel Amago (eds), *Unearthing Franco's Legacy: Mass Graves and the Recovery of Historical Memory in Spain*, Notre, Dame, Indiana: University of Notre Dame Press, 2010.

Riambau, Esteve, 'The Clandestine Militant Who Would be Minister: Semprún and Cinema' in Ferrán, Ofelia and Gina Herrmann (eds), *A Critical Companion to Jorge Semprún: Buchenwald, Before and After*, New York: Palgrave Macmillan, 2014.

Richards, Michael, 'Grand Narratives, Collective Memory, and Social History: Public Uses of the Past in Postwar Spain' in Jerez-Farrán, Carlos and Samuel Amago (eds), *Unearthing Franco's Legacy: Mass Graves and the*

Recovery of Historical Memory in Spain, Notre Dame, Indiana: University of Notre Dame Press.

Roberts, Ronald Suresh, *No Cold Kitchen—A Biography of Nadine Gordimer*, Johannesburg: STE Publishers, 2005.

Robson, James Stephen, 'Ngũgĩ wa Thiong'o's fight against colonialism and neo-colonialism: An explanation of the theme of betrayal', MA thesis, Simon Fraser University, 1987.

Rosberg, Carl Gustav and John Cato Nottingham, *The myth of "Mau Mau" nationalism in Kenya*, New York: Praeger, 1966.

Rotberg, Robert and Dennis Thompson, *Truth Versus Justice: The Morality of Truth Commissions*, Princeton: Princeton University Press, 2000.

Rousso, Henry, *Vichy Syndrome: History and Memory in France Since 1944*, Cambridge: Harvard University Press, 1991.

———— 'L'épuration en France: une histoire inachevée', *Vingtième Siècle. Revue d'Histoire.*, No. 33, Jan–March 1992, pp. 78–105, http://www.persee.fr/web/revues/home/prescript/article/xxs_0294-1759_1992_num_ _33_1_2491

Rush, Peter D. and Olivera Simić (eds), *The Arts of Transitional Justice: Culture, Activism, and Memory after Atrocity*, New York: Springer, 2014.

Sandel, Michael, J., *Justice: What's the right thing to do?*, New York: Farrar, Straus and Giroux, 2010.

Sartre, Jean-Paul, *What is Literature?* New York: Philosophical Library, 1949 (originally published as *Qu'est-ce que la littérature?*, Paris: Gallimard, 1948).

Shehadeh, Raja, *Palestinian Walks: Notes on a Vanishing Landscape*, London, Profile Books, 2nd edition, 2008.

Schwerdt, Dianne, 'Caught in the Crossfire: Writing Conflict in Two African Novels', *The Australasian Review of African Studies*, 30, 1 (2009), pp. 101–17.

Sen, Amartya, *The Idea of Justice*, London: Penguin Books, 2010.

Serote, Mongane Wally, *A Tough Tale: South Africa*, London: Kliptown Books, 1987.

Service, Robert, *Lenin: A Biography*, London: Macmillan, 2000.

Sicherman, Carol, 'Ngũgĩ wa Thiong'o and the Writing of Kenyan History', *Research in African Literatures*, 20, 3 (1989), pp. 347–70.

———— *Ngũgĩ wa Thiong'o, The Making of a Rebel: A Source Book in Kenyan Literature and Resistance*, Borough Green, Sevenoaks: Hans Zell, 1990.

Smelser, Neil J. and Paul B. Baltes (eds), *International Encyclopedia of the Social and Behavioral Sciences*, Vol. 12, Oxford: Elsevier, 2001.

Soueif, Ahdaf, *Cairo: Memoir of a City Transformed*, London: Bloomsbury, 2014.

South African Communist Party, 'Letter sent by Bram Fischer to his Counsel in February 1965 when he went underground, and read to the court', http://www.sacp.org.za/main.php?ID=2369

Sprintzen, David, *Camus: A Critical Examination*, Philadelphia: Temple University Press, 1988.

Steele, Jonathan, 'The Guardian Profile: Nadine Gordimer', *Guardian*, 27 Oct. 2001, http://www.theguardian.com/books/2001/oct/27/fiction.artsandhumanities

Sterne, Steve J., *Battling for Hearts and Minds: Memory Struggles in Pinochet's Chile, 1973–1988*, Durham, CO: Duke University Press, 2006.

Stoll, David, *Rigoberta Menchú and the Story of all Poor Guatemalans*, Boulder, Colorado: Westview Press, 1999.

Tabucchi, Antonio, *Pereira Maintains*, Edinburgh: Canongate Books, 2010.

Tidd, Ursula, *Jorge Semprún: Writing the European Other*, Oxford: Legenda, 2014.

Todd, Olivier, *Albert Camus—A Life*, New York: Carroll & Graf, 2000.

Torpey, John, *Making Whole What Has Been Smashed: On Reparations Politics*, Cambridge: Harvard University Press, 2006.

Tremlett, Giles, 'Grandsons of Grandfathers', in Jerez-Farrán, Carlos and Samuel Amago, *Unearthing Franco's Legacy: Mass Graves and the Recovery of Historical Memory in Spain*, Notre Dame, Indiana: University of Notre Dame Press, 2010.

Truth and Reconciliation Commission of South Africa, *Report—Volume 1*, 1998 http://www.justice.gov.za/trc/report/finalreport/Volume%201.pdf

Tutu, Desmond, *No Future without Forgiveness*, London: Rider, 1999.

United Nations Treaty Collection, No. 1486, *International Convention on the Suppression and Punishment of the Crime of Apartheid*, adopted by the General Assembly of the United Nations on 30 November 1973, https://treaties.un.org/doc/Publication/UNTS/Volume%201015/volume-1015-I-14861-English.pdf

United Nations, *Social Justice in an Open World: The Role of the United Nations*, New York: United Nations, Department of Economic Social Affairs, The International Forum for Social Development, 2006.

Van Delden, Maarten and Yvon Grenier, *Gunshots at the Fiesta, Literature and Politics in Latin America*, Nashville: Vanderbilt University Press, 2009.

Van der Merwe, Hugo, 'What Survivors Say about Justice: An Analysis of the TRC Victim Hearings' in Chapman, Audrey R. and Hugo Van der Merwe (eds), *Truth and Reconciliation in South Africa: Did the TRC Deliver?* Philadelphia: University of Pennsylvania Press, 2008.

Van Diepen, Maria, *The National Question in South Africa*, London: Zed Books, 1988.

Vidal, Hernán, 'Ariel Dorfman: The Residue of Hope After Public Personae Construction', *Exile, Intellectuals, and the Memory Wars. Hispanic Issues On Line Debates* 5 (Fall 2012), pp. 4–24, http://hispanicissues.umn.edu/assets/doc/01_VIDAL_EIMW.pdf

BIBLIOGRAPHY

Villa-Vicencio, Charles and Wilhelm Werwoerd (eds), *Looking Back, Reaching Forward: Reflections on the Truth and Reconciliation Commission of South Africa*, Cape Town: University of Cape Town Press, 2000.

Weaver, James and Jeanne Colleran, '"Whose Memory? Whose Justice?" Personal and Political trauma in Ariel Dorfman's Death and the Maiden', *Performance Research*, 16,1, (2011), pp. 31–42.

Weissman, Susan (ed.), *The Ideas of Victor Serge: A Life as a Work of Art*, London: Critique Books/Merlin Press, 1997.

———— *Victor Serge: The course is set on hope*, London and New York, Verso, 2001.

West, Robin, 'Re-Imagining Justice', *Yale Journal of Law and Feminism* 333, 14 (2003), Georgetown Public Law and Legal Theory Research Paper No. 11–107, http://scholarship.law.georgetown.edu/facpub/685

Wilde, Alexander, 'Irruptions of Memory: Expressive Politics in Chile's Transition to Democracy', *Journal of Latin American Studies*, 31, 2 (1999), pp. 473–500.

———— 'A Season of Memory: Human Rights in Chile's Long Transition' in Collins, Cath, Katherine Hite, and Alfredo Joignant (eds), *The Politics of Memory in Chile: From Pinochet to Bachelet*, Boulder, Co: Lynne Rienner, 2013.

Wilson, E. and Piper, J., *Spatial Planning and Climate Change*, London: Routledge, 2010.

Wilson, Ilse, 'At home with Nadine Gordimer, a very private individual', *Mail and Guardian*, 18 July 2014, http://mg.co.za/article/2014-07-17-at-home-with-nadine-gordimer-a-very-private-individual

Wolf, Christa, *What Remains and other Stories*, London: Virago 1993.

———— *Parting from Phantoms: Selected Writings, 1990–1994*, Chicago: University of Chicago Press, 1997.

Wolpe, Harold, *Race, Class and the Apartheid State*, London: James Currey, 1987.

Wood, Allen W., 'Justice and Class Interests', *Philosophica* 33, 1 (1984), pp. 9–32.

Woodworth, Paddy, *Dirty War, Clean Hands: ETA, the Gal and Spanish Democracy*, 2nd Edition Connecticut: Yale Nota Bene, 2003.

Wu, Sharon, 'Mau Mau Historiography, Ngũgĩ wa Thiong'o's *A Grain of Wheat* and M.G.Vassanji's *The In-Between World of Vikram Lall*', MA thesis, National Central University, Taiwan, 2007.

Zaretsky, Robert, *Albert Camus, Elements of a Life*, Ithaca and London: Cornell University Press, 2010.

INDEX

INDEX

INDEX

INDEX

Nazi Germany (1933–45), 3, 5, 7,
15, 27, 39, 59–61, 64, 68, 72,
73, 76, 77, 79, 81, 82, 122, 123,
125, 129–35, 144–5, 202, 215,
218, 223
necklacing, 191
'Neither Victims nor Executioners'
(Camus), 80
neo-colonialism, 4, 15, 20, 24, 31,
101–6, 107, 111, 113, 146, 215,
218, 224
*Neo-Colonialism, The Last Stage of
Imperialism* (Nkrumah), 103
neo-liberalism, 13, 18, 30–1, 113,
157–8, 163
Netherlands, 4, 123, 127–8, 155,
156, 160
New Economic Policy (NEP),
50–1, 55
Ngaahika Ndeenda (Mirii & wa
Thiong'o), 102
wa Ngũgĩ, Njeeri, 113
Niehaus, Carl, 190–1
Nietzche, Friedrich, 172
Nigeria, 226
Nkrumah, Kwame, 103
No Time Like the Present (Gordimer),
183, 208–9, 212
Nobel Prize, 10, 80, 182, 184
non-violence, 63, 138, 185, 190
None to Accompany Me (Gordimer),
203–4, 207, 211
North Atlantic Treaty Organisation
(NATO), 119
Northwestern University, 98
Novelists on the Novel (Allot), 10
Nozick, Robert, 17, 18
Nuremberg trials (1945–6), 202,
223

Odinga, Oginga, 97, 98
oil crisis (1973), 157

On Liberty (Mill), 18
One Day in the Life of Ivan Denisovich
(Solzhenitsyn), 132
Opus Dei, 121
oral tradition, 90, 102, 106, 117
Oran, Algeria, 67
Orenburg, Russia, 38
Orwell, George, 11–12, 35
othering, 99
Outsider, The (Camus), 62, 64,
65–6, 204

Pact of Forgetfulness, 139, 140
Pacto del Olvido, 139, 140
Palestine, 12, 27
Palestinian Walks (Shehadeh), 12
Para leer al Pato Donald (Dorfman &
Mattelart), 158–9, 161
Paris Soir, 63–4
Paris, France, 36, 38, 53, 59, 63,
64, 67, 70, 71, 73, 74, 76, 123,
133, 135, 155
Parti Communiste Francais (PCF),
60, 63, 69, 71, 74, 84, 123, 124
Partido Comunista de Espana
(PCE), 124–5, 129–30, 132–3,
135–9, 142, 144, 147, 215, 222
Partido Demócrata Cristiano
(PDC), 152, 164
Partido Obrero de Unificación
Marxista (POUM), 39
Partido Socialista de Chile (PS),
153, 154, 176
Partido Socialista Obrero Espanol
(PSOE), 124, 138–9, 140, 145,
222
Pasternak, Boris, 35
Paxton, Robert, 61
Paz, Octavio, 10
PEN (Poets, Essayists and
Novelists), 194
penal systems, 2, 4, 15, 26–7,

INDEX

INDEX